BEHAVING BADLY

BEHAVING BADLY

Aversive Behaviors in Interpersonal Relationships

Edited by
Robin M. Kowalski

American Psychological Association
Washington, DC

Published by
American Psychological Association
750 First Street, NE
Washington, DC 20002

Copies may be ordered from
APA Order Department
P.O. Box 92984
Washington, DC 20090-2984

In the U.K., Europe, Africa, and the Middle East, copies may be ordered from
American Psychological Association
3 Henrietta Street
Covent Garden, London
WC2E 8LU England

Typeset in Goudy by EPS Group Inc., Easton, MD

Printer: Edwards Brothers, Inc., Ann Arbor, MI
Cover Designer: NiDesign, Baltimore, MD
Technical/Production Editor: Jennifer Powers

The opinions and statements published are the responsibility of the authors, and such opinions and statements do not necessarily represent the policies of the APA.

Library of Congress Cataloging-in-Publication Data
Behaving badly : aversive behaviors in interpersonal relationships / edited by Robin M. Kowalski.—1st ed.
        p. cm.
    Includes bibliographical references and indexes.
    ISBN 1-55798-716-5 (cloth : alk. paper)
    1. Interpersonal relations.   2. Interpersonal conflict.   3. Social interaction.
  4. Disorderly conduct.   5. Gossip.   6. Invective.   I. Kowalski, Robin M.   II. Title.

HM1106 .B45 2000
158.2—dc21

                                                                        00-041611

British Library Cataloguing-in-Publication Data
A CIP record is available from the British Library.

Printed in the United States of America
First Edition

To my parents, Randolph and Frances Kowalski, with love

—R. M. K.

CONTENTS

CONTRIBUTORS

Michael Harris Bond, Department of Psychology, Chinese University of Hong Kong, Shatin, New Territories

Steve Duck, Department of Communication Studies, University of Iowa, Iowa City

Elsie Howerton, Department of Psychology, Western Carolina University, Cullowhee, NC

Thomas E. Joiner, Jr., Department of Psychology, Florida State University, Tallahassee, FL

Warren H. Jones, Department of Psychology, University of Tennessee, Knoxville

Jennifer Katz, Department of Psychology, Washington State University, Pullman, WA

Robin M. Kowalski, Department of Psychology, Western Carolina University, Cullowhee, NC

Mark R. Leary, Department of Psychology, Wake Forest University, Winston-Salem, NC

Michelle McKenzie, Department of Psychology, Western Carolina University, Cullowhee, NC

Rowland S. Miller, Department of Psychology, Sam Houston State University, Huntsville, TX

Danny S. Moore, Department of Psychology, University of Tennessee, Knoxville

Laura A. Negel, Department of Psychology, University of Tennessee, Knoxville

Ralph L. Rosnow, Department of Psychology, Temple University, Philadelphia, PA

Arianne Schratter, Department of Psychology, University of Tennessee, Knoxville

Carrie A. Springer, Department of Psychology, University of Memphis, Memphis, TN

James T. Tedeschi, Department of Psychology, State University of New York at Albany

Roos Vonk, Department of Social Psychology, University of Nijmegen, Nijmegen, the Netherlands

Alaina M. Winters, Department of Communication Studies, University of Iowa, Iowa City

PREFACE

In keeping with John Donne's oft-cited quote "No man is an island," people do not exist in isolation. Not only can they not function entirely apart from their interactions with others, but people's desire to be accepted and included by other individuals may be a fundamental human motive (Baumeister & Leary, 1995). In one study examining people's perceptions of what gives life meaning, people gave the highest rating to interpersonal relationships (Klinger, 1977). However, although no person is an island and we depend on others for our well-being and to give our life meaning, many individuals would periodically love to be alone on an island to escape the mean, nasty, petty, and otherwise aversive behaviors in which other people, particularly those closest to them, engage.

Research has shown that negative interpersonal interactions exert a disproportionate influence on mental health, relationship outcomes, and overall well-being compared to positive social exchanges (Lepore, 1992; Rook, 1998; Vinokur & van Ryn, 1993). Indeed, interpersonal conflicts rank near the top of the list of daily stressors that compromise mental health (Bolger, DeLongis, Kessler, & Schilling, 1989). Dissatisfying interpersonal relationships represent one of the most common complaints of people entering therapy (Rook, 1998).

Much of the dissatisfaction and stress that people report in their relationships with others appears to stem from the inconsiderate, mundane, annoying behaviors in which people engage. Whether purposively or mindlessly, relational partners, family members, and friends hurt our feelings, engage in breaches of propriety, tease mercilessly, spread rumors and, in general, appear to value their relationships with us less than we desire. The purpose of this book is to examine the negative and positive characteristics and motives of these aversive behaviors and relational transgressions. Given that the darker side of interpersonal relationships can affect interactions in any setting (e.g., home, work, school), anyone interested in personal relationships, social psychology, or clinical–counseling psychology will find the book useful.

This book begins with an overview of aversive behaviors and relational transgressions in chapter 1, where I discuss reasons for the slow emergence of a focus on the dark side of interpersonal relationships, variables that influence perceptions of aversiveness, and people's responses to the repetitive negative social behaviors of others. The four chapters in part 2 examine improper and distancing behaviors. Representing perhaps one of the most pervasive of the aversive behaviors that occur in our interactions with others are breaches of propriety—impolite, obnoxious behaviors, such as being selfish and failing to control one's body, with which we are all familiar. After discussing the origins of impropriety, Rowland S. Miller examines personal and social influences on people's indecorous behavior and then discusses the most prevalent types of impropriety (chapter 2). One common type of impropriety involves swearing, a behavior that is the focus of chapter 3. In this chapter, Alaina M. Winters and Steve Duck present a perspective on swearing as an aversive, yet relational behavior. They suggest that, despite its aversive qualities, swearing may have relational motivations, such as increasing intimacy or signaling one's connection with others. In chapter 4, Roos Vonk focuses on two types of aversive self-presentations: those that are intended to be aversive and those that have aversive consequences without the actor's intention. Jennifer Katz and Thomas E. Joiner, Jr., discuss (in chapter 5) three types of depressotypic behavior: excessive reassurance-seeking, negative feedback-seeking, and aggression. Each of these behaviors can disrupt social interaction, lead to social rejection of the depressed individual, and compromise the emotional and sometimes physical well-being of the interaction partner.

The five chapters in part 3 each deal with hurting others. Mark R. Leary and Carrie A. Springer discuss (in chapter 6) a theory of hurt feelings that links hurt feelings to relational devaluation, or the perception that others do not regard their relationships with us to be as close or valuable as we desire them to be. As noted by Leary and Springer, one type of hurtful event is teasing. In chapter 7, Elsie Howerton, Michelle McKenzie, and I examine the understudied phenomenon of teasing. After conceptualizing what constitutes teasing, we examine the victims and perpetrators of teasing, the functions that teasing serves, and the consequences of teasing. Ralph L. Rosnow presents a two-sided perspective on rumor and gossip in chapter 8. After discussing the dark side of rumor and gossip, he turns to an examination of the multiple social functions (some even positive) that these behaviors serve. In chapter 9, Warren H. Jones, Danny S. Moore, Arianne Schratter, and Laura M. Negel elaborate on the theme of interpersonal transgressions with a specific focus on betrayals. After providing a conceptualization of betrayals, they provide three operationalizations of the concept including betrayal narratives, betrayal as a personality variable, and betrayal as a characteristic of social networks. In chapter 10, James T. Tedeschi and Michael Harris Bond use the social interactionist theory of coercive actions to interpret aversive behaviors. Specifically, they suggest that aversive interpersonal behaviors are related to motives for social control, the establishment or re-establishment of justice, and assertion and protection of valued identities. Tedeschi and Bond point out that, although these three motives are common to people in all cultures, their form, frequency, and intensity vary across cultures. In chapter 11, I examine some of what we now know about aversive interpersonal behaviors; they are an inevitable part of relating to others and they may, despite their aversiveness, have relationship-enhancing consequences.

I would be engaging in an aversive behavior myself if I were remiss in thanking individuals who have been extremely helpful in this book's creation. Sherri Valentine spent innumerable hours in the library tracking down books and journals. Her tireless efforts along with her insights into the first chapter of this volume are very much appreciated. Mark Leary painstakingly edited my own chapters and was extremely helpful in brainstorming about ideas related to the book. My husband Tom Britt patiently tolerated a few instances of complaining and reassurance-seeking while I worked on this book. Finally, I would like to thank Susan Reynolds at the American Psychological Association, who enthusiastically endorsed this project from the beginning and has maintained that enthusiasm throughout the whole process. She has been a terrific person with whom to work.

REFERENCES

Baumeister, R. F., & Leary, M. R. (1995). The need to belong: Desire for interpersonal attachments as a fundamental human motivation. *Psychological Bulletin, 117*, 497–529.

Bolger, N., DeLongis, A., Kessler, R. C., & Schilling, E. A. (1989). Effects of daily stress on negative mood. *Journal of Personality and Social Psychology, 57*, 808–818.

Klinger, E. (1977). *Meaning and void: Inner experience and the incentives in people's lives*. Minneapolis: University of Minnesota Press.

Lepore, S. J. (1992). Social conflict, social support, and psychological distress: Evidence of cross-domain buffering effects. *Journal of Personality and Social Psychology, 63*, 857–867.

Rook, K. S. (1998). Investigating the positive and negative sides of personal relationships: Through a lens darkly? In B. H. Spitzberg & W. R. Cupach (Eds.), *The dark side of close relationships* (pp. 369–393). Mahwah, NJ: Erlbaum.

Vinokur, A. D., & van Ryn, M. (1993). Social support and undermining in close relationships: Their independent effects on the mental health of unemployed persons. *Journal of Personality and Social Psychology, 65*, 350–359.

I

AVERSIVE INTERPERSONAL BEHAVIORS: AN INTRODUCTION

1

AVERSIVE INTERPERSONAL BEHAVIORS: ON BEING ANNOYING, THOUGHTLESS, AND MEAN

ROBIN M. KOWALSKI

"Closeness often breeds undue influence, loss of identity, loss of privacy, frustrations of individual goals and personal projects, and the possibilities of great psychological and even physical harm" (Spitzberg & Cupach, 1994, p. 317).

When most people think of aversive interpersonal behaviors, they think of acts of aggression or violence, such as physical abuse, murder, and rape. In fact, these extreme forms of aversive behavior are, within the whole scheme of behaviors, relatively rare. To limit our focus to these acts of aggression or violence would be to ignore the more mundane aversive interpersonal behaviors to which most people are exposed on a much more regular basis and which in some instances may lead to more extreme aggressive actions. Although not an exhaustive list, the following behaviors fall within this category of mundane aversive behaviors:

- rudeness
- gossiping
- swearing
- failing to control bodily functions
- chronic complaining
- narcissism
- excessive reassurance-seeking

- teasing
- hurting others' feelings
- ostracism
- conflict
- deception
- infidelity
- not listening
- intentional embarrassment
- neglect
- spreading rumors
- violating confidentiality
- betrayals
- using the silent treatment
- moodiness
- criticism
- jealousy
- forgetting commitments
- disappointment
- incompetence
- contempt
- passive–aggressiveness
- defensiveness
- sabotage.

Although some of these behaviors, particularly those involving breaches of propriety, may occur with acquaintances or strangers, most are enacted within the context of intimate relationships, with friends, family members, and romantic partners. Within the context of close relationships, aversive interpersonal behaviors often involve relational transgressions in that they violate "rules for appropriate relational conduct" (Metts, 1994, p. 217). Other researchers have used the term *social undermining* to refer to interactions characterized by aversive behaviors (Vinokur & van Ryn, 1993, p. 350; see also Rook, 1998).

The labels *aversive interpersonal behaviors*, *relational transgressions*, and *social undermining* cast a very negative, dark pallor over these behaviors. Indeed, many of them (e.g., sabotage and contempt) deserve that portrayal. However, because of the frequency with which these behaviors occur within relationships and because these behaviors are often perpetrated inadvertently, with no intent whatsoever to hurt others, it seems important to understand the conditions under which they arise and their consequences for the individuals involved and for their relationships with one another. As is demonstrated throughout this book, many of these behaviors have redeeming features despite their aversive qualities.

INATTENTION TO THE DARK SIDE OF RELATIONSHIPS

Despite the prevalence of relational transgressions in our lives, researchers have been remiss in their study of aversive interpersonal behaviors in four ways. First, with the exception of research on blatant forms of relational aggression, such as domestic violence, researchers have tended to accentuate the positive side of interpersonal relationships and to neglect the negative side (Duck, 1994; Duck & Wood, 1995; Kowalski, 1997c). Second, where the dark side of interpersonal relationships has been examined, research has been conducted in a disjointed manner on particular phenomena without devoting attention to aversive interpersonal behaviors as a broader category of human behavior (Kowalski, 1997c). Although isolated studies have examined specific types of relational transgressions, such as infidelity, conflict, neglect, and ostracism, and the effects of these negative social interactions on emotional well-being (Lakey, Tardiff, & Drew, 1994; Lepore, 1992; Rook, 1984, 1998; Vinokur & van Ryn, 1993), little effort has been made to consider broader questions regarding why people often treat one another so badly. The causes and consequences of what appear to be disparate behaviors are similar when one delves below their surface manifestations. Third, investigations of particular aversive behaviors have been limited to a single context, ignoring other settings in which the behavior might occur. For example, a significant body of research has examined bullying at school but little research has examined bullying in the workplace (Duck, 1994). Fourth, studies that have examined the aversive side of relationships have portrayed "the negative side of relating . . . as a deviation from the positive rather than as a phenomenon that also composes the totality of relationship experience" (Duck, 1994, p. 5). In other words, researchers have discussed negative interpersonal interactions as aberrations in relationships stemming from basic misunderstandings rather than inherent features of those relationships.

Beginning in 1994, however, these gaps in research began to be bridged. At that time, William Cupach and Brian Spitzberg edited *The Dark Side of Interpersonal Communication*, in which they laid the foundation for studying "the dark side of human interaction" (p. vii). In 1997, I edited a volume that took a detailed look at some of the specific behaviors with which people are confronted on a regular basis, including ostracism, complaining, intentional embarrassment, and guilt induction (Kowalski, 1997a). The following year, Spitzberg and Cupach (1998) published a follow-up to their original book entitled *The Dark Side of Close Relationships*. Thus, the present volume is the fourth to examine the dark, aversive side of interpersonal relationships. All of these books not only highlight the darker side of interpersonal relationships, but also provide a framework for understanding the broader phenomenon of relational transgressions.

The relatively recent emergence of research examining the dark or aversive side of interpersonal interaction raises the question of why the study of aversive behaviors as a phenomenon was neglected for so long. Not only are relational transgressions pervasive in our interactions with other people, but they are, quite simply, an inevitable part of relating to others (Kowalski, 1997b). No matter how compatible two people are, they inevitably do things to offend, irritate, annoy, or hurt their interaction partner. At times, such behaviors may be inadvertent, as when people are sick and, thus, bad-tempered. At other times, however, the behaviors may be intentional efforts to hurt another or to change another's behavior.

At least three reasons account for why researchers have been remiss in studying the dark side of interpersonal relationships. First, the slow emergence of attention to the dark side of relationships may have stemmed from the fact that the study of relationships began rather recently. Although early research in social psychology focused on affiliation (Sarnoff & Zimbardo, 1961; Schachter, 1959) and attraction (Berscheid & Walster, 1978; Byrne, 1971; Newcomb, 1961), it was not until the early 1970s and 1980s that behavioral researchers began to investigate close relationships.

Second, once relationships began to be investigated, researchers tended to focus on the positive, pleasant features of relationships. For example, social support research initially focused on the correlation between positive social relationships and health (Cohen & Wills, 1985). Only some years later did researchers turn their attention to the role that negative social interactions play in creating psychological distress (Bolger, DeLongis, Kessler, & Schilling, 1989).

Third, it is possible that people today are simply meaner and nastier to their intimate partners than they once were, a change that necessitated increased research attention to the insidious side of relationships. As Miller (chapter 2, this volume) pointed out, societal values and norms have changed so that behaviors that once were frowned on are now more readily accepted. People are less inhibited about performing what were once considered inappropriate behaviors. Indeed, we have probably become desensitized to some aversive interpersonal behaviors to the point where we may not even recognize that they have been perpetrated by others or, perhaps worse, by ourselves. For example, standards of decorum appeared to be much stricter in the past than they are today. Thus, flatulence or belching while watching television is not only more likely today but also more likely to be disregarded by those who hear it as compared to 20 years ago.

Given that insufficient attention has been devoted to aversive interpersonal behaviors, the purpose of this book is to expand on our existing knowledge and to provide additional exemplars of what qualify as aversive interpersonal behaviors. In this chapter, I examine what is meant by the construct of aversiveness and variables that influence the perception of aversiveness. I then turn to a neglected topic within research on the dark side or "underbelly" of social interaction: people's responses when they are repeatedly treated badly by others.

DEFINING *AVERSIVENESS*

Like beauty, aversiveness is in the eye of the beholder. What one person views as insulting and offensive, another may perceive as funny and enjoyable. One person's pain is another person's pleasure. These differences in perceptions of aversiveness are clearly seen in research on bullying (Besag, 1989; Ross, 1996), hurtful exchanges (Leary, Springer, Negel, Ansell, & Evans, 1998), betrayals (Jones, Moore, Schratter, & Negel, chapter 9, this volume), interpersonal conflict (Baumeister, Stillwell, & Wotman, 1990; Orvis, Kelley, & Butler, 1976), teasing (Kowalski, 2000), and evil (Baumeister, 1997). Relative to victims, the perpetrators of these actions minimize the negative impact of their behavior, view their behaviors more benignly, perceive the behavior as rationally motivated, and see the negative consequences of the behavior as limited.

However, differences in perceptions of the aversiveness of interpersonal behaviors lie not only between victims and perpetrators, but also among victims and among perpetrators. Whereas some victims find teasing to be enjoyable and some episodes of conflict to be energizing, other victims feel victimized and, in some instances, devastated by what they perceive as very hurtful exchanges. Clearly, then, whether or not something is viewed as aversive depends on the perspective of the viewer. Because of the potential ambiguity in identifying aversive behaviors, I conceptualize *aversive interpersonal behaviors* as behaviors by another individual that are encoded by a target (i.e., victim) as stressful. Any number of variables may lead people to encode others' behaviors as stressful, including the extent to which the behavior connotes relational devaluation of the target by the perpetrator, the degree to which the behavior informs the target about undesired aspects of himself or herself, and the degree to which the behaviors disrupt ongoing interactions. Given this conceptualization, any variable that influences the degree to which a person perceives the behavior as stressful should enhance feelings of the aversiveness of the situation.

VARIABLES INFLUENCING PERCEPTIONS OF AVERSIVENESS

Elsewhere, I have suggested that four variables determine whether a behavior is aversive: (a) the degree to which the behavior interferes with basic psychological needs for belongingness, control, and self-esteem maintenance; (b) the social confrontation involved in the behavior; (c) the inappropriateness of the behavior; and (d) the ambiguity characterizing the behavior (Kowalski, 1997c). After briefly examining these four variables, I describe eight additional influences on people's perceptions of the aversiveness of others' behavior: norms, severity and frequency of transgression, intentionality, empathic accuracy, relational intimacy, relationship type, individual differences, and public nature of the transgression. What all of these variables have in common is that they influence the meaning that people attach to others' behaviors. "Aversive" and "nonaversive," "positive" and "negative" are not attributes of behaviors themselves; rather, they are determined by the meaning that a target assigns to a behavior (Duck, 1994).

Interference With Basic Psychological Needs

Behaviors that interfere with people's basic psychological needs for belongingness (Baumeister & Leary, 1995), control (Thompson, 1981; Williams, 1997), and self-esteem (Leary, 1999) are perceived as aversive (Kowalski, 1997c). When the satisfaction of these needs is perceived to be in jeopardy, people experience a number of negative affective states including anxiety, sadness, depression, jealousy, hostility, loneliness, disgust, anger, and boredom (Baumeister & Leary, 1995; Leary, in press). To the degree that the experience of these emotional states is linked to the behaviors of another, those behaviors are likely to be evaluated negatively. For example, a person might feel jealous when his or her spouse shows increased attention toward a member of the other sex. Any behaviors that are indicative of this increased attention toward another are likely to be evaluated negatively.

Social Confrontation

Social confrontation episodes are initiated when one individual confronts another person about some aspect of his or her behavior or personality (Newell & Stutman, 1988, 1991). Because few people like being confronted about aspects of themselves, particularly aspects that portray them in an undesirable light, such confrontations are generally aversive (Kowalski, 1997c). Social confrontation episodes that involve criticisms as opposed to simple statements of dissatisfaction with another's behavior (Gottman, 1994; Kowalski, 1996) are perceived as particularly aversive. For example, being told "You don't help out around the house. You are such a lazy person," connotes something very different than "I would appreciate it if you would be more helpful around the house."

Inappropriateness

As pointed out by Miller (chapter 2, this volume), many behaviors are encoded as aversive because they are inappropriate breaches of propriety. Perceptions of what is appropriate versus inappropriate depend on several factors including the age of the actor, the situational context in which the behavior is performed, and social norms. Behaviors that might be considered appropriate for a toddler, such as eating with his or her hands, are less appropriate for an adult, particularly in the presence of other people. Poking fun at the bride or groom at a wedding rehearsal is considered, by most people, par for the course. However, poking fun at a deceased person during the funeral is a breach of propriety.

Ambiguity

Many interpersonal behaviors are ambiguous (Kowalski, 1997c). It is often unclear from simply observing certain behaviors what the actor's motivation was and, thus, how the behavior should be interpreted. This uncertainty regarding the meaning of another's behavior and, thus, the type of response that is warranted is stressful. The more ambiguous a behavior and the more difficult it is to understand the motive for the behavior, the more likely the target is to perceive the behavior as aversive.

Norms

The meaning that is assigned to particular interpersonal behaviors depends on prevailing norms. As pointed out by Kowalski, Howerton, and McKenzie (chapter 7, this volume), behaviors that are perceived as relationship enhancing in one culture or subculture may be highly offensive in other cultures or subcultures. Even within a given culture, the norms may change and behaviors that were once considered inappropriate and aversive may become acceptable social exchanges (see Miller, chapter 2, this volume). As Reynolds (1998, p. 19A, cited in Miller, chapter 2, this volume) noted, "young people are hearing vulgarities so commonly that they never associate them with any sort of impropriety" (p. 30). Indeed, a great many aversive behaviors that would have been deemed unacceptable 30 years ago are given little more than passing attention today.

Severity and Frequency of the Transgression

Both the severity and the frequency of the relational transgression influence perceptions of its aversiveness. Even here, however, individual differences influence evaluations of the severity of the offense. What is a severe offense to one person and therefore perceived as hurtful and detrimental to the relationship may be a minor offense to another. In addition, whereas some people's perceptions of severity are determined by a single indiscretion, others evaluate severity on the basis of the cumulative effect of repeated transgressions.

Generally speaking, however, more severe offenses, such as extramarital affairs, are likely to be evaluated as more aversive compared to having one's feelings hurt because one's relational partner did not call when he or she promised. In addition, the more frequently a particular negative behavior occurs, the more likely it is to be perceived as aversive. An isolated incident of teasing, for example, may be easily tolerated, but repeated teasing despite requests to terminate the behavior is harder to accept. Changes in relational evaluation and the negative effects of the behavior on the relationship become more clear-cut (Leary, in press).

Evaluations of the severity of a transgression are also influenced by the explicitness of the relational rule that has been violated (Metts, 1994). Blatant disregard for rules that have been explicitly established within the relationship is perceived as more serious and more damaging to the relationship than simply violating a relational partner's assumptions regarding appropriate behavior.

The role of the severity and frequency of interpersonal behaviors in influencing aversiveness can be understood using Lazarus's (1966) model of stress. Indeed, consistent with my own conceptualization of aversiveness, many researchers have classified negative social interactions as stressors (e.g., Ross, 1996; Shinn, Lehmann, & Wong, 1984). Lazarus divided potential stressors into three categories: daily hassles (i.e., minor irritants to which people are exposed on a daily basis), chronic life strains (i.e., more long-term problems that are evaluated as taxing one's resources), and major life events (i.e., events that produce major disruptions in one's life). The degree to which each of these is appraised as stressful depends on two appraisal processes (Lazarus & Folkman, 1984). During the *primary appraisal phase*, an individual evaluates the demands that are being imposed by the environment (in this case, another person's behaviors). During the *secondary appraisal phase*, the individual evaluates his or her ability to manage these demands. The greater the stressor (e.g., the more severe or frequent the transgression), the more people perceive the environment as placing demands on them that exceed their resources to deal with them. This explains why an individual who is teased rarely views the teasing more benignly than someone who no longer wants to go to school because of persistent teasing by classmates. This model also sheds light on why two individuals exposed to the identical interpersonal stressor may react differently. Whereas one person may view the stressor as manageable, the other may perceive that it exceeds his or her resources to cope.

Not surprisingly, then, perceptions of the severity of an interpersonal behavior and, thus, its aversiveness, vary with the level of stress currently being experienced by an individual. According to the stress exacerbation hypothesis (Rook, 1990), negative social exchanges are perceived as more aversive and distressing by people who are already stressed.

Intentionality

People's interpretations of the behaviors of others are also affected by the perceived intentionality of the behavior. Discerning malicious intent in another's behavior casts the behavior in a negative light, changes the dynamics of the interaction between the two people, and potentially damages the relationship (Kowalski, 1999; Vangelisti, 1994).

Goffman's (1967; see also Argyle, Furnham, & Graham, 1981) level of responsibility construct provides a succinct model for examining intentionality. According to this model, people draw one of three types of inferences about others' behaviors. First, the target may perceive that the perpetrator intended no harm. For example, a man who is teased about his clothing may realize that the teaser had no intention of hurting his feelings. Even if he is offended by the behavior, he perceives that the perpetrator was unaware that his or her actions would be perceived as offensive.

Second, and at the other end of the continuum, are situations in which individuals' behaviors are perceived as intentionally offensive and malicious, as designed specifically to humiliate, hurt, and embarrass the target. Sometimes, behaviors that fall within this category stem from anger on the part of the perpetrator and are often labeled *revenge*. Other times, the perpetrator simply takes joy in others' suffering (*schadenfreude*; Smith et al., 1996). Intentionally malicious behaviors are difficult for a target to explain away; therefore, they are more likely than unintentional slights to have long-term, detrimental effects on a relationship.

Third, the target may perceive the perpetrator's behaviors as "incidental offenses" (Goffman, 1967). In these instances, the target feels that the perpetrator understands that his or her behavior might have aversive consequences, but the behavior is not engaged in maliciously or with the intent of hurting the target. For example, even though they know that there is the potential for misinterpretation, people may tease others to demonstrate camaraderie and to have good-natured fun, not to hurt the target of the tease. If the target is in fact hurt, the implications for the relationship are unlikely to be long term (Vangelisti, 1994). Thus, people who perceive that others either intended no harm or that harm was an inadvertent by-product of the behavior are less likely to negatively evaluate the behavior or the perpetrator than targets who view the behavior as maliciously motivated.

Empathic Accuracy

Empathic accuracy has been defined as "the ability to accurately infer the specific content of one's partner's thoughts and feelings evinced during a dyadic interaction" (Thomas & Fletcher, 1997, p. 194). Empathic accuracy is influenced both by a perceiver's ability to read the thoughts and feelings of an actor and by the actor's readability (Colvin, Vogt, & Ickes, 1997). The more easily a person's thoughts and feelings can be gleaned from his or her verbal and nonverbal behaviors and the greater the perceiver's ability to pick up on these thoughts and feelings, the higher the empathic accuracy. Some people are simply not very accurate in reading other individuals (Funder, 1995; Hancock & Ickes, 1996). Other people are difficult to read, either because they are adept at masking their thoughts and feelings or because their thoughts and feelings do not match the behaviors that they present to others (Clark, Pataki, & Carver, 1996).

Applied to perceptions of aversive behaviors, people who are high in empathic accuracy should be more accurate in interpreting the motivations behind others' behavior. If these motivations are perceived to be negative, then the behavior is interpreted as aversive. If, on the other hand, the intentions are perceived as innocuous, the same behavior is likely to be interpreted more positively.

Interpretations of another's thoughts and feelings are also influenced by people's expectations for the other's behavior. People who have idealistic perceptions of how a relational partner should behave may, on one hand, be more likely to perceive even innocuous behaviors as aversive because they do not compare favorably with ideals. On the other hand, idealistic people may impute positive motives to a partner's intentionally malicious behavior as a means of preserving an idealistic image of the existing relationship. In either case, empathic accuracy has been sacrificed (Hancock & Ickes, 1996; Thomas & Fletcher, 1997).

Relational Intimacy

Relationships differ from one another along a number of dimensions. One dimension concerns the degree of closeness or intimacy that characterizes the relationship. As connoted by the phrase "We only hurt the ones we love," the more intimate the relationship, the higher the likelihood that aversive interpersonal behaviors occur (Miller, 1997). For example, people are more likely to tease their friends and romantic partners than they are total strangers (Kowalski et al., chapter 7, this volume), and they are hurt more frequently by friends and romantic partners than by strangers (Leary & Springer, chapter 6, this volume). Similarly, people generally do not belch in front of total strangers but are much more inclined to do so in front of their intimate friends and partners (Miller, chapter 2, this volume).

People who are close to us have much greater influence over our emotional states than people who are relationally more distant (Berscheid, 1983). Being hurt or relationally devalued (Leary et al., 1998) by a loved one is much more painful than being rejected by someone with whom one is only mildly acquainted. One reason for this is that significant others are in a better position to control valued and desired outcomes (Vinokur & van Ryn, 1993). Moreover, people expect their relationship partners and friends to generally be nice to them and respect them. Thus, the pain of having these expectations violated can be particularly sharp.

It would appear, then, that relational intimacy increases an individual's tendency to perceive behaviors as aversive. At the same time, however, "relational intimacy may serve to buffer the distancing effects of some negatively perceived interpersonal behaviors" (Vangelisti, 1994, p. 69). Generally speaking, we are more likely to give the benefit of the doubt when assigning meaning to a romantic partner's behavior than to an acquaintance's behavior.

Whether relational intimacy increases or decreases people's perceptions of the aversiveness of others' behaviors depends in large part on the current affective state of the relationship (Cunningham, Barbee, & Druen, 1997; Kowalski, 1997c). For example, people who are satisfied with their relationships make different attributions for the relational transgressions of a romantic partner than people who are dissatisfied with their relationships. Specifically, people who are satisfied with their relationships are less affected by the negative social behaviors of their partner (Fincham, 1985) and are more likely than those who are dissatisfied to give their partner the benefit of the doubt. Thus, they are less likely to make negative characterological attributions to the partner for his or her behavior. Relative to happy couples, unhappy couples are significantly less likely to interpret a partner's intended positive behaviors as positive (Gottman et al., 1976; see also Noller & Ruzzene, 1991; Thomas & Fletcher, 1997). It is important to note, however, that negative interpersonal behaviors that occur within the context of a satisfied relationship do not necessarily hurt any less than those that occur among acquaintances. They are simply less likely to have long-term negative consequences for the relationship.

Relationship Type

The type of relationship within which negative social exchanges occur also influences perceptions of aversiveness (Segrin, 1993). For example, according to Vangelisti (1994), people respond to perceived aversive behaviors from family members differently than those of nonfamily members. Members of one's family are permanent. No matter how aversive the behavior in which they engage, they are still members of one's family. Thus, family members may "be less likely than nonfamily members to allow a single negative interpersonal behavior such as a hurtful message to affect their relationships with other members" (Vangelisti, 1994, p. 70). One would expect this to be particularly true for members of collectivist as opposed to individualistic cultures. People in collectivist cultures define themselves in terms of their connections with other people and, thus, generally work harder to preserve established interpersonal bonds than do members of individualistic cultures (Triandis, 1994).

In general, people tend to overlook the slights of friends and intimate partners more readily than they do those of strangers or acquaintances. One reason for this is that people have access to vast amounts of information about their close relations compared to strangers. Thus, they have more information on which to make an informed decision regarding the motivations and intentions of relational friends and partners. Although this allows for the possibility that even more negative attributions are made for the behaviors of a close intimate, typically the attributions are more favorable.

Individual Differences

Clearly, some people are more likely than others to view another's behavior as aversive. Some people are simply more tolerant of and less reactive to the behaviors of others. Moreover, people's attributional styles differ; some people are more inclined to attribute others' negative interpersonal behaviors to internal factors, whereas others are more likely to give people the benefit of the doubt (Kowalski, 1997b; Layden, 1982). Furthermore, some people are more sensitive to the self-relevant implications of others' interpersonal behaviors. For example, people who are high in their perception of risk in intimacy (Pilkington & Richardson, 1988) are more attuned to suggestions of relational devaluation than people who see little risk in social relationships. Compared to people who perceive that intimacy is not a risky business, people who perceive high risk in intimacy have fewer closer relationships and lower trust in others (Pilkington & Richardson, 1988). They tend to be more sensitive to interpersonal slights and more likely to perceive particular behaviors as indicative of relational devaluation and betrayal. Indeed, an examination of some of the items included on the Risk in Intimacy Scale (Pilkington & Richardson, 1988) shows the link between perceptions of risk and hurt feelings: "I'm afraid to get really close to someone because I might get hurt," "Most close relationships end with hurt feelings for one or both parties," and "The most important thing to consider in a relationship is whether I might get hurt." In addition, people who are high in negative affectivity may be more inclined to interpret another's behaviors in a negative light (Lakey et al., 1994).

Individual differences also exist in people's feelings of comfort with relationships. Some individuals find even positive, loving relationships to be frightening and thus aversive (Duck, 1994; Kowalski, 1997c). Others, however, can find meaning in even the most destructive, unloving relationships.

Public Nature of the Transgression

People's perceptions of relational transgressions are in part influenced by the presence of an audience. Feelings of humiliation and distress are typically heightened in the presence of an audience. As threatening to one's self-esteem as another's taunts or put-downs may be, the humiliation is magnified in the presence of other people. It is one thing to lose face in the presence of only the person who is responsible for the loss of face, but it is quite another matter to lose face before an entire audience of people. As Baumeister (1997) stated,

> the most important function of the audience is probably just that it makes the offense harder to ignore. People seem to feel that they cannot ignore, dismiss, or otherwise "take" an insult if other people see it. . . . Audiences lend social reality to events. If no one else knows about it, you can pretend it never happened. . . . If someone else knows about an ego threat, the option of ignoring it is lost. (p. 156)

Although certainly the immediate presence of other people enhances perceptions of aversiveness, the audience does not have to actually be present at the time of the transgression. Rather, the audience is conceptualized more generally to include anyone who might one day find out about the transgression (Baumeister, 1997). Thus, the perceived aversiveness of infidelity is enhanced by a spouse's concern with who else might know about the affair.

RESPONSES TO AVERSIVE INTERPERSONAL BEHAVIORS

The more aversive a behavior is perceived to be, the more likely a target is to respond aversively. Interestingly, however, little attention has been devoted to how targets respond to the repetitive aversive actions of a perpetrator (see, however, Tedeschi & Bond, chapter 10, this volume). In light of the recent school shootings, all of which stemmed, in part, from social rejection and teasing, examining people's responses to aversive interpersonal behaviors seems timely. Responses to the relational transgressions of others has implications not only for the future of the relationship between the individuals involved, but also for the physical and emotional health of the victim of the aversive exchanges. For example, people who respond by seeking revenge have much poorer relational and health outcomes than people who respond with forgiveness.

In one attempt to examine the influence of responses on behavioral and health outcomes, a researcher asked participants in her laboratory to remember an incident in which they were hurt by another person ("Should all be," 1999). They were then instructed to imagine holding a grudge against the perpetrator and inducing guilt in the perpetrator for the incident. This was followed by instructions to imagine empathizing with the perpetrator and wishing well for the perpetrator. Results showed reliable physiological differences in participants when they held a grudge as opposed to wishing the perpetrator well. When considering revenge as a response, participants reported more stress than when considering forgiveness. In addition, participants reported more feelings of control and power when they empathized with the perpetrator compared to when they harbored animosity toward the perpetrator.

Given the influence that people's responses to relational transgressions have on the long-term health of the individuals and their relationship and given that some of these responses themselves qualify as aversive behaviors, I turn to these responses now, which include revenge, forgiveness, resignation, and confrontation. It is important to note that responses to the aversive interpersonal behaviors of another are not necessarily directed at the perpetrator. Rather, they may be displaced, typically on to someone who resembles the actual perpetrator in some way (e.g., belongs to the same social or racial group).

Revenge

Revenge is probably the least adaptive and (fortunately) rarest response to aversive interpersonal behaviors. Acts of revenge can range from the common mode of passive–aggressiveness to less common methods such as physical attack and murder.

A case that was well-publicized in the media highlights the lengths to which people go to enact revenge against those whom they feel have slighted them. Ronald Shanabarger confessed to killing his 7-month-old son by suffocating him with plastic wrap. The reason he gave for killing the child was to get back at his wife who had refused to cut short a cruise when his father had died. As if this were not tragic enough, Shanabarger had planned to seek revenge in this way before the child was even born. Indeed, he married the woman, fathered a child with her, then waited for a period of time to allow her to bond with the child, all with the intention of seeking his revenge against her. He told reporters that he wanted his wife to feel how he felt when his father had died ("Father charged," 1999).

The school shootings that occurred in Colorado, Washington, and Kentucky, among other places, also illustrate revenge as a response to perceived aversive treatment by others. All of the shooters were labeled oddities and misfits. Eric Harris and Dylan Klebold, perpetrators of the Littleton, Colorado, massacre, "were shunned, made fun of, and ignored, especially by the age-old high school clique that was their antithesis: the jocks" (Cannon, Streisand, & McGraw, 1999, p. 17). Luke Woodham, who killed two students in Pearl, Mississippi, had just been dumped by his girlfriend. He also reported having been teased about his weight and about being effeminate. Mitchell Johnson, the 13-year-old who, along with Andrew Golden, killed one teacher and four students in Jonesboro, Arkansas, had been rejected by his girlfriend. He had also been teased about being overweight (Cloud, 1999). Experts commenting on the school shootings have said that these adolescent boys felt rejected and, thus, enraged (Cannon et al., 1999). As noted by Mulrine (1999),

> a growing number of experts say that a more effective deterrent to teenage violence may be curbing a practice that has long been considered just another schoolyard rite of passage. The practice is bullying —the teasing, harassing, and occasional mild violence inflicted by the supposedly powerful against the presumedly powerless. (p. 24)

The violence arises from an attempt to get revenge for the bullying. Indeed, the National School Safety Center has labeled *bullying* "the most enduring and underrated problem in American schools" (Mulrine, 1999, p. 24). The role that rejection and ridicule played in the shootings is stated most clearly in the note ostensibly written by Eric Harris. In this note, he stated "Your children who have ridiculed me, who have chosen not to accept me, who have treated me like I am not worth their time are dead" ("Possible Gunman Suicide," 1999).

The National School Safety Center (1998) has developed a checklist of characteristics associated with individuals who have been involved in school violence. Among these characteristics are "Is on the fringe of his/her peer group with few or no close friends," "Has been bullied and/or bullies or intimidates peers or younger children," and "Is involved with a gang or an antisocial group on the fringe of peer acceptance." In his statement before the U.S. House of Representatives, Dr. Ronald Stephens, executive director of the National School Safety Center, discussed the causes of school violence. The first cause he labeled *past victimization*, and he noted that 80% of bullies had been victims of bullies (Stephens, 1998). The second cause he stated was a feeling of being "isolated, neglected, ignored, and ridiculed."

Clearly, then, perceiving others' behaviors as aversive may lead people to respond with aversive behaviors of their own. Although revenge, like most other forms of violence, typically does not bring about tangible rewards or change the circumstances that have already befallen the avenger, it makes him or her feel better to see the other person experiencing pain (Baumeister, 1997).

People who are most likely to seek revenge are those whose self-esteem has been threatened (Baumeister, 1997). As pointed out by Lakey et al. (1994), negative interpersonal exchanges can alter people's perceptions of both themselves and other people. Whereas some people can deal with the esteem-threatening implications of aversive treatment, others are less able to do so. It is this latter group of individuals who are most likely to enact revenge motivated by a desire to get back at those who have threatened their favorable self-perceptions. Thus, people who have positive views of themselves but who have been put down and humiliated, particularly in front of other people, display the highest likelihood of seeking revenge (Baumeister, 1997; Brown, 1968). At times, this motive to seek revenge is so strong that people who feel humiliated seek revenge even at personal costs to themselves (Brown, 1968).

A victim's desire to seek revenge can, in some instances, be ameliorated by perpetrators who apologize or express regret over their relational transgression. People who acknowledge their actions and take responsibility for them elicit more compassionate, forgiving responses than people who do not. For example, within the United States, programs of restorative justice are on the rise. These programs are designed to bring victims and offenders in contact with one another with the hope that healing for the victims can begin. However, clearly, such programs are unlikely to be effective if the offender shows no remorse over the crime that has been committed. Indeed, within the criminal justice system, only perpetrators who actually admit their guilt are allowed to be a part of the restorative justice programs (Lampman, 1999a, 1999b).

Forgiveness

Your spouse forgets your birthday. Annoying and hurtful, but probably a forgivable offense. Your child is murdered in the mayhem created by Eric Harris and Dylan Klebold. Forgivable? Probably not. "How-to books, therapy and interventions may be useful in dealing with an unfaithful spouse, gossiping colleague, or even some cases of violence. But there are some practices—serial killing, torturing, genocide—often regarded as unforgivable" ("Should all be," 1999, p. 58). Clearly, there are variations in the degree to which people can be forgiven for their aversive behaviors. In addition, people differ in their willingness and ability to forgive someone for a particular transgression.

Part of people's willingness to forgive others depends on the degree to which they can understand the thoughts and feelings of the transgressors (Jones et al., chapter 9, this volume; McCullough et al., 1998; McCullough,

Worthington, & Rachal, 1997; Tedeschi & Bond, chapter 10, this volume). However, forgiveness follows only when this understanding yields insights into other people's benign motives for enacting aversive behaviors. If the insight yields negative information about the intentions of the transgressor, then forgiveness is unlikely to follow. Ickes and Simpson (1997) summed up this role of empathy and forgiveness by stating that

> if each partner fully comprehends the other's thoughts, feelings, hopes, fears, intentions, and desires, there is presumably no offense that cannot be forgiven. In contrast, . . . if each partner fully comprehends the other's point of view and subjective experience, there is presumably no offense that ever can be forgiven. (p. 218)

Resignation

Some people resign themselves to other people treating them badly. On the surface, anyway, these individuals appear to let the negative social exchanges with others roll off of their backs. However, this is not always the case. In fact, there are two types of resignation responses. In one— *quiet resignation*—resignation involves quietly tolerating the behaviors of others. Whether other people are teasing them, engaging in excessive reassurance-seeking, inducing guilt in them, engaging in breaches of propriety, or using excessive profanity, individuals who engage in quiet resignation, although finding the behaviors annoying, simply ignore them. In the second—*internalized resignation*—resignation takes the form of internalizing the criticisms, put-downs, or annoyances of another person. For example, if others engage in frequent breaches of propriety in their presence, people who internalize the behaviors perceive that the others do not like them; therefore, they must deserve the disrespect and bad treatment of others. Similarly, when others treat them with contempt, they internalize the message that they are disgusting human beings.

Distancing

Often, people simply try to distance themselves from the aversive interpersonal behaviors of another. In some cases, the victim can adopt a defensive posture and deny the validity of what the perpetrator is saying or doing. For example, people who are teased can deny the truth of what the teaser is saying. Because, however, all aversive interpersonal behaviors do not lend themselves to this type of response (i.e., it is difficult to deny the reality of someone's flatulence), people may opt to distance themselves through rejection and avoidance. People who swear excessively or who engage in frequent breaches of propriety may eventually be rejected by the target and all subsequent interaction with those individuals avoided.

Confrontation

Given that many negative social behaviors are inadvertent, one effective response is simply to inform people that their behaviors are annoying and hurtful. This information may be provided in a relatively passive, quiet manner or it may take the form of a reproachment in which perpetrators are informed of their transgressions in an assertive, blaming fashion. Not surprisingly, one would expect an individual's choice between these two types of confrontation to vary with the perceived motives of the perpetrator and with the frequency of the annoyance. Perpetrators who are believed to be acting maliciously or who engage in annoying behaviors on a regular basis are more likely to be reproached than quietly confronted.

CONCLUSION

An examination of the dark side of interpersonal relationships and the many mundane, oftentimes mindless slights that people perpetrate against others has, until recently, been neglected, with more attention focused on the positive facets of relationships. Reasons that account for this relative inattention to the aversive side of relationships include the short history of research on relationships in general, the tendency of researchers to focus on the positive rather than the negative features of relationships, and changing social values and norms that may have weakened people's inhibitions regarding inappropriate interpersonal behavior.

Within the past few years, however, researchers have begun to devote increased attention to the negative, more insidious side of interpersonal relationships. Among the factors currently being investigated are variables that influence people's perceptions of the aversiveness of interpersonal behaviors. Included among these variables are social norms, the severity and frequency of the behavior, the intention believed to be motivating the behavior, and the public nature of the transgression.

All of these variables influence the meaning that people assign to the behaviors of others and, thus, the response that is generated, whether that response be revenge, forgiveness, resignation, distancing, or confrontation. For example, a person who infers that the aversive behaviors of another stem not from maliciousness but from simply a lack of mindfulness is very likely to forgive the transgressor. On the other hand, a person who perceives that a perpetrator has intentionally hurt him or her is more likely to respond with anger, reproachment, or even revenge.

In turning attention to the aversive side of interpersonal interactions, I reiterate Duck's (1994) suggestion that the negative side of relating should not be depicted as a deviation from the positive, but rather as an integral, inevitable part of human relationships. No one is immune from experiencing the hurt that often accompanies negative social exchanges or from occasionally inflicting hurt on others through one's own aversive behaviors.

REFERENCES

Argyle, M., Furnham, A., & Graham, J. A. (1981). *Social situations.* Cambridge, England: Cambridge University Press.

Baumeister, R. F. (1997). *Evil: Inside human violence and cruelty.* New York: W. H. Freeman.

Baumeister, R. F., & Leary, M. R. (1995). The need to belong: Desire for interpersonal attachments as a fundamental human motivation. *Psychological Bulletin, 117,* 497–529.

Baumeister, R. F., Stillwell, A., & Wotman, S. R. (1990). Victim and perpetrator accounts of interpersonal conflict: Autobiographical narratives about anger. *Journal of Personality and Social Psychology, 59,* 994–1005.

Berscheid, E. (1983). Emotion. In H. H. Kelley, E. Berscheid, A. Christensen, J. H. Harvey, T. L. Huston, G. Levinger, E. McClintock, L. A. Peplau, & D. R. Peterson (Eds.), *Close relationships* (pp. 110–168). New York: Freeman.

Berscheid, E., & Walster, E. (1978). *Interpersonal attraction* (2nd ed.). Reading, MA: Addison-Wesley.

Besag, V. (1989). *Bullies and victims in schools.* Buckingham, UK: Open University Press.

Bolger, N., DeLongis, A., Kessler, R. C., & Schilling, E. A. (1989). Effects of daily stress on negative mood. *Journal of Personality and Social Psychology, 57,* 808–818.

Brown, B. R. (1968). The effects of need to maintain face on interpersonal bargaining. *Journal of Experimental Social Psychology, 4,* 107–122.

Cannon, A., Streisand, B., & McGraw, D. (1999, May 3). Why? There were plenty of warnings, but no one stopped two twisted teens. *U. S. News & World Report,* pp. 16–19.

Clark, M. S., Pataki, S. P., & Carver, V. H. (1996). Some thoughts on self-presentation of emotions in relationships. In G. Fletcher & J. Fitness (Eds.), *Knowledge structures in close relationships: A social psychological approach* (pp. 247–274). Hillsdale, NJ: Erlbaum.

Cloud, J. (1999, May 31). Just a routine school shooting. *Time, 153,* 34–43.

Cohen, S., & Wills, T. A. (1985). Stress, social support, and the buffering hypothesis. *Psychological Bulletin, 98,* 310–357.

Colvin, C. R., Vogt, D., & Ickes, W. (1997). Why do friends understand each other better than strangers do? In W. Ickes (Ed.), *Empathic accuracy* (pp. 169–193). New York: Guilford.

Cunningham, M. R., Barbee, A. P., & Druen, P. B. (1997). Social allergens and the reactions that they produce: Escalation of annoyance and disgust in love and work. In R. M. Kowalski (Ed.), *Aversive interpersonal behaviors* (pp. 190–214). New York: Plenum.

Cupach, W. R., & Spitzberg, B. H. (1994). (Eds.). *The dark side of interpersonal communication*. Hillsdale, NJ: Erlbaum.

Duck, S. (1994). Stratagems, spoils, and a serpent's tooth: On the delights and dilemmas of personal relationships. In W. R. Cupach & B. H. Spitzberg (Eds.), *The dark side of interpersonal communication* (pp. 3–24). Hillsdale, NJ: Erlbaum.

Duck, S., & Wood, J. T. (1995). For better, for worse, for richer, for poorer: The rough and the smooth of relationships. In S. Duck & J. T. Wood (Eds.), *Confronting relationship challenges* (Vol. 5, pp. 1–21). London: Sage.

Father charged in baby-killing plot under suicide watch. (1999, June 29). [Online]. Available: http://www.cnn.com/US/9906/29/revenge.killing.01.ap/

Fincham, F. D. (1985). Attribution processes in distressed and nondistressed couples: 2. Responsibility for marital problems. *Journal of Abnormal Psychology, 94,* 183–190.

Funder, D. C. (1995). On the accuracy of personality judgment: A realistic approach. *Psychological Review, 102,* 652–670.

Goffman, E. (1967). *Interaction ritual: Essays on face-to-face behavior.* New York: Pantheon Books.

Gottman, J. M. (1994). *Why marriages succeed or fail.* New York: Simon & Schuster.

Gottman, J. M., Notarious, C., Markman, H., Bank, S., Yoppi, B., & Rubin, M. E. (1976). Behavior exchange theory and marital decision making. *Journal of Personality and Social Psychology, 34,* 14–23.

Hancock, M., & Ickes, W. (1996). Empathic accuracy: When does the perceiver–target relationship make a difference? *Journal of Social and Personal Relationships, 13,* 179–199.

Ickes, W., & Simpson, J. A. (1997). Managing empathic accuracy in close relationships. In W. Ickes (Ed.), *Empathic accuracy* (pp. 218–250). New York: Guilford.

Kowalski, R. M. (1996). Complaints and complaining: Functions, antecedents, and consequences. *Psychological Bulletin, 119,* 179–196.

Kowalski, R. M. (1997a). *Aversive interpersonal behaviors.* New York: Plenum.

Kowalski, R. M. (1997b). Aversive interpersonal behaviors: An overarching framework. In R. M. Kowalski (Ed.), *Aversive interpersonal behaviors* (pp. 215–233). New York: Plenum.

Kowalski, R. M. (1997c). The underbelly of social interaction: Aversive interpersonal behaviors. In R. M. Kowalski (Ed.), *Aversive interpersonal behaviors* (pp. 2–9). New York: Plenum.

Kowalski, R. M. (1999). *Pleasant versus unpleasant experiences of teasing.* Unpublished manuscript, Western Carolina University.

Kowalski, R. M. (2000). "I was only kidding!": Victims' and perpetrators' perceptions of teasing. *Personality and Social Psychology Bulletin, 26,* 231–241.

Lakey, B., Tardiff, T. A., & Drew, J. B. (1994). Negative social interactions: Assessment and relations to social support, cognition, and psychological distress. *Journal of Social and Clinical Psychology, 13*, 42–62.

Lampman, J. (1999a, February 4). A new model to deal with crime and its victims. *Christian Science Monitor, 91*, p. 17.

Lampman, J. (1999b, January 28). The power of forgiveness. *Christian Science Monitor, 91*, p. 13.

Layden, M. A. (1982). Attributional style therapy. In C. Antaki & C. Brewin (Eds.), *Attributions and psychological change: Applications of attributional theories to clinical and educational practice* (pp. 63–82). New York: Academic Press.

Lazarus, R. S. (1966). *Psychological stress and the coping process.* New York: McGraw-Hill.

Lazarus, R. S., & Folkman, S. (1984). *Stress, appraisal, and coping.* New York: Springer.

Leary, M. R. (1999). The social and psychological importance of self-esteem. In R. M. Kowalski and M. R. Leary (Eds.), *The social psychology of emotional and behavioral problems* (pp. 197–222). Washington, DC: American Psychological Association.

Leary, M. R. (in press). Emotional responses to interpersonal rejection. In M. R. Leary (Ed.), *Interpersonal rejection.* New York: Oxford University Press.

Leary, M. R., Springer, C., Negel, L., Ansell, E., & Evans, K. (1998). The causes, phenomenology, and consequences of hurt feelings. *Journal of Personality and Social Psychology, 74*, 1225–1237.

Lepore, S. J. (1992). Social conflict, social support, and psychological distress: Evidence of cross-domain buffering effects. *Journal of Personality and Social Psychology, 63*, 857–867.

McCullough, M. E., Rachal, K. C., Sandage, S. J., Worthington, E. L., Jr., Brown, S. W., & Hight, T. L. (1998). Interpersonal forgiving in close relationships: II. Theoretical elaboration and measurement. *Journal of Personality and Social Psychology, 75*, 1586–1603.

McCullough, M. E., Worthington, E. L., Jr., & Rachal, K. C. (1997). Interpersonal forgiving in close relationships. *Journal of Personality and Social Psychology, 73*, 321–336.

Metts, S. (1994). Relational transgressions. In W. R. Cupach & B. H. Spitzberg (Eds.), *The dark side of interpersonal communication* (pp. 217–239). Hillsdale, NJ: Erlbaum.

Miller, R. S. (1997). We always hurt the ones we love: Aversive interactions in close relationships. In R. M. Kowalski (Ed.), *Aversive interpersonal behaviors* (pp. 13–29). New York: Plenum.

Mulrine, A. (1999, May 3). Once bullied, now bullies—with guns. *U. S. News & World Report,* 24.

National School Safety Center. (1998). Checklist of characteristics of youth who have caused school-associated violent deaths. [Online]. Available: http://www.nssc1.org/reporter/checklist.htm

Newcomb, T. M. (1961). *The acquaintance process*. New York: Holt.

Newell, S. E., & Stutman, R. K. (1988). The social confrontation episode. *Communication Monographs, 55*, 266–285.

Newell, S. E., & Stutman, R. K. (1991). The episodic nature of social confrontation. In J. A. Anderson (Ed.), Communication Yearbook 14 (pp. 359–392). Newbury Park, CA: Sage.

Noller, P., & Ruzzene, M. (1991). Communication in marriage: The influence of affect and cognition. In G. J. O. Fletcher & F. Fincham (Eds.), *Cognition in close relationships* (pp. 203–233). Hillsdale, NJ: Erlbaum.

Orvis, B. R., Kelley, H. H., & Butler, D. (1976). Attributional conflict in young couples. In J. H. Harvey, W. Ickes, & R. Kidd (Eds.), *New directions in attribution research* (Vol. 1, pp. 353–386). Hillsdale, NJ: Erlbaum.

Pilkington, C. J.,& Richardson, D. R. (1988). Perceptions of risk in intimacy. *Journal of Social and Personal Relationships, 5*, 503–508.

Possible gunman suicide note found. (1999, April 24). Available: http://aol.com/news/specials/news/denver/home.adp.

Rook, K. S. (1984). The negative side of social interaction: Impact on psychological well-being. *Journal of Personality and Social Psychology, 46*, 1097–1108.

Rook, K. S. (1990). Parallels in the study of social support and social strain. *Journal of Social and Clinical Psychology, 9*, 118–132.

Rook, K. S. (1998). Investigating the positive and negative sides of personal relationships: Through a lens darkly? In B. H. Spitzberg & W. R. Cupach (Eds.), *The dark side of close relationships* (pp. 369–393). Mahwah, NJ: Erlbaum.

Ross, D. M. (1996). *Childhood bullying and teasing*. Alexandria, VA: American Counseling Association.

Sarnoff, I., & Zimbardo, P. G. (1961). Anxiety, fear, and social affiliation. *Journal of Abnormal and Social Psychology, 62*, 356–363.

Schachter, S. (1959). *The psychology of affiliation*. Stanford, CA: Stanford University Press.

Segrin, C. (1993). Interpersonal reactions to dysphoria: The role of relationship with partner and perceptions in rejection. *Journal of Social and Personal Relationships, 10*, 83–97.

Shinn, M., Lehmann, S., & Wong, N. W. (1984). Social interaction and social support. *Journal of Social Issues, 40*, 55–76.

Should all be forgiven? (1999, April 5). *Time, 153*, 54–59.

Smith, R. H., Turner, T. J., Garonzik, R., Leach, C. W., Urch-Druskat, V., & Weston, C. M. (1996). Envy and schadenfreude. *Personality and Social Psychology Bulletin, 22*, 158–168.

Spitzberg, B. H., & Cupach, W. R. (1994). Dark side dénouement. In W. R. Cupach & B. H. Spitzberg (Eds.), *The dark side of interpersonal communication* (pp. 315–320). Hillsdale, NJ: Erlbaum.

Spitzberg, B. H., & Cupach, W. R. (1998). (Eds.). *The dark side of close relationships*. Mahwah, NJ: Erlbaum.

Stephens, R. D. (1998). Statement of Dr. Ronald D. Stephens. Available: http://www.nssc1.org/witness/testim.htm.

Thomas, G., & Fletcher, G. J. O. (1997). Empathic accuracy in close relationships. In W. Ickes (Ed.), *Empathic accuracy* (pp. 194–217). New York: Guilford.

Thompson, S. C. (1981). Will it hurt less if I can control it? A complex answer to a simple question. *Psychological Bulletin, 90,* 89–101.

Triandis, H. C. (1994). *Culture and social behavior.* New York: McGraw-Hill.

Vangelisti, A. L. (1994). Messages that hurt. In W. R. Cupach & B. H. Spitzberg (Eds.), *The dark side of interpersonal communication* (pp. 53–82). Hillsdale, NJ: Erlbaum.

Vinokur, A. D., & van Ryn, M. (1993). Social support and undermining in close relationships: Their independent effects on the mental health of employed persons. *Journal of Personality and Social Psychology, 65,* 350–359.

Williams, K. D. (1997). Social ostracism. In R. M. Kowalski (Ed.), *Aversive interpersonal behaviors* (pp. 133–170). New York: Plenum.

II

IMPROPER AND DISTANCING BEHAVIORS

2

BREACHES OF PROPRIETY

ROWLAND S. MILLER

On occasion, people surprise us with acts of thoughtful generosity, sensitivity, or righteousness. Recently, for instance, my 14-year-old son Christopher startled and delighted me by forestalling an inappropriate joke. He and several of his soccer teammates were traveling to a game in our family van when one of his friends announced, "I'm not a racist, but do you want to hear a funny joke?" To my mild astonishment, Chris said, "No, I don't. I don't want to hear it, Robert." Chastened, Robert kept the (undoubtedly demeaning) joke to himself, and the boys went on with their conversation.

I was impressed by my son's assertive effort to resist an unwanted offense to propriety. Even more striking, however, was my realization of how unusual desirable behavior of this sort is. Indeed, that is the point I wish to raise by mentioning this episode: Such behavior is uncommon, and it is conspicuous because of its rarity. More common by far is impolite, indecorous, or obnoxious behavior that inconveniences or annoys other people. In fact, later that same evening, I happened on a couple loading their purchases from a shopping cart into their car in a grocery store's parking lot. When the cart was empty, they merely pushed it aside into an adjacent parking space and climbed into their car, blithely ignoring the cart as it began to roll across the lot toward another row of cars (including mine). I trotted over to retrieve it, only to find that not only had the offending customers heedlessly imperiled others' property, they had fouled the environment by emptying their overflowing ashtray onto the pavement before departing. A pile of cigarette butts and ash began to slowly disperse in the light breeze.

Exasperating actions like these are commonplace and are far more ordinary and familiar to most of us than are notable acts of decorous propriety.[1] We are frequently confronted with behavior from others that seems boorish, impolite, selfish, insensitive, thoughtless, or obnoxious, and such irritants are becoming more prevalent all the time. We certainly think social life is less civil than it used to be; three-fourths of American citizens believe that incivility (such as vulgar language and selfish, discourteous driving) is more common now than it was 10 years ago (Marks, 1996). "When it comes to manners and morals, we all sense a continued rottening" (Eberly, 1999) of the politesse of public life. Some observers even argue that we are beset by "growing social disorder and cultural disintegration" (Stanfield & Stanfield, 1997, p. 111) that threatens to become a full-scale "cultural collapse": "Divorce, dirty language, adultery, blasphemy . . . and so on were not unknown in 1960. But today, they permeate our lives" (Buchanan, 1999, p. A10).

Our standards do seem to have changed over time. The most popular etiquette manual of 1873 advised polite diners to "never allow the conversation at the table to drift into anything but chit-chat; the consideration of deep and abstruse principles will impair digestion" (Hill, 1873, p. 21). Nowadays, in contrast, people need to be warned that "a lady does not discuss menopause or its symptoms in mixed company, particularly when a meal is being served. It absolutely ruins dinner" (Hodge, 1998, p. 2F). Indeed, some norms of etiquette and manners that were once familiar may be disappearing altogether. According to the popular social critic Miss Manners, "we are at the sad stage . . . where polite conventions have been ignored so long that even kindly disposed people no longer know what they are" (Martin, 1998, p. 12). Americans are using more coarse, indecent language than they used to (Jay, 1992), for instance, and "young people are hearing vulgarities so commonly that they never associate them with any sort of impropriety" (Reynolds, 1998, p. 19A).

Why is improper, impolite, and generally noisome behavior so commonplace? What sorts of actions are these that cause others to bristle in frustration or disgust? In this chapter, I attempt to answer these questions using a broad conceptualization of improper behavior that spans several different lines of inquiry in social psychology, sociology, and communication studies. There have been few empirical studies of impropriety per se,

---

[1]In fact, lest readers think my anecdote about Christopher to be self-serving, I should admit that he has lousy table manners and has never written anyone a thank-you note. He's a good, decent kid, but he's still guilty of frequent breaches of propriety—as most people probably are.

but the construct illuminates fundamental themes of social life and connects diverse topics in the behavioral sciences.

THE ORIGINS OF IMPROPRIETY

Social behavior seems improper when "it is judged by at least some of the other participants in the interaction to be wrong according to one or more rules" (Stebbins, 1993, p. 5). Logically, then, impropriety may be increasingly widespread either because people follow the "rules" less frequently or because there is less consensus about what the rules are. In fact, both of these broad patterns may be at work in many of the cultural, personal, and situational influences that underlie improper behavior. I first consider cultural factors that provide the context for impropriety.

Changing Cultures

At various rates and for diverse reasons, cultures change. As they evolve, their standards for appropriate behavior may be shaped by a variety of influences of at least three different general types.

Macro-Economic Factors

Historians suggest that the norms of polite conduct and manners now referred to as *etiquette* began to emerge thousands of years ago when humans first started living together in large settlements (Martin & Stent, 1990). Urban centers mixed different clans and encouraged specialized division of labor, and people needed explicit systems for dealing with strangers from different classes and groups. Such codes lent predictability to what would otherwise have been chaotic, confusing, or dangerous interactions, and they allowed the harmony that was a marker of new *civilizations*. From this perspective, etiquette was not a set of silly, trivial practices that unfairly constrained individual authenticity and honesty (see Martin, 1985); instead, it was useful and functional, allowing diverse peoples to live peaceably by avoiding misunderstanding and averting conflict.

Recently, however, long-standing divisions among the social classes in Western cultures have become less distinct. The rapid growth of an expansive middle class has diluted some of the distinctions of power and status among people that once made cautious respect for others—and thus the need for etiquette—advisable. Social norms and manners based in defensive circumspection toward one's fellows (Edwards, 1999) have gradually eroded as more people have come to feel the empowerment and entitlement that accompanies rising socioeconomic status.

Simultaneously, the participation in the labor force that has caused this modern prosperity has had us at work and on the move, displaced from our old neighborhoods and increasingly cut off from our new neighbors. As a result, our sense of community and interdependence with others has eroded: Membership in civic and fraternal organizations, participation in parent–teacher organizations, church going, and even bowling in organized leagues are all noticeably lower than they used to be (Putnam, 1995). For some observers, it is no coincidence that "community involvement, political participation, civic responsibility, and simple everyday courtesies and manners are all evidently declining" at precisely the same time (Stanfield & Stanfield, 1997, p. 114). Compared to earlier eras, people have less desire to be polite to others and less reason to behave so.

Emerging and Variable Norms

Partly as a result of the disengagement from our fellows, Western cultures have entered an "age of the individual" in which, to a new extent, one's personal pleasures and pains seem far more important than the collective good (Seligman, 1990, p. 6). One may plausibly argue that where norms of generalized reciprocity and social trust once governed behavior, we now glorify greed and the clever exploitation of one's peers. Consequently,

> we care less and less about our fellow citizens ... We may see them as obstacles or competitors, or we may not see them at all, but unless they happen to be our friends, we rarely think we owe them anything. (Carter, 1998, pp. 4–5)

This new age has also supported a variety of new social identities that have created new complexities in social life. The individualism and affluence of the culture have allowed (if not encouraged) people to assert a greater number of idiosyncratic identities with which others must deal. In the United States, for instance, past decades were simpler times in which some groups that are now influential were simply ignored: "Feminists did not exist. Homosexuals did not exist. Muslims did not exist. But John Wayne did" (Carter, 1998, p. 43). Whether or not appearances were deceiving, we once seemed to share a more singular vision of the American ideal than we do now. Today, in contrast, we seem subdivided into social pluralities with diverse and competing norms (see Magida, 1996).

At least some of these are geographical. For example, the southern United States embodies a "culture of honor" in which affronts to one's dignity are grievous harms for which redress must be sought—through violence, if necessary. Thus, insults and other indignities are much more likely to elicit an aggressive response in the American South than in the North, where different norms exist and people are more likely to shrug off insults from others (Cohen, Nisbett, Bowdle, & Schwarz, 1996).

Coupled with this newfound individualism and cultural pluralism are the shifting norms of fad and fashion that, in recent memory, have always changed from one generation to the next. (Presently, grandmothers who balked at their daughters' pierced ears are shuddering anew at their grand-daughters' pierced tongues.) Certainly, American culture is both more sexually and violently explicit than it used to be (Merida & Leiby, 1999). Consider Alfred Hitchcock's legendary film *Psycho* from 1960: In the terrifying shower scene in which a character is stabbed to death, we see blood running down the drain but we never actually see the knife cut the victim's skin;[2] an awful concept is suggested rather than shown. Now, 40 years later, any movie in that genre is almost certain to include graphic, detailed depictions of grotesque injuries. Violence that was once implied is now vividly, explicitly portrayed.

Other cultural events shape our collective norms, too. In the United States, when a President's affair with a White House intern became known to the public, journalistic "standards governing what was acceptable for public consumption were rewritten on the spot" (Vobejda, 1999, p. 22A). Americans may have wished to avoid public notice or mention of ordinarily private behaviors such as "oral sex," but, for the first time in that country, this was hard to do; the *Washington Post*, for instance, used the term in 225 different articles in the 12 months that followed disclosure of the affair (Vobejda, 1999).

New Technologies

Fueling our modern detachment from our neighbors—and the creation of new norms—are scientific advancements that often have unforeseen and unintended effects on social life. For example, new technologies that enhance our personal freedoms and leisure sometimes privatize what had been public, social endeavors, insulating us from others in the name of convenience. When people began staying home to watch television in the 1950s, they reduced their participation in organized sports and other communal activities; today, watching videotapes or shopping via the Internet at home, they less often mingle with others at theaters or shopping malls (Putnam, 1995). People are spending more time in front of their computers, where they can communicate with others, but electronic interactions may be a poor substitute for the richer contact people enjoy when they are face to face; the more time people spend exploring the Internet, the more lonely they tend to be (Kraut et al., 1998).

Scientific developments can also induce changes in existing norms of propriety. The recent profound advances in technologies of human reproduction are an excellent case in point (Friedman & Squire, 1998). The

---

[2]This description does not fit most viewers' memories of the movie, but it is undeniably true. The 45-second scene is comprised of some 40 clips of film, and the knife is shown near the victim's body three times, but no actual stabbing is ever shown.

invention of birth control pills almost certainly helped stimulate the "sexual revolution" of the 1960s that transformed our standards of acceptable sexual behavior. Before chemical contraception became widespread, for instance, very few young adults openly cohabited before marrying, but today most do (Whyte, 1990). Even more remarkably, modern procedures allow sperm donors to impregnate women they have never met and permit surrogate mothers to nurture fetuses that are not their own. The familiar convention of marriage has less to do with parenting than ever before, and our expectations, norms, and (in some cases) laws are changing as a result (e.g., Nissimov, 1999).

Technology may allow new forms of impropriety as well. The creators of computer viruses can now inconvenience or harm millions of strangers at once, creating frustration on an unprecedented scale. Other new improprieties have a smaller reach but are more widespread: There are now over 66 million active cellular telephones in the United States, and their inconsiderate use allows their owners to annoy others at movies, in restaurants, in church, or on the road in wholly new ways (Aversa, 1999).

Summary

We live in a culture that has made it easier for people to "do their own thing" than ever before. Hard work and geographic mobility have expanded the middle class but disconnected us from our neighbors and communities. Technology has brought our entertainments home, further insulating us from others. Being less interdependent, we have less reason to consider others' outcomes to be important to us and may thus be less likely to make the many small sacrifices on the behalf of others that polite propriety entails (Carter, 1998; Sober & Wilson, 1998).

Coupled with ordinary changes in fad and fashion, increasing individualism has also reduced our consensus about appropriate norms of personal conduct—so that old standards of proper behavior are no longer universally held—even as new technologies have created brand new ways to invade others' privacy or infringe on their peace. The net result is that "it has never been easier to insult people inadvertently" (Martin, 1985, p. 29).

In summary, cultural changes have probably made people generally less willing to temper their actions and restrain their impulses in the service of the collective good. They have also made social life more complex, with diverse ideological, ethnic, sexual, religious, regional, and gendered factions of various ages all demanding appropriate, but idiosyncratic, acknowledgment and respect. Perhaps more than ever before, people wishing to be decorous and polite to others must take specific, careful note of with whom, and where, their interactions take place (Axtell, 1990; Magida, 1996).

Of course some people clearly are more motivated or better able to do this than are others, and across situations, even as cultures change, there are a variety of personal factors that influence impropriety. After all, cultures do not misbehave, people do.

Personal Influences

If people were tireless beings all possessed of the same motives, knowledge, and skills, there would be many fewer breaches of propriety. However, people differ from one another in several meaningful ways, and they are often unwilling or unable to behave as others would like.

Individual Differences

Chronic differences among people in outlook and interactive style can cause frustration and misunderstanding. To a confident extravert, for instance, the inhibited timidity of someone who is socially anxious may appear to be an obnoxious lack of reciprocal warmth (Leary & Kowalski, 1995). Someone who offers a warm compliment to a person who has a negative self-concept may be surprised by an apparent lack of gratitude when the person doubts the praise (Swann, 1996). We tend to overestimate the extent to which other people share our own preferences and values, so that, in general, others are less like us than we think (Krueger & Clement, 1994); individual differences are thus a typical source of unexpected and sometimes undesirable behavior from others.

Real and expected gender differences are sometimes influential in this regard. Despite their many similarities, men and women are ordinarily expected to adopt somewhat different sex roles—with men being more instrumental and agentic than women, and women being more affective and communal than men—with the result that each sex's behavior occasionally confounds the other sex (Holmes, 1995). In particular, to be polite, men are ordinarily expected to take an active role in assisting others—opening doors, carrying packages, and picking up the check for dinner—but such behavior runs the risk of seeming patronizing and condescending (Harris, 1992). Polite women are expected to defer to the needs of others, so that a woman can seem improper and impolite if she assertively acts too much like a man (Rudman, 1998). Ironically, sex-typed men and women who do fit our culture's sex-role stereotypes may not get along with each other especially well in the long run; "feminine" women who are married to macho men tend to be less satisfied with their marriages than other women are (Miller, 1999). However, those who do not rigidly adhere to the stereotypes of usual masculine or feminine behavior—that's about half of us (O'Heron & Orlofsky, 1990)—violate others' expectations and sometimes appear to behave in an unseemly manner.

People's personalities are rather stable, and when they precipitate impropriety, their influence is likely to be long-lasting. In contrast, several other personal sources of breaches of propriety can operate either as traits, having chronic effects, or as states that come and go. Each of the following personal factors may vary reliably from person to person over time but change across situations within a particular individual as well.

Ignorance

People sometimes break the rules because they simply do not know what they are. This is a common problem in international relations; diplomats and other travelers often need substantial schooling to avoid unintentionally offending their hosts. In Japan, for instance, the process of exchanging business cards is more ceremonial than in the United States; one is expected to present one's card with both hands while making a slight bow and then read the card that is offered in return. Thereafter, that card should be respectfully placed where it can be seen; under no circumstances should it simply be pocketed. Uninitiated people are unlikely to observe such customs properly, and entire books are written to provide guidance in international etiquette (e.g., Axtell, 1990).

A more subtle form of ignorance occurs when people think they understand the rules but are actually misinformed. When "pluralistic ignorance" occurs, people misunderstand others' preferences and conform to perceived norms that, in fact, few people support. Such misinformation clearly contributes to excessive drinking on college campuses: Very few students approve of heavy drinking, but the average student believes that most others do; as a result, many students drink too much, adhering to a norm that does not really exist. Interestingly, when students are shown that most of their peers actually disapprove of heavy drinking, they drink much less, too (Schroeder & Prentice, 1998). Conceivably, such misperceptions contribute to other undesirable behaviors such as bingeing and purging, drug use, and unsafe sex. Evidently, both the things we do not know and the things we "know that ain't so" (Billings, 1874, p. 286) can be problematic.

Lack of Skill

Even when they know how they ought to behave, people are not always able to do the right thing. Temporary or chronic deficiencies in skill may cause people to behave improperly even when they wish to do better. In the United States, for instance, a sixth of the populace has obviously inadequate oral communication skills and is unable, for example, to provide comprehensible information about a fire in their homes or to sensibly describe a movie they have just seen (Vangelisti & Daly, 1989). Although they might wish to help, they would be likely to mislead or frustrate strangers who ask them for directions.

A lack of skill may also contribute to impropriety when people resort to undesirable behavior to get what they want. One correlate of verbal aggression in families, for instance, is a lack of skill in argumentation (Sabourin, 1996). Spouses who cannot develop sensible challenges to each others' views on an issue are more likely to attack each others' personalities, belittling the messenger because they cannot rebut the message. If they were more deft at polite debate, they might not resort to brusque and caustic treatment of one another.

Happily, some deficiencies in skill are temporary and improve over time. As strangers gradually become friends, for instance, they usually become much more astute in accurately reading each others' moods and judging each others' meanings (Colvin, Vogt, & Ickes, 1997). Such discernment undoubtedly helps them avoid stepping on each others' toes and reduces the likelihood that they will unknowingly do things their partners consider improper.

Lapse of Control

Even skilled people sometimes falter, however. Despite knowing how to behave and ordinarily being able to do so, people may find themselves blurting out hurtful secrets, wolfing down the last piece of pie, or sneaking peeks at a lover's diary because they are temporarily unable to resist temptation and cannot control themselves. Self-control appears to be a limited resource: If people engage in active efforts to control their impulses, they subsequently become less able to regulate their behavior for a short time while their willpower is being replenished (Muraven, Tice, & Baumeister, 1998). Thus, because avoiding impropriety often requires us to constrain impolite impulses, prolonged periods of self-regulation and careful behavior are likely to lead to occasional lapses of control.

An ironic aspect of conscious self-restraint is that, in order to do it well, one must monitor one's behavior and pay some attention to how well one is doing. This can cause one's unwanted impulses to stay on one's mind. Shameful secrets and hidden love affairs often operate in this manner (Wegner & Wenzlaff, 1996); people who try to keep secrets often find themselves preoccupied with the very facts (or people) they are trying to keep hidden. Presumably, during periods of distraction or self-regulatory fatigue, they may unwittingly be likely to let slip some hint of the improper truth simply because it is often on their minds.

Lack of Effort

People also behave improperly when they are not trying hard enough to do otherwise. Even when they are capable of controlling themselves, people will not restrain their impulses if they do not exert the effort required to do so. If they do not expend energy trying to be polite, most people lazily do things that are improper.[3] For instance, people typically work at presenting themselves to their acquaintances in a manner that makes favorable, attractive impressions; thus, someone on a blind date may go to extraordinary, desperate lengths to avoid passing gas noisily in the presence of someone they want to impress. However, people work less hard at impressing those who already like them (Leary et al., 1994); when others' acceptance is assured, people feel freer to relax and "be themselves." This reduced effort often leads to greater impropriety (Miller, 1997), so that a spouse is more likely than a casual partner to just go ahead and pass gas, perhaps with the excuse that "I couldn't help it." The point is that such people usually can "help it" and could readily avoid such improprieties if they expended the needed effort.

Lack of Care

Deficient effort causes impropriety when people misbehave because they are lazy. In such cases, people often value the norms they are breaking but do not want to work hard enough to meet their demands. In contrast, on other occasions, people misbehave because they do not value a norm sufficiently in the first place; in these cases, they choose to disobey the rules not (just) because they may be lazy, but because they do not care enough to obey them.

There are two different forms such nonconformity can take. In the first, independence, people do whatever suits them regardless of a norm's proscriptions; if they are aware of a relevant norm, they simply ignore its dictates. In these instances, people really do not care about the rules. By comparison, in the second type of nonconformity, people do take heed of the rules but are careful not to follow them. This is defiant anticonformity, and its irony is that anticonformists may be substantially governed by a salient norm, despite their wayward behavior: In their efforts to defy a norm, they may go out of their way to flaunt the rule, inconveniencing themselves to do something other than what the norm suggests. In such cases, people are not "independent" at all; their behavior is still being influenced (albeit in reverse) by the rules (Franzoi, 1996).

Malevolence

In other instances of nonconformity, people do not merely break norms of propriety, they are openly antagonistic to the norms and to other people. Here, improper behavior is intentional and deliberate, and it is motivated by the desire to do harm to others. Some cases of intentional

---

[3]This assertion assumes that, at bottom, people are self-indulgent egotists rather than selfless altruists and that socialization and training lead naturally greedy, self-centered children to become polite, considerate adults. The assumption may be incorrect, but it is not unfamiliar; it has a long history in philosophy and psychology, so I accept it uncritically here.

embarrassment are an example of this (Sharkey, 1997); people sometimes mercilessly tease or sabotage others to cause them embarrassment to "put them in their place."

Selfishness

People sometimes offend and frustrate others because it is advantageous for them to do so, and they are more concerned with their own convenience than with the well-being of others. People who empty their car ashtrays in parking lots are almost certainly being selfish; were they to consider their actions, they would probably realize that they are being a nuisance to others, but the personal benefits of their behavior are more influential than the communal drawbacks.

Perhaps if they were possessed of greater sympathy for the disgust they cause others, such people would not behave as they do. When one is sympathetic, others' distress is salient; this motivates actions that tend to take others' well-being into account (Wispé, 1991). Indeed, the antisocial behavior of people who are said to lack a "conscience" often seems to be based on disregard for the feelings of others (Millon, Simonsen, Birket-Smith, & Davis, 1998).

Summary

Whether chronically or occasionally, people who behave improperly and irritate others do so because they do not recognize and understand how they ought to behave or are unable or unwilling to do better. A variety of failings can produce impropriety when people do know how they should act instead; insufficient skill or temporary lapses of self-control can make it difficult for people to do what they ought, or they may be too fatigued, lazy, or unconcerned to invest the required effort. Greed and selfishness can make polite behavior seem less expedient and rewarding than its impolite alternatives, and people sometimes behave obnoxiously because they seek to do others harm. All of these influences may come and go in almost any of us, but stable individual differences also probably predispose some of us to more frequent impropriety than others will produce.

These various factors probably guarantee that any of us will behave improperly from time to time. Indeed, to the extent that proper behavior requires active effort, thoughtful attention, and self-control, one could argue that impropriety is the default human condition and polite decorousness is a departure from our native state. Several reasons may explain why naturally selfish people sometimes behave in unselfish ways (see Sober & Wilson, 1998), but we should not be surprised that people are often improper.

Still, there are other influences on impropriety that reside not in personal dispositions and states but in the situations from which impropriety springs. No matter who we are, we may occasionally find ourselves in situations in which we seem unable to avoid offending or irritating others despite wishing otherwise.

Situational Influences

Normative Specificity

Sociologist Erving Goffman (1963) suggested that situations vary along a continuum of "tightness" and "looseness" that describes the extent to which individuals may behave idiosyncratically without seeming untoward or disrespectful. In some settings, there are relatively strict standards for appropriate conduct, whereas in others, a wider variety of individual actions are acceptable. Situations thus differ in the specificity with which they dictate what is and is not improper, and breaches of propriety are inevitably more noticeable in "tight" settings in which less behavioral freedom is allowed. Even small children should be silent and still at a symphony orchestra's formal performance in a concert hall, for instance, but more playfulness is to be expected if the symphony is playing outdoors at a park on a sunny day.

Indeed, serious concertgoers are likely to be annoyed at the outdoor concert if they expect others to maintain the same decorum that is expected of them indoors. Norms are less precise and exacting in "loose" situations, but the potential for perceived impropriety exists there, too, if people enter such situations with conflicting expectations.

Normative Clarity and Consensus

Faced with situations in which inconsistent, uncertain, or conflicting norms are present, even skilled, well-intentioned people may not know how to act. Even genteel, generous people may offend others when no single strategy of behavior is acceptable to all those who are present. One such situation occurs when people simultaneously encounter different groups that have diverse expectations and standards for propriety (i.e., a *multiple audience problem*; Leary, 1995), and in such settings, it may simply be impossible to please all of the people all of the time: Anything one does may elicit disapproval from somebody. Stepparents may face such situations in their blended families, particularly when stepchildren marry and want both of their divorced parents to participate in the event. The bride and groom, the divorced parents, various siblings, and other family members may all have firm and heartfelt opinions about the role a stepparent should play in the wedding. There is often considerable doubt and acrimony about where the stepparent should sit or even whether he or she is welcome at all. The lack of agreement among all observers about what is proper—and the novelty and uncertainty such situations present—nearly ensure that someone will think the stepparents improper no matter what they do.

A special case of the multiple audience problem occurs when almost everyone agrees that a person's behavior is proper, but an idiosyncratic perceiver judges things to be amiss. On occasion, individuals use standards that are clearly not normative to perceive impropriety that is not apparent to anyone else; here, impropriety resides in the eye of the beholder and not in the behavior being judged. A fellow who has not been forewarned about the audience's rambunctious behavior at a screening of *The Rocky Horror Picture Show* (Sherman, 1975), for instance, may be annoyed by their interference with the show (while, at the same time, everyone else in the audience may be wondering, "what's the matter with him?").

Evolving Norms

Behavior that was once appropriate may become less desirable as a situation slowly changes and its relevant norms evolve. Unless people keep revising and updating their perceptions of propriety, their behavior may gradually become increasingly improper as time goes by. For instance, people are ordinarily more modest around their friends than they are around strangers (Tice, Butler, Muraven, & Stillwell, 1995); thus, boastful behavior that elicits favorable reactions from acquaintances is likely to be disadvantageous when a more meaningful relationship develops.

Indeed, changing norms are commonly evident when casual relationships become intimate ones. Behavior that was charming or endearing early in a relationship can become frustrating and obnoxious as a couple spends more time together or takes on important new responsibilities such as marriage or parenting. A partner who initially seems playful and spontaneous may later seem irresponsible and unreliable, and one who initially appears nurturing and attentive may later seem smothering and possessive. In fact, the very characteristics that one initially finds most attractive in a new partner often become the things one finds most obnoxious about that person as the relationship develops and its norms evolve; such self-defeating "fatal attractions" may occur in as many as 29% of all romantic relationships (Felmlee, 1998).

Dire Necessity

People sometimes find themselves in pressing situations of such exigency that they have no choice but to frustrate others with a breach of propriety. A mother rushing her terrified, bleeding child to a hospital is likely to inconvenience others with her frantic driving, but she is also likely to feel that her actions are justifiable and necessary. Situational constraints and demands can certainly cause people to do things that they would rather not do.

A nuance here is that people are probably egocentric and self-serving when they evaluate the necessity of their actions. My judgment that I simply must get home in time for the next episode of my favorite television show is unlikely to be shared by those I irritate and annoy along the way; they are likely to think that I'll be just fine if I wait for the episode to be replayed later in the year. One person's absolute necessity may sometimes seem to others to be greed and selfishness instead (Gilovich, Kruger, & Savitsky, 1999).

Summary

Situations sometimes confuse us with vague, loose norms that provide little guidance or with audiences that hold conflicting expectations that cannot all be satisfied. On other occasions, even when we know how we ought to behave, situations can pressure us into actions that we know to be improper. Specific standards of propriety may change over time as well, so that conduct that was once acceptable may gradually become less so.

Given the cultural changes that have made impropriety more commonplace, the variety of personal influences that can produce impropriety, and the inevitable situational pressures that make occasional impropriety hard to avoid, breaches of propriety are obviously an inescapable fact of social life. Moreover, several different types of impropriety may be encountered every day. With this understanding of the sources of impropriety in hand, I now turn to consideration of the specific events that constitute commonplace breaches of propriety.

TYPES OF IMPROPRIETY

As this volume attests, social scientists have recently begun to study the obnoxious "dark side" of everyday life. Several volumes (Cupach & Spitzberg, 1994; Kowalski, 1997; Spitzberg & Cupach, 1998) and a variety of empirical studies have examined distressing and destructive aspects of interaction such as insults (Harris, 1993), interruptions (LaFrance, 1992), gossip (Jaeger, Skelder, & Rosnow, 1998), guilt induction (Sommer & Baumeister, 1997), bragging (Leary, Bednarski, Hammon, & Duncan, 1997), and betrayal (Shackelford & Buss, 1996). Teasing (Keltner, Young, Heerey, Oemig, & Monarch, 1998), lying (DePaulo & Kashy, 1998), and all the other things people do to hurt others' feelings (Leary, Springer, Negel, Ansell, & Evans, 1998) have also been explored. Even the harm that may be done by being too helpful to others has been inspected (Fisher, Nadler, & Whitcher-Alagna, 1982).

However, investigations that have attempted to catalog diverse types of improper behavior have typically focused on the transgressions that anger, frustrate, or disappoint partners in close relationships (e.g., Buss, 1991; Metts, 1994). Although these are especially consequential social situations, the rules of friendship and intimacy differ in meaningful ways from communal norms of civility and politeness (Argyle & Henderson, 1984). On some dimensions, they ask more of us; whereas friends should share important news and trust and confide in one another, for example, it is generally enough for passersby simply to avoid invading others' privacy. In other areas, there are fewer restrictions on friends than on strangers; intimates can tell brutal truths that strangers should keep to themselves. This is not always a good thing: We might wish that intimates were as courteous and cordial to one another as they are to strangers but, in fact, sometime during their relationship, married people are ultimately likely to be meaner to each other than to anyone else they know (Miller, 1997). Some spouses would do well to be as polite at home as they are at work or at play with total strangers.

I sought to expand on the existing studies of relational transgressions by exploring the breaches of propriety we encounter in all phases of social life. I began by inviting 64 young adults (51 women, 13 men) to compile lists of the obnoxious, impolite, and irksome things they noticed themselves and others doing over several days time. I then produced categories of impropriety that organized these events using Bulmer's (1979) method of analytic induction, developing categories using a portion of the data and then testing their usefulness with the rest of the data. Fifteen different broad types of improper behavior emerged. The usefulness of this scheme was examined with a new set of data provided by 34 young adults (27 women, 7 men) who, for two consecutive days, provided detailed reports of the first breach of impropriety they encountered each day. Two independent judges were able to classify these accounts very reliably using the 15 categories, so the 34 participants were schooled in the coding scheme and then instructed to tabulate and rate the bothersomeness of all of the breaches of impropriety they encountered over the next 4 days (which included a weekend). A total of 991 obnoxious incidents were noted—an average of more than 7 such incidents per person per day—constituting by far the largest sample of such events on record.

What did I find? I first should note that these reports came from a sample of youthful collegians in the southwestern United States that was disproportionately female. In addition, during the 4-day survey, they categorized each instance of impropriety themselves; they did a good job of this with their own detailed accounts submitted earlier in this procedure, but there was undoubtedly some variability in their coding expertise. They also reported all of the improprieties they encountered, whether or not they were personally involved. In a few cases, the respondents were the authors of the improper action, whereas in others they were merely bystanders. Most of the time, the respondents were actually the unhappy targets of the undesirable behavior, but a variety of different perspectives are represented here. Thus, the results that follow should be treated as a suggestive snapshot of impropriety rather than a definitive exposition of the relative frequencies of these events in modern life.

The various events we observed fell into two broad classes. The first of these included actions of individuals who were not involved in contingent interactions with the observer (or anyone else) at the time. These were public actions, obviously, but many of their authors had no idea they were being observed. A solitary driver vigorously but absent-mindedly picking his nose at a stoplight was an exemplar of such cases. These behaviors clearly mattered to others (who were offended or inconvenienced), but they did not necessarily involve other people.

In contrast, the second class of events included actions directed in some way toward other people who were clearly the targets of such actions. On occasion, the targets were not even present at the time (e.g., when one was the focus of energetic gossip), and even when they were present, they were not always engaged in contingent interaction with the author of the action. Indeed, they were not necessarily even aware that the undesirable action was taking place; instances of malicious sabotage, for example, were sometimes conducted against targets who remained unaware that they had been victimized. Still, in most of these events, authors directed their actions at targets with whom they were interacting, whether at home, on the road, or out on the town.

Individual Behavior

Four types of individual impropriety were observed. Each involved the obnoxious misuse or mishandling of one's person or the surroundings.

Control of One's Body

People who distressed others by picking scabs or their noses, squeezing pimples, scratching their genitals, passing gas, burping, or otherwise misbehaving with their bodies in public places were said to have exerted inappropriate control of themselves. Representative examples included these accounts:

> A little boy that goes to my church is always picking his nose and eating what he picks. He did it again today. I thought I was going to throw up.

* * *

> I was in Wal-Mart in my hometown and I saw a man blow his nose in his hand.

* * *

> My roommate passed gas for such an extended period that the entire
> 3-bedroom, 2-bath apartment absolutely reeked of gastrointestinal
> emissions.

These actions involved personal matters of individual grooming and decorum, and they would not have caused others disgust had they simply been private. It was the public nature of the act, not any effort or intent to do others harm, that made these behaviors a nuisance.

Control of One's Props

Mismanagement of clothes, cars, and other accessories could also be obnoxious. One such example involved a professor who came to class not only with his zipper down but with his shirttail sticking out of his fly; remarkably, he did this on several occasions. (The class couldn't decide whether to be amused or annoyed, but ultimately decided on the latter.) Another "prop" that appeared in several reports was chewing gum; in one case, a passenger in a car threw her gum out of the window instead of wrapping it in a napkin, and the car's owner later found it smeared down the side of the car.

Control of One's Environment

People annoyed or inconvenienced others by fouling the physical environment. Any form of littering—such as leaving malodorous, dirty diapers in a parking lot—fit here. So did aural pollution of a sort that illustrates the influence of cultural factors such as fads and technology.

> When I was going into the grocery store there was a guy hanging out
> in his car with the music up so loud it was hurting my ears. The bass
> was up so high his car rattled with every beat. I know he had the
> volume up this high because he thought it made him cool.

Control of One's Companions

People distressed others by losing appropriate control over their animal or human companions. In these cases, fault was ordinarily attributed to an older, presumably more responsible, person who allowed dogs or children (in one instance, even a tarantula) in his or her care to run wild:

> While I was at work in a clothing store, a child walked around pulling
> the sales tags off of some clothing. The mother acted as if what her
> child had done was cute and funny. It wasn't to me. We have to figure
> out which tag goes to which item and reattach it.

As is evident from this example, some breaches of propriety did material harm to the person or possessions that were affected. Improprieties always caused emotional distress, frustrating, annoying, or disgusting others but, occasionally, physical damage was done as well.

Interactive Behavior

Individual improprieties, particularly those involving control of one's body, occurred often. Nevertheless, a wider variety of breaches of propriety involved interactive behavior in which another person was clearly the intentional or unintentional target of the act. In general, some of these were the most aggravating breaches of all.

Inattention

When people too often interrupted others, ignored them, or did not show appropriate concern, respect, or sympathy for others, they were said to be guilty of insufficient attention. At a minimum, such actions were judged to be impolite, but at their worst they were painful or humiliating rejections:

> Three weeks ago my stepson got married. On the nametag of the corsage I was given was written *Other*. That is not the way for a bride to make friends with her mother-in-law even if I am a stepmother-in-law.

> * * *

> When I spoke to my stepsister, she started walking off like I wasn't even in the same room with her. She hasn't talked to me in 5 years.

> * * *

> Tuesday night I was at a party, and my friend introduced me to one of his friends. The person I was introduced to shook my hand but didn't even look at me or say "nice to meet you." I was ignored totally. My friend was embarrassed that he introduced me to him. This was inattention.

Many of these slights could have been accidental, but some of them were obviously intentional and were meant to be apparent to the wounded recipient. If so, they were still passively aggressive actions and thus could be distinguished from more active attempts at harm such as verbal insults or physical sabotage. However, we generally did not attempt to judge the intentions of the actor, choosing instead to classify the person's observed behavior; our categories were more reliable as a result.

Violations of Privacy

The obverse of inattention was snooping, prying, eavesdropping, spying, or gossiping that invaded others' privacy. Some targets probably never knew that they had been preyed on, and these actions were sometimes private ones, conducted when no one else was present. Nevertheless, these were classified as interactive improprieties because their authors did not select their victims randomly; their existing relationships with the victims motivated the invasions of privacy:

> By serendipity, I found a letter from my aunt to her new boyfriend, so I read it.

* * *

> One evening some friends were at my apartment and we came across a letter of my roommate's. We boiled water and broke the seal on the envelope with the steam. We knew it was an invasion of privacy but we were so curious.

Insufficient Manners

A lazier, more passive behavior was the failure to do something polite, a deficiency of manners. People who did not offer thanks (much less write thank you notes) or provide other small courtesies to others committed this impropriety.

> I was invited to a friend's wedding and knew I wasn't going to be able to go, but I didn't take the time to RSVP that I wouldn't be able to make it. It was an intentional act of omission, and it was pretty lazy.

* * *

> Two weeks ago, my neighbor's hot water heater caught on fire while she was in the shower. The girl ran to our apartment completely naked and called 911. My girlfriend gave her some of her clothes to wear. The girl never thanked us or returned my girlfriend's clothes.

* * *

> People saw me coming toward the elevator, but didn't hold the door.

As these instances suggest, breaches of propriety could result either from acts of commission or from acts of omission.

Selfishness

Lazy irresponsibility also figured prominently in several accounts of selfishness but, when this category was appropriate, people gained some personal benefit by shirking their duties or tasks. Selfish actions involved some element of greed that was not present in a simple failure of manners:

> My roommate refuses to do the dirty dishes at our apartment. I left to go home over the Christmas break and there were his dirty dishes in the sink. When I came home weeks later, the dishes were still in the

sink full of mold. He had been at the apartment over the break, and he refused to do the dishes or clean the house. It is very annoying to come home to a filthy house.

Selfishness was also the verdict given to drivers who did not wait their turn in line and to companions who changed radio stations and television channels without asking first.

Rudeness

Other actions were straightforwardly discourteous and were judged to be rude. These behaviors did not provide their authors any personal benefits, but they did produce aggravation for others. Many of these improprieties involved thoughtless or intended criticism that disparaged others.

> We watched a movie on television, and my husband commented about a very attractive female and said I could look like her if I worked out.

* * *

> A co-worker pointed out that my hair would look so much better if I curled it and styled it a different way.

* * *

> This occurred while meeting my boyfriend's family. His father asked me what my major is, and I told him psychology. He informed me that all college students who major in psychology need help themselves. I was extremely offended.

* * *

People were also frequently rude while driving their cars, leaving parking places unusually slowly to frustrate other drivers or maneuvering their cars to block others on the highway.

Intentional Embarrassment or Provocation

As Sharkey (1997) suggested, people's deliberate efforts to tease or embarrass their companions are often motivated by friendly, playful intentions. However, when those actions were so crude or obnoxious that they annoyed the target or others, they were judged to be improper.

> On my way to my car after class, three young men were walking in front of me horse-playing and having a great time. All of the sudden another guy ran up from behind all of us and jerked down the warm-up pants of one of the men. This young man was wearing no underpants. They all laughed as the "mooner" chased the guy who pulled down his pants. This was a breach of propriety because I was present,

and I feel it was distasteful having to look at his butt. I know the "mooner" was very embarrassed.

Occasionally, provocations such as these did not seem playful at all, with people apparently aiming to get someone's "goat." If the actions were harmless enough to cause mere embarrassment, they fit this category. However, if they were cruel or malevolent, they fit another type of impropriety.

Maliciousness

Insults or sabotage that derisively demeaned or harmed others were judged to be malicious. Although we cannot be sure of the actor's intentions, the following account was deemed to fit this category:

> At a party last night my buddy was extremely intoxicated. He had been drinking Dickel all night and was hammered. Towards the end of the night everyone else got pretty wasted also. My buddy was almost out of his bottle of Dickel, so when he left to go to the bathroom we played a seriously rude joke on him. Another buddy of mine grabbed his bottle and began urinating in it. When the drunk returned he took a huge swallow of it and almost choked.

Categorization of events such as these required some care because they often contained elements of both playfulness and intentional embarrassment. However, no such deliberation was needed in this case:

> I had a very egotistical roommate once, and she drove me crazy. One time I had heard enough about her breast implants, etc., that I just couldn't take it anymore. I urinated in her shampoo bottle.

Drunkenness

People also behaved badly when they were intoxicated, but this was typically most apparent to those who were not drunk themselves:

> I live in a dorm, and the people tend to get a little rowdy at night after the bars close. It seems like they have a party outside my door after I decide to go to bed. They usually stay there until I go and tell them to leave. The reason I believe this is a breach of propriety is because they annoy others when they've been drinking too much.

Curiously, my respondents considered drunkenness to be the least bothersome of all these breaches of propriety, a fact that prompts me to remind you that these accounts were provided by college students. Sedate middle-aged homeowners might think drunkenness to be rather more obnoxious.

Boorishness

A similar point can be made about excessive, needless vulgarity, which I termed *boorishness*. This was the impropriety these respondents encountered least often, possibly because only an astonishing amount of vulgarity would be noticeable to young adults, who use a lot of vulgar language all the time (Jay, 1992).

Playfulness

When people were not drunk but engaged in rambunctious clowning or annoying impishness, they were said to be excessively playful.

> While I was driving on my way to the Dollar store, I honked and waved at complete strangers. I initiated it, and the strangers waved back.

Others' Sensitivity

Behavior that did not appear to break a situation's norms occasionally gives offense to idiosyncratic observers. Here, the breach of propriety seemed to have more to do with the perceiver's "thin skin" than with any misbehavior from the others involved.

> I went out to dinner at an extremely nice restaurant to meet my boy-friend's parents for the first time. I found them extremely uptight and unapproachable. I did not really want an entrée because I was too nervous and did not want to eat. I ordered oysters, which were listed as an appetizer on the menu. They freaked out and seemed extremely offended. I still don't really understand what norm I violated; maybe it had something to do with them being Jewish and I'm not, but I apparently violated some norm or another.

Interestingly, such events were typically more bothersome than several other types of impropriety.

The Worst of the Lot

There seem to be several different ways that others can annoy, irritate, or inconvenience us on any given day. In fact, these events are routine occurrences; as Table 2.1 indicates, each of these 15 breaches of propriety was encountered at least once a week, on average, and several of them occurred about once a day. Moreover, these events are typically not just trivial nuisances; instead, they are notable annoyances. As Table 2.2 reveals, two-thirds of them were ordinarily judged to be at least moderately bothersome (ratings were performed using a 7-point scale, with 1 = "not at all bothersome" and 7 = "extremely bothersome"). I did not determine how these exasperating experiences affected the respondents' subsequent moods and well-being, but they were probably not inert; the cumulative wear-and-tear of the major and mild episodes of distaste and irritation that are caused by these events may ultimately be quite burdensome (see Rook, 1984).

TABLE 2.1
Mean Frequency of Occurrence of the
Breaches of Propriety Over 4 Days

Impropriety	Frequency
Boorishness	1.2
Control of props	1.4
Intentional embarrassment	1.5
Control of companions	1.5
Drunkenness	1.7
Maliciousness	1.7
Violations of privacy	2.0
Playfulness	2.1
Others' sensitivity	2.4
Control of environment	2.9
Inattention	3.2
Insufficient manners	3.4
Selfishness	3.5
Rudeness	3.7
Control of body	4.4

With that concern in mind, I constructed an "impact index" for each of these improprieties (by multiplying its frequency of occurrence by its average bothersomeness) that summarized how common and obnoxious each event is in social life. As Table 2.3 illustrates, there were substantial differences in average "impact." (Keep in mind that these data were obtained from a collegiate sample; two of the breaches they considered least

TABLE 2.2
Mean Bothersomeness of Breaches
of Propriety

Impropriety	Bothersomeness
Drunkenness	2.8
Control of props	3.5
Boorishness	3.6
Control of body	3.7
Violations of privacy	4.0
Control of environment	4.5
Playfulness	4.5
Inattention	4.6
Intentional embarrassment	4.7
Insufficient manners	4.8
Selfishness	4.9
Control of companions	4.9
Others' sensitivity	5.0
Rudeness	5.1
Maliciousness	5.2

Note. The behaviors were rated on a 1–7 scale; 4 was the midpoint (*moderately bothersome*).

TABLE 2.3
Impact Ratings of the Breaches of Propriety

Breach of Propriety	Impact Factor
Boorishness	4.3
Drunkenness	4.8
Control of props	4.9
Intentional embarrassment	7.1
Control of companions	7.4
Violations of privacy	8.0
Maliciousness	8.8
Playfulness	9.5
Others' sensitivity	12.0
Control of environment	13.1
Inattention	14.7
Control of body	16.3
Insufficient manners	16.3
Selfishness	17.2
Rudeness	18.9

Note. The impact value for each impropriety was derived by multiplying its frequency of occurrence by its average bothersomeness. Higher numbers denote greater impact.

impactful, boorishness and drunkenness, may be of greater concern to other people.)

Four events stood out as the improprieties that had the most impact on social life: control of one's body, insufficient manners, selfishness, and rudeness. The last of these, rudeness, was both quite annoying and common and thus had the highest impact rating of them all. Nevertheless, all four of these events are exemplars of impropriety, and together they delineate an important truth: None of these nuisances would occur if people merely treated others the way they usually wish to be treated in return. Each embodies a failure of simple politeness, and each could be easily avoided if people would only invest the minimal requisite attention, effort, and self-restraint. Remarkably, each of us must endure frequent annoyance because we do not observe simple rules we should have learned in kindergarten: "Don't pick it in public"; "Say please and thank you"; "Share"; and "If you can't say anything nice, don't say anything at all."

WHY WE SHOULD CARE

I have established that breaches of propriety take various forms and are regrettably routine; my respondents were on a pace to encounter several dozen annoying breaches of propriety each week. Perhaps this should be no surprise; there are several intrapersonal, situational, and cultural influences that make it likely that such nuisances should pervade social life.

Cumulatively, such events may be quite consequential, and this is one reason why we should take notice of them. Indeed, our interdependent efforts to avoid breaches of propriety and to cope with them once they have occurred have been the focus of several lines of research in the social sciences. Theories of politeness (Brown & Levinson, 1987) and the mechanisms through which people overcome social predicaments—appeasement (Keltner, Young, & Buswell, 1997), accounting (Hodgins, Liebeskind, & Schwartz, 1996), and facework (Metts, 1997)—have generated dozens of investigations. Pangs of regret (Gilovich, Medvec, & Kahneman, 1998) and the redemption of forgiveness (McCullough et al., 1998) have come under careful study. The maintenance of decorum is apparently such a tricky undertaking, there is much to understand.

Even more important, however, is the possibility that with the insights provided by studies of impropriety we can ultimately manage to be more polite, generous, and attentive to one another. We have found that breaches of propriety are obnoxious and commonplace. Still, the improprieties with the most impact could apparently be avoided altogether if people were simply less greedy and thoughtless. Most of us are perfectly capable of behaving in courteous and considerate ways when we want to (see Miller, 1997), and most of us do act in a more desirable fashion when we are reminded to (e.g., "People treat each other nicer," 1998). Straightforward training in courtesy and etiquette can help those of us who need it ("Etiquette part of business curriculum," 1999; Wilson, Boni, & Hogg, 1997) so that others will seek out our companionship and services more often (Ford, 1995). With insight and minor effort, almost any of us can be less annoying to our fellows. Thus, we ought not passively accept the uncivil state of modern social life but should instead strive, in both our studies and personal affairs, to bring to this dark side of human interaction a more gentle light.

REFERENCES

Argyle, M., & Henderson, M. (1984). The rules of friendship. *Journal of Social and Personal Relationships, 1,* 211–237.

Aversa, J. (1999, January 23). Etiquette expert details cell phone usage no-no's. *The Bryan-College Station Eagle,* p. A3.

Axtell, R. E. (1990). *The do's and taboos of hosting international visitors.* New York: Wiley.

Billings, J. (1874). *Everybody's friend, or: Josh Billings's encyclopedia and proverbial philosophy of wit and humor.* New York: American Publishing Company.

Brown, P., & Levinson, S. C. (1987). *Politeness: Some universals in language usage.* Cambridge, England: Cambridge University Press.

Buchanan, P. (1999, February 20). Cultural war is worth the effort. *The Bryan-College Station Eagle,* p. A10.

Bulmer, M. (1979). Concepts in the analysis of qualitative data. *Sociological Review*, *27*, 651–677.

Buss, D. M. (1991). Conflict in married couples: Personality predictors of anger and upset. *Journal of Personality*, *59*, 663–688.

Carter, S. L. (1998). *Civility: Manners, morals, and the etiquette of democracy*. New York: Basic Books.

Cohen, D., Nisbett, R. E., Bowdle, B. F., & Schwarz, N. (1996). Insult, aggression, and the southern culture of honor: An "experimental ethnography." *Journal of Personality and Social Psychology*, *70*, 945–960.

Colvin, C. R., Vogt, D., & Ickes, W. (1997). Why do friends understand each other better than strangers do? In W. Ickes (Ed.), *Empathic accuracy* (pp.169–193). New York: Guilford Press.

Cupach, W. R., & Spitzberg, B. H. (Eds.). (1994). *The dark side of interpersonal communication*. Hillsdale, NJ: Erlbaum.

DePaulo, B., & Kashy, D. A. (1998). Everyday lies in close and casual relationships. *Journal of Personality and Social Psychology*, *74*, 63–79.

Eberly, D. (1999, March 11). Civility. *All Things Considered*. Washington, DC: National Public Radio. Available: www.npr.org/programs/atc/archives/1999/990311.atc.html

Edwards, D. C. (1999). *Motivation & emotion: Evolutionary, physiological, cognitive, and social influences*. Thousand Oaks, CA: Sage.

Etiquette part of business curriculum at A&M. (1999, February 7). *The Bryan-College Station Eagle*, p. A12.

Felmlee, D. H. (1998). Fatal attraction. In B. H. Spitzberg & W. R. Cupach (Eds.), *The dark side of close relationships* (pp. 3–31). Mahwah, NJ: Erlbaum.

Fisher, J. D., Nadler, A., & Whitcher-Alagna, S. (1982). Recipient reactions to aid. *Psychological Bulletin*, *91*, 27–54.

Ford, W. S. Z. (1995). Evaluation of the indirect influence of courteous service on customer discretionary behavior. *Human Communication Research*, *22*, 65–89.

Franzoi, S. L. (1996). *Social psychology*. Madison, WI: Brown & Benchmark.

Friedman, E. G., & Squire, C. (1998). *Morality USA*. Minneapolis: University of Minnesota Press.

Gilovich, T., Kruger, J., & Savitsky, K. (1999). Everyday egocentrism and everyday interpersonal problems. In R. M. Kowalski & M. R. Leary (Eds.), *The social psychology of emotional and behavioral problems: Interfaces of social and clinical psychology* (pp. 69–95). Washington, DC: American Psychological Association.

Gilovich, T., Medvec, V. H., & Kahneman, D. (1998). Varieties of regret: A debate and theoretical resolution. *Psychological Bulletin*, *105*, 602–605.

Goffman, E. (1963). *Behavior in public places: Notes on the organization of social gatherings*. New York: Free Press.

Harris, M. B. (1992). When courtesy fails: Gender roles and polite behaviors. *Journal of Applied Social Psychology*, *22*, 1399–1416.

Harris, M. B. (1993). How provoking: What makes men and women angry? *Aggressive Behavior, 19*, 199–211.

Hill, T. E. (1873). *Hill's manual of social & business forms.* New York: World Publishing.

Hodge, S. (1998, October 25). What a lady! *Houston Chronicle*, p. 2F.

Hodgins, H. S., Liebeskind, E., & Schwartz, W. (1996). Getting out of hot water: Facework in social predicaments. *Journal of Personality and Social Psychology, 71*, 300–314.

Holmes, J. (1995). *Women, men and politeness.* London: Longman.

Jaeger, M. E., Skelder, A. A., & Rosnow, R. L. (1998). Who's up on the low down: Gossip in interpersonal relations. In B. H. Spitzberg & W. R. Cupach (Eds.), *The dark side of close relationships* (pp. 103–117). Mahwah, NJ: Erlbaum.

Jay, T. (1992). *Cursing in America: A psycholinguistic survey on dirty language in the courts, in the movies, in the schoolyards, and on the streets.* Philadelphia: J. Benjamin.

Keltner, D., Young, R. C., & Buswell, B. N. (1997). Appeasement in human emotion, social practice, and personality. *Aggressive Behavior, 23*, 359–374.

Keltner, D., Young, R. C., Heerey, E. A., Oemig, C., & Monarch, N. D. (1998). Teasing in hierarchical and intimate relations. *Journal of Personality and Social Psychology, 75*, 1231–1247.

Kowalski, R. M. (Ed.). (1997). *Aversive interpersonal behaviors.* New York: Plenum Press.

Kraut, R., Patterson, M., Lundmark, V., Kiesler, S., Mukopadhyay, T., & Scherlis, W. (1998). Internet paradox: A social technology that reduces social involvement and psychological well-being? *American Psychologist, 53*, 1017–1031.

Krueger, J., & Clement, R. W. (1994). The truly false consensus effect: An ineradicable and egocentric bias in social perception. *Journal of Personality and Social Psychology, 67*, 596–610.

LaFrance, M. (1992). Gender and interruptions: Individual infraction or violation of the social order? *Psychology of Women Quarterly, 16*, 497–512.

Leary, M. R. (1995). *Self-presentation: Impression management and interpersonal behavior.* Madison, WI: Brown & Benchmark.

Leary, M. R., Bednarski, R., Hammon, D., & Duncan, T. (1997). Blowhards, snobs, and narcissists: Interpersonal reactions to excessive egotism. In R. M. Kowalski (Ed.), *Aversive interpersonal behaviors* (pp. 111–131). New York: Plenum Press.

Leary, M. R., & Kowalski, R. M. (1995). *Social anxiety.* New York: Guilford Press.

Leary, M. R., Nezlek, J. B., Downs, D., Radford-Davenport, J., Martin, J., & McMullen, A. (1994). Self-presentation in everyday interactions: Effects of target familiarity and gender composition. *Journal of Personality and Social Psychology, 67*, 664–673.

Leary, M. R., Springer, C., Negel, L., Ansell, E., & Evans, K. (1998). The causes, phenomenology, and consequences of hurt feelings. *Journal of Personality and Social Psychology, 74,* 1225–1237.

Magida, A. J. (Ed.). (1996). *How to be a perfect stranger: A guide to etiquette in other people's religious ceremonies.* Woodstock, VT: Jewish Lights.

Marks, J. (1996, April 22). The American uncivil war. *U.S. News & World Report, 120,* 66–72.

Martin, J. (1985). *Common courtesy: In which Miss Manners® solves the problem that baffled Mr. Jefferson.* New York: Atheneum.

Martin, J. (1998). *Miss Manners'™ basic training: The right thing to say.* New York: Crown.

Martin, J., & Stent, G. S. (1990). I think; therefore I thank: A philosophy of etiquette. *The American Scholar, 59,* 237–254.

McCullough, M. E., Rachal, K. C., Sandage, S. J., Worthington, E. L., Jr., Brown, S. W., & Hight, T. L. (1998). Interpersonal forgiving in close relationships: II. Theoretical elaboration and measurement. *Journal of Personality and Social Psychology, 75,* 1586–1603.

Merida, K., & Leiby, R. (1999, April 25). Are recent tragic events evidence of a decaying culture? *Houston Chronicle,* p. 12F.

Metts, S. (1994). Relational transgressions. In W. R Cupach & B. H. Spitzberg (Eds.), *The dark side of interpersonal communication* (pp. 217–239). Hillsdale, NJ: Erlbaum.

Metts, S. (1997). Face and facework: Implications for the study of personal relationships. In S. Duck (Ed.), *Handbook of personal relationships: Theory, research and interventions* (2nd ed., pp. 373–390). Chichester, England: Wiley.

Miller, R. S. (1997). We always hurt the ones we love: Aversive interactions in close relationships. In R. M. Kowalski (Ed.), *Aversive interpersonal behaviors* (pp. 11–29). New York: Plenum Press.

Miller, R. S. (1999). Dysfunctional relationships. In R. M. Kowalski & M. R. Leary (Eds.), *The social psychology of emotional and behavioral problems: Interfaces of social and clinical psychology* (pp. 311–338). Washington, DC: American Psychological Association.

Millon, T., Simonsen, E., Birket-Smith, M., & Davis, R. D. (Eds.). (1998). *Psychopathy: Antisocial, criminal, and violent behavior.* New York: Guilford Press.

Muraven, M., Tice, D. M., & Baumeister, R. F. (1998). Self-control as a limited resource: Regulatory depletion patterns. *Journal of Personality and Social Psychology, 74,* 774–789.

Nissimov, R. (1999, April 9). In vitro dad not just sperm donor, appeals panel finds. *Houston Chronicle,* p. 29A.

O'Heron, C. A., & Orlofsky, J. L. (1990). Stereotypic and nonstereotypic sex role trait and behavior orientations, gender identity, and psychological adjustment. *Journal of Personality and Social Psychology, 58,* 134–143.

People treat each other nicer after mayor scolds on civility. (1998, December 28). *The Palm Beach Post,* p. 5A.

Putnam, R. D. (1995). Bowling alone: America's declining social capital. *Journal of Democracy, 6,* 65–78.

Reynolds, J. A., III. (1998, August 24). You can't escape gutter language in today's world. *Houston Chronicle,* p. 19A.

Rook, K. S. (1984). The negative side of social interaction: Impact on psychological well-being. *Journal of Personality and Social Psychology, 46,* 1097–1108.

Rudman, L. A. (1998). Self-promotion as a risk factor for women: The costs and benefits of counterstereotypical impression management. *Journal of Personality and Social Psychology, 74,* 629–645.

Sabourin, T. C. (1996). The role of communication in verbal abuse between spouses. In D. D. Cahn & S. A. Lloyd (Eds.), *Family violence from a communication perspective* (pp. 199–217). Thousand Oaks, CA: Sage.

Schroeder, C. M., & Prentice, D. A. (1998). Exposing pluralistic ignorance to reduce alcohol use among college students. *Journal of Applied Social Psychology, 28,* 2150–2180.

Seligman, M. E. P. (1990). Why is there so much depression today? The waxing of the individual and the waning of the commons. In R. E. Ingram (Ed.), *Contemporary psychological approaches to depression: Theory, research and treatment* (pp. 1–9). New York: Plenum Press.

Shackelford, T. K., & Buss, D. M. (1996). Betrayal in mateships, friendships, and coalitions. *Personality and Social Psychology Bulletin, 22,* 1151–1164.

Sharkey, W. F. (1997). Why would anyone want to intentionally embarrass me? In R. M. Kowalski (Ed.), *Aversive interpersonal behaviors* (pp. 57–90). New York: Plenum Press.

Sherman, J. (Director). (1975). *The Rocky Horror Picture Show* [Film]. Available from Twentieth Century Fox Home Entertainment.

Sober, E., & Wilson, D. S. (1998). *Unto others: The evolution and psychology of unselfish behavior.* Cambridge, MA: Harvard University Press.

Sommer, K. L., & Baumeister, R. F. (1997). Making someone feel guilty: Causes, strategies, and consequences. In R. M. Kowalski (Ed.), *Aversive interpersonal behaviors* (pp. 31–55). New York: Plenum Press.

Spitzberg, B. H., & Cupach, W. R. (Eds.). (1998). *The dark side of close relationships.* Mahwah, NJ: Erlbaum.

Stanfield, J. R., & Stanfield, J. B. (1997). Where has love gone? Reciprocity, redistribution, and the nurturance gap. *Journal of Socio-Economics, 26,* 111–126.

Stebbins, R. A. (1993). *Predicaments: Moral difficulty in everyday life.* Lanham, MD: University Press of America.

Swann, W. B. (1996). *Self-traps: The elusive quest for high self-esteem.* New York: Freeman.

Tice, D. M., Butler, J. L., Muraven, M. B., & Stillwell, A. M. (1995). When modesty prevails: Differential favorability of self-presentation to friends and strangers. *Journal of Personality and Social Psychology, 69,* 1120–1138.

Vangelisti, A. L., & Daly, J. A. (1989). Correlates of speaking skills in the United States: A national assessment. *Communication Education, 38,* 132–143.

Vobejda, B. (1999, February 13). Case made sex a topic for a nation. *Houston Chronicle,* p. 22A.

Wegner, D. M., & Wenzlaff, R. M. (1996). Mental control. In E. T. Higgins & A. W. Kruglanski (Eds.), *Social psychology: Handbook of basic principles* (pp. 466–492). New York: Guilford Press.

Whyte, W. K. (1990). *Dating, mating, and marriage.* New York: Aldine de Gruyter.

Wilson, C., Boni, N., & Hogg, A. (1997). The effectiveness of task clarification, positive reinforcement and corrective feedback in changing courtesy among police staff. *Journal of Organizational Behavior Management, 17,* 65–99.

Wispé, L. (1991). *The psychology of sympathy.* New York: Plenum Press.

3

YOU ****!: SWEARING AS AN AVERSIVE AND A RELATIONAL ACTIVITY

ALAINA M. WINTERS AND STEVE DUCK

Why do men swear? When they swear, why do they use the words which they do? (Patrick , 1901, p. 113)

Most of what we say to others is polite, pleasant, task focused, exchange oriented, and designed to facilitate the smooth progress of an interaction toward its goals (Krauss & Fussell, 1996). All the same, a lot of everyday communication is not (Duck, Rutt, Hurst, & Strejc, 1991) and amounts to behaviors that may have detrimental effects on interpersonal relationships or that are regarded as impolite, disruptive, inappropriate, or otherwise aversive (Duck & Wood, 1995; Kowalski, 1997).

Swearing, obscene language, and profanity represent particularly challenging cases because they are "common" in both senses of the word, that is, frequent and vulgar (Bostrom, Baseheart, & Rossiter 1973). People who swear are generally perceived negatively (Cameron, 1969; Foote & Woodward, 1973; Jay, 1992b; Selnow, 1985). Swearing is discouraged in general (Lester, 1996); it is not normally permitted at all in solemn, workplace, or formal settings (Graham, 1986; Jay & Olson, 1993); it is regarded as offensive in most social interactions (Selnow, 1985); and it is ordinarily seen to cast the speaker as a socially disapproved, impolite, and coarse person (Winters, 1993). Ninety percent of women claim that swearing is so disparaged and aversive that they would never swear in a formal interview (Oliver & Rubin, 1975). In addition, swearing is regarded as potentially disruptive, demeaning of others, sexually and racially offensive, rude, disgusting, and broadly impermissible (Hughes, 1991; Jay, 1992a).

Moreover, because of the (often undefined or unspecified) damage that profane terms may do to young and impressionable minds, swearing has been the subject not only of polite and understood rules, but also of explicit legislation and active moral censure by religious sources, the Supreme Court, and governing bodies for films and television, who register censure and disapproval by means of formal codes and regulations (Hughes, 1991; Rothwell, 1971). For example, the Ten Commandments forbid taking the name of God in vain, and the Watergate tapes were published with "expletive deleted" to avoid giving offense. In 1990, the rap group 2 Live Crew was arrested in Florida on charges of obscenity because they used swear words in their most recent album, and recently the television networks have introduced a code to warn viewers of the use of "bad" language in scheduled programs. We conclude that swearing has a relevance to social experience that makes it interesting to students of aversive social behaviors, that it is regarded as aversive to the extent that it occasionally becomes the topic of legislation, and that it is regarded as not only impolite but also socially disruptive.

In part, our research interest in the phenomenon of swearing is all the greater because this disapproved, aversive activity is extremely prevalent in everyday life. Cameron (1969) reported that every 14th word in a sample of 66,767 words recorded from everyday speech was profanity. Cameron's findings indicated that from 4% to 13% of everyday speech consisted of swear words, depending on the context from which the word sample came (e.g., leisure activity or work). The sheer pervasiveness of expletives in social behavior should warrant examination of the role, functions, and effects of swearing in social interaction, given that it is both aversive and pervasive. Also of interest is that, whereas it is publicly condemned, swearing is nevertheless widely practiced in private (Montagu, 1967; Rothwell, 1971), which suggests that both social psychological processes and relational norms are at play to govern usage of swear-words. However, social psychological studies regarding swearing are rare (Jay, 1977).

There has been very little recent research on swearing and, of necessity, our discussion relies on those older works that exist for consideration. Keep in mind that, although swearing is more prevalent today, its forms and functions have remained relatively stable throughout history. Its growing public presence in social behavior surely makes it a ripe topic for deeper analysis in light of today's theoretical and empirical advances. Our modest hope is to follow the lead of the editor of this volume in raising the "underbelly" topics of social life from obscurity by conceptualizing some persistent challenges to understanding future research.

AN ANALYSIS OF SWEARING

Profane language is language that is unholy, not sacred, and therefore not permitted to be used except "outside the temple" (*pro fanum*; *Chambers 20th Century Dictionary* [MacDonald, 1978]). The *Oxford English Dictionary* calls it "lacking in refinement and good taste, uncultured, ill-bred." Hughes (1991) noted that "in many cultures swearing is fascinating in its protean diversity and poetic creativity" and that "swearing draws upon such powerful resonators as religion, sex, madness, excretion, and nationality, encompassing an extraordinary variety of attitudes including the violent, the amusing, the shocking, the absurd, the casual and the impossible" (p. 3). As discussed below, however, it is not solely the referent that makes a word into a swear word, but something to do with the manner of reference (e.g., it is not normally regarded as swearing when physicians refer to genitalia in a consulting room using the Latin term, but it might be if the Anglo Saxon term were used instead and by garage mechanics). Thus, swearing is vulgar and as such attracts disapproval as an aversive behavior in interpersonal relationships.

Noting long ago that social psychologists did not then know the principles underlying the uses of profanity, Patrick (1901) began by distinguishing between assertive and ejaculatory kinds of swearing. *Asseverative swearing* attracts the listener's attention and is intended to enhance the speaker's credibility as the swearing offers a social emphasis or a firm claim to speak the truth that adds credence to a statement and strength to an assertion. Examples are "Yes, by God!" or "Hell, no!" or the forms of swearing used in legal oaths for the same purposes. *Ejaculatory swearing*, the main focus of both Patrick's analysis and ours, refers to the sort of swearing that is simply exclamatory and may be seen as powerfully insulting, derogatory of others, crude, offensive, and even disruptive of social orders in that it can be used to register disrespect for authority.

Although both forms can still be distinguished, the form most often regarded as aversive in social behavior is the ejaculatory, a broad class that covers several different subspecies. Patrick (1901) differentiated seven classes of words and phrases used in profanity: (a) names of deities ("By God"); (b) names connected with sacred matters of religion (e.g., the old form "Zounds," referring to "God's wounds"); (c) names of saints ("Jumping Jehosaphat"); (d) names of sacred places, such as Jerusalem or one's mother's grave; (e) words related to a supposed future life ("Good heavens," "Damnation," and its minced forms such as "darn" or "tarnation"); (f) vulgar words forbidden by polite usage (Patrick gave no examples, and we will not do so either. We recognize the irony that the absence sends its own interesting message about the aversive consequences of exemplifying swearing in academic writing and the implicit rules that scholars follow in their work.); and (g) expletives having unusual force for various reasons, such as "Mercy!" "Gracious," or "For pity's sake" and "other fossil remains of religious terms or ejaculatory prayers" (p. 115).

In some cases, both forms of swearing serve simply to mark emphatic points or special moments in the flow of social interaction, or they may be used because the speaker lacks a more elaborated vocabulary for achieving social purposes (Bernstein, 1971). These latter do not concern us much here. In the more interesting cases, different levels of analysis are possible, from the individual–motivational to the social–structural. Obviously there is the essentially individual level analysis that treats swearing as letting off steam or expressing anger, outrage, or frustration. It is, for instance, a classic indicator of some personality variables, for example Type A personality, inasmuch as people classified as Type A swear forcefully and often (Innes, 1981). Swearing can also be used to shock or to create impressions of the speaker as tough, fearsome, or dominant (as in delinquent gangs; Daro & Gelles, 1992; Gregersen, 1979) or as an informed, active, and responsible social agitator (Rothwell, 1971).

Swearing may also be analyzed broadly at the group or dyadic level, where it serves intergroup purposes (e.g., stigmatizing or derogating out-groups) and can function negatively by expressing prejudices through racial and other slurs (Lester, 1996). Some of these instances not only express individual opinions and emotions but also serve subtly to reject membership in one group and claim membership of a different group, according to principles of group differentiation discovered by such social psychological researchers as Tajfel (1978) and Giles and Coupland (1991). Indeed, phrases such as "swearing like a trooper," "abusing one another like fish-wives," or "talking like a sailor/tinker" associate the broad act of cursing with particular types of people and social classes. A recent treatise on swearing supports the view that a fundamental purpose of swearing is such social differentiation and structuring (Hughes, 1991).

Although offered primarily as a social history, Hughes's book proposes that swear words act to stigmatize social practices and people and also to effect a social ordering or categorization of groups and individuals. For example, both historically and in current uses, many swear words reinforce a moral or social hierarchy that impugns illegitimacy or incest or refers disparagingly to the target's ancestry or sexual practices. Some researchers also noted that swearing is used as "sexploitation" by assigning men to the active role and women to an objective role in sexual reference, so that the female role is represented as inferior and passive (Sagarin, 1962; Scheid-lower, 1995). The same researchers indicated that women are depicted by men using a broader range of slang terms that equate them with sexual functions.

In an extension of such ideas to the dyadic level, we offer an essentially relational analysis in broader detail. First, the use of swearing is permitted more freely in interactions where the partners are familiar with each other. Second, swearing can be used to indicate familiarity and informality or acceptance of others. Third, swearing can be used to create relational boundaries, that is, rather like nicknames or personal idioms (Hopper, Knapp, & Scott, 1981), which serve to include "members" and exclude others; use of swearing serves to signal something about the relationship between speaker and hearer as well as to convey specific descriptive meanings. For example, swearing is used in relational ways in teasing, joking, relieving social tension, shocking the listener, and rebuking forcefully. It is also a means of social bonding by "playing the dozens" or other forms of mock insult that actually tease partners and help create and define relational bonds (Labov, 1972; Semin & Rubini, 1990). The maintenance of such bonds might be in positive or negative relationships. Language in this latter category, therefore, ranges from the artful exchange of nonserious insults (Schwebel, 1997) to the deliberate use of denigratory and offensive terms to insult enemies (Wiseman & Duck, 1995) or to commit verbal abuse (West, 1995). For example, "sounding" and "signifying" are long-standing and common speech acts of ritualistic exchanges of insults in African American vernacular (Labov, 1972; Mitchell-Kernan, 1972), and Schwebel (1997) even recorded that insult matches routinely occur in a jocular way in college dormitories where social scientists find their most typical social psychological experiment participants, college sophomores.

The interesting question from a social psychological point of view is why an aversive behavior is used in an affiliative way, and a corollary concern is how this is done. Can aversive behaviors actually serve bonding functions, and if so, how? To address these issues, we first review existing research on swearing and then consider how this aversive behavior is used in social interaction in paradoxical ways that turn it into a relational behavior.

PREVIOUS RESEARCH

Most previous research on swearing falls into one of the four areas below: (a) the *classification*, typologizing, and evaluation of swear words (e.g., Baudhuin, 1973; Cameron, 1969; Fine & Johnson, 1984; Jay, 1977), plus assessments of the frequencies of swear word use (e.g., Foote & Woodward, 1973; Jay, 1977, 1992a; Jay & Olson, 1993; Mabry, 1974); (b) *motivations* for using swear words (e.g., Berger, 1973; Crest, 1974; Hall & Jay, 1988; Jay 1992a; Montagu, 1967; Rothwell, 1971; Smith, 1951); (c) the *contextual elements* of swearing, such as swearing in different settings (e.g., Jay & Olson, 1993; Miller, 1989; Paradise, Cohl, & Zweig, 1980; Phillips & Kassinove, 1987; Wiley & Locke, 1982), swearing by the sexes (e.g., Coyne, Sherman, & O'Brien, 1978; Jay, 1992b; Jay & Burke, 1980; Rieber, Wiedemann, & D'Amato, 1979; Sanders & Robinson, 1979; Selnow, 1985), and swearing in various social roles and relationships (e.g., Bailey & Timm, 1976; de Klerk, 1991; Foote & Woodward, 1973; Staley, 1978); and (d) effects of swearing on *social perception* (e.g., Bailey & Timm, 1976; Baudhuin, 1973; Bostrom et al., 1973; Mulac, 1976; Powell et al., 1984; Selnow, 1985; Staley, 1978). Our review below follows this basic structuring of the literature.

Classification: What Counts?

In considering the impact and definition of swearing, it is crucial to note that swear words are not defined as aversive simply by their referent. For example, few people would be offended by being told to "copulate away." Instead the offensiveness of a swear word is partly defined by the culturally enhanced knowledge, often absent in young children, that the word is a swear word that is inappropriate for general use or that has special status in the culture only as a swear word (Davis, 1983; Jay, 1992a). For the most part this special status comes from references to something that is taboo or stigmatized in the culture (Andersson & Trudgill, 1990). However, there is more to it than that, and Davis (1983) noted that the Latin terms for taboo topics such as sexual organs and functions, for example, are regarded as socially inoffensive and are not used as swear words, whereas the Anglo-Saxon words for exactly the same parts and functions are regarded as highly offensive.

Thus, it is not the taboo function or feature itself that is offensive but the implications of the verbal register ("educated or uneducated speech") used to identify it (e.g., Battan, 1992). This observation is important for our later analysis because we believe that it is the context of usage—specifically, the membership or association with a socially stratified group implied by the register—that makes some words aversive. Because such overtones change, there are consequent changes with regard to the level of obscenity, offensiveness, and other evaluative aspects of the words with historical time and circumstances (Fine & Johnson, 1984; Hartford, 1972; Jay, 1977). Few would be much offended today by being branded a "coxcomb" or a "knave," for example, or being cursed with "the pox" or "a plague on [our] house," although these were standard offensive terms in Shakespeare's day.

Many obsolete and current forms of swearing refer not only to socially stigmatized activities, but to disparaged groups, ranks, or classes, and suggest low placement in the social order (Hughes, 1991). The above examples from history associate stigmatizing diseases with an implication of destructive moral inferiority, a usage that continues today in the use of the term "lousy." Terms such as "blackguard" (kitchen servant) and "bastard" were originally used for the same purpose, although they also had literal meaning in reference to stigmatized conditions or social positions. The style continues today in the application of insults comparing people to various stigmatized body parts or practices. "Heel" and "the pits" are the mildest examples of references to the body, whereas the strongest modern terms refer to stigmatized sexual practices such as incest with a parent and indiscriminate fellatio. Our point, then, is that social knowledge and contexts of use for such terms achieve something: They change the terms pragmatically into an allegation of social membership in a socially disparaged category.

Previous researchers have focused on frequency of occurrence or on topical issues, and so they have primarily sought to classify swear words in the absence of information about their specific contexts of use. Therefore, we believe, they have underplayed the relational circumstances of such use. In a hallmark study of swearing, Cameron (1969) sampled the speech of college students, adults at work, and adults at leisure by having "overhearers" record 15-second intervals of natural speech. He categorized the resulting list of words as primarily sexual, sacred-religious, or excretory. Mabry (1974) attempted to expand this category system by differentiating *abrasive* (crude or coarse verbal representations of sexual organs and activities), *technical* (neutral, nonslang terminology for sexual processes and organs, such as the Latin terms), *abrasive–expletive* (both abrasive and personally defaming terms), *latent* (words suggestive of sexual play such as "behind" and "goose"), and *euphemistic* (acceptable terms used in semi-guarded polite conversation—itself an implied claim to membership—such as "make love" and "cherry"). Although Mabry's (1974) typology is more extensive than Cameron's (1969), many words loaded onto several factors and could not be classified into any one dimension of his typology.

Cameron's distinction between sexual, religious, and excretory terms is a more advantageous typology in that it allows for a more comprehensive classification of swear words that is not limited to sexual terms. This system has also been the basis for other researchers to distinguish evaluative dimensions of swearing terms (Baudhuin, 1973), and Fine and Johnson (1984) expanded it to five categories of swear words: sexual anatomy, sexual acts, scatological words, words of ancestral origin, and profanity. Jay (1977) analyzed the responses of 52 college students to a sample of 60 words. His analysis produced three categories: body products, religious terms, and social deviations. Similarly, Smith (1951) classified swear words as blasphemous, scatological, or sexual.

Such approaches apparently assume that the words have a vulgar meaning in and of themselves; indeed, Winters (1993) showed that, in 24% of cases, respondents regarded the force of the swear word as the feature making a situation into an inappropriate one. The focus of much research has likewise been on vulgarity of words as an inherent quality as researchers ask participants to rate words on a scale of offensiveness, trying to determine some absolute level of vulgarity as if this were a pure characteristic of the word itself. The problem with such efforts is that they have not explored the terms as they are used in daily life and, therefore, have not differentiated the aversive dictionary meanings of the terms from the pragmatics of their use in a particular situation and as part of a larger interaction or relationship. Swearing is most often one part of a much larger social episode and so is both a cause and a result of individuals' feelings about one another, of the tone of an interaction, and of the broader flow of experience.

Studies need to distinguish between swearing expletively while alone, swearing at another person, and using profanity about other people or objects in the presence of a third party. Swearing at someone else could be an expression of disgust on the one hand or a teasing rebuke on the other, and so could have different relational and social psychological implications as a result. Swearing with someone else may be a simple indication of relaxation, or informality, and could even demonstrate a shared language and experience of target objects or people. Its function relationally could then be to indicate intimacy as much as to denote the meaning of a particular object.

These observations prompt us to recognize the relational functions served on the occasions of the use of profanity. To date, most research focuses only on denotative meanings to classify single swear words, and so the connotative, emotional meaning gained from a contextual examination of swearing has been relatively unexamined (Jay, 1977, 1992a); hence, the relational circumstances and force of swearing have remained undiscovered.

Motivation

Swear words are not always spoken in a personal vacuum with no psychological intent or social purpose. Although previous researchers have listed a variety of motivations and uses for swearing, we are not aware of any studies that have explored the relational motivations except in the broadest ways. By *relational motivations* we mean those purposes and functions of swearing that serve relational objectives such as increasing a sense of intimacy, signaling belonging, or enhancing informality. For example, Bergler (1936) stated that swearing by a man "is primarily directed toward the woman as an attempt to seduce her by the purposeful accentuation of sexual facts and relationships through the medium of conversation" (p. 226), and Smith (1951) also considered the role of swear words in sexual arousal and coitus. Crest (1974) noted that, whereas many people feel the need to limit their everyday speech in reference to words associated with sex, using taboo words during lovemaking is a common and enjoyable practice. In attempting to broaden this suggestion, Hartford (1972) listed expressing sympathy and friendliness as possible social relational functions of swearing.

Most other scholars have considered the individual motivations of speakers, such as those achieving a cathartic effect of swearing (Berger, 1973; Montagu, 1967; Patrick, 1901; Smith, 1951). For example, Smith attributed swearing to the release of pent-up frustration generally related to poor education and cultural background, possessing unsatisfactory sexual outlets, or pathology. Hall and Jay (1988) also found the same individual motivations (expressions of anger and frustration) in a study of children's swearing, but they also found that obscenities were used to describe and evaluate others, to make jokes, to communicate surprise, and to convey sarcasm, suggesting that the purpose for swearing changed as a function of the activity in which it occurred.

Fine and Johnson (1984) made broader attempts to differentiate motivation and showed three motivations for using swear words: (a) psychological motives (e.g., express anger), (b) social motives (e.g., get attention), and (c) linguistic motives (e.g., out of habit). The category of psychological motives was listed as the most important overall motive for swearing, and the specific motives of express anger and emphasize feelings were ranked the most important motivations for swearing.

Other suggested motivations are "social" at a broader sociological level, and Rothwell (1971) presented a list of obscenity functions within the historical context of the Vietnam antiwar movement and radical social change of the late 1960s and early 1970s. Reasons for swearing included gaining attention, discrediting others and the "establishment," provoking others, establishing identification with group members, and providing individual catharsis.

The analyses of motivation in previous research are, then, primarily focused on the speaker satisfying individual needs for self-expression, although some motivations are seen as devoted to broad social goals. So-called "relational motivations" are really identical to individual motivations expressed about a partner, and perhaps individual sexual gratification is not truly relational at all. Recent work on relationship awareness (Acitelli, 1993) might be adduced here to strengthen the argument that much communication in relationships is carried out in light of awareness of the relationship as a psychological entity and to recognize similarities and differences between partners, consolidate a sense of belonging to the relationship, and particularize the relationship to its participants. Building on such research, we argue that in the contexts of everyday life, swearing may be used to signal shared senses of familiarity, relaxation, jocularity, fun, and comfort with a partner (Winters, 1993). In the case of swearing at or about a third party, two persons who begin to permit or to share use of derogatory terms about another are colluding in membership; in the case of swearing with each other (or adopting informal language without a specific derogated target), the two partners are also "doing intimacy."

Context

Although researchers have considered the possible effects of various contextual factors in the production, use, and perception of swear words, there is little systematic research examining context and cursing. Where studies exist, they have generally looked only at one or two variables, not at the entire social situation—and its meaning to the participants is almost never a variable that is studied. Yet such meaning could affect perceptions or effects of swearing. Like all language, swearing occurs within a living context, and even though researchers acknowledge this, little research has so far examined the social psychological context in which swearing occurs.

Language production and interpretation in general are affected by context (Cohen & Siegel, 1991; Forgas 1985; Giles & Coupland, 1991). Swearing, as a specific form of language, is therefore not exempt from the effects of context. Jay (1977) emphasized the role of context in regard to swearing by stating that "regardless of how we or others attempt to define dirty words, the ultimate decision of the dirtiness of words relies on the communication context itself, i.e., the speaker, the listener, the social-physical setting, and the topic of discussion" (p. 236). He later recognized the intent of the message as another significant contextual variable in the use of swear words (Jay, 1992a). There is a clear interaction between these factors; a speaker's intent may itself be affected by the speaker's evaluation of context in terms of factors such as the situation and other interactants. Close relationships themselves provide a context of relaxation, comfort, and informality that seems to allow speakers to feel they may go beyond typical patterns of word use.

Several researchers (Bailey & Timm, 1976; Cameron, 1969; Graham, 1986; Jay, 1977, 1992a; Jay & Burke, 1980; Oliver & Rubin; 1975; Rothwell, 1971; Simkins & Rinck, 1982; Winters, 1993) have reported that the type of swear words used as well as the frequency and the perceived inappropriateness of their use are affected by the presence of others; the social status, role, and gender of those present; the setting; and the purpose for interaction. However, few researchers examine these factors together. Staley (1978) attempted to assess the effects of a variety of (combined) contextual variables on a respondent's production of expletives. She provided respondents with a variety of emotionally charged situations, altering the presence of listeners, the gender of listeners, the relationship of speaker with listeners, and the type of emotion (fear, anxiety, anger, happiness). Her analysis showed that the social milieu, including the individual's emotional state, did indeed affect the type of expletive elicited. For example, students used stronger expletives less frequently when they were with individuals of greater social status. Similar research attempts to manipulate or even examine multidimensional social milieus are, however, still rare.

As individual variables, however, the social identity or status, role, relationship, and gender of one's conversational partners are known to influence the use of swear words (Bailey & Timm, 1976; de Klerk, 1991; Hartford, 1972; Sanders & Robinson, 1979; Staley, 1978; Winters, 1993), as are such contextual variables as the intimacy of the physical setting, topic of discussion, or public or private nature of the communication episode (Graham, 1986; Hartford, 1972; Jay, 1977, 1990, 2000; Rothwell, 1971; Winters, 1993). For example, both male and female individuals indicated that their use of swear words was halted or modified by the presence of people who would be offended by the remark, such as elders, church members, parents, children, strangers, and members of the opposite sex (Bailey & Timm, 1976; Foote & Woodward, 1973; Simkins & Rinck, 1982; Staley, 1978). In general, gender role expectations (Mulac, 1976; Powell et al., 1984) and situational factors such as the presence of others, individual differences, and the specific swear words used have also been noted (Winters, 1993), with less swearing being found when people are trying to convey positive affect (Staley, 1978). Counselors avoid using swear words with preteenagers and are prudent about the use of swear words with adults until "a solid interpersonal relationship has been formed" (Miller, 1989, p. 59). Thus, establishment of a personal relationship is a prerequisite for use of swear words between professionals and their clients, and we argue for an extension of the principle here: Swearing between intimates is a general relational indicator, suggesting comfort and a sense of intimacy.

Social Perception

"You mean the profanity? . . . That's simply the way they talk here. Nobody pays any attention to you unless you swear every other word." [Captain Kirk to Mr. Spock regarding the 20th-century use of language in Star Trek IV: The Voyage Home]

Field, laboratory, and questionnaire studies such as those reported by Jay (1992a) provide support for the notion that swearing is a male-dominated activity. In one of his field studies, men swore over twice as frequently as women (1,482 vs. 689 episodes, respectively). Although men and women swear at different frequency levels and use different words when they do, perceptions of swearers are generally negative regardless of gender. For example, any message containing swear words is typically rated less persuasive than messages not containing swear words (Bostrom et al., 1973; Mulac, 1976; Phillips & Kassinove, 1987). However, it is also broadly true that evaluations of those who swear vary depending on the person (role, gender), the context (persuasive speech, counseling session), the word that is used, and the perceived justification of the use of swear words (Winters, 1993). Studies examining gender differences thus tend to differ in their findings. Therefore, we first examine the generalized negative perceptions of those who swear and then examine work that specifically looks at the function of gender differences in swearing.

Speakers who swore were rated lower in socio-intellectual status and aesthetic quality by a sample of 47 student and nonstudent respondents (Mulac, 1976). Counselors who swore freely were perceived less favorably and as less trustworthy by undergraduate psychology students than counselors who did not swear (Paradise et al, 1980; Phillips & Kassinove, 1987). Undergraduate and graduate psychology students enrolled in a counselor education course tended to give higher therapeutic ratings to counseling sessions that included either client-initiated or counselor-reciprocating swearing than sessions without swearing (Wiley & Locke, 1982). This indicates to us that sessions with swearing by both client and counselors are read by outsiders as indicating a relationship in much the same way that observers read other signals of the existence of relationships into forms of speech (Planalp & Garvin-Doxas, 1994).

Social attractiveness and task attractiveness are also affected by swearing. Powell et al. (1984) studied the effects of offensive language on impressions made from transcripts of job interviews. Swearing by the interviewee had a negative effect on the impressions of social attractiveness (attractiveness of the individual as a potential friend) and task attractiveness (attractiveness of the individual as a potential coworker) of the applicant.

In a study designed to specifically examine contextual elements related to the perceived inappropriateness of swearing, Winters (1993) found that the most influential factor in respondents' judgments of inappropriateness was the perceived lack of justification or purpose for the speaker's use of expletives, with ejaculatory swearing in a public place or setting (i.e., not one indicating a special relationship between participants) leading to the most aversive social perceptions of those who swear. In 27% of cases, respondents said that the situation did not warrant the use of swear words or that swearing served no purpose. Furthermore, that "others were present" defined the contextual element marking inappropriateness in 66% of the cases. These findings are of course general findings that do not distinguish the relationships of others to the swearer or the gender of others present.

Gender differences in the frequency of swearing, evaluations of swear words, and evaluations of those who swear have been reported by researchers such as Rieber et al. (1979), who found that women reacted more strongly than did men to obscenity. Bostrom et al. (1973) found that whereas the use of swear words was detrimental to the perceived credibility of a communicator during a persuasive speech, female communicators who used swear words created greater attitude changes in their audience than male communicators who used swear words. Mulac (1976), on the other hand, found no difference in the perceived image of male and female speakers who used obscenities in a taped persuasive speech. In addition, no differences were found in the perceived image of the speaker as a result of the gender of the audience.

Selnow (1985) found that women reported less swearing than men and thought swearing was less appropriate in different contexts (e.g., in formal meetings, on cable television) than men did. Supporting Selnow's (1985) findings that women swore significantly less than men, Jay (1992a) reported that, in actual speaking situations, male individuals swore more frequently than female individuals both as children and adults. Martin (1997) found that use of profanity and certain slang terms enabled readers of conversational transcripts to identify the gender of the speaker even when other identifiers of gender (e.g., pronouns) had been "neutralized." Speakers tend to use different types of swear words as a function of the gender of speakers and listeners. In their study of sexual vernacular, Sanders and Robinson (1979) and Simkins and Rinck (1982) found that the terms used to describe genitalia and sexual acts varied significantly between men and women depending on the gender of others present.

Inconsistencies in the results of research regarding social perceptions of male and female individuals who swear have been attributed to changes in gender role expectations during the 1970s, especially in the United States, because swearing has traditionally been regarded a masculine activity (Mulac, 1976; Powell et al., 1984; Rieber et al., 1979). As the American culture shifts toward more egalitarian attitudes regarding gender role expectations, perceptions of swearing as a masculine activity are being challenged (Rieber et al., 1979).

Furthermore, even though traditional gender role expectations can affect swearing and social perceptions of those who swear (Mulac, 1976; Powell et al., 1984), gender role expectations may sometimes be less salient than other role expectations (e.g., parent role expectations; de Klerk, 1991) and may affect results regarding gender differences. For example, the role of parent may restrict or prohibit swearing, especially when with younger children regardless of whether the parent is male or female. However, the boundary between gender role expectations and parent role expectations is not clear. De Klerk (1991) suggested that mothers and teachers, occupying traditionally female roles, do not generally swear in the presence of children, whereas fathers often do. Moreover, actual role behavior and role expectations are not necessarily equivalent. Oliver and Rubin (1975) found that married women reported a greater propensity to use expletives at home with their children than single (childless) women expected they would use if they had children.

However, the results summarized above are often found in studies that use results from pencil-and-paper laboratory studies and that ask for reports about the "average speaker" without specifying the gender of that speaker (Jay, 1992a). Thus, respondents may report about the generalized behavior of both male and female individuals. Furthermore, dissimilar findings from studies involving gender differences may also be due to a number of confounding individual differences. For example, the feminist women in Rieber et al.'s study (1979) reported a significantly greater frequency of obscenity use than did men or nonfeminist women. Moreover, samples taken from public and private settings in same- or mixed-sex company may vary greatly because of the highly contextual nature of the appropriateness of swearing.

IS SWEARING RELATIONAL?

We have noted that much research on swearing is based on studies that ask general questions about the use of words, often do not distinguish between public and private settings of use, rarely ask about the relationship between speaker and listener, and show a larger concern with general taboos than with the ways in which taboos may be broken in a manner that creates a relational ambiance. Yet, one well-established finding of the research on personal relationships is that the breaking down of taboos and boundaries is a familiar mechanism for increasing intimacy (Dindia, 1997; Jourard, 1971).

The asseverative form of swearing is a clear claim of power and veracity (Patrick, 1901). We can now extend that function also to the ejaculatory form: Whenever people swear they are claiming power and asserting self. Although such assertion of power may be a purely individual activity (as in the usage of swearing made by Type A personalities) or a class or gender claim (as when women were encouraged in the 1970s to swear as a means of asserting power through language; Jong, 1973), swearing can also exert power in relationships. The most obvious case is when an abusive man swears at his partner in a derogatory way, but less abusive and more informal ways of swearing can also be relational, as when African American informal speech permits the use of "the n-word" as a familiar term between members of the group but reacts to the term as a racial slur when spoken by a White person. Such possibilities are missed by studies that use only vignettes or word lists to investigate swearing and profanity and that do not study the uses in real social interaction.

These observations could be regarded as merely methodological were we not intent on accounting for the ways in which a behavior can be simultaneously aversive and widely practiced. It is our belief that a behavior that is normally aversive or abusive can be given a different connotation by the relational circumstances of its production and can, in turn, produce different relational meaning. Just as Bergmann (1993) has shown that gossip is both aversive and bonding, so we believe is profanity. In both cases, the relational context of use is an important factor in the analysis. Cohesion in social groups or dyads depends to some degree on the shared willingness to break social taboos and to collude in the expression of moral disparagement of outsiders. The development and tolerance of increasingly informal codes of speech in a relationship are social psychological mechanisms for developing greater closeness in that relationship. Willing collusion in a social practice that is otherwise aversive can be used to signal bonding and acceptance. Thus, the use of swear words is relational even though the referential meanings of the terms are aversive, and the practice is generally discouraged in the broader social group. We believe that such a proposal helps us understand why profanity occurs in informal personal relationships when it is an aversive social behavior at large.

SUMMARY

Past research focuses on several aspects of swearing, including the specific terms and the gender differences in the production and evaluation of the words. It has typically focused on the meaning of terms rather than the social functions and practices of using such words. However, even though researchers acknowledge the importance of the social psychological context in understanding the meaning and functions of swearing, little social psychological research has addressed this topic. Significant areas for future research point to the primary need to determine the social psychological and relational contextual elements present in a situation involving swear words and in which swearing is perceived as appropriate or inappropriate. There is also a need for research on the actual swear words used, the reasons behind the specific evaluation of the use of swear words as inappropriate for a situation, and the individual differences that may affect those reasons. There are, however, some broader and, we believe, more interesting, social psychological and contextual issues that need to be investigated more vigorously as social psychologists attempt a fuller explanation of this aversive social behavior. We argue that the pragmatics of swearing point to a bonding function of a behavior that is otherwise perceived only as aversive because of its use of negatively charged words.

REFERENCES

Acitelli, L. K. (1993). You, me, and us: Perspectives on relationship awareness. In S. W. Duck (Ed.), *Understanding relationship processes: Vol. 1: Individuals in relationships* (pp. 144–174.). Newbury Park, CA: Sage Publications.

Andersson, L., & Trudgill, P. (1990). *Bad language*. Cambridge, MA: Basil Blackwell.

Bailey, L. A., & Timm, L. A. (1976). More on women's—and men's—expletives. *Anthropological Linguistics, 8*, 438–449.

Battan, J. F. (1992). "The word made flesh": Language, authority, and sexual desire in late nineteenth-century America. *Journal of the History of Sexuality, 3*(2), 223–244.

Baudhuin, E. S. (1973). Obscene language and evaluative response: An empirical study. *Psychological Reports, 32*, 399–402.

Berger, A. (1973). Swearing and society. *ETC: A Review of General Semantics, 30*(3), 283–286.

Bergler, E. (1936). Obscene words. *Psychoanalytic Quarterly, 5*(2), 226–248.

Bergmann, J. R. (1993). *Discreet indiscretions: The social organization of gossip.* New York: Aldine de Gruyter.

Bernstein, B. (1971). *Class, codes and control.* London: Routledge.

Bostrom, R. N., Baseheart, C. M., & Rossiter, C. M., Jr. (1973). The effects of three types of profane language in persuasive messages. *The Journal of Communication, 23*, 461–475.

Cameron, P. (1969). Frequency and kinds of words in various social settings, or what the hell's going on? *Pacific Sociological Review, 3*, 101–104.

Cohen, R., & Siegel, A. W. (Eds.). (1991). *Context and development.* Hillsdale, NJ: Erlbaum.

Coyne, J. C., Sherman, R. C., & O'Brien, K. (1978). Expletives and woman's place. *Sex Roles, 4*, 827–835.

Crest, D. (1974). Those four-letter words of love: Why we use them. *Sexology, 41*(1), 15–18.

Daro, D, & Gelles, R. J. (1992). Public attitudes and behaviors with respect to child abuse prevention. *Journal of Interpersonal Violence, 7*, 517–531.

Davis, M. S. (1983). *SMUT: Erotic reality/obscene ideology.* Chicago: University of Chicago Press.

de Klerk, V. (1991). Expletives: Men only? *Communication Monographs, 58*, 156–169.

Dindia, K. (1997). Self-disclosure, self-identity, and relationship development: A transactional/dialectical perspective. In S. W. Duck (Ed.), *Handbook of personal relationships* (2nd ed., pp. 411–425). Chichester, England: Wiley.

Duck, S. W., Rutt, D. J., Hurst, M., & Strejc, H. (1991). Some evident truths about communication in everyday relationships: All communication is not created equal. *Human Communication Research, 18*, 228–267.

Duck, S. W., & Wood, J. T. (1995). For better for worse, for richer for poorer: The rough and the smooth of relationships. In S. W. Duck & J. T. Wood (Eds.), *Confronting relationship challenges: Vol. 5 Understanding relationship processes* (pp. 1–21). Thousand Oaks, CA: Sage Publications.

Fine, M. G., & Johnson, F. L. (1984). Female and male motives for using obscenity. *Journal of Language and Social Psychology, 3*(1), 59–74.

Foote, R., & Woodward, J. (1973). A preliminary investigation of obscene language. *The Journal of Psychology, 83,* 263–275.

Forgas, J. P. (Ed.). (1985). *Language and social situations.* New York: Springer-Verlag.

Giles, H., & Coupland, N. (1991). *Language: Contexts and consequences.* Pacific Grove, CA: Brooks/Cole.

Graham, M. (1986). Obscenity and profanity at work. *Employee Relations Law Journal, 11,* 662–677.

Gregersen, E. A. (1979). Sexual linguistics. *Annals of the New York Academy of Sciences, 327,* 3–19.

Hall, P., & Jay, T. (1988, March). *Children's use of obscene speech.* Paper presented at the meeting of the Popular Culture Association, New Orleans, LA.

Hartford, R. J. (1972). *A social penetration model for obscene language.* Doctoral dissertation, University of Maryland.

Hopper, R., Knapp, M. L., & Scott, L. (1981). Couples' personal idioms: Exploring intimate talk. *Journal of Communication, 31,* 23–33.

Hughes, G. (1991). *Swearing: A social history of foul language, oaths and profanity in English.* Oxford, England: Blackwell.

Innes, J. M. (1981). *Progress in applied social psychology.* Chichester, England: Wiley.

Jay, T. B. (1977). Doing research with dirty words. *Maledicta: The International Journal of Verbal Aggression, 1,* 234–256.

Jay, T. B. (1990, March). *What are "fighting words?"* Paper presented at the meeting of the Eastern Psychological Association, Philadelphia, PA.

Jay, T. B. (1992a). *Cursing in America.* Philadelphia: John Benjamins.

Jay, T. B. (1992b, April). *Women cursing women.* Paper presented at the meeting of the Eastern Psychological Association, Boston, MA.

Jay, T. B. (2000). *Why we curse: A neuro-psycho-social theory of speech.* Philadelphia: J. Benjamin.

Jay, T. B., & Burke, T. (1980, April). *Male and female differences in dirty word usage.* Paper presented at the meeting of the Eastern Psychological Association, Hartford, CT.

Jay, T. B., & Olson, R. (1993, April). *Cursing in the nursing home.* Paper presented at the meeting of the Eastern Psychological Association, Arlington, VA.

Jong, E. (1973). *Fear of flying.* New York: Pratt.

Jourard, S. M. (1971). *The transparent self* (rev. ed.). New York: Van Nostrand Reinhold.

Kowalski, R. (1997). The underbelly of social interaction: Aversive interpersonal behaviors. In R. Kowalski. (Ed.), *Aversive interpersonal behaviors* (pp. 1–9). New York: Plenum Press.

Krauss, R. M., & Fussell, S. R. (1996). Social psychological models of interpersonal communication. In E. T. Higgins & A. Kruglanski (Eds.), *Social psychology: Handbook of basic principles* (pp. 655–701). New York: Guilford Press.

Labov, W. (1972). Negative attraction and negative concord in English grammar. *Language, 48*, 773–818.

Lester, P. M. (1996, August). *On the N- and F-words: Quantifying the taboo.* Paper presented at the meeting of the Association for Education in Journalism and Mass Communication, Anaheim, CA.

Mabry, E. A. (1974). A multivariate investigation of profane language. *Central States Speech Journal, 35*, 39–44.

MacDonald, A. M. (Ed). (1978). *Chambers 20th Century Dictionary.* Edinburgh, UK: W. & R. Chambers.

Martin, R. W. (1997). "Girls don't talk about garages": Perceptions of conversations in same- and cross-sex friendships. *Personality Relations, 4*, 115–130.

Miller, M. J. (1989). The use of counselor profanity in counseling. *Counseling and Values, 34*, 57–60.

Mitchell-Kernan, C. (1972). Signifying, loud-talking and marking. In T. Kochman (Ed.), *Rappin' and stylin' out: Communication in urban black America* (pp. 315–335). Urbana: University of Illinois Press.

Montagu, A. (1967). *The anatomy of swearing.* New York: Macmillan.

Mulac, A. (1976). Effects of obscene language upon three dimensions of listener attitude. *Communication Monographs, 43*, 300–307.

Oliver, M. M., & Rubin, J. (1975). The use of expletives by some American women. *Anthropological Linguistics, 17*(5), 191–197.

Paradise, L. V., Cohl, B., & Zweig, J. (1980). Effects of profane language and physical attractiveness on perceptions of counselor behavior. *Journal of Counseling Psychology, 27*, 620–624.

Patrick, G. T. W. (1901). The psychology of profanity. *Psychological Review, 8*, 113–127.

Phillips, M., & Kassinove, H. (1987). Effects of profanity, touch, and sex of the counselor and behavioral compliance: Implications for rational–emotive therapists. *Journal of Rational–Emotive Therapy, 5*(1), 3–12.

Planalp, S., & Garvin-Doxas, K. (1994). Using mutual knowledge in conversation: Friends as experts in each other. In S. W. Duck (Ed.), *Dynamics of relationships: Vol. 4 Understanding relationship processes* (pp. 1–26). Newbury Park, CA: Sage Publications.

Powell, L., Callahan, K., Comans, C., McDonald, L., Mansell, J., Trotter, M. D., & Williams, V. (1984). Offensive language and impressions during an interview. *Psychological Reports, 55*, 617–618.

Rieber, R. W., Wiedemann, C., & D'Amato, J. (1979). Obscenity: Its frequency and context of usage as compared in males, nonfeminist females, and feminist females. *Journal of Psycholinguistic Research, 8*(3), 201–223.

Rothwell, J. D. (1971). Verbal obscenity: Time for second thoughts. *Western Journal of Speech, 35*, 231–242.

Sagarin, E. (1962). *The anatomy of dirty words.* New York: Lyle Stuart.

Sanders, J. S., & Robinson, W. L. (1979). Talking and not talking about sex: Male and female vocabularies. *Journal of Communication, 29,* 22–30.

Scheidlower, J. (Ed.). (1995). *The F word.* New York: Random House.

Schwebel, D. C. (1997). Strategies of verbal dueling: How college students win a verbal battle. *Journal of Language and Social Psychology, 16,* 326–343.

Selnow, G. W. (1985). Sex differences in uses and perceptions of profanity. *Sex Roles, 12*(3/4), 303–312.

Semin, G. R., & Rubini, M. (1990). Unfolding the concept of person by verbal abuse. *European Journal of Social Psychology, 20*(6), 463–474.

Simkins, L., & Rinck, C. (1982). Male and female sexual vocabulary in different interpersonal contexts. *The Journal of Sex Research, 18,* 160–172.

Smith, A. (1951). Swearing. *Journal of Sex Education, 4*(4), 256–260.

Staley, C. M. (1978). Male-female use of expletives: A heck of a difference in expectations. *Anthropological Linguistics, 20*(8), 367–380.

Tajfel, H. (Ed.). (1978). *Differentiation between social groups.* London: Academic Press.

West, J. (1995). Understanding how the dynamics of ideology influence violence between intimates. In S. W. Duck & J. T. Wood (Eds.), *Confronting relationship challenges: Vol. 5 Understanding relationship processes* (pp. 129–149). Thousand Oaks, CA: Sage Publications.

Wiley, D. A., & Locke, D. C. (1982). Profanity as a critical variable in counseling. *Counselor Education and Supervision, 27,* 245–252.

Winters, A. M. (1993). *You shouldn't talk like that: An analysis of factors that affect the perceived inappropriateness of swearing.* Unpublished master's thesis, Illinois State University, Normal.

Wiseman, J. P., & Duck, S. W. (1995). Having and managing enemies: A very challenging relationship. In S. W. Duck & J. T. Wood (Eds.), *Confronting relationship challenges: Vol. 5 Understanding relationship processes* (pp. 43–72.). Thousand Oaks, CA: Sage Publications.

4

AVERSIVE SELF-PRESENTATIONS

ROOS VONK

Generally, self-presentation is a blessing. Thanks to self-presentational behavior, people do not blatantly yawn when we tell boring stories; they do not jump with joy at funerals, even when they feel like it; and visits to in-laws do not usually end in slanging matches (in Britain, this refers to an argument in which people shout, curse, and insult each other; cf. M. R. Leary, 1995). Self-presentation is the lubricating oil of social traffic. Interactions runs smoothly because people laugh about jokes that are not funny, make compliments about bad hairstyles, and generally allow each other to save face (Goffman, 1959). Thus, self-presentation facilitates social interaction.

Notwithstanding these undeniably important benefits, there is also a dark side to self-presentation, which this chapter is about. In part, this dark side emerges because the images that people project are not always what they had in mind. That is, the secondary impression (i.e., the impression that is actually formed of the self-presenting actor) may deviate from the impression that was calculated and desired by the actor (Schneider, 1981). For instance, an employee who laughs about the corny jokes of his supervisor, aiming to please the supervisor, may cause annoyance or even unease when the extent of his laughter is disproportionate to the funniness of the jokes. Similarly, a potential son-in-law who aims to impress his new in-laws by describing his many accomplishments may become the object of boredom and aggravation rather than admiration. In these cases, the aversiveness of the self-presentation is unintentional.

In other cases, people knowingly project obnoxious images that others most assuredly find aversive. For instance, supervisors and teachers sometimes present themselves as unusually strict and intimidating toward their subordinates or pupils (E. E. Jones & Pittman, 1982). Probably their goal is not to be liked but instead to be obeyed or even feared. Similarly, members of juvenile gangs may engage in aggressive and even immoral behaviors to impress others (e.g., Horowitz & Schwartz, 1974).

This chapter addresses these two varieties of aversive self-presentations: (a) the ones that are intended to be aversive and (b) the ones that have the effect of being aversive despite the actor's intentions to the contrary. Before discussing the motives and the effects of these self-presentations in more detail, I first present a taxonomy of self-presentational behavior that includes positive as well as negative behaviors, and I describe the motives for self-presentation in general. Subsequently, I discuss the specific motives that people may have for deliberately engaging in negative self-presentations. Finally, I describe how positive self-presentations can become obnoxious, at least in the eye of the observer.

A TAXONOMY OF SELF-PRESENTATIONAL BEHAVIOR

Because people have many interpersonal goals and many ways to accomplish those goals through self-presentational tactics, it may be argued that any behavior can be the result of self-presentational concerns (M. R. Leary, 1995). Therefore, any taxonomy of self-presentational episodes is bound to be either incomprehensive or chaotic. This is also true of the widely cited five-category taxonomy of E. E. Jones and Pittman (1982). To present a reasonably exhaustive and organized inventory of different forms of self-presentation, I have combined their taxonomy with four basic dimensions of personality judgments that have come up consistently in person perception research (for reviews of studies on implicit personality theory, see Schneider, 1973; Vonk 1993a). The result is presented in Table 4.1. The table columns represent four categories of personality dimensions that have been described in the literature on person perception and interpersonal behavior; this literature is specified in the table notes. Note that these dimensions are not orthogonal to each other. In fact, they are all evaluative, and their endpoints merely denote different kinds of "good" (likability, ability, strength, and morality) and "bad" (unlikability, inability, weakness, and immorality). The table rows represent the positive and the negative pole of each dimension. In the cells, several categories of self-

TABLE 4.1
A Taxonomy of Eight Forms of Self-Presentation Based on Four Dimensions of Personality

Dimension	(Social) Evaluation,[a,b] Likeability,[b,c] Affiliation[d]	Competence, Intellectual Evaluation,[b] Ability[e]	Potency,[a,c] Control[d]	Morality[e]
Positive	*Ingratiation*	*Self-promotion*	Autonomy	Exemplification
Negative	Hostility, including Intimidation	Playing dumb	*Supplication*	Rebellion

Note. The five categories in italics are described in E. E. Jones and Pitman's taxonomy (1982). [a]Osgood, Suci, and Tannenbaum (1957): Evaluation, Potency. [b]Rosenberg, Nelson, and Vivekananthan (1968); Rosenberg (1977); M. P. Kim and Rosenberg (1980): Social Evaluation, Intellectual Evaluation/ Likeability, Competence. [c]Vonk (1993a, 1995): Likeability, Potency. [d]T. Leary (1957); Kiesler (1983); Wiggins (1985): Affiliation, Control (interpersonal circle). [e]Reeder and Brewer (1979); Skowronski and Carlston (1987); Morality, Ability.

presentation are listed. The five categories printed in italics are the ones described by E. E. Jones and Pittman's taxonomy.

Ingratiation is the positive end of the social evaluation dimension, a dimension that describes the contrast between likable, friendly and unlikable, hostile behavior. The goal of ingratiation is to present the self as likable (E. E. Jones, 1964). The negative end of this dimension encompasses all behaviors by which people present themselves as unlikable or hostile. For instance, people may want to make others believe that they are not friendly or nice because they want to avoid further contact with someone (Schneider, 1981) or because doing so increases their chances of getting a job that requires unlikable qualities (cf. Jellison & Gentry, 1978). *Intimidation*—establishing an impression of dominance and firmness so that others obey or keep quiet—is also a self-presentational style that classifies an individual as unlikable. Furthermore, people may convey that they are tough and uncompromising in, for instance, bargaining settings when they want to lower the opponents' aspirations and discourage them from asking too much (Pruitt & Smith, 1981; Wall, 1991) or when they are observed by their constituents (Carnevale, Pruitt, & Britton, 1979). In the presence of observers, people—especially men—may act aggressively and retaliate against someone who has provoked or exploited them, to demonstrate to the observers that they are not to be trifled with (Brown, 1968; Felson, 1978; cf. Hogan & Jones, 1983, and Horowitz & Schwartz, 1974, on juvenile delinquency and violence in juvenile gangs). In a recent study, S. H. Kim, Smith, and Brigham (1998) suggested that the presence of an observer also affects retaliation as a function of power imbalance. Generally, people retaliate more against a less powerful harm-doer but, in the presence of an observer, retaliation is stronger against a more powerful harm-doer. Presumably, the latter is seen as more justified or even courageous, whereas negative behavior toward a less powerful other is socially undesirable. Thus, in some cases people may actually harm a more powerful person to gain admiration from someone else.

The second dimension in the table is *competence–ability*, which describes the contrast between intelligence and other skills versus incompetence and ignorance. At the positive end of this dimension lies *self-promotion*, a self-presentational tactic that is specifically geared to convincing others of one's abilities. As for its opposite, there are many situations in which people *play dumb*, that is, hide their knowledge or their skills. In the extant literature, seven motives for this type of self-presentation have been described.

1. People may want to avoid an onerous task by acting as if they do not have the ability to perform it (Kowalski & Leary, 1990).
2. Some people deliberately lose poker games or sport matches, thus feigning incompetence to encourage a less skilled opponent to gamble with more money (*hustling*), or they present themselves as incapable to make the opponent reduce his effort or lower his guard (*sandbagging*; Shepperd & Socherman, 1997).
3. People may intentionally fail at a task for which failure is associated with a desirable personality trait (Baumeister, Cooper, & Skib, 1979), or they may engage in self-deprecation in interacting with an attractive target who prefers a self-effacing self-presentation (Gollwitzer & Wicklund, 1985).
4. Children may hide what they know about sex and drugs for the sake of their parents' peace of mind (M. R. Leary, 1995).
5. People may claim low ability to reduce expectations, so as to create lower, more obtainable standards for their performance and avoid a harsh judgment (Baumgardner & Brownlee, 1987; cf. Baumgardner & Arkin, 1987).
6. People sometimes play dumb on a date (e.g., hide their academic achievements; cf. Daubman, Heatherington, & Ahn, 1992) or in an intimate relationship (e.g., allow their partner to win a competition) to bolster the ego of their partner and, in the case of women, to fulfill societal role requirements (e.g., Dean, Braito, Powers, & Brant, 1975; Komarowski, 1946; Zanna & Pack, 1975).[1]
7. People may hide their accomplishments to avoid that others feel intimidated, threatened, or jealous (Exline & Lobel,

---

[1]According to Gove, Hughes, and Geerken (1980), playing dumb does not occur more frequently among women than among men. However, as can be seen from this overview, there are many varieties of playing dumb and many motives underlying this behavior, and it seems possible that men and women engage in different forms and are driven by different motives.

1999). A recent study by Bargh, Gollwitzer, Lee Chai, and Barndollaer (1998) suggested that this type of behavior may even emerge automatically and unintentionally, as a result of the activation of goals ("auto-motives"). In this experiment, participants who were primed with an empathy goal (by means of words such as *friendly* and *cooperation*), compared with participants primed with a performance goal (e.g., *success* and *effort*), showed decreased performance at a task when they were paired with an accomplice who was insecure about his abilities at the task. Thus, by activating an empathy goal, participants automatically played dumb to protect their partner's self-esteem.

Depending on the setting and the motives for playing dumb, this type of self-presentation may not be seen as negative and certainly not as aversive. On the contrary, it seems that many occasions of playing dumb can be regarded as instances of modesty or even ingratiation. Nevertheless, the category is included in the present chapter because ignorance and incompetence are regarded as undesirable. As will become clear in this chapter, many behaviors that are negative on one dimension may be positive on another one, but this does not alter the fact that people sometimes do present themselves in an undesirable way, at least with respect to one dimension. For now, then, all negative poles of the personality dimensions are of interest.

Potency–control is the third dimension that is useful in describing self-presentational behavior. On the negative side of this dimension, *supplication* (E. E. Jones & Pittman, 1982) means that one presents the self as dependent and helpless. The supplicator cultivates the role of a person who is needy and weak, physically ill, or even depressed (Hill, Weary, & Williams, 1986; cf. Kelly, McKillop, & Neimeyer, 1991) or mentally disturbed (Braginsky, 1981). Although this behavior is weak and powerless, it can be as annoying as intimidation and even as aggressive, because it is a strong appeal to feelings of guilt and moral responsibility on the part of the target (cf., Kowalski, 1996). On the other side of the potency dimension is *autonomy*, a self-presentational style that is sometimes confused with absence of self-presentation, that is, with being oblivious to social demands and a tendency to be guided solely by one's private thoughts and feelings (e.g., Buss & Briggs, 1984). However, as demonstrated by Schlenker and Weigold (1990), people may actually change their publicly expressed attitudes merely to demonstrate that they are autonomous. Similarly, self-presentational motives may lead people to convey that they do not need others or do not care what others think.

Finally, with respect to the *morality* dimension, exemplification (e.g., Gilbert & Jones, 1986) represents the positive end of this dimension. This behavior is enacted by (for example) parents, teachers, and religious leaders to set a moral example by projecting an image of integrity and moral worthiness. Regarding the negative end of morality, note that immoral behavior that results from self-presentational motives does not occur frequently: People do not usually aim to appear more immoral than they really are, because the very essence of morality implies that one does not ever engage in immoral behaviors, even when it is desirable (Reeder & Brewer, 1979; Reeder & Spores, 1983). Mark Leary (personal communication, August 12, 1997) has suggested that in this cell of the table, one might place the behavior of rebellious people who attempt to shock or offend the establishment by ostentatious bad behavior (e.g., shock-rock musical groups). In addition, young people may engage in immoral behaviors to avoid being seen as "goody-two-shoes" by their peers. Exline (1999) has suggested that moral, exemplifying behavior, just as competent behavior, can be seen as threatening by others. Therefore, people may swear or drink or engage in other bad behaviors for the same reasons that they play dumb (Exline & Lobel, 1999): to avoid being seen as threatening by others who might feel guilty, scolded, or "policed" by being around a person who exemplifies the things that they cannot or do not accomplish. In these cases, people may portray themselves as a little bad to make others feel comfortable and to protect themselves from being accused of self-righteousness or feeling superior to others (Exline, 1999).

Motives for Self-Presentation

In addition to facilitating social interaction, self-presentation generally serves the goal of self-enhancement and receiving social approval. This motive implies that self-presenters usually aim to create a glorifying image of the self. Positive self-presentations reduce the risk of being rejected by others, and they can serve to gain all other kinds of material or psychological rewards (e.g., pay raises, respect). However, the motive to be liked is pervasive even when no tangible outcomes are at stake (Baumeister & Leary, 1992).

Nevertheless, negative self-presentations do occur and, because they cannot be accounted for by the motive of self-enhancement and social approval, other motives must be involved. According to E. E. Jones (1964, 1990), self-presentation is a behavioral instrument that serves the goal of making others behave in desired ways. For instance, job applicants attempt to influence the impression formed of them by the interviewer, in such a way that they are more likely to get the job. It follows that self-presentation can take all sorts of forms: A job applicant might present himself or herself as confident or modest, liberal or conservative, sociable or formal, depending on whatever is most advantageous for securing the job. In some cases, it may be desirable to present the self negatively, if this affects others' behaviors in desired ways. For instance, others may obey (if one intimidates them), take their onerous business elsewhere (if one plays dumb or un-skilled), or offer help (in case of supplication).

Self-presentations need not always serve one's own personal goals only, however. Just as people may tell lies for either self-centered or altru-istic reasons (DePaulo & Bell, 1996; DePaulo & Kashy, 1998), both mo-tives may also guide self-presentational behavior. For instance, people may play dumb to prevent that they intimidate a more insecure or less educated person. Thus, self-presentational behavior—both positive and negative—may be conducted for the benefit of the target.

Negative Self-Presentations

Self-presentations may be either deliberately or inadvertently aver-sive. In the overview above, the four negative self-presentations can be classified as intentionally negative: In all four cases, there is a motive to project a negative image—that is, a motive to be seen as unlikable, in-competent, helpless, or immoral, even though self-presenters may not al-ways be fully aware of these motives. Indeed, the entire taxonomy above is based on the actor's intentions. To say that self-promotion is positive on the competence dimension means that the self-promoter intends to be seen as competent and skilled; to classify ingratiation as socially good means that the ingratiating actor has the goal of being seen as likable. However, as noted earlier, the impression intended by the actor may often deviate from the impression that is actually formed by observers. That is, from the perspective of the audience, we might arrive at an entirely different clas-sification of positive and negative self-presentations. In fact, the word *aver-sive* in the title of this book generally refers to the perspective of the observer or the target of behavior. Behaviors may produce aversive con-sequences for the actor's own well-being (Baumeister & Scher, 1988), but more usually the term refers to the consequences of a behavior for others (see Peeters & Czapinski, 1990, and Vonk, 1999b, on the distinction be-tween self-profitable and other-profitable behaviors). From the observer's perspective, self-presentations classified as positive in the taxonomy above may turn out to be aversive or vice versa. For instance, as noted earlier, playing dumb may be anything but aversive from the viewpoint of the target, because it often serves to protect the target's self-worth. Conversely, self-promotion may be quite aversive when it is not conducted with the appropriate subtlety. Especially in cases like the latter, where positive self-presentations inadvertently become obnoxious, the self-presentation is un-likely to affect the target in the way that was intended and desired by the actor.

In the next section, I address intended negative self-presentations, that is, the negative types of self-presentation in the taxonomy above.

I describe a correlational study in which the motives for these deliberately negative self-presentations were further explored, by comparing these self-presentations with their intentionally positive counterparts. In that study, self-presentation is examined from the perspective of the self-presenting actor. The subsequent section takes the perspective of the audience and considers unintended aversive self-presentations—that is, self-presentations that are intended to be positive (such as self-promotion and ingratiation), but are in fact perceived by others as aversive. A literature review is presented to address the questions when and why self-presentation becomes disagreeable from the perspective of observers.

INTENDED AVERSIVE SELF-PRESENTATIONS: AN EMPIRICAL EXPLORATION

Six of the eight self-presentations in the taxonomy above were examined in a survey among readers of the Dutch popular journal *Psychologie*, based on the same concept as *Psychology Today*. Among other things, the purpose of this study was to examine the occurrence of negative self-presentational behaviors (i.e., hostility, playing dumb, and supplication), to compare these categories with their positive counterparts (ingratiation, self-promotion, and autonomy), and to explore the motives for negative self-presentations and the settings in which they occur. The morality dimension was not included in the study; the length of the questionnaire required some restrictions and, as noted, the negative pole of this dimension seems infrequent, especially in a sample like this.

Method

In an issue of *Psychologie*, a questionnaire on self-presentation was included. Readers were encouraged to think about the ways in which they present themselves to others and to fill out the questionnaire and mail it in a postage-paid envelope provided for this purpose; they could also respond by e-mail. The questionnaire started with a brief introduction on self-presentation, in which it was explained that any behavior can be the result of the motive to present the self in some way. Six categories of self-presentation (self-promotion, playing dumb, ingratiation, hostility, autonomy, and supplication, in this order) were briefly described. For each category, a list of behaviors associated with that category was presented (e.g., for self-promotion: emphasize one's abilities, describe one's accomplishments, claim personal responsibility for a joint performance, attribute bad performance to lack of effort or situational variables, show off knowledge, use difficult language, drop names). No examples were given regarding settings or motives, because these might influence respondents. It was stressed that a behavior is self-presentational only when it is motivated by the goal to affect others' impression of the self, that is, to be seen as competent or knowledgeable, as incompetent or ignorant, as likable, as hostile or threatening, as autonomous and independent, or as helpless and dependent. It was also noted that self-presentation does not necessarily imply deceit. For instance, one may compliment a person and really mean it, but the act of complimenting may be motivated by self-presentational goals. So, self-presentation can range from making genuine compliments, vis exaggerating it a little, to blatant deceit, as long as the motive is to affect someone's impression of oneself rather than simply to express one's feelings.

For each of the six categories of self-presentation, respondents were asked to indicate how frequently they engaged in this type of self-presentation on a scale ranging from 1 (*never*) to 5 (*almost all the time*). If their response was *never*, they were routed to the next set of questions; in the other cases, they were asked to think of the most recent occasion on which they had engaged in this behavior and to describe briefly in their own words (a) the persons toward whom the behavior was enacted, (b) their intention or goal, and (c) their exact behavior.

Responses to these questions were coded by two judges. Part of the material (124 descriptions) was coded independently by both judges to examine interjudge agreement. From the descriptions of motives and behavior, the judges identified instances that did not fit the criteria of self-presentation (mostly because the behavior did not serve self-presentational goals, e.g., asking for help with a chore because one wants to be helped) or did not belong in that particular category. The persons toward whom the behavior was enacted were classified into one of 47 categories (e.g., neighbor, spouse, sibling, teacher, physician, waiter or waitress), which are described later (interjudge agreement = 92%). The motives listed by the respondents were coded on a scale from 1 (entirely self-serving) to 7 (entirely other-serving; between-judges $r = .83$). An example of a motive coded as 1 is the motive to get a job; an example of a motive coded as 7 is the motive to cheer up a friend who feels bad.

The last part of the questionnaire consisted of a Dutch adaptation of Snyder's (1974) self-monitoring scale,[2] followed by three background questions (regarding sex, age, and education).

A completed questionnaire was returned by 447 readers (116 male respondents and 321 female respondents; 10 respondents did not indicate their gender), with a mean age of 34.1 years (age range 14–82) and with mostly higher education (226 respondents had completed higher professional education or had a master's degree). These data indicate that the sample was a fair reflection of the demographics of *Psychologie* readers.

---

[2]The results of this assessment are beyond the scope of this chapter. Self-monitoring was significantly correlated with the frequency of all self-presentations (most strongly with ingratiation, $r = .38$, and self-promotion, $r = .30$) except for hostility.

Results

Occurrence

In reporting the results of the study, I describe both the three negative and the three positive self-presentations examined here. The purpose is to examine the motives and the situations that evoke negative self-presentations, so the data on the positive self-presentations are reported primarily for the sake of comparison.

Table 4.2 presents the occurrence of each of the six types of self-presentation, according to respondents' own frequency ratings. On all three dimensions, the negative category was enacted significantly less frequently than the positive one. This is hardly remarkable, considering that self-presentation typically implies that a desirable image of the self is presented. What is remarkable in these results is that the negative varieties of self-presentation are not uncommon at all, according to respondents' own indications. For hostility and playing dumb, the mean frequency is close to 3, which was the *sometimes* category on the response scale. Only supplication seems to occur less frequently, with a mean closer to *rarely*. This was the only category for which the ratings of male (M = 1.95) and female respondents (M = 2.24) were significantly different.

Table 4.3 presents the correlations between the reported frequencies of the different categories of self-presentation. Note that there are only minor negative correlations between the two poles of each dimension, that is, ingratiation–hostility, self-promotion–playing dumb, and autonomy–supplication. The two poles seem to be largely independent from each other. Overall, negative self-presentations are not inversely related to positive ones. On the contrary, several of the positive and negative self-presentations are positively correlated with each other. Ingratiation has positive correlations with all other self-presentations except for its opposite, hostility. These results suggest that, generally, negative self-presentations are enacted by the same people as positive ones.

TABLE 4.2
Frequency of Occurrence of Six Categories of Self-Presentation Behavior

Behavior	M	SD
Ingratiation	3.74	.93
Hostility–intimidation	2.89	.85
Self-promotion	3.18	.86
Playing dumb	2.93	.90
Autonomy	3.45	.97
Supplication	2.17	.86

Note. Respondents rated their self-presentation behaviors on a 5-point scale (1 = *never*, 5 = *almost all the time*).

TABLE 4.3
Pearson Correlations Between Reported Frequency of Enacting the Different Types of Self-Presentation Behaviors

Behavior	1.	2.	3.	4.	5.	6.
1. Ingratiation						
2. Hostility	−.10*					
3. Self-promotion	.30***	.08				
4. Playing dumb	.14**	.08	−.07			
5. Autonomy	.22***	.19***	.26***	.02		
6. Supplication	.24***	.09	.02	.14**	−.08	

Note. *$p < .05$. **$p < .01$. ***$p < .001$.

Note that the negative self-presentations under consideration here are intentional. Respondents were explicitly asked to report behaviors by which they knowingly set out to convey an unlikable, ignorant, or dependent impression. Having established that these intentional aversive self-presentations are not unusual, the next question is what motivates people to project undesirable images like these and in which social settings this behavior occurs.

Motives

Respondents were asked to think of the last time they engaged in each of the six self-presentation behaviors and to describe their motives for the behavior. Not surprisingly, these motives were highly divergent across the six categories. Each type of self-presentation appears to be driven by its own set of motives. The motives were classified on a self-serving versus other-serving dimension to allow some analysis at an aggregate level (see Method description above). Table 4.4 presents the results of this classification in the first column. The second column reports the number of descriptions on which the analyses in the present section are based (i.e.,

TABLE 4.4
Mean Ratings for Motive Given for the Most Recent Instance of Each Type of Self-Presentation Behavior

Behavior	Motive	Valid *N*
Ingratiation	2.75$_a$	350
Hostility	1.39$_b$	301
Self-promotion	1.35$_b$	284
Playing dumb	3.32$_c$	267
Autonomy	1.75$_d$	230
Supplication	1.16$_b$	153

Note. Motives were rated using a 7-point scale (1 = *self-serving*, 7 = *other-serving*). Means that do not share the same subscripts are significantly different at $p < .05$ (Duncan comparison test).

after excluding instances that either did not fit the present definition of self-presentation or did not fit the pertinent category; see the description in the Method section).

Overall, the behaviors were predominantly self-serving: All means are below 4, the neutral point of the rating scale. However, analysis of variance indicated that the different types of self-presentation differed from each other in this respect, $F(5, 1,585) = 85.14$, $p < .001$.[3] The most extreme self-serving category is *supplication*. The motives listed for this behavior almost invariably reflected the need to receive help or support, either materially (e.g., help with a flat tire or a clogged sink), but very often emotionally (e.g., pity, comfort, usually "attention"). To list a few examples of this category: A respondent acted "hysterically" because she wanted her mother to help her find something; another one cried and screamed to make her husband "see that I have feelings too"; a husband, in turn, acted "disappointed and depressed" to get his wife to endorse his plans; a woman attempted to make an ex-lover come back by appealing to his guilt; several high school students reported exaggerating their illness because they wanted to stay home from school; and one woman went to her physician deliberately not wearing any make-up and looking dreadful with the goal of getting him to take her illness seriously. Very rarely did supplication serve the target's interest. One of the few exceptions was a therapist who acted helplessly toward a patient to encourage him to describe his situation more clearly.

A shared second place for self-servingness can be assigned to self-promotion and hostility. Self-promotion, not surprisingly, was most frequently used to make a good impression in performance-related settings, for instance, to impress one's superior, to get a job, to be selected for a sports team, to launch an account from a client, to prove that one is worthy of a new position, or to persuade colleagues to go along with one's plans. Some respondents engaged in self-promotion to hide insecurity or simply to evoke appreciation, respect, or admiration or to be taken seriously. Occasionally, it was used in response to others who seemed too content with themselves to put them in their proper place. One respondent acted overly confident toward a car salesman to discourage him from trying to "con" her. Self-promotion rarely served the target's benefit. The exceptions were work-related settings in which respondents attempted to reassure a target who depended on their abilities (e.g., a lawyer toward a distressed client).

Regarding hostility, it should be noted that two subcategories emerged

---

[3]In the analyses reported here, the six self-presentation categories were treated as between-subjects variables, because a multivariate analysis (with categories as a within-subjects variable) would include only respondents who provided an example of each of the six categories, and the others would be treated as missing cases. Note that the present analyses are conservative because the within-subjects variance is part of the error term. All results were checked by means of the appropriate multivariate tests, and no meaningful differences between the two types of analyses were found.

from the responses in this category. One type of response clearly reflected intimidation. Here, the goal was to gain or retain control over someone by being strict and unyielding (e.g., toward pupils in the classroom or toward one's own children). More frequently, however, the emphasis was on keeping people at a distance (physically or emotionally), either by deliberately acting in a disinterested manner (e.g., ignore, give brief responses) or by being hostile and aggressive. This type of behavior was reported, for instance, in trying to discourage someone who was sexually or romantically interested in the respondent, to keep pushy strangers at arms length in bars or at parties, to avoid intimacy or sex within a relationship, to signal to a shopkeeper that one only wants to browse, or to simply give somebody the message that one is not interested in further contact. Several respondents reported being conspicuously hostile to show someone that their feelings had been hurt. Others, who had also been hurt, reported being aloof and cold, to act as though they were invulnerable. Most frequently, respondents in this subcategory aimed to create an emotional distance because they wanted to be "left alone"; to shut out others from their emotional lives, especially in difficult times; and to keep their problems private and far away from meddling family members. Sometimes, respondents acted aloof and businesslike to avoid being drawn into someone else's problems or to prevent an emotional outburst during a bad-news conversation. Whenever this type of behavior served other people's interest, it was because respondents felt they should not burden others with their emotional distress or wanted to avoid being the cause of others' concern; therefore, they walled off the other person.

The motives listed for autonomy, another primarily self-serving type of presentation, are partially similar to those for the emotional–hostility category described above: In some cases, respondents used this self-presentational style to keep others from interfering in their lives or, in case of other-serving autonomy, to keep others from worrying about them (e.g., after a divorce when they were living alone) or feeling obligated to help them. A few respondents mentioned autonomous self-presentations toward a former lover or spouse, to demonstrate that they did not need him or her anymore. For several respondents, the goal of autonomous self-presentations was to avoid being seen as weak or vulnerable or to avoid pity by emphasizing their strength and their ability to deal with their problems. Occasionally, respondents mentioned expressing unorthodox or "different" opinions to demonstrate their independent thinking or to show that they did not care to belong in a particular group. One respondent mentioned "playing hard to get" with a person in whom she was romantically interested. Similarly, autonomy was sometimes described as a way to achieve power over someone by acting as if one does not need anything from this person. As I demonstrate later in *Targets*, autonomy also occurred frequently in interactions with parents, especially among younger respondents, either because they wanted their parents not to worry about them (e.g., when they had just started living on their own) or when they were still living at home because they wanted to demonstrate their independence and maturity (sometimes with an ulterior goal, e.g., to be left at home alone during their parents' vacation). For similar reasons, respondents sometimes presented themselves as autonomous at work to acquire more independence and responsibilities.

One of the self-presentations that was less self-serving was ingratiation. This might come as a surprise, because ingratiation is the prototypical behavioral instrument to affect others (and has been described as such by E. E. Jones, 1964) and being seen as likable clearly is personally rewarding. Indeed, in many cases respondents ingratiated themselves for this reason, sometimes with specific goals in mind (e.g., to sell something, to persuade someone to have sex with them, to make a new friend; in E. E. Jones's terminology, these are instances of *acquisitive ingratiation*) but usually simply to "be liked" or to "be accepted" (*signifying ingratiation*; E. E. Jones, 1964). Nevertheless, ingratiation was also frequently used to smooth social interaction, for instance, to make everyone feel comfortable at social gatherings, to re-establish peace after a conflict, to improve the atmosphere after a sad event, to establish a friendly relationship with a new colleague, or to avoid an awkward situation (e.g., responding to a waiter that dinner was good even when it was horrible). In cases like these, the judges coded the motive as both self- and other-serving (i.e., a neutral rating of 4). In a minority of cases, ingratiation served mainly the interests of the target, for instance, putting a job applicant at ease, complimenting others to enhance their confidence, or hiding one's boredom and annoyance in response to a friend's monologue about his problems.

The most other-serving self-presentation by far was playing dumb. Some of the motives for this behavior that emerged out of the questionnaires were already mentioned previously; on the self-serving side, for instance, preventing others from asking for help with a chore; on the other-serving side, preventing threats to others' self-esteem. The responses indicated that playing dumb may serve a wide variety of additional purposes. Among other things, respondents mentioned downgrading their abilities to evoke a compliment, concealing their knowledge merely to find out what someone else knows about something, trying to belong in a group that is "less educated" or reducing the distance between them and others, making a good impression with one's new parents-in-law by pretending not to know anything about drugs, making a modest impression or avoiding drawing attention to themselves, reducing high expectations to prevent others from being disappointed or by setting a lower standard for their performance, avoiding an argument or a confrontation by hiding knowledge that contradicts someone's statements, preventing competitiveness or envy, assuring that others do not feel inferior, giving credit to others for a joint accomplishment, and allowing others (mostly one's children or pupils) to discover things for themselves. As can be seen from these examples, especially the last ones, playing dumb may often reduce tension, insecurity, competitiveness, and other social discomfort. In that respect, it is actually the least aversive type of self-presentation of them all.

But overall, as noted, the self-presentations examined in this study were more personally rewarding for the self-presenter than for the target (cf. DePaulo & Kashy, 1998, for parallel findings on lies). Interestingly, there appears to be no systematic difference in this respect between the positive and the negative self-presentations. Corroborating E. E. Jones's (1964, 1990) view, it seems that both positive and negative self-presentations can affect others' behaviors and feelings in desired ways, depending on the setting and on what is desired in that setting.

Targets

In addition to respondents' goals, I also examined toward whom the self-presentations were enacted. Table 4.5 presents the frequencies of targets classified by their role in the respondent's life. Some of the 47 categories used for this classification are not in this table because they occurred infrequently (e.g., waiter, civil servant, and real estate agent). Other categories that occurred infrequently were merged because they are similar and produced a similar pattern of results (e.g., subordinate + job applicant; a friend + best friend; siblings + other family members). Altogether, the target categories listed in this table compose 90% of the material. The entries in the table are frequencies and row percentages, for example, out of all 34 instances in which object of desire or romance was mentioned as the target of self-presentation, 62% were instances of ingratiation.

The row marginals include the proportion of occasions at which self-presentations were directed at each target category. For instance, subordinates + job applicants (0.9%) as well as children (0.6%) were infrequently the targets of self-presentation. (Note that these role labels refer to a target's role with regard to the respondent; e.g., *subordinate* refers to the *respondent's* subordinate.) This corroborates E. E. Jones's (1964, 1990) view that self-presentation is motivated by dependence, that is, the need to influence the target's behavior. Because of the asymmetry in the dependence relationship between supervisors and subordinates, selection officers and job applicants, and parents and children, it follows that self-presentation is more often directed upward (i.e., toward superiors and parents) than downward (i.e., toward subordinates and children), as the results indeed indicate. As can be seen from the row marginals, the most common targets of self-presentation are *colleagues* and *partner or spouse*. In part, this may reflect dependence in these relationships, but we should also realize that people spend a lot of time with their colleagues and their partner, so the base rate for these targets is high to begin with.

TABLE 4.5
Frequencies and Row Percentages for Targets Toward Whom the Six Categories of Self-Presentational Behaviors Were Enacted

Target of Behavior	Ingratiat.	Hostil./Intim.	Self-Prom.	Play Dumb	Auton.	Suppl.	Total
Object of desire or romance							
n	21	5/1	3	4	1	0	34
%	62	15	9	12	3	—	2
Subordinate or job applicant							
n	8	7/3	0	0	0	0	15
%	53	47	—	—	—	—	<1
Pupil or student							
n	9	8/8	5	3	1	1	27
%	33	30	19	11	4	4	2
Children							
n	1	4/4	0	2	1	1	9
%	11	44	—	22	11	11	<1
Stranger							
n	13	21/4	5	3	2	1	45
%	29	47	11	7	4	2	3
Ex-partner or ex-spouse							
n	0	5/1	0	1	4	2	12
%	—	42	—	8	33	17	<1
Neighbors or roommates							
n	11	16/0	2	3	4	3	39
%	28	41	5	8	10	8	3
In-laws							
n	13	8/1	1	6	4	1	33
%	39	24	3	18	12	3	2
Job interviewer or future superior							
n	6	0/0	39	1	4	0	50
%	12	—	78	2	8	—	3

Target							
Teacher or trainer							
n	1	2/0	18	4	4	3	32
%	3	6	56	13	13	9	2
Superior or client							
n	9	6/1	50	14	15	6	100
%	9	6	50	14	15	6	6
(Best) friend							
n	41	24/0	20	54	26	12	177
%	23	14	18	31	15	7	11
Parents							
n	9	12/1	2	3	45	10	81
%	11	15	3	4	56	12	5
Partner or spouse							
n	35	26/5	12	25	40	76	214
%	16	12	6	12	19	36	14
Physician or therapist							
n	4	0/0	1	2	1	7	15
%	27	0	7	13	7	47	<1
Colleagues							
n	66	62/4	53	55	30	9	275
%	24	23	19	20	11	3	17
Acquaintances							
n	26	25/2	8	27	11	1	98
%	27	26	8	28	11	1	6
Family members							
n	11	15/1	6	18	23	15	88
%	13	17	7	21	26	17	6
Fellow students or class mates							
n	18	14/0	19	21	3	1	76
%	24	18	25	28	4	1	5

Note. Ingratiat. = ingratiation; hostil./intim. = hostility/frequency of intimidation among hostile behaviors; self-prom. = self-promotion; auton. = autonomy; suppl. = supplication. Targets are ordered by the type of self-presentation that is predominant for this target category; percentages for predominant self-presentations are underlined. All percentages have been rounded.

The table rows are ordered by the predominance of a self-presentational category, starting with *ingratiation*, which is predominant for *object of desire—romance* and for *subordinate + job applicant*. The percentages for these predominant self-presentations are underscored. The last four rows (*colleagues*, *acquaintances*, *family members*, and *class mates*) represent target categories for which no type of self-presentation stood out.

As noted earlier, the *hostility* category consisted of two subcategories, labeled *intimidation* and *distance* hereafter. Because the two are associated with different target categories, the entries in the hostility column all have a sword entry, indicating the number of occurrences of intimidation (interjudge agreement for this distinction was 77%). Thus, for instance, out of the total of seven instances of hostile self-presentations toward subordinates or job applicants, three were instances of intimidation. For behaviors toward children (enacted by parents) and pupils (enacted by teachers), all were instances of intimidation. These results illustrate that intimidation is typically a style of self-presentation used by the more powerful to maintain or regain control. In the other target categories characterized by high proportions of hostile self-presentations, these are mostly of the distance type. Relatively often, respondents were intentionally hostile or cold toward strangers, ex-lovers, neighbors, and in-laws to create or maintain a distance (although in the case of in-laws, many other respondents did attempt to be friendly by means of ingratiation).

Quite sensibly, *self-promotion* was the primary self-presentation in the interaction with job interviewers, (future) superiors, and teachers or trainers. The negative counterpart, *playing dumb*, was used frequently toward (best) friends. This finding converges with results reported by Tice, Butler, Muraven, and Stillwell (1995), who suggested that modesty prevails in the interaction with friends because they are already familiar with one's abilities. In these cases, when their talents are already recognized, people are able to avoid the risk of being seen as arrogant. This does not necessarily explain why people would play dumb instead. It is possible that some of the motives for this self-presentation are especially relevant in the interaction with friends, in particular motives that are related to avoiding competitiveness, envy, and feelings of inferiority on the part of the target, because equality is generally seen as essential to friendships.

Autonomy was the dominant self-presentation toward parents, both for children and adult respondents (note that the youngest respondent was 14). Its negative counterpart, *supplication*, occurred primarily in the interaction with partner or spouse and physician or therapist. As noted earlier, male and female respondents differed in the estimated frequency of this particular category. The reason may be that men tended to restrict supplication to the interaction with their intimate partner, whereas women used it in other settings as well. At least two variables may contribute to these differences. First, dependent and helpless behavior is part of the negative stereotype of women, so men are probably very cautious with this behavior, especially in public settings. Indeed, in a study among intimate couples, we found that men tend to express feminine qualities only in the interaction with their intimate partner (Vonk & Van Nobelen, 1993). Second, in our society women still do not have the same power that men have, and supplication is a self-presentational ploy typically used by powerless people. It is often the only way to influence a more powerful target. Notwithstanding the rationale of this behavior in some situations, the examples of it presented earlier illustrate its aversiveness. Not only is this behavior aversive to others, it can have undesirable consequences for the actor as well, because negative self-presentations, just as positive ones, may become second nature (E. E. Jones, Rhodewalt, Berglas, & Skelton, 1981; Rhodewalt, 1986).

Summary

The data on the motives and the targets of the different categories of self-presentation show that many divergent motives and settings can evoke negative self-presentations. Of the three categories examined here —or perhaps it would be more appropriate to say four, considering the differences between intimidation and distance—each one appears to be associated with its own set of motives and settings.[4] Overall, people seem to have sensible reasons to engage in negative self-presentations. When they engage in intimidation or create a distance, it is probably true that they do not make themselves likable, but that is usually not their intention in those situations. Similarly, when people present themselves as foolish and ignorant or as helpless and dependent, they are not seen as competent or strong, but they do accomplish other purposes, which presumably are more important to them at that point. Apparently, then, people make trade-offs between the positive and negative consequences of their self-presentations, although it is conceivable that they underestimate the latter (Baumeister & Scher, 1988).

It is noteworthy that the correlations between different self-presentations are generally positive and that even diametrically opposite self-presentations (ingratiation vs. hostility, self-promotion vs. playing dumb, autonomy vs. supplication) are not strongly negatively correlated. It appears that people simply differ from each other in their tendency to engage in self-presentation (with a greater tendency among those high in self-monitoring; see footnote 2) and that, to the extent that an individual uses self-presentation as a behavioral instrument, any type of self-

---

[4]There are similarities between supplication and playing dumb, but only to the extent that these categories are themselves correlated with each other. That is, foolish or ignorant behavior may often co-occur with helpless behavior; as a consequence, the two categories share some of the same motives and settings.

presentation is more likely to be used, depending on the setting and the individual's motives. Indeed, it is characteristic of the very phenomenon of self-presentation that one's behavior is adapted to the situation at hand. Negative self-presentations may be just as functional as positive ones, depending on the setting, characteristics of the target, and the actor's goals. These goals may be either selfish or altruistic. Importantly, both negative and positive self-presentations may serve either selfish or altruistic motives.

In the study described above, self-presentation was examined from the perspective of the actor. Presumably, respondents who reported occasions where they were trying to make a hostile or stupid or helpless impression aimed to be perceived negatively, at least on the pertinent dimension of judgment, whereas efforts to make a likable or intelligent or autonomous impression reflect the goal of being perceived favorably. What we do not know is whether these goals are actually accomplished, because secondary impressions may deviate from calculated impressions. In some cases, negative self-presentations may have unintended positive effects on the audience; in other cases, positive self-presentations may have unintended negative effects and be perceived as aversive. This latter outcome is likely to occur more frequently, for two reasons. First, the positive effects of negative self-presentations are usually foreseen and even intended (e.g., being seen as modest by playing dumb), whereas the negative effects of positive presentations are usually not (e.g., being seen as arrogant by engaging in self-promotion or as self-righteous by engaging in exemplification). Second, all self-presentations, both negative and positive, may arouse unintended aversion among targets as soon as the self-presentation is recognized as such—that is, as soon as suspicion arises regarding the authenticity of the presentation. In the following section, I describe these unintended aversive effects of self-presentation and review the literature that has examined the observer's perspective.

UNINTENDED AVERSIVE SELF-PRESENTATIONS

Authenticity

In society, it is socially desirable to behave consistently with one's true inner thoughts and feelings (e.g., Gergen, 1968; M. R. Leary, 1995; Schlenker, 1980; Vonk, 1999e). People should be authentic; their words should match their deeds. As a consequence, self-presenters are judged negatively when the impressions they convey are perceived to deviate from how they really are. The effects of a discrepancy between one's perceived true self and one's self-presentational behavior are perhaps most clearly illustrated by the phenomenon of hypocrisy, which represents a failed attempt at exemplification (Gilbert & Jones, 1986; cf. Stone, Wiegand,

Cooper, & Aronson, 1997). It is one thing to lie about one's age or to spend a lot of money on vacations and give none to charity or to neglect recycling one's waste; but it becomes a lot worse if that same person publicly advocates the importance of honesty or charity or protection of the environment. Thus, we may suspect that when people proclaim certain moral or prosocial values and it is found that they themselves do not live up to their own standards, they are judged more negatively than if they had not proclaimed anything at all.

It should be noted that our disapproval of inconsistencies between words and deeds is not entirely sensible. For instance, being a vegetarian, I often receive criticism because I do eat eggs and fish sometimes and wear leather shoes. When people catch me doing things like this, which are inconsistent with my own principles, they sometimes get upset or smug with me. They may even think that I am a hypocrite. Nevertheless, I think I can make a pretty good case that I am doing a better job at contributing to protect animal welfare and end Third World starvation than those who are consistent meat eaters. Granted, it would be even better if I dropped the eggs, fish, and leather, but surely it is worse to do nothing at all. Similarly, we would probably prefer parents who smoke and warn their children about the hazards of smoking rather than parents who smoke and omit this warning. It would be better, of course, if they quit smoking, but it would be worse to make their words consistent with their behavior. Thus, it may be argued that the high value we place on consistency and authenticity is not always rational.

Moreover, considering the many social benefits of self-presentation described at the beginning of this chapter, one may wonder why authenticity and consistency are so highly valued and why adapting to situational demands is seen as undesirable.[5] One possibility is that, from the perspective of the observer, cross-situational consistency is quite functional: Forming impressions of others allows people to predict future behavior, and it provides them with a sense of control (e.g., Miller, Norman, & Wright, 1978; cf. Vonk, 1999c). If those others change like chameleons in each setting, they become unpredictable. So, if people remain true to their inner selves, we can rely on them to engage in the same sort of behavior across different occasions and to act in accordance with the views they have expressed on previous occasions. This enhances our sense of control and predictability.

In addition, it is conceivable that natural selection has made humans

---

[5]Evidence for this undesirability comes from studies on correspondence bias, in which participants read about a person's behavior and learn that the behavior was conducted either under situational pressure or by the actor's free choice. In these studies, one often obtains a main effect of the choice manipulation, such that the actor is liked less when the behavior matches situational constraints (e.g., Vonk, 1999c).

overly sensitive about duplicity. The human species spent 99% of its evo-lutionary history in a hunter–gatherer mode, characterized by social exchange among group members (Axelrod, 1984). In this setting, survival depends in part on the ability to detect cheaters, such as people who claim to invest in the commodities of the group whereas in fact they only take from it (Cosmides, 1989; Cosmides & Tooby, 1992). As a consequence, members whose behavior does not match their presentations may be judged harshly.

Based on the considerations above, it may be assumed that any kind of self-presentation, whatever its position in the taxonomy used here, is judged negatively when it is perceived as deviating from the actor's true feelings or intentions. This implies that the mere occurrence of self-presentation can be seen as aversive, regardless of its valence, when the actor is suspected of not being genuine. Converging with this assumption, a study by Schlenker and Leary (1982) demonstrated that actors are judged negatively when claims about their performance do not match their actual abilities; this effect occurs regardless of whether they claim to be better (self-promotion) or worse than is warranted (playing dumb). A recent study (Vonk, 1999e) suggested that the reduced likability of self-glorifying and self-deprecating actors is mediated by the inference that the actor's ability claims are driven by self-presentational motives rather than the motive to provide accurate information about the self. Specifically, actors claiming high ability are disliked more to the extent that their statements are assumed to reflect the need to boast or impress others; actors claiming low ability are disliked more to the extent that they are suspected of false modesty or preemptively setting up a defense against future public failure.

Thus, it can be argued that the mere occurrence of self-presentation is seen as aversive, or at least as socially undesirable, because it implies that observers do not always see what they may eventually get. However, given this negative base rate for the occurrence of self-presentation in general, some forms of self-presentation are more aversive than others. For one thing, it is worse to be duped on the positive than on the negative side: If a person's true self turns out to be worse (less likable or competent) than we have been led to believe, the discrepancy is more severe than if the person turns out to be better than the self-presentation suggested. In the latter case, the potential damage is smaller (cf. Vonk, 1999c). There-fore, self-presentations classified as positive in the taxonomy above are particularly likely to be perceived as aversive by observers.

Empirical demonstrations of observers' perceptions of self-presenting actors are mostly restricted to two positive and widely occurring categories of self-presentation: self-promotion and ingratiation. These studies are de-scribed more specifically in the next section.

Self-Promotion

In a study by Godfrey, Jones, and Lord (1986), participants interacted with each other. Some were instructed to get the other participant to see them as extremely competent. Ratings by the other participant indicated that (a) only some individuals with this instruction managed to increase their perceived competence, and (b) all participants instructed to self-promote were seen as less likable after the interaction. The authors concluded that "self-promotion is not ingratiating." A recent study by Rudman (1998) showed that this is especially true when the self-promoting actor is a woman, because self-promotion violates the female role prescription of being modest and noncompetitive. In Rudman's experiments, self-promotion was effective in producing increased hireability ratings, but generally it was also associated with decreased likability. Correlational research by Paulhus (1998) suggested that people who habitually engage in self-enhancement may be liked initially but are judged negatively (and highly discrepant from their self-evaluations) after several encounters, presumably because "examples of their self-absorption . . . may eventually have accumulated to an offensive level" (p. 1206).

Looking at the behaviors that were used by self-promoters in the Godfrey et al. study, it makes sense that they were relatively disliked. In a way, the behaviors enacted by self-promoters are the opposite of what people do when they ingratiate themselves. Ingratiators draw out the other person, direct attention to the other person's area of expertise and interest, spend more time listening than talking, express agreement with the other's opinions, and tell self-deprecating anecdotes. Self-promoters do exactly the opposite: They attempt to control the conversation, direct attention to themselves and avoid the other's area of expertise, spend more time talking than listening, express disagreement with the other person, and stress their own accomplishments. Pretty aversive indeed.

Self-promotion, then, is a very hazardous type of self-presentation. If it succeeds, one usually has to incur the cost of being seen as less likable. This may be part of the trade-off, and it may be worth it if being seen as competent is sufficiently important. However, it is conceivable that one does not even accomplish this in some cases, because reduced likability may affect perceived competence (through the halo effect). Especially in the long run, when people remember only their global evaluations of a person and not the exact facts on which their inferences are based, it seems likely that competence ratings are more affected by perceived likability than by specific recollections of a person's accomplishments (cf. Ebbesen, 1981; Lingle, Dukerich, & Ostrom, 1983; Schul & Burnstein, 1985).

Highly similar words of caution can be derived from a related area, the study of self-handicapping. E. E. Jones and Berglas (1978) initially suggested that people may privately protect their self-esteem by seeking or creating impediments to performance, so that bad performance can be attributed to these impediments rather than low ability (discounting), whereas good performance makes the individual's ability all the more impressive (augmentation). In later research (e.g., T. W. Smith, Snyder, & Handelsman, 1982; T. W. Smith, Snyder, & Perkins, 1983), self-handicapping was examined as a public, self-presentational strategy, whereby people claim or exaggerate impediments to performance. In effect, this type of self-handicapping is a self-promotional tactic, intended to make the actor look more competent.

Like other varieties of self-promotion, self-handicapping appears to be a tricky business. Indeed, the few researchers who have considered self-handicapping behavior from the perspective of the observer have all concluded that the self-presentational utility of the behavior is small (Arkin & Baumgardner, 1985; Luginbuhl & Palmer, 1991; Rhodewalt, Sanbonmatsu, Tschanz, Feick, & Waller, 1995). The effect may be either that the actor is disliked or is not seen as more competent (or both). The most favorable outcome, just as in other cases of effective self-promotion, is that perceived competence is effectively increased whereas likability is reduced (Luginbuhl & Palmer, 1991; D. S. Smith & Strube, 1991). Even in this case, however, the increase in perceived competence appears to be restricted to specific judgments of the task under consideration, rather than overall intelligence or ability (Luginbuhl & Palmer, 1991). In the worst-case scenario, the self-handicapper is seen as relatively incompetent as well as unlikable (Rhodewalt et al., 1995). This result seems most likely when the ability under consideration is relatively ambiguous (e.g., creativity in the Rhodewalt et al. study); in this case, the actor's performance may be assimilated toward the expectation induced by the self-handicapping claims. That is, when a person claims test anxiety or low effort, we do not expect superior performance; as a consequence, the outcome may be perceived as mediocre when there are no clear-cut diagnostic data indicating otherwise.

Self-handicappers apparently cannot overcome these potentially negative effects by means of the type of handicap they use. The disadvantage of claiming external impediments is that it violates the general "norm for internality" (Beauvois & Dubois, 1988; Jellison & Green, 1981), by which people should be responsible for their own behaviors and outcomes. Trying to evade this responsibility by pointing to external factors is socially undesirable and, hence, unlikable. On the other hand, the drawback of claiming internal impediments is that these may affect competence judgments because they are often associated with perceived ability. This appears to be the case even for effort, a variable that logically should have a compensatory relationship to ability in evaluating performance (Heider, 1958). In fact, attributions to ability and effort are positively related, so perceptions of reduced effort are associated with perceptions of reduced ability (e.g.,

Felson & Bohrnstedt, 1980). In addition, because effort is a controllable internal variable (Weiner, 1986), low effort produces decreased liking in comparison with other internal handicaps, such as test anxiety (Rhodewalt et al., 1995). These, in turn, have their own problems. For instance, a person who claims test anxiety may be seen as more likable but certainly not as confident and able to maintain good performance under pressure.

In summary, the extant literature suggests that the effects of self-promotion and self-handicapping are often not what the self-presenter had in mind. At best, the actor is seen as relatively capable with regard to the ability under consideration. In many cases, however, self-promoting and self-handicapping behaviors are mainly perceived as unlikable, and the trade-off with perceived competence is unfavorable because the observer does not even acknowledge the ability claimed or implied by the self-presenter. This seems to be likely when there is no diagnostic, unambiguous information about the actor's accomplishments.

In this context, it is important to note that, in the studies described above, the self-presenters' claims were not corroborated by information about their actual performance. The presence of such information would no doubt make it much easier to convince the audience of one's abilities (Reeder & Fulks, 1980). In most circumstances, it is probably undesirable and "not done" to claim abilities that cannot be verified by the audience. Indeed, self-promotion is more effective when actor and observer are aware that the claims can be publicly tested (Vonk, 1999e). In this case, observers assume that the actor is as capable as he says he is, because he would not want to run the risk of being exposed as pretentious or boastful. As a consequence of this perceived truthfulness, likability is not reduced either.

There appear to be several subtle variables that make self-promoters more credible and likable. Corroboration by actual performance is one of them (or, in the case of self-handicapping, clear evidence of the claimed impediment), but common sense suggests there are many others, such as the extent to which the actor is willing to self-deprecate in other domains (a person who claims high ability in all domains is obviously less credible and less likable) and the setting in which the behavior is enacted (e.g., self-promotion among friends is seen as more undesirable than among strangers; cf. Tice et al., 1995). Everyday life provides self-promoters with many means to soften and cover up their attempts at self-glorification, so things may not be as bad as they appear in laboratory studies. (If they were, self-promotion and self-handicapping would probably have vanished from our behavioral repertoire.) Nevertheless, blatant and embarrassing instances of self-promotion and self-handicapping can be observed regularly, so apparently the fine art of this self-presentational ploy has not been mastered by many of us.

Ingratiation

In the competence domain, a trade-off can be made between likability and competence. Self-glorification may decrease likability, but it may also accomplish that one is seen as capable, and in some settings this is more important than being liked. When it comes to ingratiation, on the other hand, there is only one dimension that matters: likability. As a consequence, self-presentational failures cannot be offset by successes on other dimensions. In this domain, truthfulness is everything. To the extent that there are doubts as to whether one's behavior is genuine, these doubts are immediately reflected on perceived likability (cf. Vonk & Van Knippenberg, 1994).

Two other variables complicate the predicament of the ingratiator. First, whereas claims of high competence can be corroborated by evidence of one's performance, claims of high likability cannot. Anyone can help or support others, donate money to charity, make friendly remarks, and so on, so this type of behavior is far less informative than behaviors reflecting high ability, which can only be enacted by people with at least some level of real competence (Reeder & Brewer, 1979). As a consequence, likable and friendly behaviors contribute little to the impression formed, whereas the slightest indication of unfriendliness may be seen as evidence of a person's true nature (Reeder & Brewer, 1979; Skowronski & Carlston, 1987). This implies that, once a negative impression has inadvertently been established, it becomes difficult to turn things around: Even the most sincere and well-intended gesture of friendliness may be interpreted as mere ingratiation or even manipulation. Conversely, a previously established positive impression may be disqualified as soon as a few unlikable behaviors are observed (Vonk, 1993b).

A second complication is referred to as the *ingratiator's dilemma* (E. E. Jones, 1964): Ingratiation is most difficult precisely in those situations where it matters most—namely, when one depends on another person. This is because observers strongly rely on dependence as a cue in determining whether likable behavior is genuine (Vonk, 1998b, Exp. 2). As noted, likable behavior is relatively ambiguous because it can result from a variety of traits and intentions, including the motive to ingratiate or conform to social demands (E. E. Jones & Davis, 1965). Therefore, in determining the meaning of these behaviors, perceivers tend to use cues about the dependence relationship between the actor and the target (Vonk, 1999a).

When likable behaviors are enacted toward a target on whom the actor depends, these behaviors evoke suspicion of ulterior motivation (cf. Fein, 1996; Fein, Hilton, & Miller, 1990). This suspicion is reflected in moderate inferences about the underlying disposition, that is, the actor's true likability level: The observer is uncertain whether the actor is genuinely likable or is driven by ulterior, self-presentational motives. At this point, the actor's behavior is not yet seen as aversive. The observer is merely considering two competing hypotheses: (a) Either the behavior reflects the actor's true likability, which is good, or (b) it reflects ulterior motives, which is bad. This attributional ambiguity can be resolved by means of additional information about the actor (Fein et al., 1990). For instance, when a person engages in likable behaviors toward more powerful target people (e.g., superiors), it becomes important to know how the person behaves toward less powerful targets (subordinates). In this case, the slightest indication that the person is unlikable toward the latter is sufficient for observers to instantly categorize the person as a detestable "brown-noser" (Vonk, 1998b, Exp. 3).

This type of behavioral pattern (referred to in Dutch as "licking upward, kicking downward") is seen as highly aversive in Western culture. It is also a pattern that is recognized relatively easily by observers. People appear to have a readily available "slime schema" (Vonk, 1998b) about this type of person, which is activated spontaneously when likable behaviors toward more powerful targets are observed. Thus, the identification of self-presentational motives does not always require a thoughtful attributional analysis; instead, the process may be quick and dirty (like other schema-driven operations)—quick, because it does not require any cognitive effort (Vonk, 1998b, Exp. 5; cf. Vonk, 1999e), and dirty, because it is diffuse and prone to error, so that an actor may erroneously be included into the schema once it has been activated (Vonk, 1998b, Exp. 4).

People who are likable toward more powerful targets and unlikable toward less powerful targets are judged negatively. In fact, they are judged just as negatively as people who are unlikable toward everyone (Vonk, 1998b, Exp. 1). There are at least two reasons for the aversiveness of this behavioral pattern. First, the likable behaviors toward more powerful targets are not only discounted as uninformative about the actor's true likability, but they also demonstrate that the actor has violated the authenticity norm. Second, unlikable behaviors toward powerless targets are judged more negatively than the same behaviors toward powerful targets (Vonk, 1999a), perhaps because it is worse to harm those who are not in a position to stand up for themselves or retaliate (cf. the previously mentioned study by S. H. Kim et al., 1998, which suggests that self-presenters are aware of the norm against negative treatment of a less powerful other).

In sum, the dependence relationship between the actor and the target is a crucial cue used by observers in inferring whether likable behaviors are genuine. If likable behavior is directed upward only, it is dismissed as utterly uninformative. Thus, although likability cannot be demonstrated by means of performance, it seems that observers rely on a person's behaviors toward less powerful others when they want to verify whether an actor is truly likable. If these behaviors are less favorable, observers instantly form a disagreeable picture of the actor.

In addition to dependence, other cues are used by observers in determining whether likable behavior is truthful. In the case of flattery or opinion conformity, observers can examine whether the flattery is consistent with the actual qualities of the target. For instance, when a lecturer with fancy video materials but a lousy lecture is complimented on the clarity of the talk, the flatterer is more likely to be suspected of ingratiation than when the compliment concerns the video. From the perspective of the uninvolved observer, this means the flattery has to be deserved: When the observer feels the compliment is not justified by qualities of the target, the flatterer is more likely to be suspected of ulterior motives.

From the perspective of the target, the flattery has to match the target's self-concept to be seen as credible (cf. S. C. Jones & Schneider, 1968). Because most people have a positive self-concept, this may explain why ingratiators are generally judged more favorably by those who are the target of the ingratiation than by uninvolved observers (E. E. Jones, Stires, Shaver, & Harris, 1968; see Gordon, 1996, for a meta-analysis). In the example above, the lecturer may have a more optimistic view of his or her speech than the audience and, hence, be more likely to assign credibility to a compliment about the speech. E. E. Jones (1964) has described this difference in terms of "vain distortion" (p. 77): It is more rewarding to uncritically accept lavish praise directed toward the self than toward someone else, because it boosts one's ego.

It should be noted that this "vain distortion effect" may be produced by both motivational and cognitive variables (Vonk, 1999d). On the motivational side, people aim to protect and enhance their self-esteem, so they are motivated to accept flattery at face value. In addition, people are not only motivated to be liked, but also to like those with whom they interact because they want the interaction to be pleasant (e.g., Berscheid, Graziano, Monson, & Dermer, 1976; Vonk, 1998a). So, they are probably not keen on questioning the motives of their interaction partners, because this might produce decreased liking for these people.

On the cognitive side, several variables work against a critical examination of an ingratiator's behavior toward oneself. First, because one is involved in the interaction oneself, cognitive resources are consumed by having to manage one's own part of the interaction (Osborne & Gilbert, 1992). As a result, it is more likely that the actor's behavior is taken at face value, because one lacks the attention resources required to engage in a sophisticated attribution analysis of the actor's motives (Gilbert, Krull, & Pelham, 1988). Second, most people have a positive self-concept. Therefore, an ingratiator typically confirms what they already knew—that they are likable, competent people whose opinions are accurate. Expectancy-consistent information, whether it pertains to the self or to others, is unlikely to be examined critically. Therefore, it makes sense that targets of ingratiation assign more credibility to the behavior than uninvolved observers, who have no existing positive expectancy about the target.

In everyday life, there is still another reason why targets of ingratiation may often fail to recognize the ulterior motives of the flatterer. In many cases, people only know how they themselves are treated by a person, and not how this person treats others—others who are perhaps less powerful and treated less nicely. As noted earlier, this kind of information is essential in allowing a confident inference of ulterior motivation. Unfortunately, powerful people in particular often lack information about how their subordinates behave toward other subordinates, if only because they often do not have the time and the motivation to keep track of all the behaviors of their employees (cf. Fiske, 1993). Seeing that a subordinate is friendly and supportive toward them, they are bound to like this person. We may assume that many leaders remain in this sweet state of ignorance, while their subordinates gnash their teeth watching how one of their colleagues "butters up" the boss (Vonk, 1998b, p. 861).

In summary, from the perspective of the target, ingratiation is not aversive at all. Therefore, it is likely to have the desired effect precisely with those for whom it is intended. In this scenario, there are clearly payoffs for everyone involved (cf. E. E. Jones, 1964). The target's self-concept is bolstered and verified. The target probably reciprocates the liking expressed by the ingratiator and admires his or her good judgment of character. As a result, the ingratiator is more likely to achieve the desired goal (e.g., a promotion). In the end, everybody is happy—except the observer; the subordinate who knows how the ingratiator has treated the less powerful and who becomes an involuntary witness to the excruciatingly unjust success of "brownnosing." This particular scenario probably illustrates the true meaning of aversive better than any of the examples described in this chapter.

SUMMARY AND DISCUSSION

In many ways, self-presentation has both positive and negative facets. First, desirable as well as undesirable behaviors can result from self-presentational motives. The survey among readers of the journal *Psychology* indicates that, although positive behaviors are more frequently motivated by self-presentational concerns, everyday life provides plenty of instances of intentional negative self-presentations. People present themselves as foolish and ignorant, hostile and threatening, cold and aloof, dependent and helpless, all for reasons that seem sensible enough. That is, people often have good reasons to engage in bad behaviors, and they are willing to incur losses in some domains to achieve gains in others.

Second, behaviors that are positive from the perspective of the actor may be negative from the observer's perspective or vice versa. For instance, we have seen that playing dumb, a behavior that may be classified as negative, very often serves to protect the self-esteem of others or to avoid envy and competitiveness. Hence, this behavior is often beneficial in social interaction. Conversely, positive self-presentations such as self-promotion and ingratiation may be perceived negatively by others, as became evident in the last part of this chapter.

Third, in addition to the different perspectives of the actor and the audience, there is also a difference between targets and uninvolved observers. This difference is germane to ingratiation, where the behavior is highly hedonically relevant to the target. In these cases, targets and observers may differ widely in their assessment of the behavior. In fact, the more pleasing the behavior is for the target, the more aversive it usually is for the observer.

Finally, the phenomenon of self-presentation can be evaluated both positively and negatively. On the one hand, we expect people to flexibly adapt their behavior to the setting, to stick to certain role requirements, and to suppress their natural instincts at least part of the time. On the other hand, there is also a strong authenticity norm in our society, which prescribes that people show their true thoughts and feelings and present themselves the way they really are. As a consequence, the mere occurrence of self-presentation is often evaluated negatively. This implies that, in a way, members of our culture receive two conflicting messages. On the one hand, they should show their true nature, behave in the same way in different settings and toward different people, and not be bothered with what others think (cf. M. R. Leary, 1995). On the other hand, they should conform to social roles, care about others' feelings, and thus refrain from expressing their every thought and enacting their every urge. In addition, it is also clear enough that, to get ahead in life, it is necessary to be likable toward the more powerful and to stress one's accomplishments and hide one's weaknesses. However, these are precisely the self-presentational behaviors judged as most undesirable by others.

There is only one way out of this catch-22, and it is what we all probably do most of the time: We engage in self-presentation, but not conspicuously so. We walk a fine line between the two competing requirements from our culture. We carefully dose the level of true self that we reveal—not too much, not too little, depending on the setting. We can fall on either side of the line. On some occasions, we let ourselves go. We talk too much or too loudly, we forget table manners, or we show our superiors what we really think of them. On other occasions, our presentation becomes too blatant. We laugh at our supervisor's joke before it's finished, we drop just one accomplishment too many saying that "It was nothing," or we use a foreign word but pronounce it incorrectly (e.g.,

Americans attempting to pronounce Van Gogh in Dutch). It's hard to tell which side of the line is more aversive.

REFERENCES

Arkin, R. M., & Baumgardner, A. H. (1985). Self-handicapping. In J. H. Harvey & G. Weary (Eds.), *Attribution: Basic issues and applications* (pp. 169–202). New York: Academic Press.

Axelrod, R. (1984). *The evolution of cooperation.* New York: Basic Books.

Bargh, J. A., Gollwitzer, P. M., Lee Chai, A., & Barndollaer, K. (1998). *Bypassing the will: Nonconscious self-regulation through automatic goal pursuit.* Manuscript submitted for publication.

Baumeister, R. F., Cooper, J., & Skib, B. A. (1979). Inferior performance as a selective response to expectancy: Taking a dive to make a point. *Journal of Personality and Social Psychology, 37,* 424–432.

Baumeister, R. F., & Leary, M. R. (1992). The need to belong: Desire for interpersonal attachments as a fundamental human motivation. *Psychological Bulletin, 117,* 497–529.

Baumeister, R. F., & Scher, S. J. (1988). Self-defeating behavior patterns among normal individuals: Review and analysis of common self-destructive tendencies. *Psychological Bulletin, 104,* 3–22.

Baumgardner, A. H., & Arkin, R. M. (1987). Coping with the prospect of social disapproval: Strategies and sequelae. In C. R. Snyder & C. E. Ford (Eds.), *Clinical and social psychological perspectives on negative life events* (pp. 323–346). New York: Plenum Press.

Baumgardner, A. H., & Brownlee, E. A. (1987). Strategic failure in social interaction: Evidence for expectancy-disconfirmation processes. *Journal of Personality and Social Psychology, 52,* 525–535.

Beauvois, J. L., & Dubois, N. (1988). The norm of internality in the explanation of psychological events. *European Journal of Social Psychology, 18,* 299–316.

Berscheid, E., Graziano, W., Monson, T., & Dermer, M. (1976). Outcome dependency: Attention, attribution, and attraction. *Journal of Personality and Social Psychology, 34,* 978–989.

Braginsky, B. (1981). On being surplus: Its relation to impression management and mental patienthood. In J. T. Tedeschi (Ed.), *Impression management theory and social psychological research* (pp. 295–309). New York: Academic Press.

Brown, B. R. (1968). The effects of need to maintain face in interpersonal bargaining. *Journal of Experimental Social Psychology, 4,* 107–122.

Buss, A. H., & Briggs, S. R. (1984). Drama and the self in social interaction. *Journal of Personality and Social Psychology, 47,* 1310–1324.

Carnevale, P. J. D., Pruitt, D. G., & Britton, S. D. (1979). Looking tough: The negotiator under constituent surveillance. *Personality and Social Psychology Bulletin, 5,* 118–121.

Cosmides, L. (1989). The logic of social exchange: Has natural selection shaped how humans reason? *Cognition, 31,* 187–276.

Cosmides, L., & Tooby, J. (1992). Cognitive adaptations for social exchange. In J. H. Barkow, L. Cosmides, & J. Tooby (Eds.), *The adapted mind* (pp. 163–228). Oxford, England: Oxford University Press.

Daubman, K. A., Heatherington, L., & Ahn, A. (1992). Gender and the self-presentation of academic achievement. *Sex Roles, 27,* 187–204.

Dean, D., Braito, R., Powers, E., & Brant, B. (1975). Cultural contradictions and sex roles revisited: A replication and reassessment. *Sociological Quarterly, 16,* 207–215.

DePaulo, B. M., & Bell, K. L. (1996). Truth and investment: Lies are told to those who care. *Journal of Personality and Social Psychology, 71,* 703–716.

DePaulo, B. M., & Kashy, D. A. (1998). Everyday lies in close and casual relationships. *Journal of Personality and Social Psychology, 74,* 63–79.

Ebbesen, E. B. (1981). Cognitive processes in inferences about a person's personality. In E. T. Higgins, C. P. Herman, & M. P. Zanna (Eds.), *Social cognition: The Ontario Symposium* (Vol. 1). Hillsdale, NJ: Erlbaum.

Exline, J. J. (1999, April). Woeful winners, lonely leaders, and holy rollers: STTUC in the gaze of the green-eyed monster. Seminar conducted at the annual meeting of the Christian Association for Psychological Studies, Colorado Springs, CO.

Exline, J. J., & Lobel, M. (1999). The perils of outperformance: Sensitivity about being the target of a threatening upward comparison. *Psychological Bulletin, 125,* 307–337.

Fein, S. (1996). Effects of suspicion on attributional thinking and the correspondence bias. *Journal of Personality and Social Psychology, 70,* 1164–1184.

Fein, S., Hilton, J. L., & Miller, D. T. (1990). Suspicion of ulterior motivation and the correspondence bias. *Journal of Personality and Social Psychology, 58,* 753–764.

Felson, R. B. (1978). Aggression as impression management. *Social Psychology, 41,* 205–213.

Felson, R. B., & Bohrnstedt, G. W. (1980). Attributions of ability and motivation in a natural setting. *Journal of Personality and Social Psychology, 39,* 799–805.

Fiske, S. T. (1993). Controlling other people: The impact of power on stereotyping. *American Psychologist, 48,* 621–628.

Gergen, K. J. (1968). Personal consistency and the presentation of the self. In C. Gordon & K. J. Gergen (Eds.), *The self in social interaction* (Vol. 1). New York: Wiley.

Gilbert, D. T., & Jones, E. E. (1986). Exemplification: The self-presentation of moral character. *Journal of Personality, 54,* 593–615.

Gilbert, D. T., Krull, D. S., & Pelham, B. W. (1988). Of thoughts unspoken: Social inference and the self-regulation of behavior. *Journal of Personality and Social Psychology, 55,* 685–694.

Godfrey, D., Jones, E. E., & Lord, C. (1986). Self-promotion is not ingratiating. *Journal of Personality and Social Psychology, 50*, 106–115.

Goffman, E. (1959). *The presentation of self in everyday life*. Garden City, NY: Doubleday/Anchor Books.

Gollwitzer, P. M., & Wicklund, R. A. (1985). Self-symbolizing and the neglect of others' perspectives. *Journal of Personality and Social Psychology, 48*, 702–715.

Gordon, R. A. (1996). Impact of ingratiation on judgments and evaluations: A meta-analytic investigation. *Journal of Personality and Social Psychology, 71*, 54–70.

Gove, W. R., Hughes, M., & Geerken, M. R. (1980). Playing dumb: A form of impression management with undesirable side effects. *Social Psychology Quarterly, 43*, 89–102.

Heider, F. (1958). *The psychology of interpersonal relations*. New York: Wiley.

Hill, M. G., Weary, G., & Williams, J. (1986). Depression: A self-presentation formulation. In R. Baumeister (Ed.), *Public self and private self* (pp. 213–239). New York: Springer.

Hogan, R., & Jones, W. H. (1983). A role theoretical model of criminal conduct. In W. S. Laufer & J. M. Days (Eds.), *Personality theory, moral development, and criminal behavior*. Boston: Lexington.

Horowitz, R., & Schwartz, G. (1974). Honor, normative ambiguity and gang violence. *American Sociological Review, 39*, 238–251.

Jellison, J. M., & Gentry, K. W. (1978). A self-presentational interpretation of the seeking of social approval. *Personality and Social Psychology Bulletin, 4*, 227–230.

Jellison, J. M., & Green, J. (1981). A self-presentation approach to the fundamental attribution error. *Journal of Personality and Social Psychology, 40*, 643–649.

Jones, E. E. (1964). *Ingratiation*. New York: Appleton-Century-Crofts.

Jones, E. E. (1990). *Interpersonal perception*. New York: Freeman.

Jones, E. E., & Berglas, S. (1978). Control of attributions about the self through self-handicapping strategies: The role of alcohol and underachievement. *Personality and Social Psychology Bulletin, 4*, 200–206.

Jones, E. E., & Davis, K. E. (1965). From acts to dispositions: The attribution process in person perception. In L. Berkowitz (Ed.), *Advances in experimental social psychology* (Vol. 2, pp. 220–266). New York: Academic Press.

Jones, E. E., & Pittman, T. S. (1982). Toward a general theory of strategic self-presentation. In J. Suls (Ed.), *Psychological perspectives on the self* (Vol. 1, pp. 231–262). Hillsdale, NJ: Erlbaum.

Jones, E. E., Rhodewalt, F., Berglas, S. E., & Skelton, J. A. (1981). Effects of strategic self-presentation on subsequent self-esteem. *Journal of Personality and Social Psychology, 41*, 407–421.

Jones, E. E., Stires, L. K., Shaver, K. G., & Harris, V. A. (1968). Evaluation of an ingratiator by target persons and bystanders. *Journal of Personality, 36*, 349–385.

Jones, S. C., & Schneider, D. J. (1968). Certainty of self-appraisal and reactions to evaluations from others. *Sociometry, 31*, 395–403.

Kelly, A. E., McKillop, K. J., & Neimeyer, G. J. (1991). Effects of counsellor as audience on internalization of depressed and nondepressed self-presentations. *Journal of Counseling Psychology, 38*, 126–132.

Kiesler, D. J. (1983). The 1982 interpersonal circle: A taxonomy for complementarity in human transactions. *Psychological Review, 90*, 185–214.

Kim, M. P., & Rosenberg, S. (1980). Comparison of two structural models of implicit personality theory. *Journal of Personality and Social Psychology, 38*, 375–389.

Kim, S. H., Smith, R. H., & Brigham, N. L. (1998). Effects of power imbalance and the presence of third parties on reactions to harm: Upward and downward revenge. *Personality and Social Psychology Bulletin, 24*, 353–361.

Komarowski, M. (1946). Cultural contradiction and sex roles. *American Journal of Sociology, 52*, 184–189.

Kowalski, R. M. (1996). Complaints and complaining: Functions, antecedents, and consequences. *Psychological Bulletin, 119*, 179–196.

Leary, M. R. (1995). *Self-presentation: Impression management and interpersonal behavior*. Dubuque, IA: Brown & Benchmark.

Leary, T. (1957). *Interpersonal diagnosis of personality*. New York: Ronald.

Lingle, J. H., Dukerich, J. M., & Ostrom, T. M. (1983). Accessing information in memory-based impression judgments: Incongruity versus negativity in retrieval selectivity. *Journal of Personality and Social Psychology, 44*, 262–272.

Luginbuhl, J., & Palmer, R. (1991). Impression management aspects of self-handicapping: Positive and negative effects. *Personality and Social Psychology Bulletin, 17*, 655–662.

Miller, D. T., Norman, S. A., & Wright, E. (1978). Distortions in person perception as a consequence of the need for effective control. *Journal of Personality and Social Psychology, 36*, 598–602.

Osborne, R. E., & Gilbert, D. T. (1992). The preoccupational hazards of social life. *Journal of Personality and Social Psychology, 62*, 219–228.

Osgood, C. E., Suci, G. J., & Tannenbaum, P. H. (1957). *The measurement of meaning*. Urbana: University of Illinois Press.

Paulhus, D. L. (1998). Interpersonal and intrapsychic adaptiveness of trait self-enhancement: A mixed blessing? *Journal of Personality and Social Psychology, 74*, 1197–1208.

Peeters, G., & Czapinski, J. (1990). Positive–negative asymmetry in evaluations: The distinction between affective and informational negativity effects. In W. Stroebe & M. Hewstone (Eds.), *European review of social psychology* (Vol. 1, pp. 33–60). Chichester, England: Wiley.

Pruitt, D. G., & Smith, D. L. (1981). Impression management in bargaining: Images of firmness and trustworthiness. In J. T. Tedeschi (Ed.), *Impression management theory and social psychological research* (pp. 247–267). New York: Academic Press.

Reeder, G. D., & Brewer, M. B. (1979). A schematic model of dispositional attribution in interpersonal perception. *Psychological Review, 86,* 61–79.

Reeder, G. D., & Fulks, J. L. (1980). When actions speak louder than words: Implicational schemata and the attribution of ability. *Journal of Experimental Social Psychology, 16,* 33–46.

Reeder, G. D., & Spores, J. M. (1983). The attribution of morality. *Journal of Personality and Social Psychology, 44,* 736–745.

Rhodewalt, F. (1986). Self-presentation and the phenomenal self: On the stability and malleability of self-conceptions. In R. F. Baumeister (Ed.), *Public self and private self* (pp. 117–142). New York: Springer-Verlag.

Rhodewalt, F., Sanbonmatsu, D. M., Tschanz, B., Feick, D. L., & Waller, A. (1995). Self-handicapping and interpersonal trade-offs: The effects of claimed self-handicaps on observers' performance evaluations and feedback. *Personality and Social Psychology Bulletin, 21,* 1042–1050.

Rosenberg, S. (1977). New approaches to the analysis of personal constructs in person perception. In J. K. Cole & A. W. Landfield (Eds.), *Nebraska symposium on motivation*. Lincoln: University of Nebraska Press.

Rosenberg, S., Nelson, C., & Vivekananthan, P. S. (1968). A multidimensional approach to the structure of personality impressions. *Journal of Personality and Social Psychology, 9,* 283–294.

Rudman, L. A. (1998). Self-promotion as a risk factor for women: The costs and benefits of counterstereotypical impression management. *Journal of Personality and Social Psychology, 74,* 629–645.

Schlenker, B. R. (1980). *Impression management: The self-concept, social identity, and interpersonal relations*. Monterey, CA: Brooks/Cole.

Schlenker, B. R., & Leary, M. R. (1982). Audiences' reactions to self-enhancing, self-denigrating, and accurate self-presentations. *Journal of Experimental Social Psychology, 18,* 89–104.

Schlenker, B. R., & Weigold, M. F. (1990). Self-consciousness and self-presentation: Being autonomous versus appearing autonomous. *Journal of Personality and Social Psychology, 59,* 820–828.

Schneider, D. J. (1973). Implicit personality theory: A review. *Psychological Bulletin, 79,* 294–309.

Schneider, D. J. (1981). Tactical self-presentations: Toward a broader conception. In J. T. Tedeschi (Ed.), *Impression management theory and social psychological research* (pp. 23–40). New York: Academic Press.

Schul, Y., & Burnstein, E. (1985). The informational basis of social judgments: Using past impression rather than the trait description in forming a new impression. *Journal of Experimental Social Psychology, 21,* 421–439.

Shepperd, J. A., & Socherman, R. E. (1997). On the manipulative behavior of low machiavellians: Feigning incompetence to "sandbag" an opponent. *Journal of Personality and Social Psychology, 72,* 1448–1459.

Skowronski, J. J., & Carlston, D. E. (1987). Social judgment and social memory: The role of cue diagnosticity in negativity, positivity, and extremity biases. *Journal of Personality and Social Psychology, 52,* 689–699.

Smith, D. S., & Strube, M. J. (1991). Self-protective tendencies as moderators of self-handicapping impressions. *Basic and Applied Social Psychology, 12,* 63–80.

Smith, T. W., Snyder, C. R., & Handelsman, M. M. (1982). On the self-serving function of an academic wooden leg: Test anxiety as a self-handicapping strategy. *Journal of Personality and Social Psychology, 42,* 314–321.

Smith, T. W., Snyder, C. R., & Perkins, S. C. (1983). The self-serving function of hypochondriacal complaints: Physical symptoms as self-handicapping strategies. *Journal of Personality and Social Psychology, 44,* 787–797.

Snyder, M. (1974). The self-monitoring of expressive behavior. *Journal of Personality and Social Psychology, 30,* 526–537.

Stone, J., Wiegand, A. W., Cooper, J., & Aronson, E. (1997). When exemplification fails: Hypocrisy and the motive for self-integrity. *Journal of Personality and Social Psychology, 72,* 54–65.

Tice, D. M., Butler, J. L., Muraven, M. B., & Stillwell, A. M. (1995). When modesty prevails: Differential favorability of self-presentation to friends and strangers. *Journal of Personality and Social Psychology, 69,* 1120–1138.

Vonk, R. (1993a). Individual differences and common dimensions in Implicit Personality Theory. *British Journal of Social Psychology, 32,* 209–226.

Vonk, R. (1993b). The negativity effect in trait ratings and in open-ended descriptions of persons. *Personality and Social Psychology Bulletin, 19,* 269–278.

Vonk, R. (1995). Effects of inconsistent behavior on person impressions: A multidimensional study. *Personality and Social Psychology Bulletin, 21,* 674–685.

Vonk, R. (1998a). Effects of cooperative and competitive outcome dependency on attention and impressions. *Journal of Experimental Social Psychology, 34,* 265–288.

Vonk, R. (1998b). The slime effect: Suspicion and dislike of likeable behaviors toward superiors. *Journal of Personality and Social Psychology, 74,* 849–864.

Vonk, R. (1999a). Differential evaluations of likeable and dislikeable behaviours enacted toward superiors and subordinates. *European Journal of Social Psychology, 29,* 139–146.

Vonk, R. (1999b). Effects of other-profitability and self-profitability on evaluative judgements of behaviours. *European Journal of Social Psychology, 29,* 139–146.

Vonk, R. (1999c). Effects of outcome dependency on correspondence bias. *Personality and Social Psychology Bulletin, 25,* 110–117.

Vonk, R. (1999d). *Self-serving interpretations of flattery: The dilemma of being ingratiated.* Manuscript submitted for publication.

Vonk, R. (1999e). Impression formation and impression management: Motives, traits, and likeability inferred from self-promoting and self-deprecating behavior. *Social Cognition, 17,* 390–412.

Vonk, R., & Van Knippenberg, A. (1994). The sovereignty of negative inferences: Suspicion of ulterior motives does not reduce the negativity effect. *Social Cognition, 12,* 169186.

Vonk, R., & Van Nobelen, D. (1993). Masculinity and femininity in the self with an intimate partner: Men are not always men in the company of women. *Journal of Personal and Social Relationships, 10,* 627–630.

Wall, J. A., Jr. (1991). Impression management in negotiations. In R. A. Giacalone & P. Rosenfeld (Eds.), *Applied impression management* (pp. 133–156). Newbury Park, CA: Sage Publications.

Weiner, B. (1986). *An attributional theory of motivation and emotion.* New York: Springer.

Wiggins, J. S. (1985). The interpersonal circle: A structural model for the integration of personality research. In R. Hogan (Ed.), *Perspectives in personality* (Vol. 1, pp. 1–47). New York: JAI Press.

Zanna, M. P., & Pack, S. J. (1975). On the self-fulfilling nature of apparent sex differences in behavior. *Journal of Experimental Social Psychology, 11,* 583–591.

5

THE AVERSIVE INTERPERSONAL CONTEXT OF DEPRESSION: EMERGING PERSPECTIVES ON DEPRESSOTYPIC BEHAVIOR

JENNIFER KATZ AND THOMAS E. JOINER, JR.

"Since most people in the depressed person's environment (and eventually even his family) find his behavior aversive, they will avoid him as much as possible." (Lewinsohn, Weinstein, & Shaw, 1969, cited in Coyne, 1976b)

It is widely accepted that an individual's depression adversely affects his or her social functioning. A number of studies have reported an association between depression and negative interpersonal outcomes (see Segrin & Dillard, 1992, for a review; see also literature on stress generation, e.g., Hammen, 1991). However, null results reported by other researchers suggest that depression is not always linked to interpersonal difficulties (e.g., King & Heller, 1984; McNeil, Arkowitz, & Pritchard, 1987). How can we account for these mixed findings?

One potential answer involves the role of depressotypic interpersonal behavior. We posit that depression is associated with interpersonal problems only to the extent that the depressed person engages in depressotypic behavior. That is, interacting with a depressed person should be only interpersonally aversive when distress is clearly and repeatedly signaled to

We gratefully acknowledge Paul Kwon for his helpful comments on an earlier draft.

other people. Depressotypic behaviors may communicate several types of aversive messages to relationship partners. For example, these behaviors may communicate that the partner is implicated in the development of the problem (e.g., "you don't really love me anymore, do you?") or that the relationship is no longer satisfying and rewarding (e.g., "we just aren't close like we used to be"). In addition, depressotypic behaviors may overwhelm relationship partners with demands, whether implicit or stated, for help (e.g., "I just wish someone could help me feel better").

In this chapter, we focus on three classes of depressotypic behaviors: (a) excessive reassurance-seeking, (b) negative feedback-seeking, and (c) interpersonal aggression. Definitions, relevant theory, central predictions, and empirical work on each are summarized. We argue that these behaviors may be classified as depressotypic on the basis of research linking these behaviors to depression and depressive symptoms. We also argue that these behaviors are aversive on the basis of research linking these behaviors with negative interpersonal outcomes. Measurement issues relevant to research of these behaviors are highlighted. Finally, we briefly discuss theory and research relating each behavior to other theoretically important constructs that influence both mood and social behavior: self-esteem and attachment style. We conclude that focused attention to depressotypic behaviors and their effects on others should broaden and enhance the understanding of the social aspects of depression.

EXCESSIVE REASSURANCE-SEEKING

These persons, in their continuous need of supplies that give sexual satisfaction and heighten self-esteem simultaneously, are "love addicts." (Fenichel, 1945, p. 387)

Excessive reassurance-seeking has been defined as the relatively stable tendency to persistently seek assurances from others that one is lovable and worthy. The excessive reassurance-seeker seeks these assurances regardless of whether such assurance has already been provided (Joiner & Metalsky, 1998a; Joiner, Metalsky, Katz, & Beach, 1999). Although reassurance temporarily soothes the excessive reassurance-seeker, these adaptive benefits are short-lived; doubts begin to settle in soon afterward. Subsequently, additional reassurance is sought.

Relationship to Depression

Reassurance-seeking as a depressotypic interpersonal behavior was first described within Jim Coyne's (1976b) interpersonal theory of depression. Coyne proposed that initially nondepressed but mildly dysphoric individuals seek reassurance from others to alleviate self-doubts regarding their own worth and to determine whether others truly care about them. Others often respond with reassurance, but to little avail; the person doubts the reassurance and attributes it instead to others' sense of pity or obligation. Potentially depressed people thus face an intractable dilemma: They both need and doubt others' reassurance.

The need for reassurance is emotionally powerful and thus temporarily predominates, compelling the individual to again request feedback from others. Once received, however, the reassurance is again doubted, and the pattern is repeated. Because the pattern is repetitive and resistant to attempts to change it, the significant others of the increasingly depressed person become frustrated and irritated. Consequently, these significant others are increasingly likely to reject the depressed individual as well as to become depressed themselves. Rejection furthers the shrinkage and disruption of the depressed person's interpersonal environment, which in turn maintains or exacerbates his or her symptoms. The theory thus describes an interpersonal process involving the gradual worsening of depressive symptoms within the crucible of close relationships. This process has implications for the causes, maintenance, exacerbation, consequences, treatment, and prevention of depression (for research stemming from the model, see, e.g., Coyne, 1976a; Coyne et al., 1987; Hokanson, Rubert, Welker, Hollander, & Hedeen, 1989).

Elsewhere (e.g., Joiner, Alfano, & Metalsky, 1992, 1993; Katz, Beach, & Joiner, 1998), we have argued that excessive reassurance-seeking constitutes the theory's main ingredient, in that it serves as a type of interpersonal vehicle that transmits the distress and desperation of depression from one person to another, with untoward consequences for everyone involved. The focus on excessive reassurance-seeking, in the context of Coyne's (1976b) theory, has produced two main strands of research, one having to do with the causes of depression, and the other with its consequences.

Covariation

Reassurance-seeking is conceptualized as one interpersonal cause of depression, and this is supported in studies establishing both covariation and temporal antecedence. In all samples studied to date, a significant correlation between excessive reassurance-seeking (as measured by the Reassurance-Seeking Scale; (e.g., Joiner et al., 1992) and depression has emerged. Studies have examined this covariation in 3,465 individuals from a variety of settings. Findings hold across samples of college students (Joiner, 1994; Joiner et al., 1992, 1993; Joiner & Metalsky, 1995, 1998a; Potthoff, Holahan, & Joiner, 1995), U.S. Air Force cadets (Joiner & Schmidt, 1998), various clinical samples (Joiner & Metalsky, 1998b), and women in heterosexual dating relationships (Katz & Beach, 1997a; Katz et al., 1998). Given this diversity, the consistency of the magnitude of the correlation (with a median value of about .36) is notable.

Temporal Antecedence

High reassurance-seeking at one point in time may represent a harbinger for the development of depressive symptoms at a later point in time, consistent with the criterion of temporal antecedence. To date, six studies have examined this postulate. Joiner and Schmidt (1998) tested this prediction in a study of 1,005 Air Force cadets who were undergoing basic training. Participants completed measures of excessive reassurance-seeking and depressive symptoms before basic training, and they completed symptom measures following basic training. Consistent with the criterion of temporal antecedence, baseline levels of reassurance-seeking were significantly predictive of increases from baseline to follow-up in depressive symptoms.

Other studies have taken a diathesis–stress approach to the relation between excessive reassurance-seeking and future depression, framing stress and reassurance-seeking as interactive, contributory causes of depressive symptoms. For example, Joiner and Metalsky (1998a, Study 5) showed that when high-reassurance-seeking college students were faced with the stress of an unsatisfactory grade on a midterm exam, they exhibited depressive reactions, whereas low-reassurance-seeking students did not. Similarly, Joiner and Metalsky (1998a, Study 4) found that when high-reassurance-seeking students were paired with a roommate who viewed them negatively, they experienced increased depressive symptoms, but low-reassurance-seeking students did not. Katz et al. (1998) obtained a similar finding: High-reassurance-seeking women reported increases in depressive symptoms when in a dating relationship with men who viewed them negatively, but low-reassurance-seeking women did not experience depression increases, even if they were in a devaluing relationship.

Potthoff and colleagues (1995), too, found that excessive reassurance-seeking, together with interpersonal stress (e.g., disagreements with friends), predicted subsequent depressive symptoms. Using structural equation modeling techniques, these researchers reported that latent variables corresponding to excessive reassurance-seeking and to interpersonal stress were contributors to prospective increases in depression; Metalsky and Johnson (1997) reported similar results.

Taken together, these six studies support the contention that excessive reassurance-seeking satisfies the criterion of temporal antecedence in its relation to depressive symptoms as a contributory cause. Notably, none of these studies examined clinical forms of depression, leaving open the question of whether excessive reassurance-seeking is relevant regarding more severe forms of depression (cf. Coyne, 1994; Tennen, Hall, & Affleck, 1995; Vredenburg, Flett, & Krames, 1993).

Why does reassurance-seeking increase risk for depression? One possibility—especially relevant in the later stages of the process described by Coyne (1976b)—is that, as depression mounts, excessive reassurance-seeking becomes difficult for significant others, who withdraw from or reject the reassurance-seeking person, which in turn encourages yet more symptoms.

Interpersonal Consequences

Researchers have focused on two broad categories of consequences: (a) interpersonal rejection and (b) "contagious depression."

Interpersonal Rejection

Several studies have found that people who report depressive symptoms are negatively evaluated by significant others, but only if they are also excessive in their reassurance-seeking. For example, in a study of women involved in heterosexual dating relationships, Katz and Beach (1997a) found that women with depressive symptoms were negatively evaluated by their dating partner, but only if they were high in reassurance-seeking. Joiner and Metalsky (1995; see also Joiner et al., 1992, 1993) have obtained similar findings among college students and their same-sex roommates: Students who experienced depressive symptoms were negatively evaluated by their roommates if they were excessive in reassurance-seeking. Joiner and Metalsky (1995) found that the same did not hold for anxious students—they were not likely to be negatively evaluated by roommates, even if excessive in reassurance-seeking. A notable aspect of this series of studies is that the predicted "devaluation effect" occurs even in presumably supportive relationships, such as romantic relationships and roommate relationships in which students have chosen to live together.

Joiner (1999) extended these findings to psychiatric youth inpatients. High-reassurance-seeking youth reported interpersonal difficulties, particularly when also experiencing depressive symptoms. Benazon (1998) reported a replication of the rejection effect among a sample of married dyads, each with one clinically depressed member. Excessive reassurance-seeking on the part of the depressed member predicted the partner's negative evaluation of the depressed member, even beyond variance contributed by marital dissatisfaction, a very strong correlate of negative spousal evaluation.

"Contagious" Depression

Joiner and Katz (1999) meta-analyzed the literature on "contagious" depression (i.e., one person's depression inducing symptoms in another person) and concluded that 40 findings from 36 studies ($N = 4,952$) provided substantial overall support for the proposition that depressed mood and particularly depressive symptoms are contagious.

Based on two studies, we believe that excessive reassurance-seeking may be implicated in the interpersonal contagion of depression. In a study of college students and their dating partners, Katz, Joiner, and Beach (1999) reported that partners' depression levels significantly corresponded, even controlling for relationship satisfaction. Furthermore, partners of those who reported both high levels of reassurance-seeking and depressive symptoms were especially likely to report substantial depressive symptoms themselves. In a study of college roommates, Joiner (1994) reported a similar finding: Even after controlling for negative events that may affect both members of a roommate pair, one roommate's depression level prospectively predicted the other's, particularly if reassurance-seeking was high.

Contagious depression is a reasonably well-documented phenomenon (Joiner & Katz, 1999). Moreover, excessive reassurance-seeking may explain, in part, when depression will be interpersonally transmitted. Taken together with research on interpersonal rejection, the work on contagious depression suggests that the joint operation of depressive symptoms and excessive reassurance-seeking disaffects significant others by distancing them actually (e.g., ending the relationship) or functionally (e.g., emotional unavailability because of frustration or contagious depression).

Measurement Issues

All of the research described earlier used the Reassurance-Seeking Scale developed by Joiner and Metalsky (e.g., Joiner et al., 1992; Joiner & Metalsky, 1995). Can the scale bear the weight of this research? Joiner and Metalsky (1998a, Studies 1 and 2) reported very strong factorial rigor for the scale, as well as significant relations between the scale and (a) actual reassurance-seeking behavior in the lab and (b) self-reported reassurance-seeking in a particular relationship. Other studies have supported discriminant validity, even with regard to conceptually similar constructs (e.g., dependency; negative affectivity; Joiner & Metalsky, 1998a; Joiner & Schmidt, 1998). Internal consistency coefficients have ranged from .85 to .95.

Is reassurance-seeking necessarily a bad thing? We have been careful to use the term *excessive reassurance-seeking* to emphasize a key distinction between this variable and one involving the acquisition of social support, which has been shown to be protective in relation to health problems (e.g., Collins, Dunkel-Schetter, Lobel, & Scrimshaw, 1993). We suggest that there is a considerable difference between the routine and adaptive solicitation of social support across distinct situations and the repeated and persistent seeking of reassurance within the same situation, even when reassurance has already been provided. This distinction is borne out by the positive association between support-seeking and health in the social support literature, and the negative association between excessive reassurance-seeking and mental health in our program of research.

Summary

Excessive reassurance-seeking predisposes people to the development of depressive symptoms. Initially, this may occur as a function of growing demoralization of the high-reassurance-seeking person, who has struggled to gain—but been disappointed with—others' responsiveness. As depressive symptoms emerge, they may interact with continued excessive reassurance-seeking to induce negative interpersonal consequences (e.g., rejection, contagion), which in turn further encourage symptom expression. (Potthoff et al., 1995, modeled this process using structural equation modeling.) Ongoing reverberations of depression, reassurance-seeking, and interpersonal problems thus appear to be self-perpetuating, perhaps in part accounting for the chronic and recurrent nature of depression.

NEGATIVE FEEDBACK-SEEKING

Your face-saving promises, whispered like prayers, I don't need them. I need the darkness, the sweetness, the sadness, the weakness. (Merchant, 1998)

Negative feedback-seeking may be broadly defined as behaviors that people use to elicit critical or other forms of unfavorable feedback about themselves from others. It is intimately tied to self-verification theory. Derived from theories concerned with self-concept and self-consistency, this theory describes how people tend to value social information about the self that is consistent with their self-views (Swann, 1983, 1987). Stimuli that are predictable and familiar and that reduce uncertainty may be perceived as especially trustworthy and accurate (Swann, Griffin, Predmore, & Gaines, 1987). Accordingly, feedback that confirms or verifies already-existing schemata is more likely to be remembered and evaluated as valid than information that runs counter to expectations and beliefs (cf. Swann & Read, 1981). People remember (Swann & Read, 1981) and believe (Swann et al., 1987) self-verifying evaluations rather than nonverifying evaluations, independent of the positivity or negativity of the feedback provided. That is, people appear to seek and value positive feedback concerning their positive self-conceptions, but in fact they seek and value negative feedback concerning their negative self-conceptions.

Negative feedback-seeking is thought to stem from self-verification strivings. From the self-verification perspective, a primary motive of interpersonal behavior is to preserve the self-concept. It has been suggested that self-verification processes occur as an attempt to increase the individual's sense of predictability and control within social situations rather than for the sake of consistency itself (Swann, Stein-Seroussi, & Giesler, 1992). Specifically, self-verification strivings are thought to be motivated by intrapsychic, epistemic concerns about promoting existential security (e.g., "I really do know myself") and interpersonal, pragmatic concerns about promoting fluid interpersonal transactions (e.g., "My partner really does know me"). For people with negative self-conceptions, the emotional costs of receiving negative feedback are presumed to be outweighed by the benefits of a more stable, predictable sense of both the self and of the self as related to others. As such, there may be short-term adaptive consequences of negative feedback-seeking behaviors.

Self-verification theory often is misunderstood as suggesting that people with negative self-views uniformly reject positive self-relevant feedback. Clearly, the self-verification motive does not exist in a vacuum. People also seek and value positive, affectively pleasing feedback from others (e.g., reassurance-seeking). From a self-verification perspective, however, people with negative self-conceptions are more likely to seek and prefer negative feedback despite its negative affective consequences. This perspective is supported by general research in the area of self-esteem. For instance, relative to people with low self-esteem, people with high self-esteem are more likely to engage in behaviors that elicit positive self-relevant feedback (see Taylor & Brown, 1988, for a review). In contrast, people with low self-esteem seek positive feedback only when there is little risk for humiliation or failure (Wood, Giordono-Beech, Taylor, Michela, & Gaus, 1994).

Relationship to Depression

Research suggests a concurrent relationship between negative feedback-seeking and depression: Negative-feedback-seeking occurs at higher rates among depressed than among nondepressed people, and such feedback is perceived to be more accurate among depressed people. Some research also suggests that seeking and receiving negative feedback from relationship partners may lead to future depressive symptoms. These studies have been conducted with clinically depressed individuals as well as with samples of people with subthreshold levels of depression.

Covariation

Swann, Wenzlaff, Krull, and Pelham (1992) proposed that depressed people gravitate toward relationship partners who view them unfavorably for reasons of self-verification. In a series of four studies, they investigated whether depressed people with negative self-views sought unfavorable appraisals from others. Inclusion criteria for status as "depressed" varied somewhat across studies, but generally it was based on a Beck Depression Inventory (BDI; Beck, Ward, Mendelson, Mock, & Erbaugh, 1961) score of 9 or higher. This criteria is similar to that used by other researchers interested in individuals with nonclinical levels of depression. However, it should be noted that the BDI is not a diagnostic instrument and that scores of 9 represent only moderate elevations in symptoms. In Study 1, depressed persons were inclined to prefer an unfavorable evaluator, whereas nondepressed persons were inclined to prefer a favorable evaluator. In Study 2, depressed persons preferred friends who viewed them less positively than nondepressed persons. Both studies provide support for the notion that depressed people display greater preferences for negative feedback than do nondepressed people.

Study 3 was a prospective study of negative feedback-seeking tendencies and the rejection of depressed participants by their roommates. Results suggested that dysphoric people (classified on the basis of a BDI score of 6 that remained stable over repeated administrations over the semester) were more inclined to report interest in unfavorable feedback from their roommates with regard to various self-attributes (e.g., intellectual ability) than nondepressed people. Finally, in Study 4, cognitive and affective precipitants of negative feedback-seeking were examined among undergraduate women. Participants sought positive feedback about positive self-views but negative feedback about negative self-views, and these effects occurred independent of manipulations made to induce positive, negative, or neutral affect. People with negative self-views were significantly more likely to elicit unfavorable feedback than people with positive self-views, even though negative feedback was related to increases in both depressive and anxious symptoms.

These initial and provocative studies of self-verification and depression were criticized on a number of theoretical and methodological grounds (Alloy & Lipman, 1992; Hooley & Richters, 1992). The major points made by these critiques are reviewed briefly herein. First, the classification of chronic depression and dysphoria was inconsistent across studies and was based solely on scores from the BDI, which cannot be used in isolation to diagnose clinical depression. Next, the construct of negative feedback-seeking was criticized for being poorly operationalized and not reflective of actual feedback-seeking behaviors (see Measurement Issues, below). Finally, these critics argued that the motivational underpinnings of the self-verification effects were not substantiated by the research methods used. That is, although depressed people appeared motivated to seek negative feedback, it was unclear whether these tendencies were enacted to promote predictability and control over the social environment, as predicted by the theory.

In reply to these criticisms, Swann, Wenzlaff, and Tafarodi (1992) conducted two additional studies of depression and negative feedback-seeking behaviors. The first study was designed to test the hypothesis that dysphoric individuals would prefer evaluators who appraised them unfavorably. Data were collected from 20 students with mild elevations on the BDI and from 30 nondysphoric students who became acquainted with an evaluator and then received either a positive or negative evaluation ostensibly from that evaluator. Results were consistent with predictions based on self-verification theory. Dysphoric participants preferred to interact with an evaluator whose appraisal was unfavorable, whereas nondysphoric participants preferred to interact with an evaluator whose appraisal was favorable. Furthermore, all participants were more interested in interacting with the evaluator when the participant believed the evaluation to be accurate. The second study was designed to test the hypothesis that people are motivated to seek self-verifying feedback from others to maintain a sense of predictability and control. Again, data were collected from dysphoric students with mild depressive symptoms and nondysphoric controls. Each was provided with either self-verifying or self-discrepant feedback about one set of self-relevant characteristics and was then allowed to seek feedback about another set of characteristics. Swann et al. predicted and found that dysphoric participants responded to positive feedback by eliciting negative feedback about his or her self-reported limitations. That is, mildly depressed people sought negative, self-verifying feedback after receiving positive, nonverifying feedback.

This rebuttal article addressed some (but not all) of the major criticisms of the original article regarding negative feedback-seeking behaviors and the motivational underpinnings of self-verification strivings among people with depressive symptoms. Subsequently, other researchers (e.g., Joiner et al., 1992, 1993; Joiner & Metalsky, 1995; Katz & Beach, 1997a) also have documented elevated levels of interest in negative feedback among dysphoric people, further supporting this view.

The issue of negative feedback-seeking among clinically depressed people was addressed later in two additional studies. Giesler, Josephs, and Swann (1996) compared preferences for favorable versus unfavorable feedback among adults with high self-esteem, low self-esteem, and depression. Participants were identified as clinically depressed using both a structured clinical interview (the *Diagnostic and Statistical Manual of Mental Disorders*, 3rd ed., rev.; *DSM-III-R*; American Psychiatric Association, 1987) and a minimum score of 16 or higher on the BDI. Each individual was provided with two bogus summaries about the self, one positive and one negative, that ostensibly summarized longer, more in-depth evaluative reports. Participants were asked to read the summaries and to choose the one in-depth evaluative report (favorable or unfavorable) they would be most interested in reading. Selection of the unfavorable report served as the index of negative feedback-seeking. Results indicated that 82% of the depressed group, 64% of the low self-esteem group, and 25% of the high self-esteem group selected the unfavorable evaluation. Results also suggested that depression exerted effects on preference ratings through influences of accuracy. That is, people in the depressed group perceived the unfavorable summaries as more accurate (i.e., self-verifying) than the favorable summaries, and this perceived accuracy accounted for the effect of group membership on feedback preference.

Joiner, Katz, and Lew (1997) examined depressive symptoms, interest in negative self-verifying feedback, and peer relationship functioning in a clinical sample of psychiatric youth inpatients. Approximately one-half of the sample was diagnosed with major depression, depressive disorder not otherwise specified, or bipolar disorder. Consistent with Giesler et al.'s (1996) findings, level of depression was associated with interest in negative feedback from others. Interest in negative feedback also was more strongly associated with the cognitive rather than emotional symptoms of depression, and it was associated with depression specifically rather than emotional distress more generally. Therefore, a correlational link between depression and negative feedback-seeking has been established in a variety of laboratories with different populations.

Temporal Antecedence

To date, only one longitudinal study has investigated the hypothesis that negative feedback-seeking serves to increase risk for depression. Joiner (1995) hypothesized that people with negative self-views who seek self-verifying feedback from others are vulnerable to future increases in depression. He tested this hypothesis in a longitudinal study of same-sex roommate pairs. Consistent with prediction, target individuals who were both interested in negative feedback from their roommates and who were evaluated negatively by their roommates were at increased risk for later depression, even after controlling for the targets' level of self-esteem. Thus, it was concluded that negative feedback-seeking may lead to the onset or maintenance of depressive symptoms, at least among people who are successful at soliciting negative, self-verifying feedback from others.

Taken together, studies of people experiencing both clinical and subclinical levels of depression provide some support for the notion that negative feedback-seeking is a depressotypic behavior. Findings suggest that (a) depression is related to interest in negative self-relevant feedback, (b) depressed people perceive negative self-relevant feedback to be both accurate and self-verifying, and (c) people who seek and receive negative self-relevant feedback experience increases in depressive symptoms over time. These findings provide support for the role of negative feedback-seeking as a concurrent correlate of depression and as a vulnerability for future depression. Interest in negative, self-verifying feedback by depressed people may help to perpetuate their emotional distress and may cause impaired social functioning.

Interpersonal Consequences

According to self-verification theory, one of the presumed benefits of confirming one's beliefs about oneself is to promote fluid social interactions. Indeed, a growing body of research suggests that people are most satisfied with self-verifying relationship partners (e.g., Katz, Beach, & Anderson, 1996; Schafer, Wickrama, & Keith, 1996; Swann, De La Ronde, & Hixon, 1994). However, it appears that this strategy backfires for depressed or dysphoric people with negative self-views.

Depressed people tend to be rejected by relationship partners because interactions with depressed people tend to be aversive. Negative feedback-seeking behaviors appear to contribute significantly to this phenomenon. In their study of psychiatric youth inpatients, Joiner et al. (1997) found that interest in negative feedback was associated with rejection by peers within relatively long-standing peer relationships. Swann, Wenzlaff, Krull, and Pelham (1992; Study 3) found that the more that dysphoric participants sought unfavorable feedback, the more likely their roommates were to derogate them later, intend to terminate the relationship, and plan to have a new roommate in the future.

Negative feedback-seeking may be particularly toxic for relationships when coupled with excessive reassurance-seeking, as described by the integrative interpersonal theory of depression (Joiner et al., 1992, 1993; Joiner & Metalsky, 1995). According to this theory, the receipt of each type of depressotypic behavior generates interest in the other type of behavior. Reassurance provided to depressed persons may be emotionally satisfying but cognitively displeasing. The receipt of positive nonverifying feedback thus triggers depressed persons to seek negative, verifying feedback from partners. In turn, this feedback is cognitively pleasing but emotionally unsatisfying. This prompts the depressed person to seek more reassurance, creating a cycle of reassurance-seeking and negative feedback-seeking. The confusing interpersonal demands of the depressed person, whose needs for confirmation and enhancement are at odds with each other, may generate relationship stress. The partner may sense, rightly so, that the depressed person is never satisfied with the feedback that the partner provides. In addition to relationship stress, these interpersonal demands may contribute to rejection by the partner, the partner's dissatisfaction with the relationship, or both. In turn, partner rejection may exacerbate the depressed person's depressive symptoms (Katz et al., 1998).

Empirical support for the integrative interpersonal theory of depression is growing. Findings suggest that the three-way interaction of depression, interest in reassurance, and interest in negative feedback is associated with interpersonal disruption in close dyads. More specifically, reassurance-seeking and negative feedback-seeking behaviors among depressed undergraduates predict rejection among same-sex roommates, both cross-sectionally (Joiner et al., 1993) and longitudinally (Joiner & Metalsky, 1995), and partner relationship dissatisfaction (but not rejection per se) among heterosexual dating couples (Katz & Beach, 1997a).

More recently, an entrainment model has been proposed (Katz & Joiner, 2000). Building on the integrative interpersonal theory, research efforts have focused on the relationship between reassurance-seeking and negative feedback-seeking within dyads. Preliminary data suggest that the relationship between reassurance-seeking and negative feedback-seeking as indexed by self-report measures is moderated by level of depression. Among dysphoric people, reassurance-seeking and negative feedback-seeking tendencies are significantly correlated. Among nondysphoric people, these two types of feedback-seeking are not significantly correlated. Efforts currently are under way to examine feedback-seeking behaviors among depressed individuals and their relationship partners' responses to both reassurance-seeking and negative feedback-seeking using observational methods.

Measurement Issues

Defining negative feedback-seeking in terms of specific behaviors poses a challenge to researchers in the field. In part, this challenge is due to the inconsistency between the topography of a behavior and its function. For example, direct requests for negative feedback (e.g., "Don't you think that I'm a rotten cook?") may actually elicit positive, reassuring responses (e.g., "No, of course not"). We believe that the function of the behavior, rather than the topography, is the key to defining a behavior as negative feedback-seeking. As a result, actual negative feedback-seeking may occur at relatively covert levels.

What does negative feedback-seeking look like? Negative feedback-seeking presumably can take many forms. One manifestation may involve the selection of negative feedback, particularly when this choice is made over favorable, neutral, or no feedback options. Another may involve the rejection of positive self-relevant feedback. Yet another may have to do with selection of relationship partners who do not provide high levels of positive feedback or who tend to provide negative feedback. Additional possibilities include requests for agreement with self-derogation, excessive passive or withdrawn behavior, or the provision of negative feedback to others, which may be reciprocated.

The elusive topography of negative feedback-seeking may be directly related to the more elusive topography of negative feedback provision. Strong social norms prohibit the expression of blatantly negative feedback to others in most cases (e.g., Goffman, 1955), so negative feedback provision may be expressed through nonverbal and other less overt channels. Both self-report and behavioral indices of the negative feedback-seeking construct have been developed and used in previous research. In some studies, negative feedback-seeking has been operationalized in terms of motivational strivings for negative feedback. In other studies, negative feedback-seeking has been operationalized in terms of behavior.

Swann, Wenzlaff, Krull, and Pelham (1992) developed a self-report measure of negative feedback-seeking. This measure assesses interest in seeking self-relevant feedback within five distinct domains: intellectual ability, athletic ability, social competence, musical–artistic talents, and physical attractiveness. Respondents are asked to pick 5 of 10 possible questions that they would like to have their relationship partners answer about them at a future time. (It is unclear whether the researchers ask these partners to provide the respondent with the feedback they request.) Each of the five self-relevant domains are framed both positively from the perspective of the relationship partner (e.g., "What do you see as your girlfriend's most physically attractive features?") and negatively (e.g., "What do you see as your girlfriend's least physically attractive features?"). The negative feedback-seeking score is calculated as the number of negatively valenced topics selected. Possible negative feedback-seeking scores range from 0 to 5, with higher scores reflecting more interest in negative feedback. Adequate construct validity for this measure has been established (e.g., Joiner et al., 1993; Swann, Wenzlaff, & Tafarodi, 1992). To date, however, no studies have examined correspondence between this measure and actual negative feedback-seeking behaviors.

Other research on negative feedback-seeking has examined respondents' behavioral preferences for negative feedback over other types of feedback or over no feedback. For instance, respondents may provide self-descriptive information and then may be offered a choice to review evaluative feedback that is positively, negatively, or neutrally valenced in tone. Selection of the negatively valenced feedback is the index of negative feedback-seeking.

Another methodological issue with important conceptual implications involves the difference between negative feedback from partner and partner abuse. Swann, Hixon, and De La Ronde (1992) speculated that interpersonal abuse functions to verify recipients who have negative self-views. However, abusive partner behavior differs in important ways from the types of partner feedback typically measured within a self-verification framework, rendering generalization to abuse potentially problematic. In all likelihood, people seek negative feedback only under certain "safe" conditions. When negative feedback is excessively unfavorable and damaging to the self-view, this feedback would not be experienced as self-verifying. Given that abusive behavior involves one person's attempt to diminish and coerce another, it seems unlikely that such feedback would be actively solicited by people in order to verify their self-views, even if negative. Katz, Arias, and Beach (1999) empirically studied self-verification effects on relationship quality on the basis of discrepancies between self-esteem and both psychological abuse and self-esteem support. They concluded that the application of self-verification theory to the context of partner abuse is misguided but may be useful in understanding support-based relational processes. Therefore, some research evidence suggests that negative feedback should be differentiated from partner abuse.

Summary

The idea that depressed people engage in behaviors that may unwittingly lead to further distress is not new (e.g., Coyne, 1976b). However, self-verification theory provides an avenue for understanding some of the ways in which people may inadvertently perpetuate their depressive symptoms as well as related interpersonal problems. In particular, the types of feedback that depressed people are interested in and feel comfortable with may have negative consequences for both themselves and their relationship partners. Although typically it may be adaptive to maintain self-knowledge and predictability–control, negative feedback-seeking strategies, particularly when combined with other depressotypic interpersonal behaviors (e.g., reassurance-seeking), may lead to both individual and social disruption.

AGGRESSIVE BEHAVIOR

> They may exploit the depression for the justification of the various aggressive impulses toward external objects, thus closing the vicious circle. (Bibring, 1953, cited in Coyne, 1976b, p. 186)

Aggressive behavior may be defined as behavior with intent to harm the individual who is its object (e.g., Berkowitz, 1993). Within the context of ongoing relationships, such behaviors may take many forms, including psychological, physical, and sexual aggression against others. Given the severe physical and psychological consequences of interpersonal aggression, aggressive behaviors typically are experienced as aversive by others.

Numerous theoretical accounts link aggressive behavior to depressive symptoms, and a sampling of these accounts are described herein. Traditional psychoanalytic theorists have suggested that aggression and depression are inversely related (Bleichmar, 1996). Specifically, anger and aggression are the result of externalizing defense mechanisms (e.g., projection), whereas sadness and depression are the result of internalizing defense mechanisms (e.g., turning against the self). However, other researchers (e.g., Jakubaschk & Hubschmid, 1994) have rejected this traditional view because of empirical findings suggesting a positive, rather than negative, relationship between aggressive behavior and depressive symptoms. The direction of causality is not clear. Some theorists have suggested that depression and other negative affective states may cause aggression (e.g., Berkowitz, 1989); others have suggested that individuals who engage in aggressive behavior are at risk for developing depression, largely because of the negative effect of aggressive behavior on interpersonal relationships (e.g., Patterson & Stoolmiller, 1991).

According to the dual-failure model proposed by Patterson and Stoolmiller (1991), an individual's aggressive behavior elicits rejection from peers. Peer rejection, in turn, leads to internalizing problems such as depression. Depression also is viewed as secondary to aggression from a fairly recent psychobiological perspective. Van Praag (1994, 1996) has identified a subtype of depression termed the "anxiety and/or aggression-driven, stressor-precipitated depression" (1996, p. 57). In this type of depression, called *5-HT related depression*, depressed mood occurs as a derivative of anxiety and aggression dysregulation, which are the primary symptoms in need of treatment. According to these perspectives, then, aggression can precipitate depression, either indirectly through peer rejection or directly through psychobiological mechanisms.

In summary, many theoretical perspectives link depression and aggressive behavior. Contemporary theories and a growing body of empirical research suggest a positive link between aggressive behavior and depressive symptoms. The direction of causality between aggression and depression has not been definitively established, and the relationship most likely is a dynamic process. We argue that, in at least some cases, aggressive behavior serves as a predisposing factor to depression. Support for this thesis is provided in the review of empirical studies herein. A comprehensive review of the literature on aggression, its relationship to depression, and its consequences for others is beyond the scope of this chapter; here we simply provide a review of recent and representative studies.

Relationship to Depression

Covariation

In studies of children and adolescents, researchers have found a significant but moderate correlation between aggressive behavior and depression. For example, Weiss and Catron (1994) examined the relationship between aggression and depression in a sample of 350 third to sixth graders and found a correlation of .46. They concluded that the relationship between aggression and depression may represent a more broadband relation between externalizing and internalizing problems generally (see also Capaldi, 1991; Cole & Carpenitieri, 1990). Reiss and Rojahn (1993) studied children, adolescents, and adults diagnosed with mental retardation. They found that aggressive study participants were four times more likely to meet diagnostic criteria for depression than nonaggressive study participants. They also found that anger was significantly associated with both aggression and depression and postulated that anger may mediate the relationship between aggression and depression.

Covariation of aggression and depression has been found in a number of studies of adults as well. These findings hold true among unselected samples of adults. For example, in a laboratory experiment, Bjork, Dougherty, and Moeller (1997) examined self-ratings of depression as related to aggressive behavior in response to provocation. A significant positive correlation emerged between level of aggressive responding and depression for women but not for men. Furthermore, an association between aggression and depression has been found in selected samples of violent offenders. Dewhurst, Moore, and Alfano (1992) studied adult male sexual offenders, wife batterers, violent men, and control participants and investigated attitudes and mood. They found that hostility toward women and depression were the two best predictors of violence against women. Hastings and Hamberger (1988) similarly found that wife batterers showed higher levels of dysphoria, anxiety, and somatic complaints than age-matched nonviolent men. Pan, Neidig, and O'Leary (1994) also showed that depressive symptoms increased the odds of husbands' use of both mild and severe physical aggression against wives. Furthermore, Vivian and Malone (1997) found that husbands who engaged in severe marital violence were more depressed than husbands who engaged in either verbal or mild levels of physical marital aggression. Findings are not restricted to male samples. For instance, in a study of 64 female prison inmates, participants with higher depressive symptoms as measured by the BDI also had significantly higher scores on measures of aggression, as well as lower mean scores on assertion (Varese, Pelowski, Riedel, & Heiby, 1998).

The association between aggression and depression has held among clinical samples of depressed people. Korn, Plutchik, and Van Praag (1997) studied aggression and homicidal impulses among patients diagnosed with panic disorder and patients diagnosed with comorbid panic and major depression. Compared to the pure panic group, patients in the comorbid panic and major depression group reported twice as many episodes of assaults and a fivefold increase in homicidal ideation. In a study of depressed outpatients, Nierenberg, Ghaemi, Clancy-Colecchi, and Jerrold (1996) found significant relationships among measures of anger, aggression, hostility, and depressive symptoms, although only cynicism was related to suicidal ideation.

Temporal Antecedence

Does aggressive behavior temporally precede depressive symptoms? Dumas, Neese, Prinz, and Blechman (1996) studied 478 first and third graders who were rated by teachers and peers with regard to aggression, rejection, and depressive symptoms over the school year. Ratings of aggression were more stable than rejection or depression over time. The authors also reported that a child who displayed aggression at Time 1 had a 49% chance of displaying depressive symptoms at Time 2. Kerr, Tremblay, Pagani, and Vitaro (1997) studied 10-year-old boys over 5 years. They found that social withdrawal (but not behavioral inhibition) combined with aggressive behavior was associated with later depressive symptoms as well as continued aggression.

Although much of the longitudinal data have been collected among youth, some available data with adult samples also suggest temporal antecedence. Windle and Windle (1995) examined retrospective data from 4,462 military veterans. Four patterns of physical aggression were examined: childhood-only aggression, adult-onset aggression, continuous child and adult aggression, and a contrast group with low levels of aggression in childhood and adulthood. They found that the adults who continuously engaged in aggressive behaviors throughout childhood and adulthood, as well as the adult-onset group, showed the highest levels of psychiatric disturbance in the form of major depression, alcohol disorders, or both.

Interpersonal Consequences

Interpersonal aggression has severe negative consequences for others. One class of aversive consequences involves physical injury and mortality. Social and psychological consequences for the aggressor's targets can include rejection of the aggressor and psychological distress on the part of the targets, including posttraumatic stress disorder (PTSD) and depression.

Physical Injury

Rates of violent crime, such as murder, forcible rape, and aggravated assault, doubled from 1970 to 1990 (Federal Bureau of Investigation [FBI], 1991). Rates of violent crime have further increased 23% from 1988 to 1997 (FBI, 1997). In 1992, it was estimated that between 1.5 and 2.5 million children were abused or neglected, more than 1.5 million individuals were victims of assault, and more than 650,000 women were victims of rape (Novello, Shosky, & Froehlke, 1992). Various physical injuries are associated with these different violent crimes. One physical consequence of violent crime is death. Homicide is a leading cause of death for male and female individuals, especially for individuals in urban, poverty-stricken environments (Fontanarosa, 1995). In many cases, homicide victims are in ongoing relationships with their assailants. In 1997, 48% of murder victims knew their assailants. Furthermore, 29% of female murder victims were slain by husbands or boyfriends, and 3% of male murder victims were slain by wives or girlfriends (FBI, 1997).

Rejection and Impaired Social Functioning

In addition to causing physical injury and death, aggression disrupts interpersonal relationships among both children and adults. Common areas of research involve the study of peer rejection in aggressive children and relationship functioning and dissolution among adults who engage in domestic violence.

It is well-established that aggressive children are at high risk for rejection by their peers. In fact, research has demonstrated a causal link between aggression and rejection, such that aggressive behavior in the school years actively encourages peer rejection (Dodge, 1983). In a recent study of 7- to 9-year-old boys, participants who were either aggressive or depressed were more disliked by their peers than nonaggressive and nondepressed boys. Furthermore, being disliked was associated with more aggressive behavior subsequently. The association between boys' initial aggression and their subsequent aggression with peers was mediated by dislike by their peers (MacKinnon-Lewis & Lofquist, 1996). These findings are consistent with the dual-failure model proposed by Patterson and Stoolmiller (1991), who proposed that aggressive behavior increases the risk for social disruption and, subsequently, depression.

Domestic violence is a commonly studied form of interpersonal violence among adults. Disturbed social functioning in violent romantic relationships may manifest as marital discord and relationship dissolution. Windle and Windle (1995) found that aggressive men endorsed higher levels of marital discord than did nonaggressive men. Furthermore, violent behavior by one spouse generally is associated with greater marital dissatisfaction and more intentions toward ending the relationship in the other (e.g., Bauserman & Arias, 1992). Women who hold their partners accountable for engaging in violent behavior tend to report greater intentions to leave the relationship (e.g., Pape & Arias, 1995). Unfortunately, many women remain in relationships with aggressive partners despite high levels of marital dissatisfaction. Factors such as economic dependence, social isolation, and fears of retaliation by the violent partner may contribute to the maintenance of violent relationships (e.g., Strube, 1988).

Psychological Distress and Depression

Victims of interpersonal violence in childhood and adolescence perpetrated by parents, other caregivers, or peers show a variety of emotional and behavioral problems. These problems may include aggression, anxiety, and depression (Garbarino, Dubrow, Kostelny, & Pardo, 1992; Singer, Anglin, Song, & Lunghofer, 1995).

Depression and symptoms of PTSD among adult victims of aggression are common. The effects of exposure to violence and victimization on adult functioning have been studied most extensively among samples of women. Female victims of sexual assault also are at elevated risk for onset of depression and substance abuse disorders (e.g., Burnam et al., 1988). Women in physically violent marital relationships show elevated levels of depressive symptoms (Andrews & Brown, 1988; Cascardi & O'Leary, 1992). Furthermore, psychological aggression by marital partners may have even stronger negative effects than physical aggression (e.g., Folingstad, Rutledge, Berg, Hause, & Polek, 1990). Although causal relationships are difficult to establish within ecologically valid settings, temporal antecedence has been established. One recent longitudinal study showed that psychological abuse in the form of dominance and isolation behaviors by male dating partners led to future increases in depressive symptoms for dating women (Katz & Arias, 1999).

The literature on vicarious traumatization suggests that exposure to aggression, even when one is not the direct target of the aggressor's behavior, may increase risk for psychological distress. For instance, although findings have been somewhat inconsistent, some evidence suggests that children exposed to family violence may be at risk for emotional problems including depression, anxiety, and low self-esteem (e.g., Holden & Ritchie, 1991; Kolbo, 1996). Furthermore, therapists who work with victims of violent crime may experience burnout as a result of vicarious exposure to aggression (McCann & Pearlman, 1990). The concept of vicarious traumatization, like the concept of contagious depression, involves the interpersonal transmission of negative affect from one individual to others. Accordingly, the interpersonal psychological consequences of aggression in terms of depression and traumatic stress for its targets may be far-reaching in cases of vicarious traumatization.

Measurement Issues

Researchers who study interpersonal aggression are challenged by many methodological issues. Assessing aggressive behavior through observation in a laboratory or naturalistic setting involves complex ethical considerations. Measuring aggression through self-report measures may be compromised by factors such as memory for violent events and social desirability considerations. In addition, the most commonly used self-report measures of aggression within family and couple relationships (e.g., the Conflict Tactics Scale; CTS; Straus, 1979) assess frequency of violent behavior, but not motivation for engaging in aggressive behavior and impact of the aggression on the target. Measures of other types of aggression (e.g., psychological abuse, sexual coercion) are plagued by a lack of consensus in defining and labeling different types of aggressive behaviors.

Many innovative measures of aggression have been developed and used in psychological research. In laboratory settings, some indices have included administration of shock (real or fictitious) to other participants (e.g., Hammock & Richardson, 1992), verbal assault (e.g., Cohen, Nisbett, Bowdle, & Schwarz, 1996), and administration of excessive amounts of hot sauce on another person's food (e.g., McGregor et al., 1998). Outside of the laboratory, researchers have used a variety of self-report measures of aggressive behavior with different groups. Among children, commonly used measures include use of teacher or parent checklists, for instance the *Child Behavior Checklist* (e.g., Edelbrock & Achenbach, 1980) as well as peer nomination methods (e.g., Weiss & Catron, 1994). Among couples and other intimate dyads, the CTS is used to assess frequency of aggressive behavior (but not intent or impact). A psychological abuse scale, ordinary violence scale, and severe violence scale comprise this measure. Another measure of verbal aggression is the Psychological Maltreatment of Women Scale (Tolman, 1989), which assesses dominance and isolation and emotional and verbal forms of abuse.

Although tremendous progress has been made in the field of interpersonal aggression over the past few decades, there is room for additional development. For instance, assessment of the motivations of the assailant seems important in studies of interpersonal aggression. This would clarify instances in which aggression is used against others for self-defense purposes, as a means of expressing strong emotions, or as a means of punishing, coercing, or controlling the target individual. Assessment of the impact of interpersonal aggression on targets also could provide valuable information with regard to the level of social disruption that results from aggressive behavior.

Summary

Aggressive behavior may predispose people to the development of depressive symptoms. In large part, this may occur because of the disrupted social environment that results from aggressive behavior. The negative interpersonal consequences of aggression for others include physical injury, social disruption, and psychological distress. After experiencing an aggressive episode, relationship partners may withdraw from their assailant emotionally through relationship dissatisfaction or physically by ending the relationship. Aggressive individuals may continue to engage in aggression because they are frustrated with an unrewarding social environment. Ongoing episodes of aggressive behavior may further increase the risk for depression and social disruption, perhaps creating a cycle of emotional dysregulation and interpersonal problems.

DISPOSITIONAL VARIABLES RELATED TO THE USE OF DEPRESSOTYPIC BEHAVIORS

The relationship between depressotypic behaviors and dispositional factors has not been the subject of much empirical inquiry to date. However, each behavior can be conceptually linked to other dispositional constructs that affect individuals' social functioning. Specifically, we briefly outline theory of and research on these depressotypic behaviors as related to self-esteem level, self-esteem stability, and adult attachment styles. It should be noted, however, that conceptual links can be made to other socially relevant dispositional constructs as well, such as sociotropy and autonomy (Beck, 1983).

Level and Stability of Self-Esteem

Low or uncertain self-esteem appears to be related to the depressotypic behaviors of reassurance-seeking, negative feedback-seeking, and aggression. First, the more proximal precursors of heightened reassurance-seeking may be negative life events and associated increases in anxiety and decreases in self-esteem. Joiner, Katz, and Lew (1999) hypothesized that the occurrence of negative events engenders a sense of concern and uncertainty about one's self (cf. self-esteem) and about the future (cf. anxiety). In response to increased anxiety and to the threat to self-esteem, people may engage in reassurance-seeking to assuage their sense of doubt about the self and about the future. Results have supported the view that negative life events predicted an increase in reassurance-seeking as a function of increases in anxiety and decreases in self-esteem.

Second, the basis of negative feedback-seeking is negative self-views or low self-esteem. According to self-verification theory, negative feedback-seeking behaviors occur to confirm one's own self-views, despite the negative emotions such feedback engenders. Self-esteem is robustly related to depression, although this association holds true only for people who have stable, rather than unstable, self-esteem (Butler, Hokanson, & Flynn, 1994; Kernis, Grannemann, & Mathis, 1991). People in self-verifying relationships tend to have relatively stable self-conceptions (e.g., Swann & Predmore, 1985). Accordingly, people who are in self-verifying relationships should show a stronger association between self-esteem level and depressive symptoms, given that their self-esteem levels are presumed to be more stable. Research conducted with women in close heterosexual relationships supports this hypothesis (Katz & Beach, 1997b).

Third, both low and unstable self-esteem are implicated in understanding aggressive behavior. Low self-esteem has long been conceptually linked to aggression (see review in Baumeister, Smart, & Boden, 1996, pp. 6–7). However, in their critical review of the literature on aggression,

Baumeister et al. concluded that domestic violence seems like the most promising milieu in which to find low self-esteem effects on aggression. In other cases, these authors described a typical aggressor as one who has a favorable, often inflated, view of self who encounters someone who communicates a negative (or less positive) appraisal of the individual. This nonverifying appraisal is threatening for people with unstable self-views. As a result of this threat, the individual may engage in aggressive behavior in defense of the unstable favorable self-view (Kernis, Cornell, Sun, Berry, & Harlow, 1993).

Attachment Style

Depressotypic interpersonal behavior may vary as a function of individuals' dispositional attachment styles. Bowlby's (1973, 1980, 1982) theory on infant attachment specifically describes depressotypic interpersonal behaviors used by infants under conditions of stress or discomfort. He proposed that infants develop a behavioral attachment system to keep caregivers nearby. Bowlby observed that young infants' responses to stress were characterized by a predictable sequence of observable emotions: protest, despair, and detachment. Protest involves active behavioral signals of distress (e.g., crying and resistance to soothing). Despair involves infant's passivity and despondent behaviors, and emotional detachment involves behaviors that promote physical and psychological distance between the infant and attachment figure.

Although considerable controversy exists regarding whether infant attachment persists into adulthood and about the stability of attachment style over time (e.g., Baldwin & Fehr, 1995), there is accumulating evidence that attachment processes operate in adulthood and are consequential for social functioning. In adulthood, one would expect behavior reflecting the attachment system to take different forms, because conceptual continuity, rather than literal continuity, should exist over time (West, Livesly, Reiffer, & Sheldon, 1986). Most likely, depressotypic behaviors in adulthood are more complex than in infancy. Regardless, however, people experiencing depressive symptoms may be thought to have activated attachment systems leading to depressotypic behaviors. We suggest that the depressotypic behaviors discussed in this chapter may fit well into this framework. Specifically, reassurance-seeking behaviors actively communicate despair and may be a form of protest. Depending on its topography, negative feedback-seeking may be a way of communicating either despair or despondency about the self. Aggression may either cause or result from emotional detachment.

Although reassurance-seeking, negative feedback-seeking, and aggression among depressed people have not yet been studied within an attachment framework, other research suggests that such endeavors might be fruitful. Undergraduate women who report less positive childhood experiences with their parents are often insecurely attached and mildly depressed, and they endorse avoidant and preoccupied beliefs about their current romantic relationships (Carnelley, Pietromonaco, & Jaffe, 1994). Furthermore, attachment styles appear to influence general interactional behaviors among distressed, nondepressed individuals. For instance, in a study of dating couples, Simpson, Rholes, and Nelligan (1992) showed that when securely attached women were nervous, they sought more support from their partners, whereas avoidant women sought less. The securely attached men in this study offered more support to their nervous partners, whereas those who were more avoidant offered less.

Summary

In summary, certain dispositional factors may be related to use of depressotypic interpersonal behaviors, which may be experienced as aversive by others. Both level and stability of self-esteem appear to be dispositional factors related to depression more generally, as well as to depressotypic interpersonal behavior more specifically. Furthermore, attachment theory may provide a useful framework for conceptualizing about the interpersonal origins behind the use of depressotypic interpersonal behaviors.

CHAPTER SUMMARY

In this chapter, we have advanced theory and research regarding three modes of depressotypic behavior: excessive reassurance-seeking, negative feedback-seeking, and aggression. Over the recent past, each class of behaviors has become the focus of empirical inquiry by researchers on depression. We believe that a better understanding of the ways in which depression is interpersonally communicated may help explain the aversive effects of depression on others. From an interpersonal perspective, depressotypic behaviors appear to be implicated in the cause and maintenance of depressive episodes, in part through their effects on social disruption. When depressed people are experienced as aversive by others, they are rejected. Rejection may manifest as withdrawal, relationship dissatisfaction, and relationship dissolution. These aversive social consequences also affect relationship partners' individual well-being. More specifically, close others may be affected by contagious depression and stress, and in the case of interpersonal aggression, by physical as well as psychological harm. Attention to these and other forms of depressotypic behaviors should enhance our ability to understand and assist depressed individuals and their close relationship partners.

REFERENCES

Alloy, L. B., & Lipman, A. J. (1992). Depression and selection of positive and negative social feedback: Motivated preference or cognitive balance? *Journal of Abnormal Psychology, 101,* 310–313.

American Psychiatric Association. (1987). *Diagnostic and statistical manual of mental disorders* (3rd ed., rev.). Washington, DC: Author.

Andrews, B., & Brown, G. W. (1988). Marital violence in the community: A biographical approach. *British Journal of Psychiatry, 153,* 305–312.

Baldwin, M. W., & Fehr, B. (1995). On the instability of attachment style ratings. *Personal Relationships, 2,* 247–261.

Baumeister, R. F., Smart, L., & Boden, J. M. (1996). Relation of threatened egotism to violence and aggression: The dark side of high self-esteem. *Psychological Review, 103,* 5–33.

Bauserman, S. A. K., & Arias, I. (1992). Relationships among marital investment, marital satisfaction, and marital commitment in domestically victimized and nonvictimized wives. *Violence and Victims, 7,* 287–296.

Beck, A. T. (1983). Cognitive therapy of depression: New perspectives. In P. Clayton & J. E. Barret (Eds.), *Treatment of depression: Old controversies and new approaches* (pp. 265–290). New York: Raven.

Beck, A. T., Ward, C. H., Mendelson, M., Mock, J., & Erbaugh, J. (1961). An inventory for measuring depression. *Archives of General Psychiatry, 4,* 561–571.

Benazon, N. R. (1998). *Predicting negative partner attitudes toward depressed persons: An empirical evaluation of two theories.* Manuscript submitted for publication.

Berkowitz, L. (1989). Frustration–aggression hypothesis. Examination and reformulation. *Psychological Bulletin, 106,* 59–73.

Berkowitz, L. (1993). *Aggression: Its causes, consequences, and control.* Philadelphia: Temple University Press.

Bjork, J. M., Dougherty, D. M., & Moeller, F. G. (1997). A positive correlation between self-ratings of depression and laboratory measured aggression. *Psychiatry Research, 6,* 33–38.

Bleichmar, H. B. (1996). Some subtypes of depression and their implications for psychoanalytic treatment. *International Journal of Psychoanalysis, 7,* 935–961.

Bowlby, J. (1973). *Attachment and loss: Vol. 1. Separation.* New York: Basic Books.

Bowlby, J. (1980). *Attachment and loss: Vol. 2. Attachment.* New York: Basic Books.

Bowlby, J. (1982). *Attachment and loss: Vol. 3. Loss.* New York: Basic Books.

Burnam, M. A., Stein, J. A., Golding, J. M., Siegel, J. M., Sorenson, S. B., Forsythe, A. B., & Telles, C. A. (1988). Sexual assault and mental disorders in a community population. *Journal of Consulting and Clinical Psychology, 56,* 843–850.

Butler, A. C., Hokanson, J. E., & Flynn, H. A. (1994). A comparison of self-esteem lability and low trait self-esteem as vulnerability factors for depression. *Journal of Personality and Social Psychology, 66,* 166–177.

Capaldi, D. M. (1991). Co-occurrence of conduct problems and depressive symptoms in early adolescent boys: I. Familial factors and general adjustment. *Development and Psychopathology, 3,* 277–300.

Carnelley, K. B., Pietromonaco, P., & Jaffe, K. (1994). Depression, working models of others, and relationship functioning. *Journal of Personality and Social Psychology, 66,* 127–140.

Cascardi, M., & O'Leary, K. D. (1992). Depressive symptomatology, self-esteem, and self-blame in battered women. *Journal of Family Violence, 7,* 249–259.

Cohen, D., Nisbett, R. E., Bowdle, B. F., & Schwarz, N. (1996). Insult, aggression, and the southern culture of honor: An "experimental ethnography." *Journal of Personality and Social Psychology, 70,* 945–960.

Cole, D. A., & Carpenitieri, S. (1990). Social status and the comorbidity of child depression and conduct disorder. *Journal of Consulting and Clinical Psychology, 58,* 748–757.

Collins, N. L., Dunkel-Schetter, C., Lobel, M., & Scrimshaw, S. C. M. (1993). Social support in pregnancy: Psychosocial correlates of birth outcomes and postpartum depression. *Journal of Personality and Social Psychology, 65,* 1243–1258.

Coyne, J. C. (1976a). Depression and the response of others. *Journal of Abnormal Psychology, 85,* 186–193.

Coyne, J. C. (1976b). Toward an interactional description of depression. *Psychiatry, 39,* 28–40.

Coyne, J. C. (1994). Self-reported distress: Analog or ersatz depression? *Psychological Bulletin, 116,* 29–45.

Coyne, J. C., Kessler, R. C., Tal, M., Turnbull, J., Wortman, C. B., & Creden, J. F. (1987). Living with a depressed person. *Journal of Consulting and Clinical Psychology, 55,* 347–352.

Dewhurst, A. M., Moore, R. J., & Alfano, D. P. (1992). Aggression against women by men: Sexual and spousal assault. *Journal of Offender Rehabilitation, 18,* 39–47.

Dodge, K. A. (1983). Behavioral antecedents of peer social status. *Child Development, 54,* 1386–1399.

Dumas, J., Neese, D. E., Prinz, R. J., & Blechman, E. A. (1996). Short term stability of aggression, peer rejection, and depressive symptoms in middle childhood. *Journal of Abnormal Child Psychology, 24,* 115–119.

Edelbrock, C., & Achenbach, T. (1980). A typology of Child Behavior Profile patterns: Distribution and correlates for disturbed children aged 6–16 years. *Journal of Abnormal Child Psychology, 8,* 441–470.

Federal Bureau of Investigation. (1991). *Uniform crime reports.* Washington, DC: US Government Printing Office.

Federal Bureau of Investigation. (1997). *Uniform crime reports.* Washington, DC: US Government Printing Office.

Fenichel, O. (1945). *The psychoanalytic theory of neurosis.* New York: W.W. Norton.

Folingstad, D. R., Rutledge, L. L., Berg, B. J., Hause, E. S., & Polek, D. S. (1990). The role of emotional abuse in physically abusive relationships. *Journal of Family Violence, 5,* 107–120.

Fontanarosa, P. B. (1995). The unrelenting epidemic of violence in America: Truths and consequences. *Journal of the American Medical Association, 273,* 1792–1793.

Garbarino, J., Dubrow, N., Kostelny, K., & Pardo, C. (1992). *Children in danger: Coping with the consequences of community violence.* San Francisco: Jossey-Bass.

Giesler, R. B., Josephs, R. A., & Swann, W. B., Jr. (1996). Self-verification in clinical depression: The desire for negative evaluation. *Journal of Abnormal Psychology, 105,* 358–368.

Goffman, E. (1955). On face work: An analysis of ritual elements in social interaction. *Psychiatry: Journal for the Study of Interpersonal Processes, 18,* 213–231.

Hammen, C. (1991). Generation of stress in the course of unipolar depression. *Journal of Abnormal Psychology, 100,* 555–561.

Hammock, G., & Richardson, D. (1992). Aggression as one response to conflict. *Journal of Applied Social Psychology, 22,* 298–311.

Hastings, J. E., & Hamberger, L. K. (1988). Personality characteristics of spouse abusers: A controlled comparison. *Violence and Victims, 3,* 31–48.

Hokanson, J. E., Rubert, M. P., Welker, R. A., Hollander, G. R., & Hedeen, C. (1989). Interpersonal concomitants and antecedents of depression among college students. *Journal of Abnormal Psychology, 98,* 209–217.

Holden, G. W., & Ritchie, K. L. (1991). Linking extreme marital discord, child rearing, and child behavior problems: Evidence from battered women. *Child Development, 62,* 311–327.

Hooley, J. M., & Richters, J. E. (1992). Allure of self-confirmation: A comment on Swann, Wenzlaff, Krull, and Pelham. *Journal of Abnormal Psychology, 101,* 307–309.

Jakubaschk, J., & Hubschmid, T. (1994). Aggression and depression: A reciprocal relationship? *European Journal of Psychiatry, 8,* 69–80.

Joiner, T. E., Jr. (1994). The interplay of similarity and self-verification in relationship formation. *Social Behavior and Personality, 22,* 195–200.

Joiner, T. E., Jr. (1995). The price of soliciting and receiving negative feedback: Self-verification theory as a vulnerability to depression theory. *Journal of Abnormal Psychology, 104,* 364–372.

Joiner, T. E., Jr. (1999). A test of interpersonal theory of depression in youth psychiatric inpatients. *Journal of Abnormal Child Psychology, 27,* 75–84.

Joiner, T. E., Jr., Alfano, M. S., & Metalsky, G. I. (1992). When depression breeds contempt: Reassurance-seeking, self-esteem, and rejection of depressed college students by their roommates. *Journal of Abnormal Psychology, 101,* 165–173.

Joiner, T. E., Jr., Alfano, M. S., & Metalsky, G. I. (1993). Caught in the crossfire: Depression, self-consistency, self-enhancement, and the response of others. *Journal of Social and Clinical Psychology, 12,* 113–134.

Joiner, T. E., Jr., & Katz, J. (1999). Contagion of depressive symptoms and mood: Meta-analytic review and explanations from cognitive, behavioral, and interpersonal viewpoints. *Clinical Psychology: Science and Practice, 6,* 149–164.

Joiner, T. E., Jr., Katz, J., & Lew, A. (1997). Self-verification and depression among youth psychiatric inpatients. *Journal of Abnormal Psychology, 106,* 608–618.

Joiner, T. E., Jr., Katz, J., & Lew, A. (1999). Harbingers of depressotypic reassurance-seeking: Negative life events, increased anxiety, and decreased self-esteem. *Personality and Social Psychology Bulletin, 25,* 630–637.

Joiner, T. E., Jr., & Metalsky, G. I. (1995). A prospective test of an integrative interpersonal theory of depression: A naturalistic study of college roommates. *Journal of Personality and Social Psychology, 69,* 778–788.

Joiner, T. E., Jr., & Metalsky, G. I. (1998a). *Reassurance-seeking: Delineating a risk factor involved in the development of depressive symptoms.* Manuscript submitted for publication.

Joiner, T. E., Jr., & Metalsky, G. I. (1998b). *The relative specificity of excessive reassurance-seeking to depressive symptoms among adult and youth psychiatric inpatients.* Manuscript submitted for publication.

Joiner, T. E., Jr., Metalsky, G. I., Katz, J., & Beach, S. R. H. (1999). Depression and excessive reassurance-seeking. *Psychological Inquiry, 10,* 269–278.

Joiner, T. E., Jr., & Schmidt, N. B. (1998). Excessive reassurance-seeking predicts depressive but not anxious reactions to acute stress. *Journal of Abnormal Psychology, 107,* 533–537.

Katz, J., & Arias, I. (1999). Psychological abuse and depressive symptoms in dating women: Do different types of abuse have differential effects? *Journal of Family Violence, 14,* 281–295.

Katz, J., Arias, I., & Beach, S. R. H. (1999). *Psychological abuse, self-esteem, and dating relationship outcomes: A critical examination of the self-verification perspective.* Manuscript submitted for publication.

Katz, J., & Beach, S. R. H. (1997a). Romance in the crossfire: When do women's depressive symptoms predict partner relationship dissatisfaction? *Journal of Social and Clinical Psychology, 16,* 243–258.

Katz, J., & Beach, S. R. H. (1997b). Self-verification and depressive symptoms in marriage and courtship: A multiple pathway model. *Journal of Marriage and the Family, 59,* 903–914.

Katz, J., Beach, S. R. H., & Anderson, P. (1996). Self-enhancement versus self-verification: Does spousal support always help? *Cognitive Therapy and Research, 20,* 345–360.

Katz, J., Beach, S. R. H., & Joiner, T. E., Jr. (1998). When does partner devaluation predict depression? Prospective moderating effects of reassurance-seeking and self-esteem. *Personal Relationships, 5,* 409–421.

Katz, J., & Joiner, T. E., Jr. (2000). *On the entrained nature of excessive reassurance-seeking and negative feedback-seeking among people with depressive symptoms.* Manuscript in preparation.

Katz, J., Joiner, T. E., Jr., & Beach, S. R. H. (1999). Contagious depression in dating couples. *Journal of Social and Clinical Psychology, 18*, 1–13.

Kernis, M. H., Cornell, D. P., Sun, C. R., Berry, A., & Harlow, T. (1993). There's more to self-esteem than whether it is high or low: The importance of stability of self-esteem. *Journal of Personality and Social Psychology, 65*, 1190–1204.

Kernis, M. H., Grannemann, B. D., & Mathis, L. C. (1991). Stability of self-esteem as a moderator of the relation between level of self-esteem and depression. *Journal of Personality and Social Psychology, 61*, 80–84.

Kerr, M., Tremblay, R. E., Pagani, L., & Vitaro, F. (1997). Boy's behavioral inhibition and the risk of later delinquency. *Archives of General Psychiatry, 54*, 809–816.

King, D., & Heller, K. (1984). Depression and the response of others: A reevaluation. *Journal of Abnormal Psychology, 93*, 477–480.

Kolbo, J. R. (1996). Risk and resilience among children exposed to family violence. *Violence and Victims, 11*, 113–128.

Korn, M. L., Plutchik, R., & Van Praag, H. M. (1997). Panic-associated suicidal and aggressive ideation and behavior. *Journal of Psychiatric Research, 31*, 481–487.

MacKinnon-Lewis, C., & Lofquist, A. (1996). Antecedents and consequences of boys' depression and aggression: Family and school linkages. *Journal of Family Psychology, 10*, 490–500.

McCann, I. L., & Pearlman, L. A. (1990). Vicarious traumatization: A framework for understanding the psychological effects of working with victims. *Journal of Traumatic Stress, 3*, 131–149.

McGregor, H. A., Lieberman, J. D., Greenberg, J., Solomon, S., Ardnt, J., Simon, L., & Pyszczynski, T. (1998). Terror management and aggression: Evidence that mortality salience motivates aggression against worldview-threatening others. *Journal of Personality and Social Psychology, 74*, 590–605.

McNeil, D., Arkowitz, H., & Pritchard, B. (1987). The response of others to face-to-face interaction with depressed patients. *Journal of Abnormal Psychology, 96*, 341–344.

Merchant, N. (1998). My Skin. On *Ophelia* [Album]. New York: Talking Dwarf Studios.

Metalsky, G. I., & Johnson, J. G. (1997, May). *Cognitive and interpersonal vulnerability to depression.* Paper presented at the annual meeting of the Midwestern Psychological Association, Chicago, IL.

Nierenberg, A. A., Ghaemi, S. R., Clancy-Colecchi, K. R., & Jerrold, F. (1996). Cynicism, hostility and suicidal ideation in depressed outpatients. *Journal of Nervous and Mental Disease, 184*, 607–610.

Novello, A. C., Shosky, J., & Froehlke, R. (1992). A medical response to violence. *Journal of the American Medical Association, 267*, 3007.

Pan, H. S., Neidig, P. H., & O'Leary, K. D. (1994). Predicting mild and severe husband-to-wife physical aggression. *Journal of Consulting and Clinical Psychology, 62*, 975–981.

Pape, K. T., & Arias, I. (1995). Control, distress, and victimization among married and cohabiting women. *Violence and Victims, 10,* 43–54.

Patterson, G. R., & Stoolmiller, M. (1991). Replications of a dual failure model for boys' depressed mood. *Journal of Consulting and Clinical Psychology, 59,* 491–498.

Potthoff, J. G., Holahan, C. J., & Joiner, T. E., Jr. (1995). Reassurance-seeking, stress generation, and depressive symptoms: An integrative model. *Journal of Personality and Social Psychology, 68,* 664–670.

Reiss, S., & Rojahn, J. (1993). Joint occurrence of depression and aggression in children and adults with mental retardation. *Journal of Intellectual Disability Research, 37,* 287–294.

Schafer, R. B., Wickrama, K. A. S., & Keith, P. M. (1996). Self-concept disconfirmation, psychological distress, and marital happiness. *Journal of Marriage and the Family, 58,* 167–177.

Segrin, C., & Dillard, J. P. (1992). The interactional theory of depression: A meta-analysis of the research literature. *Journal of Social and Clinical Psychology, 11,* 43–70.

Simpson, J. A., Rholes, W. S., & Nelligan, J. S. (1992). Support seeking and support giving within couples in an anxiety-provoking situation: The role of attachment styles. *Journal of Personality and Social Psychology, 62,* 434–446.

Singer, M. I., Anglin, T. M., Song, L. Y., & Lunghofer, L. (1995). Adolescents' exposure to violence and associated symptoms of psychological trauma. *Journal of the American Medical Association, 273,* 477–482.

Straus, M. A. (1979). Measuring intrafamily conflict and violence: The Conflict Tactics (CT) Scale. *Journal of Marriage and the Family, 41,* 75–86.

Strube, M. J. (1988). The decision to leave an abusive relationship: Empirical evidence and theoretical issues. *Psychological Bulletin, 104,* 236–250.

Swann, W. B., Jr. (1983). Self-verification: Bringing social reality into harmony with the self. In J. Suls & A. G. Greenwald (Eds.), *Social psychology perspectives* (Vol. 2, pp. 33–66). Hillsdale, NJ: Erlbaum.

Swann, W. B., Jr. (1987). Identity negotiation: Where the two roads meet. *Journal of Personality and Social Psychology, 53,* 1038–1051.

Swann, W. B., Jr., De La Ronde, C., & Hixon, J. G. (1994). Authenticity and positivity strivings in marriage and courtship. *Journal of Personality and Social Psychology, 66,* 857–869.

Swann, W. B., Jr., Griffin, J. J., Predmore, S. C., & Gaines, B. (1987). The cognitive-affective crossfire: When self-consistency confronts self-enhancement. *Journal of Personality and Social Psychology, 52,* 881–889.

Swann, W. B., Jr., Hixon, J. G., & De La Ronde, C. (1992). Embracing the bitter "truth:" Negative self-concepts and marital commitment. *Psychological Science, 3,* 118–121.

Swann, W. B., Jr., & Predmore, S. C. (1985). Intimates as agents of social support: Sources of consolation or despair? *Journal of Personality and Social Psychology, 49,* 1609–1617.

Swann, W. B., Jr., & Read, S. J. (1981). Self-verification processes: How we sustain our self-conceptions. *Journal of Experimental Social Psychology, 17,* 351–372.

Swann, W. B., Jr., Stein-Seroussi, A., & Giesler, R. B. (1992). Why people self-verify. *Journal of Personality and Social Psychology, 62,* 392–401.

Swann, W. B., Jr., Wenzlaff, R. M., Krull, D. S., & Pelham, B. W. (1992). Allure of negative feedback: Self-verification strivings among depressed persons. *Journal of Abnormal Psychology, 101,* 293–306.

Swann, W. B., Jr., Wenzlaff, R. M., & Tafarodi, R. W. (1992). Depression and the search for negative self-evaluations: More evidence of the role of self-verification strivings. *Journal of Abnormal Psychology, 101,* 314–317.

Taylor, S. E., & Brown, J. D. (1988). Illusion and well-being: A social psychological perspective on mental health. *Psychological Bulletin, 103,* 193–210.

Tennen, H., Hall, J. A., & Affleck, G. (1995). Depression research methodologies in the *Journal of Personality and Social Psychology*: A review and critique. *Journal of Personality and Social Psychology, 68,* 870–884.

Tolman, R. M. (1989). The development of a measure of psychological maltreatment of women by their male partners. *Violence and Victims, 4,* 159–177.

Van Praag, H. M. (1994). 5-HT-related anxiety and/or aggression-driven depression. *International Clinical Psychopharmacology, 9,* 5–6.

Van Praag, H. M. (1996). Serotonin-related, anxiety/aggression driven, stressor-precipitated depression: A psychobiological hypothesis. *European Psychiatry, 11,* 57–67.

Varese, T., Pelowski, S., Riedel, H., & Heiby, E. M. (1998). Assessment of cognitive behavioral skills and depression among female prison inmates. *European Journal of Psychological Assessment, 14,* 141–145.

Vivian, D., & Malone, J. (1997). Relationship factors and depressive symptomatology associated with mild and severe husband-to-wife physical aggression. *Violence and Victims, 12,* 3–18.

Vredenburg, K., Flett, G. L., & Krames, L. (1993). Analogue versus clinical depression: A critical appraisal. *Psychological Bulletin, 113,* 327–344.

Weiss, B., & Catron, T. (1994). Specificity of the comorbidity of aggression and depression in children. *Journal of Abnormal Child Psychology, 22,* 389–401.

West, M., Lively, W. J., Reiffer, L., & Sheldon, A. (1986). The place of attachment in the life events model of stress and illness. *Canadian Journal of Psychiatry, 31,* 202–207.

Windle, R. C., & Windle, M. (1995). Longitudinal patterns of physical aggression: Associations with adult social, psychiatric, and personality functioning and testosterone levels. *Development and Psychopathology, 7,* 563–585.

Wood, J. V., Giordono-Beech, M., Taylor, K. L., Michela, J. L., & Gaus, V. (1994). Strategies of social-comparison among people with low self-esteem: Self-protection and self-enhancement. *Journal of Personality and Social Psychology, 67,* 713–731.

III

HURTING OTHERS

6

HURT FEELINGS:
THE NEGLECTED EMOTION

MARK R. LEARY AND CARRIE A. SPRINGER

Psychologists have shown considerable interest in the negative experiences and emotions that undermine the quality of human life. In particular, researchers and clinicians alike have devoted a great deal of attention to emotional reactions such as depression, anxiety, anger, loneliness, and shame, and the size and breadth of the extant literature dealing with dysphoria and dysfunction are staggering. After more than 100 years of work on such topics, one might imagine that behavioral researchers would have, by now, plumbed the depths of human unhappiness and despair. Curiously, however, one common and painful experience has virtually escaped scholarly attention—the emotional experience that people colloquially call *hurt feelings*.

Hurt feelings are surprisingly common. When we asked university students to rate how often their feelings were hurt by other people, 60% indicated that on average they experienced hurt feelings more often than once a month, and 20% said that they were hurt at least once each week. Although the incidence of hurt feelings likely differs by age, personality, and culture, it is clearly a frequent experience for a large number of individuals.

People's feelings are hurt by a wide array of interpersonal events that range from seemingly minor incidents to momentous, life-changing experiences. Obviously, people are hurt when they are abandoned or betrayed by lovers and close friends, criticized harshly, or publicly humiliated. However, people's feelings are also hurt by relatively trivial things, such as forgotten birthdays, teasing, and thoughtless remarks. Whether big or small, hurtful events often cause profound distress and damage people's interpersonal relationships, sometimes irreparably. Furthermore, hurt feelings are associated with many maladaptive, if not antisocial behaviors. Sometimes people try to emotionally or physically hurt the person who has hurt them (which, in some primitive sense, is understandable), but often they also take their revenge out on others who are not in the least bit involved. Moreover, once people have been hurt, they find it difficult to trust the person who hurt them, and their wariness may generalize to other people and other relationships. Because hurt feelings are so unpleasant, people try to avoid situations and relationships in which they might be emotionally hurt. Being hurt is one of the "risks" inherent in forming relationships and developing intimacy that may deter people from becoming close to others (L'Abate, 1997; Pilkington & Richardson, 1988).

Our goal in this chapter is to provide an overview of what is currently known about hurt feelings and to speculate regarding its causes and functions. We begin by examining the status of hurt feelings as an emotion. Given that the emotion of hurt feelings have not been widely studied and do not appear in most taxonomies of emotion, we have only partial answers regarding the characteristics of hurt feelings and how they relate to other emotions.[1] After discussing the features of hurt feelings, we offer a theoretical perspective that attempts to explain why people's feelings are hurt, and then we review the sparse empirical findings that bear on this theory. Given that the capacity for emotional experience presumably evolved because it conferred an adaptive advantage, we also speculate regarding the possible function of hurt feelings. After doing so, we examine common behavioral reactions to being hurt; then we conclude with a discussion of why people hurt one another's feelings in the first place. Throughout the chapter we sprinkle in some exemplars of hurtful experiences that have been provided by participants in our research (collected as part of the studies reported in Leary, Springer, Negel, Ansell, & Evans, 1998, and Leary, Hechenbleikner, Strausser, Higgins, & Stiles, 1999).

---

[1] In writing this chapter, we have wrestled with the question of whether the term *hurt feelings* should be treated as singular or plural. *Feelings* is obviously a plural noun, but the experience it describes is best regarded as a singular entity. We find ourselves being inconsistent on this count. Sometimes a singular verb sounds better, but often hurt feelings clearly requires a plural verb (although we used a singular one in this sentence).

CONCEPTUALIZING HURT FEELINGS

We are intrigued by the semantics of the label *hurt feelings*, and we wonder what they indicate about the nature of the experience itself. Unlike every other common emotion, *hurt feelings* has no clear synonym in the English language. Most emotions have many English equivalents or near-equivalents. For example, *sad, depressed, blue, down, despondent, melancholy, glum,* and *unhappy* all connote the same general experience (with slightly different emphases). However, no other word reflects the same experience as *hurt feelings*. Certain words, such as *wounded* and *pained*, seem to capture aspects of the feeling, but people rarely use those terms to describe it.

This is not only an interesting semantic issue, but it also raises problems for the measurement of hurt feelings. Typically, self-report measures of feeling-states ask respondents to rate themselves on a set of synonyms (such as *anxious, tense, nervous,* and *fearful* in the case of a measure of anxiety), but this tack is difficult when an emotion such as *hurt feelings* has no close synonyms.

We are also struck by the fact that *hurt feelings* is a peculiar label given that other emotions often "hurt" in the sense of creating intense psychological distress or emotional "pain." People who are grief-stricken, for example, may say they hurt deeply, but they would be unlikely to say that the loved one's death had "hurt their feelings." Thus, the experience that we call *hurt feelings* is not precisely the same as that of feeling *hurt* in a more generic sense. *Hurt,* broadly defined, seems to involve any experience that is "harmful, traumatic, threatening, stressful, destructive, discounting, and debilitating to one's welfare, importance, well-being, and existence" (L'Abate, 1997, p. 115). Thus, people may "hurt" emotionally when they lose loved ones, are the victim of sexual aggression, or suffer irretrievable losses, but again, these feelings are different from what people mean when they say that others have hurt their feelings. As a result, the meaning of *hurt* is sometimes ambiguous as a label for a type of emotional distress. In this chapter, what we have to say about *hurt feelings* does not necessarily apply to the more general experience of *hurt.*

Although everyone knows what it feels like to be hurt, the precise nature of the emotional experience is far from clear. Emotion theorists have not discussed hurt feelings in their analyses of human emotions (Frijda, 1986; Izard, 1991; Plutchik, 1980) and, indeed, few writers have even mentioned the term in any scholarly context. To complicate matters, when people are hurt, they invariably experience not only hurt feelings but other negative emotions as well (Leary, Springer, et al., 1998; Leary et al., 1999; Strausser, 1997). In light of these facts, two fundamental questions arise: Is hurt a unique emotion that can be distinguished from other feeling states and, if so, why are hurt feelings so strongly associated with other negative emotions?

Emotional Nature of Hurt Feelings

Early in our research, we considered the possibility that hurt feelings was not a distinct emotional experience but rather a blend or conglomerate of other emotions. People whose feelings are hurt typically experience one or more other aversive emotions, so perhaps the experience of hurt emerges from combinations of other feelings. Indeed, it is difficult to imagine a situation in which a person's feelings were hurt but the individual did not feel simultaneously sad, angry, anxious, jealous, lonely, or otherwise upset. Even so, as we talked to people about their experiences with being hurt and reflected on our own hurtful experiences, we came to the conclusion that, even with other concomitant emotions stripped away, the subjective experience of hurt feelings has a poignant quality that distinguishes it from other feeling states. People have a difficult time articulating precisely what this quality is; we have heard it described as a "psychic ache," "cutting stab," "sinking inner pain," "painful emotional twinge," and so on. Although these phrases may be obtuse, they do not seem to characterize other common emotions that tend to occur with hurt feelings (such as anger, fear, and sadness). Rightly or wrongly, people generally think that they are able to tell the subjective difference between hurt feelings and other emotions.

To examine the emotional features of hurt feelings empirically, we conducted two studies to see whether the experience of being hurt is, in fact, reducible to other emotions (Leary et al., 1999). In the first study, participants recalled a specific time when someone had hurt their feelings, then rated how they felt at the time on 29 emotion adjectives. These adjectives, most of which were taken from the Positive and Negative Affect Schedule (PANAS; Watson & Clark, 1994), were chosen to reflect a comprehensive array of negative feelings. In the second study, a laboratory experiment, we induced mild hurt feelings by leading some participants to believe that a "team captain" (who was actually a confederate) had selected them last for a 5-person laboratory "team" that would subsequently work on an unspecified task. (This procedure was inspired by childhood experiences of being chosen last for schoolyard teams.) Participants then completed all 60 items on the PANAS and the 25 items on the revised Multiple Affect Adjective Check List (MAACL–R; Zuckerman & Lubin, 1985; Zuckerman, Lubin, & Rinck, 1983).

In both studies, two measures of hurt feelings were also administered that assessed hurt feelings in different ways. We were interested in whether one measure of hurt feelings could predict the other measure of hurt feelings after all of the other emotional measures were partialed out. If hurt feelings is nothing more than a blend or conglomerate of other feelings, then comprehensive measures of negative emotions (such as the PANAS and MAACL–R) ought to account for all of the reliable variance in hurt feelings, leaving no additional variance that is unique to feeling hurt. However, if hurt feelings is somehow distinct from other negative emotions, then unique variance in hurt feelings should remain even after dozens of other emotional ratings are partialed out.

The results for both studies were clear: After partialing out all of the other emotional measures (including items that assessed general emotional distress, such as being upset and distressed), one measure of hurt feelings could still account for variance (ranging from 6 to 13% depending on the analysis) in the other measure of hurt feelings. Thus, our tentative conclusion is that hurt is a distinct emotional experience that cannot be reduced to other negative emotions. This conclusion is buttressed by the fact that hurt feelings were predicted by different features of our respondents' experiences than the other emotions that they reported. For example, hurt feelings were predicted by the degree to which participants felt that other people did not value having a relationship with them, whereas sadness, anger, guilt, and fear were predicted by other factors (Leary et al., 1999).

Relationships to Other Emotions

Although these studies provided evidence that hurt feelings is a distinct emotional experience, they also showed that hurt is related to other negative emotions. In both studies, hurt feelings correlated positively with feeling sad, guilty, anxious, and angry. The question arises, then, of why hurt feelings tend to be associated with other negative emotions.

One possibility is that negative emotions are intercorrelated because they share a common core of undifferentiated negative affect. Dimensional models of emotion (as opposed to models that are based on taxonomies of discrete emotions) suggest that the primary dimension of emotional experience involves affective valence—whether the emotion is pleasant or unpleasant (Larsen & Diener, 1992; Russell, 1980; Watson & Tellegen, 1985). All of the emotions that tend to accompany hurt feelings share a common aversive quality, which is then colored by feelings that are specific to each particular emotion. Leary et al. (1999) found that between 60% and 70% of the variance in participants' ratings of various negative emotions—anger, sadness, fear, hurt, distress, and so on—appeared to involve a core of aversive affect that is common to most if not all unpleasant emotions.

Beyond the fact that all negative emotions are unpleasant, hurt feelings may be accompanied by other negative emotions because the situations that induce hurt feelings trigger other emotions as well. For example, a rejecting experience that causes a person's feelings to be hurt may also involve a loss of a relationship (thereby triggering sadness), decreased security (leading to anxiety), or an unjustified attack (causing anger). Thus, these various emotions may be co-effects of a single situation that has implications for various kinds of personal concerns (Frijda, 1986).

A THEORY OF HURT FEELINGS

Emotion theorists have expended great effort identifying the necessary and sufficient conditions that elicit common emotions. Most perspectives that have been offered to distinguish one emotion from another focus on how people appraise and interpret events that have personal relevance. For example, theorists have explained emotions in terms of cognitive appraisals (Lazarus, Kanner, & Folkman, 1980), personal concerns (Frijda, 1986), and attributions (Weiner, 1986). However, with the exception of Vangelisti's (1994; Vangelisti & Young, 1999) attributional analysis, the cognitive underpinnings of hurt feelings have not been explored.

Our view is that the cognitive appraisal that lies at the core of all instances of hurt feelings involves *relational devaluation*—the perception that another person does not regard his or her relationship with the individual to be as close, important, or valuable as the individual desires (Leary, Springer, et al., 1998). In extreme cases, relational devaluation may be total and unambiguous, as when people are told explicitly that another person wants nothing whatsoever to do with them ever again. In less extreme cases, relational devaluation may be subtle and implicit, as when people have the sense that others are simply not interested in interacting with them or are unwilling to expend effort and energy to maintain a relationship. In all cases, however, hurt feelings arise from perceived relational devaluation.

We are intentionally using the term *relational devaluation* rather than *low relational value* because simply believing that another person does not value one's relationship or regards it as unimportant does not, by itself, cause hurt feelings. One must feel relationally *devalued* in the sense of believing that another person values one's relationship less than one desires or, often, less than the other person valued it previously. Relational devaluation must be judged relative to the degree to which the person wants particular people to value their relationships with him or her.

Several pieces of evidence support the idea that perceived relational devaluation lies at the heart of hurt feelings. First, the intensity of people's hurt feelings correlates highly (.63) with how rejected (i.e., relationally devalued) they felt at the time (Leary, Springer, et al., 1998). Although hurt feelings correlate highly with feelings of rejection, hurt does not correlate with feelings of being disliked. Apparently, events must have direct implications for relational devaluation in order to hurt. Second, when relational devaluation is measured more directly—as the difference between how much people want others to value relationships with them and how relationally valued they think they actually are—perceived devaluation correlates moderately with how hurt people think they would feel in hypothetical situations (Hechenbleikner & Leary, 1999). Finally, when we content analyzed 118 respondents' descriptions of hurtful experiences, we found evidence of relational devaluation in every one of their narratives (Leary et al., 1999).

Hurt feelings may be triggered even long after the initial hurtful event when the person later thinks about the experience. Even though the majority of the hurtful events they reported had occurred more than a year earlier (and some as much as 10 years before), more than 90% of the respondents in one study indicated that the event still evoked negative feelings for them, and 33% characterized those feelings as "strong or painfully negative" (Leary, Springer, et al., 1998). Presumably, memories of the event evoke a sense of relational devaluation each time the experience is recalled, causing hurt feelings all over again.

Conceptualizing hurt feelings as a response to perceived relational devaluation has a couple of intriguing implications. First, people may feel hurt even when they know that others like and value them if they believe that others do not value their relationship as much as they desire or as much as the others did before. So, a man may be hurt even though he believes that a particular woman loves him if he feels that she does not love him "enough." Similarly, friends may hurt one another when they do not seem to value the friendship sufficiently even though they know that they are, in fact, friends (and thus each values the relationship to some degree). In fact, many instances of hurt feelings occur within ongoing relationships in which people are assured of the ongoing love and support of the other individual. Yet, particular events can nonetheless induce a sense of relational devaluation that hurts their feelings.

A second implication is that the perceived cause of relational devaluation is only weakly related to whether or not one is hurt by it. For example, a man who is abandoned by his romantic partner would likely be hurt whether he attributed the rejection to himself (e.g., "my partner left me because I'm a loser"), to the partner (e.g., "my partner left me because she isn't ready to settle down"), or to interpersonal or relational factors (e.g., "my partner left because we weren't getting along"). In a study of people's attributions for hurtful events, Vangelisti (1994) found that participants most commonly attributed the hurtful event to the other person but also made attributions to the relationship and to external factors. It appears, then, that the nature of one's attributions is not a strong determinant of whether or not people feel hurt as long as they experience relational devaluation. Even so, certain attributions may lower the likelihood of hurt if they diminish the degree to which the action connotes relational devaluation (e.g., "my partner left me because she was in a fugue state").

TYPES OF HURTFUL EVENTS

People's feelings are hurt by a wide variety of verbal and nonverbal behaviors, involving both acts of commission (what other people say or do) and acts of omission (what other people do not say or do). One of the goals in our study of 168 participants' accounts of hurtful experiences (Leary, Springer, et al., 1998) was to identify the primary categories of hurtful events. In that study, we ultimately classified respondents' hurtful experiences into one of six basic categories: active disassociation, passive disassociation, criticism, teasing, betrayal, and feeling unappreciated. As we demonstrate, each kind of event appears to evoke hurt feelings because it connotes relational devaluation.

Active and Passive Disassociation

Hurtful events that most clearly connote relational devaluation involve interpersonal disassociation—situations in which one person conveys a desire not to associate with another (Leary, Springer, et al., 1998). In cases of *active disassociation*, the person is explicitly rejected, abandoned, or ostracized by other people. The dissolution of a romantic relationship constitutes an example of active disassociation, for example, as do cases of being disowned by one's family, expelled from groups, and otherwise ostracized (Williams, 1997). An example of active disassociation is shown in the account of a male participant in our research who wrote about the breakup of his friendship with a woman (DS) to whom he was attracted:

> I had been best friends with DS for a while, and I was beginning to develop deeper feelings for her. I wanted to be more than friends, so I told her how I felt. But DS told me that she couldn't do that and, now that she knew how I felt about her, we couldn't ever be friends again either. She told me to get out of her life. (As a side note, he added "my feelings were hurt bad, and I was depressed for months.")

In this example, the respondent received explicit information that DS did not value her relationship with him as much as he had desired.

In cases of *passive disassociation*, people are ignored, shunned, or simply not included but not rejected outright. Passive disassociation is exemplified by the narrative of a female participant who was not included in others' plans:

> It was the day of the homecoming game, and plans were being made to go. None of the girls on my hall [in the dorm] thought to include me in the plans or ask if I needed a ride to the game.

Similarly, another respondent reported being hurt when a friend who knew that she was in the hospital did not call or visit to see how she was doing.

In cases of passive disassociation such as these, people have not received any kind of explicit indication that others do not value their relationship, but they nonetheless infer relational devaluation on the basis of others' actions. Nothing in these women's accounts, for example, suggested that they were actually rejected by their dormmates or friends, yet their feelings were hurt. It is interesting that people feel rejected in cases of passive disassociation (and may even say that they were rejected) even though rejection has not actually occurred and the event is more accurately characterized as noninclusion. From an outsider's perspective, many instances of passive disassociation involve neither rejection nor relational devaluation, but they are experienced as such.

A particular event may be interpreted as either outright rejection or as simply not being included depending on the pre-existing relationship between the people involved and their expectations regarding whether they ought to have been included. For example, although a friend may feel left out, and perhaps even mildly hurt, when not told that one was having major surgery, he or she would not necessarily feel rejected. In contrast, one's spouse might well feel explicitly rejected (and hurt, if not angry) if not informed about one's operation.

Many cases of disassociation occur when an individual chooses to spend time with one person rather than another or decides to spend time in a solitary activity rather than with the other person. In these cases, an observer could not tell whether the choice reflected a true devaluation of the relationship or merely a temporary preference for doing something else other than spending time with the individual. Yet, people sometimes interpret the other person's choice as an indication that he or she does not sufficiently value the relationship. This reaction was reflected in the account of a female respondent whose feelings were hurt because her boyfriend chose to work overtime rather than spend time with her. She noted that she understood that he needed the money, but she nonetheless felt "unimportant and rejected."

Elections are interesting cases of relational devaluation. Although defeated candidates undoubtedly feel that others do not value their relationships with them as much as they would desire, it is usually not clear whether the results of an election reflect the "acceptance" of one candidate and the "rejection" of the other, or simply a slight preference for one of two acceptable candidates. As we have noted, people often experience others' reactions as rejection even when they were not rejected in an objective, absolute sense. In the case of a close election, the defeated candidate knows that many voters did in fact prefer him or her over the victor, yet the fact that more people preferred the other candidate may hurt his or her feelings. It is informative that, after losing the 1980 presidential election to Ronald Reagan, incumbent Jimmy Carter acknowledged in his concession speech that "I can't stand here and tell you that it doesn't hurt" even though more than 36 million people (over 42% of the voters in a three-candidate election) voted for him. In Carter's case, the defeat was experienced as devaluation because he had won the previous election. Clearly, people did not value their relationship with him as much as they did previously and certainly not as much as he had desired.

Criticism

Criticism accounted for the greatest proportion of cases of hurt feelings reported by Leary, Springer, et al. (1998). In our view, people's feelings are hurt by criticism not because criticism threatens their self-image or ego (as some have supposed), but rather because it inherently conveys a negative evaluation of the individual and, by implication, a devaluation of the relationship. The hidden (or, sometimes, not so hidden) message behind criticism is often that undesirable aspects of the individual's behavior, personality, or performance have led the criticizer to value the relationship less than he or she otherwise would.

For example, one of our respondents indicated she was hurt when her boyfriend told her that another woman was thinner and prettier than she was. (In her defense, the respondent added that, "although it was true that she may have been thinner, she was a trashy slut.") In some cases, the criticism is tied explicitly to a breach in the relationship, as in the account of a male participant who wrote about his father's reaction to a high school soccer game:

> I was playing in a soccer match and wasn't playing all that well. I was already disappointed in myself for not playing well, but after the game my dad said that I should just quit soccer and to remind him never to come to watch one of my games again.

Criticisms such as this one that are directly linked to a breach in the relationship should be particularly hurtful, but criticisms that clearly do not imply relational devaluation should not hurt people's feelings (although individuals may find them troubling for other reasons). As noted earlier, simply feeling disliked does not appear to hurt people's feelings unless the disliking implies a potential for rejection (Leary, Springer, et al., 1998).

Knowing this, people often preface their criticisms of loved ones with assurances that no relational devaluation is intended. So, when a person says to a romantic partner "You know I adore you honey, but I can't stand it when you (fill in the blank)," he or she is trying to minimize the effects of the negative judgment on the partner's feelings. Previous research shows that both adults and children who imagine rejecting another person expect that the other person will be hurt more if he or she feels personally responsible for the rejection (Folkes, 1982; Weiner & Handel, 1985). From our perspective, the important consideration is not whether the person's attribution is internal or external, but rather whether he or she interprets the criticism as evidence of relational devaluation. Thus, when people try to buffer the impact of criticism and other potentially hurtful behaviors, they try to lead the other person not to infer relational devaluation from what they say or do.

Betrayal

People who feel betrayed often experience intense hurt (Auerback, 1987; Fitness, in press; Meyerling & Epling-McWherter, 1987). Although people tend to think of betrayal primarily in terms of romantic or sexual infidelity, our respondents have recounted other kinds of hurtful betrayals. For example, one woman wrote,

> I was angry with my best friend, who happened to be involved with one of my good male friends. They had a fight, and I was sympathetic to him and told him that maybe he should find someone else. Although he'd promised not to (and even thanked me for my support at the time), he told my best friend everything I said about her. My best friend never spoke to me again.

In her ratings, this respondent rated herself as maximally hurt by her male friend's betrayal of her confidence (marking a 12 on a 12-point scale) and indicated that his behavior indicated to her that he did not regard their relationship as valuable or important at all (1 on a 12-point scale).

Certain kinds of broken promises fall into the betrayal category. Not all broken promises cause hurt feelings, but when they convey a lack of concern for the relationship, people feel hurt. The implications of broken promises for relational devaluation help explain why people sometimes become upset when others do not follow through on what they said they were going to do even when, in an objective sense, the broken promise has no real importance. In cases such as these, people are reacting to the implications of the broken promise for relational devaluation rather than to the broken promise itself. The victim's reaction seems predicated on the idea that "If you valued our relationship, you would have done what you told me you were going to do!" The guilty party, on the other hand, often does not understand the strength of the person's reactions to the broken promise because no relational devaluation was intended ("What does it matter if I forgot we were going out to dinner tonight? We can go tomorrow night.").

Teasing

Some participants in our studies recounted situations in which they were hurt by being teased. Like betrayal, teasing often involves behaviors that presumably would not have occurred if the perpetrator had adequately valued his or her relationship with the target of the tease. People do not meanly tease those whose relationships they value. One woman wrote about having her feelings hurt when she was teased by one of her male friends:

> I was walking on the quad [on campus] one day and saw GT. I was wearing jeans and a white sweatshirt, and he said "You look like a white marshmallow."

Another respondent recounted being teased for "liking an ugly girl" when he was in the fifth grade. He reported feeling "completely rejected" and "very hurt." (He also noted that he "got mad and started yelling and screaming," which got him into trouble with his teacher.)

Of course, not all teasing hurts people's feelings, and, in fact, it can sometimes create or bolster a sense of camaraderie (Kowalski, Howerton, & McKenzie, chapter 7, this volume). Sharkey (1992, 1997) has discussed the conditions under which intentionally embarrassing someone can increase rather than decrease solidarity and closeness. We predict that teasing hurts people's feelings to the degree that the victim interprets the tease as an indication of relational devaluation. Teases that appear intended to hurt and or that disregard the relationship between the individuals should hurt people's feelings, but those that are interpreted as good-natured kidding should not. In fact, teases that are interpreted as reflecting a strong bond between two people should actually create a sense of relational appreciation and positive feelings.

Feeling Unappreciated

Some participants recounted instances in which they felt hurt because other people did not adequately appreciate them. Clearly, lack of appreciation connotes that the unappreciative party does not value his or her relationship with the person as much as the person would like. One male participant, for example, reported feeling hurt as he sat on the bench for long periods during basketball games, feeling unappreciated by his coach and teammates. In a different vein, a female participant wrote about feeling unappreciated by her boyfriend. Although she worked very hard to make him happy, he seemed not to notice or appreciate everything that she did for him, and his lack of appreciation hurt her feelings. In cases such as these, the sense of relational devaluation is palpable.

RELATIONAL MODERATORS OF HURTFULNESS

Not only do some events typically cause greater hurt than others (e.g., sexual infidelity usually hurts more than a forgotten birthday), but a particular event may induce different degrees of hurt depending on the nature of the relationship between the individuals involved. Most of the hurtful events described by the participants in our studies were caused by people whom our participants not only knew well, but were in relationships with at the time of the hurtful episode. For example, close friends and romantic or dating partners figured in more than 70% of the hurtful events, and family members, acquaintances, and authority figures (such as teachers and coaches) were involved in an additional 26%. Instances in which strangers caused the hurt accounted for only 2% of the cases (Leary, Springer, et al., 1998). These data support L'Abate's (1997) observation that people tend not to be hurt by

> discourteous strangers, rude salespersons, or occasional acquaintances. We may be annoyed or offended by them, but the power to hurt is usually reserved to those few, important individuals, family and friends, who are linked to us by attachment and love ties. . . . Thus, we are not only vulnerable to being hurt by those we love, but we are also fallible in hurting them, often without intending to do so. (p. 135)

People who are close to us not only have many more opportunities to hurt us than strangers, but the hurtful behaviors enacted by friends, romantic partners, family members, and other loved ones often involve more important matters than the hurtful actions of strangers. Furthermore, because hurt feelings arise when people feel that others do not adequately value their relationships, people are more hurt by those whose relational appreciation they desire. According to relational devaluation theory, the more that a person desires to be relationally valued, the more likely he or she is hurt by indications of relational devaluation. Because people want their friends, partners, and family members to value their relationships more than acquaintances and strangers, they are more vulnerable to being hurt by intimates. A behavior that may cause little reaction when coming from a stranger may hurt one's feelings deeply if performed by a person by whom one desires to be relationally valued.

When people are hurt by those with whom they are in relationships, their reactions may be moderated by the degree of closeness and satisfaction they feel in the relationship prior to the hurtful event (Vangelisti & Crumley, 1998). People who are satisfied with the relationship and who generally feel close to the other person may feel less hurt, particularly by minor infractions, than those who feel less satisfied and close. In support of this notion, relationship satisfaction correlated negatively not only with how hurt people felt after a hurtful event but also with the degree to which the event had a negative effect on the relationship (Vangelisti & Crumley, 1998). This finding may reflect the fact that people are less likely to interpret potentially hurtful behaviors that occur in the context of an otherwise close and satisfying relationship as evidence of relational devaluation than the same behaviors enacted in a troubled, unsatisfying relationship. A person who feels loved and valued is more likely to attribute occasional hurtful behaviors to factors other than the other person's lack of regard. More generally, research shows that people who are happy with their close relationships make more benevolent attributions for their partners' negative behaviors (Bradbury & Fincham, 1990).

Although we appear to be hurt more often and more deeply by those who are close to us (or at least by those with whom we desire to be close) than by strangers, we should not conclude that people are never hurt by strangers. In fact, experimental studies show that people who are barely acquainted can, in fact, hurt one another's feelings. When Strausser (1997) experimentally manipulated hurt feelings by leading participants to believe that a confederate had selected them either first or last for a 5-person laboratory team, participants who were selected last reported feeling more hurt than those who were selected first, presumably because being selected last connoted relational devaluation. More importantly, participants were hurt even though they had only 20 seconds of prior contact with the rejecting confederate.

In another study, Snapp and Leary (in press) experimentally manipulated how well a confederate (posing as another participant) knew each participant. Some participants had brief, superficial interactions with the confederate, whereas other participants had extended interviews in which the confederate learned a great deal about them. Then, two participants were placed in separate booths and told to talk about themselves over an intercom to the confederate who was listening from another room. The participants were instructed to talk continuously, and they were told that the confederate could listen to only one of them at a time by switching back and forth between them. Each participant could ostensibly tell when the confederate was listening to him or her (as opposed to the other participant) when a light on his or her microphone illuminated. Relational evaluation was manipulated by the percentage of time that the participant's light was turned on. Half of the participants thought that the confederate listened to them about 75% of the time, and the other half thought he or she listened only 25% of the time. Participants reported the greatest hurt feelings when they were ignored by a confederate who was only minimally and superficially familiar with them. One possible explanation for this finding is that, when people are rejected by those who have very little information about them, they may conclude that the other person had an unusually strong, immediate, and negative reaction to them based on the short and superficial contact. Immediate rejection by someone who barely knows us conveys greater relational devaluation than rejection by someone who knows us a bit better.

INDIVIDUAL DIFFERENCES IN HURT-PRONENESS

To date, none of the research participants whom we have asked to recall a situation in which their feelings were hurt has been unable to do so. Every individual can be hurt; in fact, the inability to have one's feelings hurt probably indicates the presence of a serious psychological disorder. Yet, although virtually everyone experiences hurt feelings, people obviously differ in how frequently they are hurt and in the intensity of their experiences. Some, particularly "thick-skinned" individuals are rarely hurt, whereas other individuals are highly susceptible to hurt feelings. To explore individual differences in the propensity to experience hurt feelings, we developed the brief, 6-item Hurt-Proneness Scale shown in Exhibit 6.1. We started with a larger pool of items that appeared to be face-valid indicators of hurt feelings, then whittled them down until we had a short, reasonably reliable measure. (Cronbach's alpha coefficient for the Hurt-Proneness Scale is .80.)

The Hurt-Proneness Scale is a measure of the frequency with which people's feelings are hurt and not the degree to which they feel hurt by hurtful events. Although scores on the Hurt-Proneness Scale correlate significantly with how often people report being hurt in everyday life ($r = .65$), the scores do not correlate with the intensity of people's hurt feelings in a particular hurtful situation ($r = .11$, ns). Thus, the scale seems to tap into how easily people's feelings are hurt, which does not necessarily reflect their subjective experience when they are hurt.

According to relational devaluation theory, people with easily hurt feelings should be those who place a great deal of emphasis on having other people value relationships with them. We have administered the Hurt-Proneness Scale along with other measures in a number of contexts, and the picture that is emerging of the hurt-prone person is consistent with this hypothesis. Hurt-prone individuals are characterized by a high need for social acceptance and approval. For example, scores on the Hurt-Proneness Scale correlate significantly (.59) with scores on the Need to

---

EXHIBIT 6.1
The Hurt-Proneness Scale

1. My feelings are easily hurt.
2. I am a sensitive person.
3. I am "thick-skinned."
4. I take criticism well.
5. Being teased hurts my feelings.
6. I rarely feel hurt by what other people say or do to me.

Note. Respondents rate the degree to which each statement is true or characteristic of them on a 5-point scale, where 1 = *not at all*, 2 = *slightly*, 3 = *moderately*, 4 = *very*, and 5 = *extremely characteristic of me*. The respondent's score is obtained by reverse-scoring Items 3, 4, and 6 and then summing the responses.

Belong Scale, a measure of the degree to which people desire to be accepted and included by other people (Leary, 1997). Hurt-proneness also correlates with various forms of interpersonal dependency that reflect the desire to be accepted and esteemed (Pincus & Gurtman, 1995; $r = .37–.54$). Furthermore, hurt-proneness correlates with endorsing personal values that reflect an emphasis on close relationships. When we administered the Hurt-Proneness Scale along with Rokeach's (1973) Value Survey to 85 undergraduate students, hurt-proneness correlated with the degree to which respondents valued both "true friendship" and "mature love." Given their interest in forming and maintaining relationships, it is not surprising that hurt-prone people are particularly sensitive to the judgments and evaluations of other people. For example, hurt-proneness correlates with the degree to which people are afraid of being evaluated negatively by other people ($r = .61$). Clearly, hurt-prone individuals place a great deal of emphasis on being approved of, accepted, and valued as relational partners.

Hurt-proneness also correlates moderately with trait self-esteem (rs range from $-.31$ to $-.45$, depending on the measure of self-esteem). Trait self-esteem reflects the degree to which people believe that they are valued and accepted by other people (Leary, Haupt, Strausser, & Chokel, 1998; Leary, Tambor, Terdal, & Downs, 1995), and people with low self-esteem feel less certain that others value their relationships than people with high self-esteem (although they do not necessarily feel rejected per se). Because they feel less relationally valued, people with lower self-esteem are more attuned to the possibility of rejection and, thus, react more strongly when they detect cues that connote relational devaluation. As a result, they are more prone to being hurt than people with high self-esteem.

People who tend to have their feelings hurt also score higher on measures of negative affectivity ($r = .36$) and neuroticism ($r = .58$) than people who are less disposed to be hurt, but they do not score lower on measures of positive affect. (Neuroticism is the only one of the "big five" personality factors that correlates with hurt-proneness.) It is unclear whether they tend to be high in negative affectivity because they are hurt more frequently or whether a tendency to experience negative affect predisposes people to experience hurt feelings.

EVOLUTIONARY UNDERPINNINGS OF HURT FEELINGS

Although cross-cultural data regarding hurt feelings have not been collected, anecdotal evidence suggests that hurt feelings are widespread, if not universal. That hurt feelings appear to be an inherent feature of human nature suggests that the capacity for hurt feelings evolved because it conferred an adaptive advantage. Virtually all emotion theorists since Darwin (1872/1998) have assumed that the capacity to experience various emotions evolved because it enhanced inclusive fitness. The adaptive signifi-cance of many social emotions—including anxiety, embarrassment, grief, and shame—has been considered (see Baumeister & Tice, 1990; Frijda, 1986; Leary, Koch, & Hechenbleikner, in press; Miller & Leary, 1992; Neese, 1990; Plutchik, 1980; Tooby & Cosmides, 1990), but not hurt feelings.

The notion that hurt feelings arise from perceived relational deval-uation helps answer the functional question by focusing on the adaptive benefits of being valued by other people. Baumeister and Leary (1995) have argued that the need to belong is a fundamental human motivation—that "human beings have a pervasive drive to form and maintain at least a minimum quantity of lasting, positive, and significant interpersonal rela-tionships" (p. 497). Put differently, people inherently desire that other people value having relationships with them. The origin of such a moti-vation is easy to understand in evolutionary terms. Because solitary human beings are rather helpless and defenseless creatures, natural selection would have favored homonids and early human beings who sought the company of other people. Prehistoric people who formed mutually supportive rela-tionships and lived in groups undoubtedly fared better in terms of survival and, hence, reproduction, than those who were content to live alone or who avoided other humans (Tooby & Cosmides, 1996). Thus, over time, biopsychological systems arose that motivated sociality and group living.

One system involved emotional responses to real and potential social rejection. Because ostracism or abandonment by others deprived the re-jected individual of the protective affordances of other people, even the prospect of rejection came to elicit strong emotional reactions. Like all social emotions, these responses to real or potential rejection served to energize the person's behavior and to communicate his or her inner state to others (Frijda, 1986). Most importantly, however, the mere prospect of experiencing aversive emotions helped the individual avoid doing things that would lead to rejection in the first place. Just as one function of pain is to help us avoid damaging ourselves physically, one function of negative affect—psychic pain—is to avoid damaging ourselves socially (which, in the ancestral environment, would have had dire physical consequences as well; Baumeister & Tice, 1990).

Several emotions appear to be reactions to real, potential, and imag-ined relational devaluation. For example, people feel socially anxious when they do not think they make impressions on others that lead others to accept them, jealous when relational ties are threatened because of the intrusion of a third party, and lonely when they feel that their relational connections are inadequate (Leary, 1990; Leary et al., in press). Hurt feel-ings appear to be among the emotions that occur when relational bonds are threatened. The potential for hurt feelings motivates people to protect their social relationships and to treat other people in ways that lead to high relational evaluation. In addition, the actual experience of hurt feelings alerts people to threats to their relationships with others and motivates remedial actions.

BEHAVIORAL REACTIONS TO HURTFUL EVENTS

People react to hurtful events in a variety of ways. In this section we examine four common responses to being hurt: crying, aggressing, derogating, and seeking other relationships.

Crying

People often cry when their feelings are hurt. Although people tend to think of crying as a relatively involuntary response to distressing events, data suggest that people have some degree of control over whether they cry when hurt. For example, a much higher proportion of our participants indicated that they had cried later when they were alone than cried in front of the person who had hurt them, suggesting that some of them purposefully withheld their crying while in the presence of other people. Not surprisingly, the likelihood of crying is related to how badly the person's feelings were hurt (rs = .37 and .60 between hurt feelings and crying in front of the person and crying when alone, respectively; Leary, Springer, et al., 1998).[2]

A gender difference also emerged that reflects the effects of the social context on hurt-induced crying. Women were as likely to cry in front of women who hurt them as in front of men. In contrast, although men were as likely as women to cry in front of women who hurt them, they were far less likely to cry in front of men. (In fact, none of the male respondents reported crying in front of other men who hurt their feelings; Leary, Springer, et al., 1998.) Although not at all surprising, this pattern shows that people often control where and when they cry when others hurt them. Whether people allow others to see them cry may reflect an interpersonal strategy as much as an expression of emotion. People may be most likely to cry when they want the person who hurt them to know it (perhaps to make the other person feel guilty or to offer reassurance), but they may suppress crying when they do not want the other person to know they are hurt (so as not to appear overly sensitive, or to deny the other person the "satisfaction" of knowing that they were hurt). In support of this idea,

---

[2]Vangelisti and Crumley (1998) reported that only 9% of their participants indicated crying in response to the hurtful event that they recounted. However, their data involved coding participants' narrative accounts of hurtful experiences, and participants may not have always remembered or mentioned everything they did when hurt. In contrast, our participants indicated whether or not they had performed each of several specified behaviors.

verbally telling the other person that one was hurt correlated with crying in that person's presence ($r = .51$).

Aggressing

People often get angry when they are hurt, so it is not surprising that they often lash out at those who hurt them (and sometimes at others as well). In our initial study of people's narratives about hurtful events (Leary, Springer, et al., 1998), 80% of the respondents indicated that they had expressed anger to the person who had hurt them, and over half indicated that they had said something critical or nasty to the person. Not surprisingly, aggressive verbal reactions were correlated with how angry and hostile the person felt at the time. Unfortunately, we lacked the foresight to ask whether our respondents had reacted with physical aggression when they were hurt, but we suspect that people sometimes do. In fact, many cases of violence among spouses and dating partners appear to be precipitated by events in which one person interprets the another's behaviors as relational devaluation (Mack, 1989; Makepeace, 1989).

Retaliatory aggression would seem to be most likely when people believe that the person behaved intentionally and particularly when they think that the person specifically intended to hurt them. Research on roommates and married couples shows that aggressive responses to negative behaviors—conflict escalation, criticism, and the like—are increased by attributions of intentionality (Doherty, 1982; Sillars, 1980). Along these lines, we found a positive correlation (.28) between respondents' beliefs that the person had purposefully tried to hurt their feelings and the degree to which they reacted in a critical, nasty fashion after being hurt.

Derogating

Being hurt also leads people to derogate the person who hurt them and to depreciate their relationship with that person. In the study described earlier in which participants were chosen either first or last for a laboratory team (Strausser, 1997), participants who were hurt by being chosen last subsequently rated the team captain less positively than those who were selected first. Given that their interactions with the team captains were constant across conditions, this effect reflects a post hoc reevaluation of the individuals who hurt them.

Hurtful events also lead people to reevaluate their interest in the relationship and often to conclude that they did not want to be accepted after all (Strausser, 1997). For example, Leary et al. (1995) found that participants who were excluded from a group by a vote of the other group members—presumably a hurtful experience—subsequently indicated that they did not want to be a member of the group anyway.

Derogating the other person and one's relationship with him or her may reflect attempts to retaliate for the hurtful experience. As noted, people often want to hurt those who hurt them, and derogation is one means of doing so. In addition, however, derogating one's hurter may help buffer the individual from feeling hurt. A sour-grapes rationalization—that the hurtful person is not a desirable relational partner and that the relationship was not important anyway—may help lower the hurt one feels after relational devaluation.

Seeking Other Relationships

The narratives that our participants wrote about hurt feelings commonly concluded with a statement indicating that the participant found an alternative relationship to replace the one that was damaged by the hurtful event. Predictably, this resolution is most likely when the relationship was irreparably damaged by the experience. For example, the female student described earlier who was left out of her dormmates' homecoming plans concluded her narrative by writing, "I found another ride to the homecoming game. I've also found other friends to hang out and do things with." Similarly, a male respondent told about being hurt when he was jilted by a woman he dated, which prompted him to "hook up with" (i.e., have sex with) another woman the same evening.

Given the strong drive to maintain close interpersonal relationships, such reactions are not surprising. The loss of a valued relationship should lead the person to seek replacements (Baumeister & Leary, 1995). Even if the hurtful event does not cause the relationship to end, feeling that one is not adequately valued as a relational partner should induce people to explore other relationships in which they may be more highly valued. In addition, this substitution pattern may reflect a simple desire to promote positive feelings. Forming new relationships may represent a more pleasant way to spend one's time after experiencing relational devaluation than pining away by oneself.[3]

WHY PEOPLE HURT OTHERS

Thus far, we have focused on people's feelings and behavior when they are hurt and more or less ignored the motives, behaviors, and feelings of those who hurt them. To conclude the chapter, we turn our attention briefly to the perpetrators of hurt feelings. Given the strong human drive

---

[3]We also have the sense that some participants may have mentioned their newfound relationships for our benefit. Having described an event in which they were ostracized or rejected by other people, participants may have wanted to convince whoever would later read the essay that the hurtful event was not a reflection on their own acceptability or desirability.

to form and maintain interpersonal relationships, why do people so often do things that convey to others that they do not value having relationships with them?

Perhaps the best answer to this question is that people do not usually intend to hurt other people's feelings but rather do so out of thoughtlessness, lack of consideration, or indifference. After participants wrote about an episode in which they had hurt someone else's feelings, we asked why they had done so. The vast majority of the participants maintained that they had not meant to hurt the other person—that it had been an accident or that they had simply been insensitive or inconsiderate. In fact, less than 20% of our respondents gave any indication that they had intended to hurt the other person. Although we might suspect these hurt perpetrators of denying personal responsibility for self-serving reasons, the victims of others' hurtful actions tell roughly the same story. Only about 30% of the victims of hurtful actions thought that the other person had intended to hurt them, and most thought that the person had simply been insensitive or inconsiderate (Leary, Springer, et al., 1998).

We were initially surprised that people were so often hurt by behaviors that they believed were unintentional. Our explanation for this finding is that even unintended actions may convey information about how highly one person values his or her relationship with another. If a friend forgets one's birthday, for example, the lapse of memory was clearly not intended. Even so, the individual may have difficulty shaking the conclusion that the friend would have remembered the birthday if he or she truly valued the individual and the relationship. People appear to assume that those who value their relationships do not behave in inconsiderate and insensitive ways.

This is not to say that perceptions of intentionality are unimportant, however. People clearly feel more hurt when they perceive that the person intended to hurt them (Leary, Springer, et al., 1998; Vangelisti & Young, 1999). We assume that this pattern emerges because intentionally hurting someone implies greater relational devaluation than unintentionally doing so.

Although most people do not intend to hurt others, some do. It is not completely clear why people intentionally try to hurt others' feelings, but in at least some cases, the action is in retaliation for perceived mistreatment. About one-third of our respondents admitted that they had acted in a hurtful manner in order to "get the person back" for something he or she had done.

CONCLUSION

Although people are frequently hurt and hurtful events result in both aversive feelings and maladaptive reactions that can undermine (if not destroy) personal relationships, psychologists and other behavioral researchers have not devoted sufficient attention to the phenomenon of hurt feelings. Hurt feelings cut to the core of human relationships, signaling that other people do not value their relationships with us as much as we desire. Given the importance of supportive relationships to human well-being, indications that others do not adequately value their relationships with us trigger strong emotions.

Thus, as unpleasant as they may be, hurt feelings are fundamentally adaptive. Of course, some people are excessively prone to experience hurt feelings, presumably because they are overly concerned about being appreciated as a relational partner or tend to interpret others' behaviors as reflecting relational devaluation. Such individuals not only experience a great deal of psychological distress, but their fears of being hurt may impede the formation of trusting relationships and lead them to behave maladaptively when they are hurt.

As L'Abate (1997) has suggested, hurt is a fundamental but neglected emotion. Indeed, if hurt feelings were a person, its feelings would be hurt by the generations of researchers who have shunned it in favor of studying other emotions. We hope that this chapter and the theory of relational devaluation that we described stimulate a great deal of future research on this neglected emotion.

REFERENCES

Auerback, S. (1987). Groups for wives of gay and bisexual men. *Social Work, 32,* 321–325.

Baumeister, R. F., & Leary, M. R. (1995). The need to belong: Desire for interpersonal attachments as a fundamental human motivation. *Psychological Bulletin, 117,* 497–529.

Baumeister, R. F., & Tice, D. M. (1990). Anxiety and social exclusion. *Journal of Social and Clinical Psychology, 9,* 165–195.

Bradbury, T. N., & Fincham, F. D. (1990). Attributions in marriage: Review and critique: *Psychological Bulletin, 107,* 3–33.

Darwin, C. (1998). *The expression of the emotions in man and animals.* New York: Oxford University Press. (Original work published 1872)

Doherty, W. J. (1982). Attribution and negative problem solving in marriage. *Family Relations, 317,* 23–27.

Fitness, J. (in press). Betrayal and rejection, revenge and forgiveness: An interpersonal script approach. In M. R. Leary (Ed.), *Interpersonal rejection.* New York: Oxford University Press.

Folkes, V. S. (1982). Communicating the causes of social rejection. *Journal of Experimental Social Psychology, 18,* 235–252.

Frijda, N. (1986). *The emotions.* Cambridge, England: Cambridge University Press.

Hechenbleikner, N., & Leary, M. R. (1999, March). *Hurt feelings and relational devaluation*. Paper presented at the meeting of the Southeastern Psychological Association, Savannah, GA.

Izard, C. E. (1991). *The psychology of emotions*. New York: Plenum Press.

L'Abate, L. (1997). *The self in the family: A classification of personality, criminality, and psychopathology*. New York: Wiley.

Larsen, R. J., & Diener, E. (1992). Promises and problems with the circumplex model of emotion. In M. S. Clark (Ed.), *Emotion* (pp. 25–59). Newbury Park, CA: Sage Publications.

Lazarus, R. S., Kanner, A. D., & Folkman, S. (1980). Emotions: A cognitive–phenomenological analysis. In R. Plutchik & H. Kellerman (Eds.), *Theories of emotion: Vol. 1. Emotion: Theory, research, and experience* (pp. 189–217). New York: Academic Press.

Leary, M. R. (1990). Responses to social exclusion: Social anxiety, jealousy, loneliness, depression, and low self-esteem. *Journal of Social and Clinical Psychology, 9*, 221–229.

Leary, M. R. (1997, March). *People who need people: Individual differences in the need to belong*. Paper presented at the meeting of the Southeastern Psychological Association, Atlanta, GA.

Leary, M. R., Haupt, A., Strausser, K., & Chokel, J. (1998). Calibrating the sociometer: The relationship between interpersonal appraisals and state self-esteem. *Journal of Personality and Social Psychology, 74*, 1290–1299.

Leary, M. R., Hechenbleikner, N. R., Strausser, K. S., Higgins, K., & Stiles, K. (1999). *The emotional nature of hurt feelings*. Manuscript submitted for publication.

Leary, M. R., Koch, E. J., & Hechenbleikner, N. R. (in press). Emotional responses to interpersonal rejection: A theory of social emotion. In M. R. Leary (Ed.), *Interpersonal rejection*. New York: Oxford University Press.

Leary, M. R., Springer, C., Negel, L., Ansell, E., & Evans, K. (1998). The causes, phenomenology, and consequences of hurt feelings. *Journal of Personality and Social Psychology, 74*, 1225–1237.

Leary, M. R., Tambor, E. S., Terdal, S. K., & Downs, D. L. (1995). Self-esteem as an interpersonal monitor: The sociometer hypothesis. *Journal of Personality and Social Psychology, 68*, 518–530.

Mack, R. N. (1989). Spouse abuse: A dyadic approach. In G. R. Weeks (Ed.), *Treating couples* (pp. 191–214). New York: Brunner/Mazel.

Makepeace, J. (1989). Dating, living together, and courtship violence. In M. M. Pirog-Good & J. E. Stets (Eds.), *Violence in dating relationships* (pp. 94–103). New York: Praeger.

Meyerling, R., & Epling-McWherter, E. A. (1987). Decision making in extramarital relationships. *Lifestyles, 8*, 115–129.

Miller, R. S., & Leary, M. R. (1992). Social sources and interactive functions of emotion: The case of embarrassment. In M. S. Clark (Ed.), *Emotion and social behavior* (pp. 202–221). Beverly Hills, CA: Sage Publications.

Neese, R. M. (1990). Evolutionary explanations of emotions. *Human Nature, 1,* 261–289.

Pilkington, C. J., & Richardson, D. R. (1988). Perceptions of risk in intimacy. *Journal of Social and Personal Relationships, 5,* 503–508.

Pincus, A. L., & Gurtman, M. B. (1995). The three faces of interpersonal dependency: Structural analysis of self-report dependency measures. *Journal of Personality and Social Psychology, 69,* 744–758.

Plutchik, R. (1980). *Emotions: A psychoevolutionary synthesis.* New York: Harper & Row.

Rokeach, M. (1973). *The nature of human values.* New York: Free Press.

Russell, J. A. (1980). A circumplex model of affect. *Journal of Personality and Social Psychology, 39,* 1161–1178.

Sharkey, W. F. (1992). Uses and responses to intentional embarrassment. *Communication Studies, 43,* 257–275.

Sharkey, W. F. (1997). Why would anyone want to intentionally embarrass me? In R. M. Kowalski (Ed.), *Aversive interpersonal behaviors* (pp. 57–90). New York: Plenum Press.

Sillars, A. L. (1980). Attributions and communication in roommate conflicts. *Communication Monographs, 47,* 180–200.

Snapp, C., & Leary, M. R. (in press). Hurt feelings among new acquaintances: Moderating effects of interpersonal familiarity. *Journal of Social and Personal Relationships.*

Strausser, K. S. (1997). *The determinants and phenomenology of hurt feelings.* Unpublished master's thesis, Wake Forest University, Winston-Salem, NC.

Tooby, J., & Cosmides, L. (1990). The past explains the present: Emotional adaptations and the structure of the ancestral environment. *Ethology and Sociobiology, 11,* 375–424.

Tooby, J., & Cosmides, L. (1996). Friendship and the banker's paradox: Other pathways to the evolution of adaptations for altruism. *Proceedings of the British Academy, 88,* 119–143.

Vangelisti, A. L. (1994). Messages that hurt. In W. R. Cupach & B. H. Spitzberg (Eds.), *The dark side of interpersonal communication* (pp. 53–82). Hillsdale, NJ: Erlbaum.

Vangelisti, A. L., & Crumley, L. P. (1998). Reactions to messages that hurt: The influence of relational contexts. *Communication Monographs, 65,* 173–196.

Vangelisti, A. L., & Young, S. L. (1999, June). *Messages that hurt: The effects of perceived intentionality on interpersonal relationships.* Paper presented at the meeting of the International Communication Association, San Francisco, CA.

Watson, D., & Clark, L. A. (1994). *The PANAS-X: Manual for the Positive and Negative Affect Schedule—Expanded Form.* Unpublished manuscript, University of Iowa.

Watson, D., & Tellegen, A. (1985). Toward a consensual structure of mood. *Psychological Bulletin, 98,* 219–235.

Weiner, B. (1986). *An attributional theory of motivation and emotion.* New York: Springer-Verlag.

Weiner, B., & Handel, S. (1985). Anticipated emotional consequences of causal communications and reported communication strategy. *Developmental Psychology, 18,* 278–286.

Williams, K. D. (1997). Social ostracism. In R. M. Kowalski (Ed.), *Aversive interpersonal behaviors* (pp. 133–170). New York: Plenum Press.

Zuckerman, M., & Lubin, B. (1985). *Manual for the Multiple Affect Adjective Check List Revised.* San Diego, CA: Educational and Industrial Testing Service.

Zuckerman, M., Lubin, B., & Rinck, C. M. (1983). Construction of new scales for the Multiple Affect Adjective Check List. *Journal of Behavioral Assessment, 5,* 119–129.

7

PERMITTED DISRESPECT: TEASING IN INTERPERSONAL INTERACTIONS

ROBIN M. KOWALSKI, ELSIE HOWERTON, AND MICHELLE MCKENZIE

Of the many mean and unpleasant things that people do to one another (Kowalski, 1997), one of the more enigmatic is teasing, sometimes referred to as *permitted disrespect*.[1] Few people can claim that they have never been teased or that they have never teased someone else. Indeed, teasing is one of the most universal of all human behaviors. Despite the prevalence of teasing in everyday life, however, little systematic research attention has been devoted to teasing, leaving unanswered innumerable questions about this phenomenon. What is teasing? When does something qualify as a tease and when is it something more ominous, such as bullying? Why do people tease? When people say "I was only kidding!" were they? Why does a particular tease make one person laugh and another cry? Do adolescents tease more than adults? Does teasing vary cross-culturally? These questions are addressed in this chapter. Where appropriate, narrative accounts of teasing encounters from our research studies are inserted to illustrate the multifaceted nature of teasing.

---

[1]Pawluk (1989) and Radcliffe-Brown (1977) discussed teasing as a variant of permitted disrespect.

DEFINING *TEASING*

The word *tease* has roots that date back many years. In Toller's *Anglo-Saxon Dictionary* (1898, cited in Pawluk, 1989), *taesan* or *toosen* means to tear to pieces, as in to tease wool or to tear a person's flesh with a weapon. *Tease* also has roots in the French *attiser* or *tiser*, meaning "to feed a fire with fuel" (Pawluk, 1989, p. 146; see also Feinberg, 1996). More current uses define *teasing* as "a verbal thrust whose meaning goes beyond the words that bear it . . . the very essence of a tease is that its meaning is always open to interpretation particularly by persons on the receiving end" (Blau, 1993, p. 66). Shapiro, Baumeister, and Kessler (1991) defined *teasing* as "a personal communication directed by an agent toward a target that includes three components: aggression, humor, and ambiguity" (p. 460). Others have suggested that

> as a form of humor or play, teasing is a language "nip" that can signal and enhance speaker enjoyment and rapport. At the same time, however, teasing is thought to be closely bound to real antagonism: the playful nip may easily be mistaken for a hostile bite. (Straehle, 1993, p. 211)

"It is a source of universal suffering as well as a means of expressing power, sadism, and friendly humor" (Warm, 1997, p. 97).

Today, multiple meanings are attached to the word *tease*. Commerce thrives on a good tease. For example, a preview of a movie or play is known as a *tease*. The advertising industry uses the concept of a tease frequently with its eye-catching campaigns that offer little sound information but aim to entice the consumer to buy. They tease consumers with unspoken promises of youth, beauty, happiness, and wealth. Animal husbandry uses a "second-string" bull or stallion as a tease to sexually excite the female before the stud arrives to perform his duty. A woman who slowly takes off her clothing article by article engages in a strip tease. Women who intentionally arouse men but do not follow through with a sex act are referred to as *sexual teases*.

Confusion surrounding teasing and how it should best be conceptualized led us to define teasing as identity confrontation couched in humor. Teasing always involves some degree of confronting or challenging an individual about some aspect of his or her self or identity. We use the phrase *couched in humor* to capture the fact that, although neither the teaser nor the target may actually perceive a teasing encounter to be humorous, the exchange is framed as if it were playful or humorous.

PROBLEMS WITH CONCEPTUALIZING TEASING

Although everyone can easily recall instances in which they were teased, conceptualizing teasing is much more difficult, as should be evident from the preceding discussion. Two reasons may account for this difficulty. First, teasing seems to mean different things to different people. Whereas people may have some experiences with teasing that are positive and light-hearted, other experiences are likely to be negative and darker, filled with memories of hurt feelings and sadness. As noted by Keltner, Young, Heerey, Oemig, and Monarch (1998), "Teasing is paradoxical. Teasing criticizes yet compliments, attacks yet makes people closer, humiliates yet expresses affection. In teasing, people intentionally embarrass and shame each other . . . , yet people go to great lengths to avoid these emotions" (p. 1231). Teasing is full of hidden meaning. Indeed, that hidden meaning makes up the essence of a tease. Depending on a number of factors, including an individual's history of being teased, mood at the time of the teasing incident, relationship to the teaser, and affect experienced as a result of being teased, the hidden meaning of a tease can take on either positive or negative connotations. Thus, perceptions of teasing can vary widely among the teaser, the target, and witnesses to the interpersonal exchange.

Second, teasing is often difficult to distinguish from related constructs and behaviors. For example, given that well over half of the bullying episodes reported by children involve teasing, do teasing and bullying represent similar phenomena (Whitney & Smith, 1993)? How do teasing and joking differ from each other? Is flirting a type of teasing? According to Feinberg (1996), flirting, gossiping, sarcasm, bullying, and sexual harassment all represent subcategories of teasing. The diversity of these phenomena, however, leads one to question whether classifying them together is the most useful way of viewing these different behaviors, particularly when one is attempting to empirically investigate the topic of teasing.

We believe that all of these constructs are, indeed, distinct from one another. However, they are linked in that they all involve the same three elements: humor, ambiguity, and identity confrontation (cf. Shapiro et al., 1991). The ways in which these elements are combined are what distinguish among behaviors such as teasing, bullying, gossiping, sarcasm, flirting, and sexual harassment (See Table 7.1.). At a general level, for example, good-natured or prosocial teasing involves high humor, moderate identity

TABLE 7.1
Distinguishing Perceptions of Teasing From Perceptions
of Related Constructs

Construct	Humor	Ambiguity	Identity Confrontation
Prosocial teasing	High	Low	Medium
Cruel teasing	Medium	Medium	High
Bullying	Low	Low	High
Flirting	Medium	High	Low
Sexual harassment	Low	Medium	Medium
Joking	High	Low	Low

confrontation, and low to moderate ambiguity. In other words, good-natured teasing is generally funny, not overly threatening to the target, and fairly straightforward in its intent. Bullying, on the other hand, is characterized by low humor, low ambiguity, and moderate to high identity confrontation. Flirting involves moderate humor, high ambiguity, and low identity confrontation. Thus, depending on how the three elements combine, behaviors are created that differ in their function, interpretation, and impact.[2]

Teasing and joking may also be distinguished from one another using this same classification scheme. Although both teasing and joking can be considered forms of humor, teasing requires the presence of the target, whereas joking does not (Boxer & Cortes-Conde, 1997; Eder, 1991). Teasing is most frequently carried out at the expense of the target of the tease (Pawluk, 1989). With joking, however, no particular individual in the interpersonal interaction is being made the center of attention; thus, there is less ambiguity and less potential for hurt feelings and miscommunication and, thus, less identity confrontation.

PREVALENCE

Everyone probably can remember occasions on which he or she was teased as well as occasions on which he or she teased someone else. In one study examining the teasing experiences of 7- and 11-year-old children, Mooney, Cresser, and Blatchford (1991) found that 96% of the children in each age group reported that teasing occurred at their school. Sixty-seven percent of the 7-year-olds and 66% of the 11-year-olds said that they had been the victims of teasing. Fifty percent of the 7-year-olds and 57% of the 11-year-olds said that they had teased others. When asked about the types of teasing, participants in this sample most frequently mentioned name-calling and verbal abuse (e.g., comments about physical appearance or race). Girls were more likely than boys to report being teased about their appearance.

These statistics focusing on the prevalence of teasing among children are not meant to imply that teasing does not persist into adulthood. Most, if not all, adults can easily recall instances in which their feelings were hurt by being teased. However, to date, no prevalence data are available regarding the instances of teasing in adulthood. We would speculate that the rate of teasing in adulthood at least equals that in childhood, although the form that the teasing takes may change with age.

---

[2]We propose these three elements as depicted in Table 7.1 as a working model, with the recognition that the classification of a particular behavior as *low*, *moderate*, or *high* in each of the three factors depends, in large part, on whether one is the perpetrator or the victim of a tease. Thus, we would suggest that, although we have used the separate labels of *low*, *medium*, and *high*, that each of these be viewed as a continuum from low to high.

WHO TEASES?

The answer to the question "Who teases?" is "everyone." Everyone, at least on occasion, teases other people. The more important question, then, is "Who initiates teasing on a regular and frequent basis?" In other words, for whom is teasing a regular part of their behavioral repertoire? Research addressing this topic is in its infancy. Shapiro et al. (1991) asked elementary and middle school children to identify the types of children who tease most frequently. The most common response from the children was aggressive bullies (51%), followed by popular and fun children (23%). Although these two types of individuals may seem very different from one another, Shapiro et al. suggested that children in both groups occupy a dominant status. Both bullies and popular children are the most powerful within the school and social setting, and, therefore, they are in a position to use teasing as a means of controlling others and demonstrating their superiority.

However, knowing the social group to which teasers most likely belong (e.g., bullies or popular children) tells us little about the personal characteristics of people who frequently tease others. To explore these characteristics, Watts (1998) used an act nomination procedure (Buss & Craik, 1984) in which participants listed characteristics, behaviors, or acts that they associate with people who tease others. After eliminating redundancies, 125 characteristics and behaviors were retained that were then rated by a second group of participants using a 9-point scale (0 = *not at all characteristic*, 8 = *extremely characteristic*) for the likelihood that each characteristic or behavior described a chronic tease. The most frequently endorsed characteristics are listed in Exhibit 7.1. As can be seen from this list, the descriptors of people who tease frequently vary widely and reflect both the positive and negative connotations associated with teasing.

Other researchers have recently investigated personality characteristics that moderate the experience of teasing for the teaser. For example, Georgensen, Harris, Milich, and Bosko-Young (1999) examined the relationship between teasing and the big five personality characteristics of neuroticism, openness, conscientiousness, agreeableness, and extraversion. They found a positive correlation between agreeableness and the amount of remorse experienced after teasing another person. Keltner et al. (1998) found a positive relationship between agreeableness and the degree of prosocial teasing. Georgensen et al. (1999) found an inverse relationship between extraversion and empathy for the target. Extraverted individuals also teased others more frequently, whereas conscientious and agreeable persons teased less frequently.

Although empirical research on gender and teasing is far from clear, in large part because of the problems in adequately conceptualizing teasing, data seem to suggest that men tease more frequently than women (Alberts,

EXHIBIT 7.1
Characteristics of Chronic Teasers

Seeks attention from others	Likes to joke
Laughs and cuts up	Talkative
Picks on others	Finds faults in others
Speaks their thoughts freely	Often flirts with others
Wants to be accepted	Sarcastic
Acts immature	Amused with themselves
Annoys and irritates others	Acts without thinking
Is a pain in the butt	Acts like a big-shot
Agitates others	Invades physical and emotional
Shows affection or love by teasing	boundaries
Likes to degrade, demean, or put	Acts in sneaky and mischie-
others down	vous ways
Has a sense of humor	A playful person
Wants to control other people	Is self-centered and selfish
Likes to get revenge on others	Is curious
Pretends to be someone they are	A know-it-all
not	Manipulative
Exploits faults in others that he or	Acts in aggressive or assertive
she has	ways

Note. Adapted from *"You Are Such a Tease!" Identifying and Describing the Chronic Teaser*, by A. Watts, 1998, Unpublished master's thesis, Western Carolina University. Copyright 1998 by A. Watts.

1992; Alberts, Kellar-Guenther, & Corman, 1996; Eisenberg, 1986; Hopper, Knapp, & Scott, 1981; Keltner et al., 1998; Kowalski, 1998). Relative to women, men are raised in a culture where teasing is perceived as a means of toughening them up. As teasing among adolescents attests, boys more than girls "go for the jugular" (Ross, 1996, p. 160) and engage in direct put-downs of other people. Ironically, this may explain why men typically react less negatively to being teased than women. They may simply be more accustomed to the face-threatening nature of the teases and, thus, less likely to interpret teases literally or negatively (Keltner et al., 1998).

In addition to differences in the frequency of teasing, men and women also seem to differ in the content of their teases. For example, in a study examining men's and women's patterns of teasing children, Eisenberg (1986) found not only that men were more likely to tease children than women but also that women were more likely to tease children by threatening some aspect of the relationship (e.g., teasing that they were going to leave the child behind while they went somewhere else), whereas men were more likely to tease about aspects of appearance (e.g., teasing that the child was ugly) or inflicting bodily harm (e.g., teasing a child that he or she was going to be hit). Similarly, Keltner et al. (1998) found that women were more inclined to tease about personal habits and sexual issues, whereas men were more likely to tease about physical appearance.

From her study of peer interactions in middle school, Eder (1993) concluded that boys and girls differ in their styles of teasing. She found that girls are more likely than boys to tease playfully and in a way that allows the target of the tease to participate. In addition, whereas boys often resort to aggressive, physical means of teasing, girls use more indirect methods, such as gossip and social exclusion (Eder, 1993; see also Besag, 1989; Ross, 1996). Boys report that they enjoy being the teaser, but they dislike being teased. Instead of joining in, they tend to become angry and aggressive or simply withdraw from the interaction altogether. Relative to girls, boys are less concerned with the face-threatening nature of their teases. In other words, boys are less concerned than girls with inducing shame or embarrassment in their teasing victims.

WHO GETS TEASED?

Although everyone is teased on occasion, some people seem to be more frequent targets for teasing than others. Because teasing involves confronting another person about an aspect of his or her identity, it is not all that surprising that people who are readily targeted for teasing are those who are different (Pearce, 1989). Thus, children with unusual names, people who stutter, individuals with strong accents, and people with physical defects frequently find themselves being teased. However, people with the most obvious physical or social difficulties or stigmatizing characteristics are typically teased less than those whose "difference" is less pronounced. One reason for this may be that major differences are off-limits for teasing. Thus, people are less inclined to tease a person with an amputation or paraplegia than someone with a limp. In addition, according to Pearce (1989), people with glaring differences learn quickly how to cope with teasing in the event that it occurs, whereas individuals with less obvious difficulties tend to react by crying or getting upset, leading themselves to be further victimized. As noted by Pearce (1989, p. 18), "it is therefore the reaction to being teased or bullied that is the key to the problem." Not surprisingly, then, children who are sensitive and prone to experience anxiety in their interactions with others are likely targets for teasing.

In addition, some people seem to set themselves up as targets for teasing. If teasing were always enjoyable, such a situation might be understandable. However, the type of teasing for which some people seem to set themselves up is negative teasing that is high in identity confrontation. People who are most likely to do this are those who are low in self-esteem and who feel most comfortable in situations in which their negative self-conceptions are confirmed (Swann, Wenzlaff, Krull, & Pelham, 1992). Low self-esteem people may engage in behaviors that set them apart from others and, therefore, make them likely targets for teasing. Although it is probably erroneous to contend that low self-esteem individuals actively seek to be teased, it is more accurate to say that they do not actively resist being targeted by teasers and bullies.

DEVELOPMENTAL TRENDS

Research has shown that children as young as 9 months of age enjoy both teasing others and being teased (Reddy, 1991). For example, infants hold a toy out as if to hand it to another only to pull their hand back when the other reaches for the toy, a behavior typically accompanied by a large grin on the face of the young child and often referred to as the *offer-withdrawal game* (Reddy, 1991).[3]

Among children in the first couple of years of life, teasing is generally perceived as delightful. When a parent or sibling says to a child in a sing-songy voice "You can't get me" and when the child "gets" the parent or sibling, the child laughs. For children at this age for whom verbal ability is not yet fully developed, teasing is a form of social communication (Reddy, 1991; Warm, 1997).

As children age, the nature and tone of their teasing changes. Whereas the teasing of preschoolers rarely contains hostile intent, the teasing of adolescents is more ambiguous and potentially more negative and hurtful (Eder, 1991). According to Eder (1991), children between the ages of 6 and 10 not only use more ambiguous forms of teasing but learn to "frame" (e.g., use contextual cues, such as tone of voice or winks) their teases in a way that connotes their playful versus harmful intent. Indeed, some types of teasing as well as related behaviors, such as sarcasm, appear to require a certain level of linguistic sophistication. Some have suggested that, to intentionally hurt another person, children must have achieved a certain level of cognitive sophistication (Maccoby, 1980). In other words, they must have learned how to differentiate self from others and have developed an understanding of empathy for others (Ross, 1996). However, because of the effects of modeling (which are observed very early in a child's development), children can engage in teasing behaviors without, perhaps, understanding fully the potential ramifications of their behavior (Chazen, 1989).

Oswald, Krappman, Chowdhuri, and von Salisch (1987) compared teasing behaviors among 6-year-olds and 10-year-olds and found age variations. Six-year-olds teased both same-sex and other-sex peers approximately the same in terms of both the frequency of teasing and the nature of the tease. Only rarely was the teasing perceived negatively by targets. Among 10-year-olds, however, the teasing assumed a decidedly nastier

---

[3]Some people might question whether such behavior actually qualifies as teasing, believing that teasing requires a certain level of cognitive development on the part of the teaser (see Maccoby, 1980). Reddy (1991) addressed this issue in her article.

tone. Although the teases were typically intended as play, they more frequently ended up being misperceived by targets, compared to the 6-year-old teases. Ten-year-old girls were more likely than boys to view the teases as annoying. Whereas 6-year-old boys teased by imitating one another's behaviors, 10-year-olds were more likely to engage in verbal teasing. Thus, the gender of the interactants becomes more relevant to teasing as children progress through elementary school (Voss, 1997).

Developmental variations in teasing parallel developments in the self-concept (Pearce, 1989). Among young children with a malleable self-concept, teases are perceived as humorous and identity confrontation as nonthreatening.[4] As a child's self-concept develops with age, however, teases may be perceived as more threatening to his or her views of the self. As a result, among adolescents, for example, who have many insecurities surrounding their identity, even good-natured teases tend to be taken seriously (Drew, 1987).

No developmental studies to date have specifically addressed age-related changes in teasing from adolescence to adulthood. Indeed, much of the empirical research on teasing has, until recently (see Kowalski, 1998) used children and adolescents as participants. In the absence of empirical data, we speculate that patterns of teasing observed among adolescents continue into adulthood, although the specific functions served by teasing may vary as one moves through the adult years. One would also expect developmental variations from adolescence through adulthood in the ability of an individual to deal with being teased. Perhaps through experience, adults more than adolescents can buffer the negative emotional effects of teasing.

WHY PEOPLE TEASE

Teasing may serve a number of functions, some more malevolent than others. The function that teasing serves depends on the age of the teaser as well as the nature of the relationship between the teaser and the person being teased. For example, parents may tease their children to teach them how to respond to others' taunts and jeers. However, peer teasing is unlikely to serve the same function. In addition, the functions that teasing serve are largely dependent on the developmental stage of the interactants (Warm, 1997). Finally, the motivations depend on whether the teasing is positive or negative. The motives of an individual who is just trying to

---

[4]One exception to this idea of young children having malleable self-concepts concerns their gender identity. Children as young as age 2 can identify whether or not they are girls or boys. Around age 6, they acquire gender constancy whereby they realize the permanence of their gender identity (Kohlberg, 1966). Not surprisingly, then, young children who are teased about their gender identity tend to react negatively.

have a little fun differ greatly from those of an individual who is maliciously trying to embarrass or humiliate another person.

Part of the ambiguity underlying teasing arises from the target's difficulty in understanding the motives of the person initiating the tease. Is the teaser just joking around, or is he or she attempting to ridicule or humiliate? When asked to list people's motives for teasing, participants in one study (Watts, 1998) displayed considerable diversity in the motives that they cited. Among the factors participants listed for why people tease were "for fun," "as a joke," "to be liked," "to hurt others," "to make others laugh," "to aggravate and annoy others," and "to make others feel inferior." Clearly, then, teasing may serve multiple functions that may be interpreted as prosocial or damaging.

In an examination of the motives stated by children who perpetrated teases, Shapiro et al. (1991) found that the most common reasons that people reported for teasing were to get someone back for teasing them, to play or joke around, to indicate that they disliked the target, or to make themselves feel better when they were in a bad mood. A similar study with 7- and 11-year-old children in London revealed similar motives: They wanted to provoke others, to entertain themselves, or to enhance their status; they were envious of the person they were teasing; they meant what they were saying; and they disliked the target (Mooney et al., 1991). From the results of their own study, Shapiro et al. concluded that teasing was a way of establishing social dominance, a means of promoting conformity within a group, and a mechanism for disguising one's true feelings and intentions. We want to expand on these motives by discussing four functions that we believe teasing serves: socialization, self-disclosure, power and control, and self-presentation and identity regulation.

Socialization

From a developmental perspective, one of the earliest functions of teasing, especially parent–child teasing, is to socialize children to deal with teasing later in life (Ross, 1996). Parents begin teasing their children very early in life. We have all seen parents good-naturedly tell their children "I'm going to get you" and make a playful lunge toward the child (Blau, 1993; Warm, 1997). The response to this type of teasing is typically a laughing child who is scrambling to get away. Although parents tease to have fun with their children, in the process teasing may help to indoctrinate them in the ways of teasing (Eisenberg, 1986). Teasing may also frequently be used by parents as a means of control to bring the behavior of their children in line with expectations or to put a stop to aversive behaviors, such as complaining (Drew, 1987; Eder, 1993). In this way, children learn about teasing and how to respond to it in a nonthreatening environment.

Adults can also use teasing as a socialization tool with their friends (Eder, 1991) and their romantic partners (Baxter, 1992). One of the most frequent uses of teasing is to make others' aware of norm violations or instances in which their behavior deviates from acceptable standards (Keltner et al., 1998). For example, a romantic partner whose clothes are mismatched may be the target of teasing to induce him or her to change clothes. In this sense, teasing is a means of promoting conformity by discouraging others from being different (Feinberg, 1996; Schieffelin, 1986; Shapiro et al., 1991).

Self-Disclosure

Teasing is an effective way of communicating information that one might otherwise be motivated to avoid disclosing. For example, it is often difficult to confront others with negative information about their appearance or behavior. Through "playful" teasing, however, one can convey this information in a way that removes the sting and allows the relationship with the other to remain intact.

In a similar vein, people are often reluctant to express their frustration or anger for fear of damaging their relationship with others (Straehle, 1993). One means by which people can disclose their frustrations at minimal risk to the relationship is through teasing. For example, a person's frustration with the failure of their spouse to help with the household chores might translate into chronic teasing regarding the spouse's laziness. In this way, the person is able to express his or her frustration with the "laziness" of the partner without creating an unpleasant situation. Similarly, adolescents may attempt to deal with the some of the stressors associated with adolescence by "talking about them" through teasing (Eder, 1991). For example, many adolescents are uncomfortable and even embarrassed by some of the physical changes that are occurring. Teasing is one means by which they can express their discomfort and embarrassment with certain topics.

People may also use teasing to reveal information without actually disclosing it, "a form of shorthand for . . . true feelings" (Blau, 1993, p. 2). For example, were elementary school boys and girls to openly express their liking for an other-sex person would be to risk being teased and criticized by one's peer group. In lieu of this, however, they can tease to convey their interest indirectly. Boys tease girls in whom they are interested and vice versa (Oswald et al., 1987). In one of the narratives that we collected (Kowalski, 2000), one student wrote

> My best friend was being made fun of. People would call him Booger Banks—someone saw him picking his nose [in] elementary school. I thought it was funny. I laughed and would somewhat jokingly call him Booger Banks but not to his face. I guess I would do it to be cool. I

mean he was my best friend and neighbor. I did not want people to think I liked him—like a boyfriend. Boys were icky back then.

Power and Control

Teasing, in and of itself, can be a very powerful tool. A simple statement, gesture, or action that almost always gets a reaction out of others is certainly a method of establishing dominance or control (Pechter, 1982). By demonstrating their power over "weaker" individuals, teasers can take the focus off of themselves and their personal qualities.

Teasing may be used to establish one's place in a social hierarchy, much like a pecking order, whether among one's peers or within a family. For example, people who tease to show that targets of the tease are not part of the group can cement their own position within the group (Ross, 1996). This was illustrated by a student in one of my studies (Kowalski, 2000):

> In junior high it was very important to be popular and hang with the in crowd. Not to be stuck up, but I was in the in crowd and there were always girls wanting to hang out with us. On this particular occasion there was a girl who wanted to hang around with us, and she was new at school. She never matched what she was wearing and looked very dirty. Everyday at lunch she used to come talk to us and we would call her names and push her away as being an outcast. Everyone laughed and usually stared at her. Once she got so upset she stayed out of school for a week. It was all in good fun—sort of—but now I feel bad about it and wonder what ever happened to her.

Within a family, "some children may feel they have more rights, power, and position than other children in the house, and they may wish to exert their power by taunting, bullying, and assaulting the others" (Feinberg, 1996, p. 204). Children may also tease their siblings as a means of garnering the attention of their parents. By gauging the reactions of the parents to the behavior, children can assess where they stand with their parents relative to their siblings (Feinberg, 1996).

Teasing also allows individuals to gain a feeling of control over things that scare them. In other words, teasing may be a means of distancing oneself from the unfamiliar and the frightening (e.g., people with disabilities or stigmas; Blau, 1993; Chazen, 1989). Indeed, many of the teasing sites on the Internet deal with children who are different, such as those suffering from chronic illnesses, stuttering, albinism, or learning disabilities. According to one child, "Sometimes when you see someone who looks different it's scary. Like you might think the same thing could happen to you. Teasing is like a magic shield for some kids" (BandAides and Blackboards, 1997). As noted by a participant in my study (Kowalski, 2000), "I was teased when I was riding the school bus. I was the only person on the bus who had brown skin, and so the other kids teased me about it. The people who were teasing me had never known anyone who was not white."

Self-Presentation and Identity Regulation

Because the impressions that we make on others affect how they perceive, evaluate, and treat us, we regularly manage our behaviors in ways that make desired impressions on others (Leary, 1995; Leary & Kowalski, 1990). Depending on one's self-presentational goals, however, these desired impressions could be positive or negative. For example, an individual who wants to project an image of being funny and humorous may engage in good-natured teasing. On the other hand, an individual who wants to be perceived as tough and someone to be reckoned with may engage in malicious teasing.

Interestingly, one type of teasing that is used, perhaps most frequently, for self-presentational purposes is self-teasing, in which the teaser takes himself or herself as the object of the tease. In this way, the person conveys to others that he or she is humorous and approachable (Boxer & Cortes-Conde, 1997). As stated by Norrick (1993):

> funny personal anecdotes end up presenting a positive self-image rather than a negative one . . . They convey a so-called sense of humor, which counts as a virtue in our society. They present a self with an ability to laugh at problems and overcome them—again an admirable character trait. So apparently, self-effacing personal anecdotes redound to conversational rapport and positive face for the teller in several ways at once. (p. 47)

Similarly, Rosner (1998) stated that "There's one person we can always tease, and that's ourselves. A little self-deprecating humor can liven up a boring meeting, lighten up a serious situation and brighten up a tarnished image."[5]

By regulating the impressions that others form of them, then, people can establish and maintain a personal identity. In addition, however, people may use teasing self-presentationally to establish a relational identity (Boxer & Cortes-Corde, 1997). Rarely if ever do people tease strangers. They may joke but not tease. Thus, teasing is a means of conveying to others the camaraderie or intimacy that one shares with the target of the tease. It may also be used to enhance one's relationship with others, because almost everyone can enjoy the fun involved in good-natured teasing.

---

[5]Whether self-teasing and other-teasing are phenomenologically equivalent is open to debate. However, because we believe that people can "confront" aspects of their own identity in a humorous way, we believe that self-teasing fits within the broader rubric of teasing.

VICTIMS' AND PERPETRATORS' PERCEPTIONS OF TEASING

Research on aversive interactions, such as bullying (Besag, 1989; Ross, 1996), hurtful exchanges (Leary, Springer, Negel, Ansell, & Evans, 1998), and interpersonal conflict (Baumeister, Stillwell, & Wotman, 1990), suggests that victims and perpetrators frequently form very different perceptions of the interaction. Relative to victims, perpetrators minimize the negative impact of their behavior, view their behaviors more benignly, perceive the behavior as motivated by rational motives, and see the consequences of their behavior as more limited in scope. Applied to teasing, Hopper et al. (1981) found that perpetrators responded more positively to teasing than did victims (see also Keltner et al., 1998). Shapiro et al. (1991) also found that children who teased viewed the behavior more favorably than children who infrequently teased.

To examine victims' and perpetrators' perceptions of teasing more completely, I had participants each write two narratives (Kowalski, 2000), one in which they recounted an instance in which they were teased and another in which they related an experience where they teased someone else. The results revealed that victims and perpetrators perceived teasing episodes differently. Relative to victims, perpetrators perceived teasing encounters to be more humorous and less annoying. Perpetrators also reported feeling guiltier about the teasing event than victims. Victims reported more negative effects on their self-esteem relative to perpetrators. Victims perceived that they were viewed less positively than perpetrators said that they viewed them. On the other hand, perpetrators thought they were viewed more favorably by victims than they actually were. Thus, consistent with other research examining differences in the perceptions of victims and perpetrators in anger and conflict situations, victims and perpetrators also differ from one another in their views on teasing.

CONSEQUENCES

Depending on how teasing is perceived, the consequences may be positive or negative. On one hand, teasing may be perceived as good-natured and as a reflection of the degree of intimacy and camaraderie between the interactants. In this case, positive, relationship-enhancing consequences would follow. On the other hand, teasing may be interpreted as an indication of relational devaluation, that is, it may indicate to the target that the teaser "does not regard his or her relationship with the person to be as important, close, or valuable as the person desires" (Leary et al., 1998, p. 1225; see also Leary & Springer, chapter 6, this volume). According to Leary et al. (1998), who found teasing to be one of the seven primary elicitors of hurt feelings, "teasing may be interpreted as veiled criticism, or as an indication that the perpetrator does not adequately value the victim or the relationship" (p. 1233). The relational devaluation may be unintentional on the part of the teaser, but the feelings of embarrassment, identity challenge, and in some instances exclusion are enough to suggest its presence to the target of the tease. According to Rosner (1998) in a discussion of teasing among children and adults, "most grown-up teasing hurts people's feelings too, even if it starts out all in good fun and isn't meant to." The consequences of teasing are not limited to the teasing target, however. They also extend to the teaser and to any witnesses to the teasing encounter. The consequences of teasing for the target, teaser, and witnesses are discussed in turn.

Target

Teasing can have both positive and negative consequences for the individual being teased. On the positive side, teasing may enhance the social bonds and camaraderie between the teaser and the target (Eder, 1991, 1993; Eisenberg, 1986; Sharkey, 1992, 1997). Indeed, the very act of teasing conveys some degree of relationship between the two individuals involved. In addition, experiences with teasing may allow an individual, particularly one who is fairly young, to develop social skills and an ability to respond appropriately to episodes of identity confrontation. Finally, teasing may simply allow for enjoyable, humorous, playful interactions with others.

On the other hand, teasing can have serious aversive consequences for the target, particularly if the teasing is persistent. Short-term consequences include feelings of shame, embarrassment, and humiliation. In some instances these emotions are experienced because of the content of the tease itself. In other instances, however, the target is ashamed or embarrassed because of his or her inability to effectively deal with being teased (Mooney et al., 1991; Pearce, 1989; Ross, 1996). As noted by a participant in one of my studies (Kowalski, 2000) who was teased on the school bus when he was in the first grade: "I kept it to myself because I was too ashamed. But still today I can remember how bad I felt." The individual may avoid school or work, as indicated by the narrative provided earlier in which the young girl was so upset as a result of being teased that she stayed out of school for a week.

Long-term consequences of teasing include learned helplessness, anxiety, depression, and low self-esteem (Hazler, 1994; Hazler, Hoover, & Oliver, 1993; Kowalski, 2000). Many individuals who were teased during adolescence often report negative repercussions of the teasing even into adulthood. For example, women's histories of being teased about physical appearance are correlated with the development of eating disorders and physique anxiety (Thompson, Cattarin, Fowler, & Fisher, 1995). Similarly, a study on the effects of peer ridicule on young girls with Turner's syndrome (a condition characterized by short stature, a weblike configuration around the neck, and eyelid folds; Paludi, 1998) revealed that "peer teasing was the most significant predictor of both depression and self-image among the Turner's Syndrome adolescents studied, even more than body image and height dissatisfaction" (Rickert, Hassed, Hendon, & Cunniff, 1996, p. 37). In my study (Kowalski, 2000), victims, particularly women, reported that teasing was detrimental to their self-esteem. As noted by one of our participants who had been teased in elementary school about her appearance: "Although I had never considered myself ugly before, after that I became very obsessed with my appearance, and I felt ugly for a long time afterward." Another participant who was teased in elementary school about her lisp stated "I was devastated no one ever told me that before, and I continued to be embarrassed for years after. I still am self-conscious about speaking, sometimes even now." In rare cases, long histories of teasing or bullying may lead to aggressive behavior by the target directed either toward himself or herself in the form of suicide or outwardly as in the shooting incidents in (for example) Paducah, Kentucky, in 1997; Pearl, Mississippi, in 1997; or Littleton, Colorado, in 1999. In all of the publicized school shootings within the past 3 years, the shooters reported that they were "sick" of being constantly harassed, bullied, and teased (Cloud, 1999).

We examined the long-term consequences of teasing in one of my own studies (Kowalski, 1998). Participants in this study wrote teasing narratives about one of five aspects of the self about which they had been teased: physical appearance, relationships, performance, social confidence, and social group. After completing their narratives, participants were asked the basis on which they had selected their particular teasing topic. The responses clearly reflected the lasting effects of teasing: "It was a horrible experience that I probably will never forget"; "It impacted my social life and self-esteem greatly throughout my school years"; "It was the most unforgettable experience of my life"; "It is the aspect that hurts me most and is still causing problems in my life"; "Because I feel that incidents such as these leave permanent scars and are never really forgotten"; "It was a very crucial time in my life, and the main thing I wanted was to be accepted by my peers. This was a time when self identity was important."

Negative effects of teasing on the self-image of the target are not surprising. By definition, teasing involves identity confrontation. Teases involve negative characterizations of the target that often impose an identity on the target that is inconsistent with his or her self-perception. At least four variables influence the degree to which teasing has an adverse influence on the self. First, the more the victim perceives the tease to be an indication that the teaser devalues his or her relationship with the victim, the more his or her self-esteem is likely to be affected (Kowalski, 2000; Leary et al., 1998). One variable that may influence perceptions of relational devaluation is the frequency of teasing. The more frequently an individual is teased, the more likely he or she is to perceive the teasing to indicate relational devaluation and, thus, the more likely his or her self-esteem is to be negatively affected (Besag, 1989; Hargreaves, 1967). Second, a victim is more likely to internalize the identity imposed by the teaser if the perpetrator is an important or significant person to the victim (Hargreaves, 1967). Aversive identity confrontations from significant others carry more weight than those from people who are less important to us. Third, the more support the perpetrator appears to have from the victim's peers, the more validating the imposed identity is perceived by the victim and the more threatening it is to the victim's identity. Fourth, identity confrontations that take place in public have a more detrimental effect on a person's self-esteem than those that are private (Hargreaves, 1967).

The adverse consequences often associated with being teased may have a secondary effect on the target's own teasing behavior. Specifically, unpleasant experiences with being teased may actually decrease the likelihood of the target subsequently teasing others, as observed in the following narrative:

> When I was young and even in middle school I recall people picking on me about my nose. They would call me "banana nose" and "Pinnochio" and ask if they could slide down my nose sometime. Ridiculous stuff, but I was very insecure, and it killed me. I would go home or in the bathroom at school and cry and cry. It was miserable. I have grown into my nose now and do not feel so insecure about the way I look. I learned from that, though. Remembering how it made me feel, I would not dare want to cause someone else the same feelings of pain and loneliness. (Kowalski, 2000, p. 234)

The positive versus negative experience of being teased may be moderated by the degree to which people, particularly children, feel that someone understands their accounts of teasing episodes. What may to an adult appear to be trivial and insignificant banter may appear overwhelming to a child. Indeed, according to Ross (1996),

> the most common reason for children not getting help with the problems of teasing and bullying is that the members of their social networks, particularly their parents, siblings, and teachers, refuse outright to give it. They may brush the child's complaints aside . . . [or] mask their unwillingness to help their children by blaming them. (p. 10)

The effects of teasing on the target rest largely on how the target evaluates the tease and his or her own ability to deal with the tease. Because of the ambiguity associated with most teasing, some researchers have labeled it a potential stressor (Ross, 1996). Consistent with Lazarus's (1966) model of stress and coping, when confronted with a stressor, people evaluate the degree of threat posed by the stressor (i.e., primary appraisal), and they evaluate their own resources for coping with the stressor (i.e., secondary appraisal). As with other stressors, teasing for some individuals is appraised as a stressor that exceeds their perceived ability to cope (Ross, 1996). Thus, two individuals exposed to the identical teasing situation can have very different responses to the situation.

Teaser

Although perpetrators may experience both positive and negative consequences as a result of teasing, the positive effects typically outweigh the negative. Because perpetrators view the behavior more benignly than victims, they experience fewer negative and more positive emotional reactions. Even when the motives for teasing are malicious, as in instances of bullying, the perpetrator experiences positive consequences. He or she experiences a temporary rise in self-esteem as result of the influence he or she has wielded over another (Hazler et al., 1993). In other instances, malicious teasing may allow the bully to successfully obscure personal shortcomings by highlighting the deficiencies in another.

Our own research examining victims' and perpetrators' perceptions of teasing illustrated that many perpetrators experience guilt after teasing another person. However, we found this effect to be moderated by the gender of the perpetrator. Men's reports of the amount of guilt they felt following the encounter did not vary as a function of whether they were the victim or the perpetrator. Women, however, reported significantly more guilt when they initiated the tease than when they were the victim (Kowalski, 2000). This may reflect women's concerns with the adverse relational consequences that may follow teasing (Eder, 1991). Indications of the guilt experienced by teasers is nowhere more apparent than in some of the narratives that they recounted.

> When I was a child my brothers and I went to the same school. My little brother had a severe stuttering problem. All of the other kids would make fun of him and call him "Porky pig." I always felt terrible when they would tease him, but he always would laugh it off. One day I got very angry with him so I started to tease him about his stuttering because I knew deep down inside it really hurt him. I got in really big trouble with my mom for this, and now when I think about it, I feel terrible. (Kowalski, 2000)

This quote highlights the little brother's response, the perpetrator's intention to use teasing to hurt, and the guilt that she felt.

Teasers also often report feeling embarrassed when they recall instances in which they perpetrated teases against others. A participant in my study (Kowalski, 2000) recalled a time in the eighth grade when her best friend who had been overweight lost all of the weight and became the most beautiful girl in the school. She stated that

One day me and this other girl were writing notes about her and she found the note which I said in it that she has horse teeth. She really does not. I guess I was jealous. Not too long ago she said, "Do you remember when I found that note and you said I had horse teeth?" I was so embarrassed.

Audience

In addition to the target and the teaser, teasing can also have favorable and unfavorable consequences for those who witness it. Specifically, teasing can have one of three effects on those who witness the teasing event. First, witnesses to the tease may have empathy with the victim of the tease and attempt to take up for him or her. They can accomplish this by either defending the target of the tease or by telling the teaser that enough is enough. The risk here, however, is great. As a function of coming to the defense of the underdog in the teasing encounter, an audience member may become the butt of the next joke. Second, and in an attempt to avoid such an outcome, witnesses to the teasing encounter may themselves join in on teasing the target. To the extent that they know the individual being teased and are familiar with the content of the tease, they can join the perpetrator in teasing the individual. However, this behavior may produce subsequent feelings of guilt. To use Goffman's (1967) face-threat analysis of social interaction, such individuals are saving their own social identity or face at the expense of the individual being teased. A third option is that the witnesses may remain innocent, idle bystanders. On one hand, audience members may be uncertain regarding how best to intervene, leading to feelings of helplessness, passivity, awkwardness, and discomfort (Ross, 1996). On the other hand, some people may simply not have enough empathy to truly understand another's embarrassment and humiliation.

The audience may also experience a degree of empathic embarrassment not with the target of the tease, although that might also happen, but perhaps even more so with the teaser. In reading the narratives in one of my teasing studies (Kowalski, 2000), one could not help but feel embarrassed with the teaser who had said, "all in good fun," something that should have never been said. Two examples follow:

> When in eleventh grade Spanish class, there was a male student in the class that I laughed at. Due to the nature of the class you had to speak out a lot when the teacher called on you to answer. Brent was shy and quiet, and when she called on him he answered in a high squeaky voice. I just started laughing and couldn't stop. The whole class did. . . . One day when he was absent the teacher explained why he talked that way. He had had cancer of the vocal cords, and they removed the ones that cause a man's voice to deepen.

* * *

One afternoon while sitting with some friends one of them said something really lame-brained. One of those comments you realize the answer to as soon as you make it. Teasingly, I made this stupid Mongoloid sounding impersonation of her asking the same question. She stood up and walked off. I was then informed that her younger sister had Down's syndrome. Needless to say, many apologies and peace offerings followed.

Thus, teasing can have both favorable and unfavorable consequences for the target, the teaser, and those who witness the tease. The reactions on the part of the target, teaser, or audience member to the tease go a long way toward determining the consequences for the other individuals involved. For example, if the target clearly perceives the tease to be good-natured and laughs along with the teaser, then audience members experience favorable consequences as well. On the other hand, if the target feels rejected and embarrassed as a result of being teased, the teaser may feel guilt, and the audience may experience empathy with the target.

CULTURAL VARIATIONS IN TEASING

Teasing has been shown to vary cross-culturally (Eisenberg, 1986, p. 182). Although research on cross-cultural variations in teasing is scarce (Boxer & Cortes-Conde, 1997), comparisons can be drawn on the basis of research conducted on individual cultures or subcultures. For example, in some cultures where teasing is indicative of close relationships, teasing between antagonistic groups is forbidden (Howell, 1973). In other cultures, however, teasing among antagonistic groups is initiated as a means of socializing the group members to maintain their cool under pressure.

For example, a popular verbal game played among members of minority and low socioeconomic status youth groups called "playing the dozens" involves the exchange of insults or taunts between groups (Abrahams, 1962; Bruhn & Murray, 1985). These insults typically involve insulting or sexual comments about the mother of one of the group members. As "inappropriate" as some cultures might consider this form of behavior to be, the function of the behavior is to "teach one to take insults in stride while encouraging verbal retorts" (Bruhn & Murray, 1985, p. 484). The game helps individuals learn how to use language creatively to express anger and vent the frustrations of daily life. Among Native Americans and other cultural groups, a behavior similar to playing the dozens is called *razzing* (Pratt, 1996). Razzing typically is used to socialize individuals and to determine the extent of their in-groupness. In other words, from the type of response generated by razzing, Native Americans and other groups can determine the degree to which particular individuals possesses culturally bound social attributes that they value.

The meaning assigned to teasing also varies cross-culturally. For example, among the Kaluli of Papau New Guinea, name-calling is a frequently used form of teasing by parents with their small children (Schieffelin, 1986). "For example, a caregiver might say to a child who has taken more than his share of food *Gasa ge!* 'You are a dog!,' referring to the habit of dogs taking what is not theirs" (p. 169). Kaluli adults often call their infant children names such as "retard" and then smile at the child so that the child understands the spirit with which the teasing is intended. Most American children would be hurt by such name-calling, but Kaluli children appear to view it all in good fun. Rather than leading others to feel excluded, such teasing among the Kaluli is intended to make children and others feel included.

Interestingly, understanding the motives behind teasing is more clear in some cultures than in our own. Among the Kaluli, for example, there are different names for different kinds of teasing. *Enteab* means "tease to make angry," whereas *kegab* means "tease in mock anger." Similarly, they have different names for the type of response that is generated by the target of a tease. *A:la:nyab* refers to an individual who is not angered or provoked by the tease, whereas *debah* refers to a target who teases back (Schieffelin, 1986).

At a general level, comparisons between individualistic and collectivist cultures would yield important information about the multifaceted nature of teasing. Several differences between these two types of culture can easily be applied to teasing. One might expect differences in teasing behavior among people from individualistic and collectivist cultures. Whereas individualistic cultures focus on the individual and his or her independence from others, collectivist cultures focus on unity and interdependence among group members (Kowalski, 1997; Triandis, 1994). Relationships among members of collectivist cultures tend to be more permanent than those in individualist cultures. Thus, not surprisingly, members of collectivist cultures more readily engage in mutual face-saving than people in individualistic cultures (Sharkey, 1997; Triandis, 1995). Given the face-threatening nature of teasing (Alberts et al., 1996; Keltner et al., 1998), people in collectivist cultures should be less likely to tease other members of their own group than individuals from individualistic cultures. Furthermore, on those occasions when teasing does occur, it would likely be more prosocial in collectivistic as opposed to individualistic cultures.

Motives and consequences of teasing would also be expected to vary between individualistic and collectivist cultures. Relative to people in individualistic cultures, people in collectivist cultures tease more for social control. As noted by Triandis (1995), collectivist cultures tend to operate according to very strict rules with which everyone is expected to comply. Those who break with the norms might be teased as a means of bringing their behavior back in line with what is culturally deemed acceptable. In support of this, in Japan, "bullying, called *ijime*, occurs when a person does not 'fit in'" (p. 52). Although people from individualistic cultures might also tease as a means of "normalizing" another's behavior, the goals are more self-serving. In other words, members of individualistic cultures are not trying to make another's behavior culturally acceptable. Rather, they are trying to alleviate their own feelings of discomfort with another's physical, social, or behavioral differences.

Comparing the long-term consequences of teasing in individualistic versus collectivist cultures is more ambiguous. On one hand, the consequences of malicious teasing would be expected to be more negative and more long-lasting in individualistic than in collectivist cultures. Emotional reactions of collectivists to events tend to be of shorter duration and more situationally prescribed relative to the emotional reactions of individualists (Triandis, 1995). Furthermore, because of concerns with the feelings of in-group members among collectivists, teasing is less likely to have the strong negative qualities to it that teasing in individualistic cultures frequently has. On the other hand, because the nature of teasing in collectivist cultures is to bring another's behavior within culturally prescribed realms, targets may be more likely to internalize teases, with accompanying feelings of shame and embarrassment. Indeed, members of collectivist cultures experience embarrassment more readily than members of individualistic cultures (Triandis, 1995).

CONCLUSION

Defined as identity confrontation couched in humor, teasing is an interpersonal behavior with which everyone is familiar. Although most people can easily recall pleasant experiences with teasing, they can more readily recall times when they felt devalued and rejected as a result of being teased. Despite others' often good intentions, few people enjoy being teased, particularly on a regular basis, and they often experience long-term negative consequences as a result. Self-esteem is often lowered and relationships damaged. Furthermore, the negative consequences that may result from teasing extend beyond the target to the teaser and audience members as well. The nature of these consequences, the meaning that is assigned to a particular tease, and the response that is offered to the tease are all constrained by the nature of the relationship between the target and teaser, past histories with teasing, current affect, and the culturally determined meaning of teasing. Clearly, the old adage that "Sticks and stones may break my bones, but words will never hurt me" is simply not true.

REFERENCES

Abrahams, R. D. (1962). Playing the dozens. *Journal of American Folklore, 75*, 209–220.

Alberts, J. K. (1992). An inferential/strategic explanation for the social organization of teases. *Journal of Language and Social Psychology, 11*, 153–177.

Alberts, J. K., Kellar-Guenther, Y., & Corman, S. R. (1996). That's not funny: Understanding recipients' responses to teasing. *Western Journal of Communication, 60*, 337–357.

BandAides and Blackboards. (1997). Who ya gonna call? The teasebusters. Available: http://funrsc.fairfield.edu/jfleitas/tease.html.

Baumeister, R. F., Stillwell, A., & Wotman, S. R. (1990). Victim and perpetrator accounts of interpersonal conflict: Autobiographical narratives about anger. *Journal of Personality and Social Psychology, 59*, 994–1005.

Baxter, L. A. (1992). Forms and functions of intimate play in personal relationships. *Human Communication Research, 18*, 336–363.

Besag, V. E. (1989). *Bullies and victims in schools: A guide to understanding and management.* Philadelphia: Open University Press.

Blau, M. (1993, July/August). Just teasing. *American Health Magazine, 12*, 66–68.

Boxer, D., & Cortes-Conde, F. (1997). From bonding to biting: Conversational joking and identity display. *Journal of Pragmatics, 27*, 275–294.

Bruhn, J. G., & Murray, J. L. (1985). Playing the dozens: Its history and psychological significance. *Psychological Reports, 56*, 483–494.

Buss, D. M., & Craik, K. H. (1984). Acts, dispositions, and personality. In B. A. Maher & W. B. Maher (Eds.), *Progress in experimental personality research* (pp. 241–301). New York: Academic Press.

Chazen, M. (1989). Bullying in the infant school. In D. P. Tattum & D. A. Lane (Eds.), *Bullying in schools* (pp. 33–43). Staffordshire, England: Trentham Books.

Cloud, J. (1999, May 31). Just a routine school shooting. *Time, 153*, 34–43.

Drew, P. (1987). Po-faced receipts of teases. *Linguistics, 25*, 219–253.

Eder, D. (1991). The role of teasing in adolescent peer group culture. *Sociological Studies of Child Development, 4*, 181–197.

Eder, D. (1993). "Go get ya a French!": Romantic and sexual teasing among adolescent girls. In D. Tannen (Ed.), *Gender and conversational interaction* (pp. 17–31). New York: Oxford University Press.

Eisenberg, A. R. (1986). Teasing: Verbal play in two Mexicano homes. In B. B. Schieffelin & E. Ochs (Eds.), *Language socialization across cultures* (pp. 182–198). Cambridge, England: Cambridge University Press.

Feinberg, L. S. (1996). *Teasing: Innocent fun or sadistic malice?* Far Hills, NJ: New Horizon Press.

Georgesen, J. C., Harris, M. J., Milich, R., & Bosko-Young, J. (1999). "Just teasing

. . .": Personality effects on perceptions and life narratives of childhood teasing. *Personality and Social Psychology Bulletin, 25,* 1254–1267.

Goffman, E. (1967). *Interaction ritual.* New York: Pantheon Books.

Hargreaves, D. (1967). *Social relations in a secondary school.* London: Routledge and Kegan Paul.

Hazler, A. J. (1994). Bullying breeds violence: You can stop it. *Learning, 94, 22,* 38–41.

Hazler, A. J., Hoover, J. H., & Oliver, R. (1993). What do kids say about bullying? *Education Digest, 58,* 16–20.

Hopper, R., Knapp, M. L., & Scott, L. (1981). Couples' personal idioms: Exploring intimate talk. *Journal of Communication, 31,* 23–33.

Howell, R. (1973). *Teasing relationships* (Addison-Wesley Module in Anthropology, No. 46). Reading, MA: Addison Wesley.

Keltner, D., Young, R. C., Heerey, E. A., Oemig, C., & Monarch, N. D. (1998). Teasing in hierarchical and intimate relations. *Journal of Personality and Social Psychology, 75,* 1231–1247.

Kohlberg, L. (1966). A cognitive-developmental analysis of children's sex-role concepts and attitudes. In E. E. Maccoby (Ed.), *The development of sex differences* (pp. 82–173). Stanford, CA: Stanford University Press.

Kowalski, R. M. (Ed.). (1997). *Aversive interpersonal behaviors.* New York: Plenum Press.

Kowalski, R. M. (1998, June). *Teasing and the self.* Paper presented at the meeting of the International Nags Head Conference, Boca Raton, FL.

Kowalski, R. M. (2000). "I was only kidding!": Victims' and perpetrators' perceptions of teasing. *Personality and Social Psychology Bulletin, 26,* 231–241.

Lazarus, R. S. (1966). *Psychological stress and the coping process.* New York: McGraw-Hill.

Leary, M. R. (1995). *Self-presentation: Impression management and interpersonal behavior.* Boulder, CO: Westview Press.

Leary, M. R., & Kowalski, R. M. (1990). Impression management: A literature review and two-component model. *Psychological Bulletin, 107,* 34–47.

Leary, M. R., Springer, C., Negel, L., Ansell, E., & Evans, K. (1998). The causes, phenomenology, and consequences of hurt feelings. *Journal of Personality and Social Psychology, 74,* 1225–1237.

Maccoby, E. E. (1980). *Social development: Psychological growth and the parent–child relationship.* New York: Harcourt, Brace, Jovanovich.

Mooney, A., Cresser, R., & Blatchford, P. (1991). Children's views on teasing and fighting in junior schools. *Educational Research, 33,* 103–112.

Norrick, N. R. (1993). *Conversational joking: Humor in everyday talk.* Bloomington: Indiana University Press.

Oswald, H., Krappman, L., Chowdhuri, I., & von Salisch, M. (1987). Gaps and bridges: Interactions between girls and boys in elementary school. *Sociological Studies of Child Development, 2,* 205–223.

Paludi, D. (1998). *Sex and gender: The human experience.* New York: McGraw-Hill.

Pawluk, C. J. (1989). Social construction of teasing. *Journal for the Theory of Social Behaviour, 19,* 145–167.

Pearce, J. (1989). *Fighting, teasing, and bullying: Simple and effective ways to help your child.* Wellingborough, England: Thorsons.

Pechter, K. (1982, December). "It never hurts when I laugh!" *Prevention,* 68–72.

Pratt, S. B. (1996). Razzing: Ritualized uses of humor as a form of identification among American Indians. In H. B. Mokros (Ed.), *Interaction and identity: Information and behavior* (Vol. 5, pp. 237–255). New Brunswick, NJ: Transaction.

Radcliffe-Brown, A. R. (1977). On joking relationships. In A. Kuper (Ed.), *The social anthropology of Radcliffe-Brown* (pp. 174–188). London: Routledge & Kegan Paul.

Reddy, V. (1991). Playing with others' expectations: Teasing and mucking about in the first year. In A. Whiten (Ed.), *Natural theories of mind* (pp. 143–158). Cambridge, MA: Basil Blackwell.

Rickert, V. I., Hassed, S. J., Hendon, A. E., & Cunniff, C. (1996). The effects of peer ridicule on depression and self-image among adolescent females with Turner syndrome. *Journal of Adolescent Health, 19,* 34–38.

Rosner, B. (1998). Stop teasing me! Available: http://abcnews.go.com/sections/business/working wounded/ww980821.

Ross, D. M. (1996). *Childhood bullying and teasing.* Alexandria, VA: American Counseling Association.

Schieffelin, B. B. (1986). Teasing and shaming in Kaluli children's interactions. In B. B. Schieffelin & E. Ochs (Eds.), *Language socialization across cultures* (pp. 165–181). Cambridge, England: Cambridge University Press.

Shapiro, J. P., Baumeister, R. F., & Kessler, J. W. (1991). A three-component model of children's teasing: Aggression, humor, and ambiguity. *Journal of Social and Clinical Psychology, 10,* 459–472.

Sharkey, W. F. (1992). Uses of and responses to intentional embarrassment. *Communication Studies, 43,* 257–275.

Sharkey, W. F. (1997). Why would anyone want to intentionally embarrass me? In R. M. Kowalski (Ed.), *Aversive interpersonal behaviors* (pp. 57–90). New York: Plenum Press.

Straehle, C. A. (1993). "Samuel?" "Yes, dear?" Teasing and conversational rapport. In D. Tannen (Ed.), *Framing in discourse* (pp. 210–230). New York: Oxford University Press.

Swann, W. B., Jr., Wenzlaff, R. M., Krull, D. S., & Pelham, B. W. (1992). The allure of negative feedback: Self-verification strivings among depressed persons. *Journal of Abnormal Psychology, 101,* 293–306.

Thompson, J. K., Cattarin, J., Fowler, B., & Fisher, E. (1995). The Perception of Teasing Scale (POTS): A revision and extension of the Physical Appearance Related Teasing Scale (PARTS). *Journal of Personality Assessment, 65,* 146–157.

Triandis, H. C. (1994). *Culture and social behavior*. New York: McGraw-Hill.

Triandis, H. C. (1995). *Individualism and collectivism*. Boulder, CO: Westview Press.

Voss, L. S. (1997). Teasing, disputing, and playing: Cross-gender interactions and space utilization among first and third graders. *Gender and Society, 11*, 238–256.

Warm, T. R. (1997). The role of teasing in development and vice versa. *Developmental and Behavioral Pediatrics, 18*, 97–101.

Watts, A. (1998). *"You are such a tease!" Identifying and describing the chronic teaser.* Unpublished master's thesis, Western Carolina University.

Whitney, I., & Smith, P. K. (1993). A survey of the nature and extent of bullying in junior/middle and secondary schools. *Educational Research, 35*, 3–25.

8

RUMOR AND GOSSIP IN INTERPERSONAL INTERACTION AND BEYOND: A SOCIAL EXCHANGE PERSPECTIVE

RALPH L. ROSNOW

Implicit in the notion that humans are social beings is the assumption that the giving and receiving of socially valued resources is essentially "wired into" human nature. However, humans are not totally rational animals, and thus it would be a mistake to think that a process akin to Bentham's (1781/1988) hedonic calculus is always operating in interpersonal relations. Nonetheless, social exchange is a convenient schema that can illuminate the instrumentality of perhaps the most common resources in our daily lives—rumor and gossip. The term *social* should not be mis-

I express my gratitude to a long line of former and current students with whom I have had the good fortune to work, directly or indirectly, in the three substantive areas that are discussed in this chapter (rumor, gossip, and interpersonal acumen): Ram Aditya, Susan Anthony, Prashant Bordia, Sean Cherry, Nicholas DiFonzo, James Esposito, Gary Alan Fine, Eric Foster, Leo Gibney, Marianthi Georgoudi, Susan Hilbert, Marianne Jaeger, Allan Kimmel, Jack Levin, Aaron Pomeroy, Bruce Rind, Anne Skleder, Jerry Suls, and John Yost. I thank Robin Kowalski for her helpful comments and suggestions, and I thank Temple University for the support that I have received through the Thaddeus Bolton Professorship.

construed as a synonym for *geniality* or *affability*, however, because rumor and gossip can also be undeniably aversive. They can steal illusions, wreck relationships, and stir up a cauldron of trouble.

My purpose in this chapter is to bring together various empirical and theoretical observations from psychology, sociology, and cultural anthropology in order to sketch an evolving conceptualization of why, how, and when rumor and gossip are generated and transmitted. I begin by giving a flavor of the prevalence of rumor and gossip and mentioning the occasionally perverse effects of each. I then examine both more closely, updating a classic psychological definition of *rumor* and reviewing the identifying characteristics of gossip. Next, I turn to the psychology of rumor and gossip, focusing on their circumstances and functions. I conclude the chapter by underscoring the purposive role of rumor and gossip in the social world.

THE DARK SIDE OF RUMOR AND GOSSIP

The word *rumor*, which comes from a Latin word meaning "noise" or "din," refers to an unconfirmed statement or report that is in widespread circulation, or as sociologist Tamotsu Shibutani (1966) characterized it in the title of his classic text, "improvised news." *Gossip* is from the Old English "god-sibbs," for godparents, meaning those with spiritual affinity to the person being baptized. Christenings were occasions for distant relatives to be present, leading to much small talk; hence, *god-sibbs* led to *gossip*. Later, the term came to denote a woman of light and trifling character who engaged in "idle talk" (Rysman, 1977). Current popular use emphasizes that gossip is small talk or idle talk, usually by women, typically focusing on someone else's private or intimate relations. Evidence of gender differences in the propensity to gossip is limited, but available data suggest that women may have a greater affinity for gossip than do men (Levin & Arluke, 1985; Nevo, Nevo, & Derech-Zehavi, 1993a, 1993b).

One factor that can make rumor and gossip more appealing to both sexes, however, is secrecy (Bok, 1983). As Sabini and Silver (1982) observed, "The juiciest things to gossip about are, after all, the things we most want to conceal, the things few people are likely to know directly" (p. 93). When wanted information is unstated or suppressed, rumor and gossip are likely to increase, as people look for more than they can get from just the face value of news. Before the surprise attack by Japan on Pearl Harbor on December 7, 1941, some American communication experts questioned the U.S. government's extreme use of censorship. Although they conceded that some secrecy was necessary, they argued that exaggerated censorship encouraged people to think that more information was being hidden than was really the case, leading to rumor and gossip to fill the suspected void (Shibutani, 1966).

Clearly we all have a need to know our circumstances, and when the sources from which we receive information are crafty, disingenuous, or simply not forthcoming, we devise our own theories. However, humans also have a habit of misreading the motives of others, which can be spun into rumor and gossip when believing leads to seeing, and more and more people are drawn into the web. Some actions and intentions are intrinsically more difficult to read than others, and interpersonal acumen can vary greatly among individuals (e.g., Aditya, 1997; Rosnow, Skleder, Jaeger, & Rind, 1994), which can lead to interpersonal problems when one party reads too much into a situation. For example, when someone acts in a way that seems on the surface to be helpful or compassionate, but his or her intention is not intrinsically benevolent, we describe this action–intention combination as *synthetic benevolence* (Rosnow et al., 1994, p. 96). To misread such a situation is to become vulnerable, because if the perception of interpersonal problems is incorrect, any solution devised to fix the problems would also be incorrect. Cognitive, developmental, and social psychologists have repeatedly demonstrated that human beings wear causal spectacles and that causality is central in human thought. When rumor and gossip ascribe incorrect causes, they can churn misperceptions into conflicts and conflicts into crises.

However, rumor and gossip are also more than simply attempts to shake loose secrets or to fill in the gaps of missing information. Moreover, both forms can be found circulating almost anywhere and any time, not only in conflicts and crises, but in normal everyday situations; when people are not talking about other people, it may be a sign of social alienation or indifference. Most specimens of rumor and gossip are harmless, to be sure, but some can be threatening or even damaging to individuals and their relationships with others. Le Gallienne (1912) used the expression "martyrs of gossip" (p. 125) to characterize how certain unsavory stories can destroy people's reputations. In fact, there are many documented instances in which negative gossip has had grave consequences for the person targeted, such as when it fed the fantasies of jealous, unsympathetic, antagonistic, or overzealous individuals (cf. Almirol, 1981; Klemke & Tiedeman, 1981; Rosnow & Georgoudi, 1985).

When menacing rumors are set free in a community, they can exacerbate an already tense situation, with devastating consequences (Knopf, 1975). In the 1960s, the Report of the National Advisory Commission on Civil Disorder (Kerner et al., 1968) concluded that rumors had appreciably aggravated racial tensions in more than 65% of the civil disorders investigated. Company managers are also sensitive to the unpleasant consequences of mischievous rumors, including the time drain on key personnel who are forced to channel their energies into combating the stories, profit losses caused by boycotts of products, legal costs, the deterioration of consumer confidence and a sullied public image for the company, a decline in employee morale, and other detrimental effects (Esposito & Rosnow, 1983).

Not surprisingly, the terms *rumor* and *gossip* have acquired a derogatory character, implying that it is not respectable to believe or spread such stories (cf. DiFonzo & Bordia, 1997; Kamins, Folkes, & Perner, 1997; Levin & Arluke, 1987; Smith, 1947). The disparaging stereotype of the rumor-monger goes back to the personification of Rumor (Fama) in Roman mythology and the Hellenic equivalent Ossa. "Monstrous, deformed, titanic," Virgil called rumor in the *Aeneid*, adding

> By night she flies between the earth and heaven
> Shrieking through darkness, and she never turns
> Her eye-lids down to sleep. By day she broods,
> On the alert, on rooftops or on towers,
> Bringing great cities fear, harping on lies
> And slander evenhandedly with truth. (Virgil, 19 A.D./1990, p. 102)

Rumor's current bad reputation is often reinforced by sensational stories that feed on fears, prejudices, and misunderstandings sustained by contemporary stresses.

To cite an instance, in Detroit in the winter of 1967–1968, an appalling rumor erupted in an atmosphere that was filled with suspicion and trepidation from racial riots the summer before (Rosenthal, 1971). The rumor alleged that a young boy, who had briefly left his mother's side to go into the lavatory of a downtown department store, had been savagely attacked and castrated. In this grisly horror tale, the race of the victim and the race of the perpetrators were always in opposition, whereas the teller of the story was usually of the same race as the victim. In another case, sociologist Edgar Morin (1971) described the circumstances surrounding a scurrilous rumor circulating in May 1969 in the city of Orléans, France. The rumor alleged that a number of Orléans women who had gone shopping in six Jewish-owned dress shops had been drugged in the stores' fitting booths and then abducted into slavery. (Ironically, no women were listed as missing in Orléans, according to police reports.) Although there was not a kernel of truth to the abduction rumor, susceptible minds were nevertheless quick to embrace the possibility that it was true and could have some basis in the Jewish character. Morin investigated the particulars of the false rumor, tracing its roots to a tabloid story (set in another city), which had previously appeared in a scandal magazine. The rumor in Orléans, Morin theorized, was sustained by prejudices as much as by fidgety feelings regarding the shopkeepers' financial success in the community.

Cases like these help explain why most people dislike the gossip or rumor spreading of others and yet do it all the time (Jaeger, Skleder, & Rosnow, 1998; Levin & Arluke, 1987). Viewed from the perspective of the person who passes the communication, rumor and gossip can be understood as instrumentally related to some personal outcome of benefit to the story-teller (e.g., G. W. Allport & Postman, 1947; Gluckman, 1963; Goodman & Ben-Ze'ev, 1994; Jung, 1910/1959; Kapferer, 1990; Knapp, 1944; Koenig, 1985; Levin & Arluke, 1987; Morin, 1971; Ojha, 1973; Prasad, 1935; Rosnow, 1974, 1977, 1988, 1991; Rosnow & Fine, 1975; Rosnow & Georgoudi, 1985; Shibutani, 1966; Sugiyama, 1996; R. H. Turner & Killian, 1957). An understanding of their functional and purposive nature is also funda-mental to any attempt to quell potentially damaging rumors or gossip (DiFonzo, Bordia, & Rosnow, 1994; Iyer & Debevec, 1991; Kamins et al., 1997; Koller, 1992), because they cannot simply be controlled by fiat. For example, there is a New York Stock Exchange rule that forbids the cir-culation of sensational rumors that could influence financial conditions on the exchange (New York Stock Exchange, 1966). As everyone who reads a daily newspaper or watches television knows, however, hot tips and dire warnings that affect stock trading flash on and off daily. Corporate takeover rumors in *The Wall Street Journal* have been associated with short-term price run-ups in the market (Pound & Zeckhauser, 1990; Zivney, Bertin, & Torabzadeh, 1996), whereas "microworld" simulation studies reported by DiFonzo and Bordia (1997) indicated that rumors can also spawn predic-tions that adversely affect trading decisions.

DIFFERENTIATING RUMOR AND GOSSIP

Updating a Classic Definition of *Rumor*

In their seminal text on the psychology of rumor, Gordon W. Allport and Leo Postman (1947) defined *rumor* as "a specific (or topical) propo-sition for belief, passed along from person to person, usually by word of mouth, without secure standards of evidence being present" (p. ix). This definition, which for years was widely cited by social psychologists, conveys several ideas, some of which can now be seen as outmoded assumptions. For example, the print and electronic media are also a conduit for rumors and may inadvertently reinforce belief in some rumors (e.g., Zerner, 1946). In the case of the castration rumor mentioned previously, a newspaper published a story to refute the rumor, but some people then quoted the article as "proof" that the incident actually happened (Rosenthal, 1971). Furthermore, millions of people now interact daily on the Internet, which is another way that rumors (and gossip) are circulated other than word of mouth (e.g., Bordia, 1996; Fisher, 1998; Harrington & Bielby, 1995).

A classic example of the intermediary role of radio in creating and spreading a rumor was the one started in 1938 about an invasion of Earth by Martians (Cantril, Gaudet, & Herzog, 1940). The rumor originated in a dramatization over CBS Radio by Orson Welles of H. G. Wells's (1946) novel *The War of the Worlds*. The broadcast came within a month of the Munich crisis, and for weeks the American people had been listening closely to their radios for live news coverage. This timeliness, combined with the sheer technical realism of the broadcast, created an atmosphere of apprehension and contagious suggestibility, which swept across the United States. Westrum (1979) observed that there is a natural tendency to credit the media's reporting of anomalies that give rise to rumors as being more representative and complete than frequently is the case. In this instance, it helped to sustain a rumor that was completely untrue.

Another tenuous assumption implicit in the traditional definition is that rumors are only of temporary interest (i.e., specific and topical). Hall (1965, 1977), however, described an ironic rumor that had periodically resurfaced since its first appearance in the 1940s. The "great cabbage hoax" concerned an alleged 26,911-word U.S. government memorandum on regulating the sale of cabbages. The irony, according to the rumor, was that the Gettysburg Address contains only 266 words; the Ten Commandments, 297 words; and the Declaration of Independence, 1,348 words. Hall noted a number of occasions on which the rumored cabbage memorandum had appeared over four decades. In 1977, the rumor popped up once again, this time in a Mobil Corporation advertisement in leading American newspapers (Rosnow & Kimmel, 1979). In the ad, a cartoon character named Pipeline Pete states the number of words in The Lord's Prayer, the Gettysburg Address, and the Declaration of Independence and then asks, "So how come it took the federal government 26,911 words to issue a regulation on the sale of cabbages?" (Rosnow & Kimmel, 1979, p. 92). The news media had a field day. Walter Cronkite mentioned the cabbage memorandum on a regional segment of the CBS Evening News. This time, the rumor went international, undergoing another metamorphosis in the process. The *London Times* quoted a speaker at a food conference as saying "The Lord's Prayer contains 56 words; the Ten Commandments, 297 words; the American Declaration of Independence, 300 words; and the European Common Market directive on the export of duck eggs, 26,911" (Rosnow & Kimmel, 1979, p. 92). The cyclic pattern of the cabbage memorandum rumor presumably reflects people's anxious feelings about government, intermittently reinforcing their beliefs about its inefficiency and the maddening bureaucratic habit of issuing verbose, incomprehensible rules and regulations.

Although the specific embodiment of a rumor may be short-lived, the symbolic themes of some rumors may endure virtually forever. Carl G. Jung (1959) discussed the longevity of what he termed *visionary rumors* (p. 5), which erupt into numerous variations after lying fallow for a period of time. Some visionary rumors become so deeply enmeshed in a society that they persist as part of its folklore. Those dealing with the power of evil seem especially robust, as illustrated by a group of tales concerning "devil-babies." In 1914, Jane Addams described the havoc created at Hull House (the Chicago settlement house that she had founded) when streams of people arrived to see the rumored devil-baby with cloven hoofs and pointed ears. No amount of denial could convince them that it did not exist. Another fascinating case in the United States concerns the devil-baby born to a Mrs. Leeds of Leeds Point, New Jersey, in 1735. According to the story, she was discontented with her lot in life and already the mother of 12 children, and she prayed to Lucifer to curse her 13th pregnancy. Her prayers were answered: The baby sprouted wings and a lizard-like tail, developed cloven hoofs, and had a face like a horse. The Leeds Devil, renamed the "Jersey Devil," would never die. For years, there were reported sightings in the swamps of the Pine Barrens in southern New Jersey. In the 1800s, it was said that a local judge befriended the demon and that the two of them often had breakfast together and discussed politics. In 1966, news stories in Philadelphia and New Jersey told of a state trooper who had seen "a cloven hoof print larger than a man's hand," thus setting off a new wave of speculation (Rosnow & Kimmel, 1979, p. 91).

In another variant on the Satanism theme, Procter & Gamble has for years been plagued by a preposterous rumor asserting that the company is in league with the "Church of Satan." The company's century-old trademark, a circle depicting a man in the moon (a popular design in the mid-1800s) and 13 stars (to honor the 13 original colonies) was purported to be a symbol of devil worship (Esposito & Rosnow, 1983; Koenig, 1985). Frantic calls and letters to Procter & Gamble reached a peak in the summer of 1982 and seemed to stop only after libel suits were filed against various individuals. The story surfaced again in 1984, when the principal of a nonsecular elementary school in Clymer, a mining town in western Pennsylvania, received an anonymous leaflet claiming that Procter & Gamble's president had gone on a television talk show to confess the company's collusion with Satan. Believing this ridiculous allegation, the principal appended a note of her own—urging parishioners to get on the anti-Satanism bandwagon to "prove we *do* make a difference"—and sent the leaflet flying (Solomon, 1984, p. 1). Procter & Gamble was deluged by several thousand angry telephone calls from Clymer residents off on a fourth crusade. In 1995, Procter & Gamble filed a lawsuit against the Amway Corporation, a competitor, for using a voice-mail system to spread rumors linking Procter & Gamble to Satanism ("Rumors of Satanism," 1995). Implicit in these examples is that rumors are theory-driven by assumptions that can impose the appearance of logical order on circumstances that may be irrelevant or mere happenstance and, therefore, may withstand the effect of time.

Another important lesson is that whether an item of communication is defined as a fact or a rumor depends largely on the situation or the individual's frame of mind. For example, Smedley D. Butler, a legendary Marine Corps General, told about an allegation with devastating consequences for a young Marine who accepted it on faith, when in actuality, according to Butler (1931), it was a baseless rumor. During the Boxer Rebellion, a story circulated that captured Marines had been subjected to blood-curdling tortures. Believing the story to be true, the young Marine became so anxious and distraught that he shot himself through the heart, killing himself instantly. Butler explained that this was how he himself "learned about Dame Rumor and her evil, lying, trouble-making ways. For the reports were nothing but rumors" (p. 24). For Butler, who was ostensibly close to the facts, the story was a malicious rumor; for the young Marine, however, hysteria and suspension of disbelief colored his perception of the story as a fact, with terrifying implications.

Three Identifying Characteristics of *Gossip*

Gossip, rumor's close cousin, is also defined by the situation in which it occurs (Hannerz, 1967). For example, discussing the divorce situation of a friend with a therapist might not be seen as gossiping, because both the style and context of the discussion do not constitute idle talk, the popular notion of gossip. The communication is focused on a specific issue, which may be vital for the purposes of the interactants. At a party or café, however, the participants would not be trying to sustain a focused interaction on a particular topic. If the divorce story came up again, it would presumably be in an "idle" fashion, characterized by a kind of *belle indifference*, indicating that it is gossip. However, were the setting and ambience to lose their quality of idleness, we would say that the people were not gossiping or at least not *just* gossiping. This notion that gossip is "packaged" to appear as idle talk, even if the ulterior motive or purpose of the exchange is profound, can be understood as one of gossip's three identifying characteristics (Rosnow & Georgoudi, 1985). Thus, gossip may begin with a show of disinterest, or even a vague contempt for the story (Almirol, 1981).

A second identifying characteristic of gossip is its moral or judgmental orientation, that is, an evaluative tone (either positive or negative) that may be explicitly or implicitly attached to the personal or intimate event, action, or scandal being discussed (Gluckman, 1963; Sabini & Silver, 1982). A recent case involved events surrounding the December 19, 1998, vote by the U.S. Congress to impeach President William Jefferson Clinton, in which gossip found fertile breeding ground in tawdry secrets, half-truths, scandal, and partisan bickering. In fact, political scandals are a wellspring of gossip, especially presidential politics. Adams (1932) observed that, going back to the beginning of this country, presidential campaigns have been composed in reality of two parts, one open to the public in speeches, debates, and media advertisements and the other a relentless whispering campaign of morally oriented gossip. On James A. Garfield's assassination, stories circulated that Chester A. Arthur, then vice-president, had been carrying out illicit relations in the White House. What helps identify this story as gossip is not that it is true or false, but that, although it is trifling and insignificant at one level, it begs to be taken seriously because it deals with moral or normative character or quality.

A third identifying characteristic of gossip involves the content of the message exchanged or received, or what might be thought of as the "legitimacy factor" (Rosnow & Georgoudi, 1985). What counts is not simply that the message is of a personal nature—many rumors also focus on personal affairs—but that the news is "nonessential" in the context of the exchange. For example, suppose that members of a faculty selection committee were discussing the academic credentials of a potential faculty member. We could say that these people were literally "talking behind the candidate's back" (because the target individual is absent), but we could hardly call this gossiping. However, what if the discussion drifted to the candidate's marital situation or culinary preferences or political affiliation? These go beyond the legitimate boundaries of the question at hand, which is whether the person merits a faculty appointment. When information seems superfluous (in the sense of being unnecessary or excessive), it constitutes gossip; that is, it goes beyond the requisite context of the exchange (Sabini & Silver, 1982).

Nebulous Forms

This does not mean that it is always a simple matter to declare that something is gossip or rumor, but it is usually possible to say that something is primarily gossip or rumor. For example, if the story is that a female executive is said to have "slept her way to the top," most people would intuitively think of it as gossip—although if it is an unfounded allegation, then it is also a rumor. Thus, gossip and rumor might be represented by two slightly overlapping circles, with nebulous forms contained in the overlapping area. That is, gossip is always about people and can involve either fact or supposition; rumors, on the other hand, might or might not involve people, but are always speculative (unlike most urban legends, for example, which are generally presented as "facts" attributed to friends of friends). Some items of communication have a flavor of both rumor *and* gossip.

A famous example of the nebulous form was a story that began circulating in 1969 that Paul McCartney of the Beatles had been decapitated in a car accident and replaced by a double. The story, which had characteristics of both rumor and gossip, swept across American college campuses at the height of the Beatles's popularity (Rosnow & Fine, 1974; Suczek, 1972). What made it a rumor was that, like some well-constructed murder mystery, the story was constructed around perceived circumstantial evidence. What gave it the appearance of gossip was that it was petty information. Even denials could be interpreted as circumstantial evidence in support of the story, because belief in it was theory-driven. At one point, McCartney himself denied his death in a cover article in the November 7, 1969, *Life* magazine. Coincidentally, on the reverse side of the cover there was an automobile advertisement. Held up to the light, it revealed a picture of a car that appeared to be superimposed across McCartney's chest so that the top of his head was blocked out. For true believers, this "clue" merely added credence to the story, which for them was hardly a rumor.

THE PSYCHOLOGY OF RUMOR

G. W. Allport and Postman's Seminal Work

When I first became interested in the psychology of rumor, the then-accepted view emphasized what G. W. Allport and Postman (1947) called the "basic law of rumor" (p. 33). It was not an empirically derived principle based on controlled studies of rumor, but one recycled by Allport and Postman from Douglas McGregor's (1938) significant contribution in another area of psychology. McGregor had studied a number of factors that he theorized lawfully affected the course of people's predictions about current events. Out of these investigations he had developed the principle that "the influence of subjective factors upon the prediction is limited by the *degree of ambiguity* of the stimulus situation, but also that this influence is dependent upon the *importance* for the predictor of the issues involved" (p. 192). Allport and Postman recast McGregor's assertion to serve as a conceptual stepping stone to argue that rumor also was generated and transmitted in a social medium of ambiguity and importance. According to the basic law of rumor, "first, the theme of the story must have some *importance* to speaker and listener; second, the true facts must be shrouded in some kind of *ambiguity*" (G. W. Allport & Postman, 1947, p. 33). Allport and Postman's thinking was similarly influenced by Gestalt psychology, which asserted that perceptions strive toward simplicity, order, and a feeling of closure. Allport and Postman took this idea one step further, arguing that by explaining confusing events that are important to us, rumor acts as a catharsis to relieve the tension of uncertainty.

The notion that humans have a desire to know their circumstances, and that rumors are a reflection of this process of explanation, remains at the heart of most theories of rumor, including my own. However, there is no convincing evidence for G. W. Allport and Postman's idea of a cathartic effect of rumormongering. Various writers have also implied that missing from the basic law of rumor was an emotional component, which I have conceptualized as a form of anxiety (Rosnow, 1980, 1991). This anxiety is a natural outgrowth of a world in flux, because people's assumptions about how the world works are often confronted by unexpected events or challenged by unforeseen favorable or unfavorable consequences of anticipated events. The more perplexing these events, the more that people need to invent stories to put their anxiety to rest (even if the attempt proves unsuccessful, or the positive effect is only temporary) and to furnish cues to guide their future behavior. Previously, Shibutani (1966) had theorized that rumors may be a given society's way of maintaining or maneuvering control over a particular situation in the face of some external threat to the existing order. That is, the flux of social change can give rise to emotional crises whenever some novel event cannot be understood in terms of established assumptions. Once people's expectations are violated, new sensitivities and new ideas emerge along with other ongoing changes in the society. For people to act in concert, they must alter their orientations together, which they do by consulting with each other via rumors and then comparing one another's impressions of their experiences and conjectures. Thus, the difference between the psychological and the sociological perspective is an emphasis on the individual versus the collective nature of this process of explanation.

G. W. Allport and Postman (1947) also claimed that, given the porosity of human memory, rumors must inevitably become shorter and more concise as they are passed from one person to another in successive versions. This assertion was based on results obtained in classroom demonstration studies they conducted, which used a classic serial reproduction paradigm previously used by memory researchers such as Stern (1902) and Bartlett (1932) and used by Kirkpatrick (1932) for the study of rumor. Bartlett's study participants had been shown a picture or given a story to read and were then asked to tell what they had seen or heard. Memory is not simply an aggregation of fixed images; it reflects a process of change that seems to start the moment a picture or story is encoded, Bartlett's research implied. In this process, perception, imagination, and reasoning play a role that is directed toward an effort to impose meaning on images in the mind's eye.

In G. W. Allport and Postman's work, a study participant first examined a depiction of a highly detailed social situation presented in a slide. This person then described the salient features to a second participant, who in turn passed the information that he or she recalled to a third participant, and so on. The consistent result was that the initial description shrank to a striking brevity as the recalled details were communicated from one person to the next. This empirical finding can, in fact, be easily replicated. However, as Buckner (1965) and others have argued, the serial transmission procedure used by Allport and Postman may not be typical of the rumor transmission process, because there was no opportunity for feedback and revision. Allport and Postman observed the leveling (or elimination of certain details) and sharpening (the underscoring of certain details) of information that was passed from one person to another in a one–way chain of communication. Buckner and others argued that whether a word-of-mouth rumor undergoes leveling or sharpening might depend on the availability of feedback, the social structure of the situation, and the teller's critical orientation toward the story. In a similar vein, Baron, David, Brunsman, and Inman (1997) showed experimentally that the perspicuousness of word-of-mouth communication is also moderated by distracting noise and verbal disorganization.

Generation and Transmission

My interest in rumor generation and transmission was first piqued by the way that the Paul McCartney rumor was unfolding, because G. W. Allport and Postman's (1947) argument did not seem to apply. Instead of shrinking, this rumor was expanding to colossal proportions as new meaning was attributed to what seemed perfectly innocent and insignificant before the rumor appeared (Rosnow & Fine, 1974). For example, the album cover of *Sgt. Pepper's Lonely Hearts Club Band* was said to show the lower part of a grave with yellow flowers shaped to resemble McCartney's bass guitar or else the letter "P." Inside the cover "McCartney" wears an arm-patch reading OPD, which was purported to signify that he had been "officially pronounced dead." The medal on his chest was said to commemorate heroic death, and on the back cover everyone is facing forward, except for McCartney's "look-alike." The album cover of *Abbey Road* shows John Lennon dressed in white, resembling a minister; Ringo Starr dressed as an undertaker; George Harrison as a gravedigger; and "McCartney" barefoot to suggest the way that corpses are supposedly buried in England. The Beatles were said to be leaving a cemetery, and a Volkswagen Beetle parked along the road carries the license plate "28 IF"—said to indicate how old McCartney would have been if he had lived. Various auditory cues and other visual effects were also interpreted as "clues" by a susceptible public (Rosnow & Fine, 1974, 1975; Suczek, 1972).

One need not assume that most of the rumor's audience really thought that McCartney was dead, but they did consider the question, lending credence to the idea of a conspiracy. It was primarily FM rock stations, college newspapers, and word of mouth that kept the conspiracy idea alive and growing through the discovery of new "evidence." The establishment media spread a version of the story that was colored with worldly cynicism, but mistrust of the establishment media raised the question of how truth can be gauged by a rumor's audience. The standard measure of truth at that time"—If I read it in the newspaper, it must be true"—was not always reliable or valid. Routine assumptions about practical epistemology could also be questioned, implying that certain truths are only accepted when they are consistent with one's frame of reference. What is truth to one person may be part of a massive conspiracy to another (Rosnow & Fine, 1974). In the context of these and other issues, my co-workers and I began investigating the circumstances of rumor. The results of these studies now point to four conditions that affect and may even predict rumor generation and transmission: general uncertainty, outcome-relevant involvement, personal anxiety, and credulity (Rosnow, 1980, 1988, 1991).

Uncertainty implies doubt, confusion, or unpredictability—or what some also have called "cognitive unclarity" (see Festinger et al., 1948; Schachter & Burdick, 1955). For example, uncertainty is produced by what are perceived as unstable, capricious, or problematic events—that is, events that seem ambiguous to the person involved. *General uncertainty* means that the uncertainty is widespread or nonexclusive in the group or community in which the rumor is being spread, and that, as others also have suggested, where there is no free-floating doubt or confusion, there is no contagion of rumor (e.g., G. W. Allport & Postman, 1947; Belgion, 1939; Knapp, 1944; Knopf, 1975; Koenig, 1985; Larsen, 1954; Nkpa, 1977; Peterson & Gist, 1951; Prasad, 1935, 1950; Shibutani, 1966; Sinha, 1952). For example, office workers know how quickly rumors travel the corridors when a new supervisor takes over, when offices are being moved to a new location, or when any curious or perplexing event creates an air of confusion or unpredictability. In a classic field experiment, Schachter and Burdick (1955) showed how the uncertainty created by a curious event (the abrupt removal of a student from a class) stirred up rumors. Recently, Prashant Bordia content analyzed the cyberspace discussion of a particular rumor, providing support for the idea that the generation of rumors on the Internet may thrive on uncertainty, as users seek out information to corroborate or challenge a perplexing story (Bordia, 1996; Bordia & Rosnow, 1998).

Outcome-relevant involvement refers to a reconceptualization of what G. W. Allport and Postman (1947) termed *importance* and Brissey (1961) called *relevance*. G. W. Allport and Postman argued that rumors emerge to explain ambiguous events that are important to people. A recent study by Anthony and Gibbins (1995) implied some support for this idea in the deaf community, but there is no distinction between rumor and gossip in American Sign Language, and it is possible that rumor and gossip were confounded in this study. Several other studies implied a more complex relationship between importance and rumor spreading. For instance, Kurt Back and his co-workers planted rumors in an organization and then had observers record each time that a rumor was transmitted (Back et al., 1950). Two rumors of prime importance were disseminated quickly, but the spread of another rumor was interpreted as having been inhibited rather than facilitated by its thematic importance. In another study, Scanlon (1977) examined the effectiveness of communications systems in the aftermath of a devastating windstorm in Sydney, Nova Scotia. Finding that

4 out of 7 individuals in one rumor chain rated a rumor they passed as relatively low in importance, he concluded that "people are, if anything, more inclined to spread rumors they do not consider important to them" (p. 125). Although Allport and Postman did not specifically define what they meant by *importance*, they implied that they meant the relevance of a situation and whether the person for whom it was relevant really cared about the outcome. Johnson and Eagly (1989), in another context, used the term *outcome-relevant involvement* (p. 292) to describe a similar situation. Although the results of different studies have diverged, it now appears that outcome-relevant involvement may be implicated as a moderator variable, for instance, moderating the extent to which people contemplate what they are about to say or do (Rosnow, Esposito, & Gibney, 1988).

Personal anxiety refers to an affective state that is produced by, or associated with, apprehension about an impending, potentially disappointing outcome—a variable that was first empirically linked with the awareness of rumor by Susan Anthony (1973). Here, the notion is that rumors persist not only because they play on uncertainty, but also because they can give expression to emotional tensions (Ambrosini, 1983; Hart, 1916; Jung, 1910/1959; Loewenberg, 1943; Rosnow, 1980). However, although tellers may want the story to put their anxieties to rest, rumors do not always erase anxieties (Anthony, 1973). Sometimes rumors can create anxiety (e.g., Cheng, 1997; DeClerque, Tsui, Abul-Ata, & Barcelona, 1986; Knopf, 1975; Miller, 1992; Naughton, 1996; Nkpa, 1977; P. A. Turner, 1992). Furthermore, although anxiety and uncertainty can be defined as separate variables that produce degrees of discomfort, they might be better understood as intimately linked in the rumor generation process (Rosnow, 1980). For example, the degree of uncertainty might be strategically exaggerated for some calculated purpose to heighten anxiety (Lerner, 1978); it also appears that uncertainty is less easily tolerated in stressful circumstances (Smock, 1955). There is now, in fact, much support for the role of personal or situational anxieties in the rumor generation process (e.g., Jaeger, Anthony, & Rosnow, 1980; Rosnow, 1991; Walker & Beckerle, 1987).

The variable of credulity, or trust, means that the likelihood that a rumor is transmitted generally depends on whether the teller finds it at least plausible or trustworthy. This idea can be best explained by envisioning two general classes of rumors, called "wish" and "dread" rumors (Rosnow, Yost, & Esposito, 1986). Wish rumors connote hoped-for consequences, whereas dread rumors imply feared or disappointing consequences. Financial rumors that are fueled by people's fantasies of a quick killing in the stock market would be examples of wish rumors (e.g., Mathur, Mathur, & Rangan, 1997; Rose, 1951). When we are anxiously awaiting a piece of news, it is easy to fantasize that it has finally arrived. Passing a wish rumor might be a way of showing off one's privileged status or an attempt to validate one's wishful thinking to savor the anticipation of a desired outcome. In either case, if the involving outcome does not materialize as predicted (i.e., false hopes or false expectations were raised), the frustration or annoyance that resulted could lead recipients to harbor resentment, even anger, toward the teller. Hence, there should be a vested interest in not passing a wish rumor unless the teller believed (even if mistakenly so) that it contained a kernel of plausibility. Dread rumors, on the other hand, emerge like hobgoblins to spook people into believing the most horrific claims (e.g., F. H. Allport & Lepkin, 1945; Cheng, 1997; DeClerque et al., 1986; Kimmel & Keefer, 1991; Knopf, 1975; Miller, 1992; Naughton, 1996; Nkpa, 1977; P. A. Turner, 1992). Because dread rumors are intrinsically disturbing, passing them may be a means of validating one's prejudices as much as sharing one's fears in an attempt (not always successful) to dissipate discomfort. If the dread rumor proved false, recipients could interpret this as evidence of the teller's unreliability or even instability. Of course, depending on the situation, it might also provoke a more aggressively hostile response. Generally, people do not start or pass disturbing rumors that they find implausible or untrustworthy, unless energized by some devious ulterior motive (e.g., Mihanovic, Jukic, & Milas, 1994) or else they are represented as a joke.

As a rudimentary model to pull these four conditions together, I have used the analogy of loading and firing a gun to explain the circumstances in which rumors are generated (loading the gun) and disseminated (pulling the trigger). The gun can be thought of as the rumor public and the bullet as the rumor, which is loaded in an atmosphere of anxiety and uncertainty. The gun is fired when it is believed the bullet will hit the mark, much as an involving rumor is usually more likely to be passed if it is perceived as plausible or credible. Kimmel and Keefer (1991), who studied rumors about AIDS, concluded that anxiety-provoking rumors perceived as personally consequential were most likely to be believed, whereas classic research by F. H. Allport and Lepkin (1945) implied that credulity is also fostered by repetition of a rumor. However, there is evidence to indicate that when people are terribly anxious or when outcome-relevant involvement is low or when the rumor takes on a life of its own, then passing it is like a "shot in the dark" (Buckhout, 1968; Rosnow et al., 1988). That is, people are not as likely to scrutinize the plausibility of a rumor when they are highly agitated, or when they do not care or are unable to assess its content, or when the situation is a bedlam of rumors. It should also be noted that rumor communication is not always a one-way transmission of a message. Rumor communication can instead involve a rich verbal transaction in which people seek information; try to establish the veracity of comments they receive; and express their anxiety, belief, and disbelief (e.g., Bordia & Rosnow, 1998; Harrington & Bielby, 1995). Although the gun analogy may provide insights into when and why rumors are active, this model may not exhaust the full range of variables that are actually operating in the generation and transmission process (see, e.g., Anthony, 1992; Anthony & Gibbins, 1995; Chelcea, Motescu, & Tighel, 1993; Chorus, 1953; Koller, 1995; Ojha, 1973; Pendleton, 1998), implying the need for further investigation in this area.

THE PSYCHOLOGY OF GOSSIP

Transactional Role

Compared to the study of rumor, gossip has proved a more slippery subject to pin down in controlled studies. Although a considerable amount of everyday conversation is devoted to gossip (Dunbar, 1997; Goldsmith & Baxter, 1996; Lumley, 1925), Almirol (1981) called it "the elusive butterfly" (p. 293). Sometimes its identity is concealed under an assumed name, like "shop talk" or "shooting the breeze" (the masculine euphemisms for gossip). Whatever name it goes by, however, it is abundantly clear that gossip can titillate the imagination, comfort or excite, and manipulate or maintain the status quo. Most of what we know about this phenomenon comes from ethnographic studies, sociometric studies of small groups, content and thematic analyses, questionnaire studies, unobtrusive observations, and various anecdotal reports.

Jerry Suls (1977) pulled some of this work together within the conceptual framework of Festinger's (1954) social comparison theory, by arguing that gossiping allows its participants to obtain needed comparisons of information in an ostensibly indirect and painless way. Interestingly, recent findings by Leaper and Holliday (1995) suggest that women may be more inclined than men to use and encourage gossip in this transactional way in conversations with same-gender friends. Dunbar (1997) theorized that, like primate grooming, gossip evolved in hominids for the purpose of socializing or to establish and maintain relationships. Based on their content analysis of gossip columns over three decades, Levin and Kimmel (1977) concluded that media gossip does indeed serve as a mechanism of socialization and social control, emphasizing norms and values that constitute the "small rules" of society. In a similar vein, recent sociometric research on gossiping and friendship networks suggests that gossip is used at times to shepherd social deviants or isolates back into the group (Jaeger, Skleder, Rind, & Rosnow, 1994; Jaeger et al., 1998).

The social exchange schema seems particularly applicable to gossiping in interpersonal relations and groups, including the kind of rhetorical gamesmanship documented by Gluckman (1963). It appears that the more exclusive the group, the greater is the amount of gossip within it. Although Gluckman noted, however, gossip may be so tightly woven into some groups that it is hard for an outsider to see the "personal knockdown" or the "sneer" that is implicit in a personal gibe. In fact, there is a fascinating parallel between the small rules of gossiping and the principles of economic exchange (Rosnow, 1977). For example, the value of news increases in direct proportion to its scarcity; as the market for news expands, the amount of gossip in circulation proliferates. Consumers have their own brand loyalties—columnists, tabloids, magazines, all of which divulge gossip in return for a fee. Gossip can be entertaining, in which case the social exchange principle would seem to be one of "reciprocity," or an even-handed interaction. Gossiping may ultimately operate to the disadvantage of a third party, but usually the defining characteristic of the transaction is that it mutually benefits the interacting parties. The two-step flow of gossip from "reliable sources" to opinion-influencing reporters who redistribute it to the public at large might be compared to the economic trading pattern in which resources are brought to a central operation and from there dispersed. Thus, in psychological and economic terms, gossiping can be seen as an instrumental transaction in which people trade small talk for status, power, fun, intimacy, money, information, or some other resource with the capacity to fulfill preconditioned needs, wishes, or expectations.

Gossiping obviously is also more than merely the strategic management of information (Yerkovich, 1977). For example, it constitutes the dramaturgical format of certain of our art forms—theater, the novel, television, soap operas—which reflect and articulate role expectations that guide everyday behavior (Spacks, 1985). Recognizing that gossip is a valued commodity in the marketplace of social exchange, Benjamin Franklin, in 1730, reintroduced the gossip column to the Colonies in his *Pennsylvania Gazette*. He was already a fearless gossip reporter by the time he arrived in Philadelphia from Boston, where he had developed his acerbic column using the pen name "Silence Dogood." Few who were famous or socially prominent escaped Franklin's notice. His lineal descendents in the press have included such luminaries as Mark Twain, Franklin P. Adams, Eugene Field, Walter Winchell, Hedda Hopper, Louella Parsons, and Drew Pearson. On radio and television, reporters and talk show hosts now compete with one another to be first with the most scintillating stories, resulting in massive daily doses of tabloid gossip. The most prominent gossip reporters are "gate keepers" (White, 1950) who channel the flow of gossip (and rumor), in return for which the potential rewards are money, recognition, and power.

Influence, Information, and Intimacy Functions

In work begun with Marianthi Georgoudi (Rosnow & Georgoudi, 1985) and resumed with Marianne Jaeger, Anne Skleder, Aaron Pomeroy, and Eric Foster, we have attempted to boil down the various functions of gossip to a few primary ones. Pomeroy (1998), working with Jaeger and myself, operationalized and quantified these functions in a preliminary questionnaire, following the lead of Nevo, Nevo, and Derech-Zehavi (1994), who developed and validated a "tendency to gossip" questionnaire. Previously, Georgoudi and I had described the news-bearing (information) and influence functions of gossip, and we included entertainment as a third possibility (Rosnow & Georgoudi, 1985). Consider, for example, the tabloid mania of the print and electronic media in the giddy name of "news" for voyeuristic readers and viewers, weary of the serious issues, whose natural reaction is to believe what they read or hear. It seems that every newspaper and local television newscast has a "people in the news" section that tries to turn small talk into entertaining fact. If enough people are drawn in, the gossip may initiate a full-blown rumor that takes on a life of its own, which in turn may entail more gossip (people talking about the rumor). Thus gossip can be both a generative mechanism and the result of rumor—that is, both process and product. On the assumption that entertainment is a thread that runs through virtually all gossip, Pomeroy (1998) substituted intimacy as a third major function (i.e., information, influence, and intimacy), and I now describe each in more detail.

First, there is the informational, or news-bearing, function (e.g., Mishra, 1990; Rosnow, 1977; Suls, 1977; Tucker, 1993; Watkins & Danzi, 1995). Gossip can be as opulent a source of knowledge about the community as any information, because its structure and content are responsive to local tensions (Klapp, 1972). In some cases, children might be informally constituted as "gossip gatherers," using their unassuming social role to gain entry to closed adult society. By way of illustration, children in western Newfoundland were used by their parents as "informers" to ferret out news regarding the drinking patterns of inhabitants in a Roman Catholic parish (Szwed, 1966). The children's "nonperson" status secured them freedom of access to private exchanges, and in turn protected them from the risk of critical sanctions for divulging information they gathered. The calculated use of gossip to spread or collect information is not limited to adults, however, nor are children unable to immerse themselves in the culture of the community by means of gossip (Taylor, 1977). By the age of 3, children have been reported to exchange small talk about other children who are not present. The nature of children's gossip is remarkably similar to the gossip of adults (Fine, 1977; Galen & Underwood, 1997), but one intriguing difference is that children often gossip in front of the target person (Goodwin, 1982). To represent the information function of gossip in the context of a work setting, Pomeroy (1998) created items such as "I like to know what is going on with the people around me, that is, who is dating whom, who is getting fired, who is getting a raise"; "I gossip about other people simply because I am interested in what is happening with other people's lives"; and "I spend a lot of time talking with my peers, trying to figure out what is going on in the lives of the people around us."

Second is the influence function, implying that gossip is also used to control attitudes and actions (Gluckman, 1963; Jaeger et al., 1994; Jaeger et al., 1998; Levin & Arluke, 1987; Levin & Kimmel, 1977; Tucker, 1993). An example, alluded to previously, is the gossip columnist who provides readers with news about the behavior of prominent individuals (Levin & Kimmel, 1977). The news has a moral as well as a normative orientation, which may serve as an effective mechanism of socialization and social control. Pomeroy (1998) used factor analysis and item analysis to differentiate the information function from the influence function, but they are not always easy to separate in a given situation. For example, people like to idolize other people, but having "idols" can make people see their own shortcomings; when we spread negative information about them, we can bring them down a peg in the eyes of others. Stirling (1956) interpreted the strategy of destroying someone's reputation in this way as Western society's "civilized" alternative to witchcraft and sorcery in more "primitive" cultures. Of course, people might also "innocently" gossip to their relational partners about other people to bring about changes in the behaviors of those relational partners who engage in the same behaviors as the other people. Pomeroy (1998) tapped into the influence function creating items such as "When someone does something inappropriate, I think everyone has a right to know so that the person will be less likely to do it again"; "Hearing the latest gossip about one of my peers often influences the decisions I make (for example, decisions to wear a certain outfit or to ask for a raise)"; "I can often improve one employee's work habits by telling him or her about the habits of other, better employees"; and "I gossip about people at work whom I dislike in order to get even with them or to put them in their place."

Third is the intimacy function of gossip, that is, its role in socializing and in establishing and maintaining relationships (e.g., Dunbar, 1997; Fine & Rosnow, 1978; Goldsmith & Baxter, 1996; S. Johnson, 1994; Jones, 1980; Mishra, 1990; Noon & Delbridge, 1993; Watkins & Danzi, 1995). Altman and Taylor (1973) invoked the metaphor of peeling away the skins of an onion to characterize the process in which people establish increasing levels of rapport and intimacy. They might, for example, share secrets about themselves (i.e., self-gossip), gradually leading to more intimate exchanges until the exploration of mutual selves results in a commitment between them. The exchange of small talk is a way of signaling to both parties that they have similar interests or are members of the same social group, but also that they share a certain level of trust (cf. Gluckman, 1963; Jones, 1980; Suls & Miller, 1977). In the case of the Paul McCartney rumor, one finding was that those who reported they had spread this gossipy story also stated that they dated and got together with friends less often than did "dead-enders," those who heard the story but did not repeat it (Rosnow & Fine, 1974). This finding seemed to imply that gossiping might be a way

of trying to gain esteem by building a friendship, because "status" is be-
stowed on the teller merely by accepting the story. Pomeroy's (1998) intimacy items were of a general nature, such as "If I didn't spend any time
talking about the personal lives of the people around me, I would feel out
of touch with my social circle"; "You can tell how close your friendship to
someone is by the amount of gossip you exchange with them"; and "When
I am trying to make friends with someone at work, it is convenient to use
information about third parties as a starting point for conversations." From
data he collected using a convenience sample of college men and women,
Pomeroy (1998) noted that the women scored higher on the information
and intimacy subscales than did the men, whereas the men scored higher
on the influence subscale.

Preconditions in Interpersonal Behavior

This and other work has led to further insights into the preconditions
of gossip, including why it arises and the interpersonal contexts in which
it is most likely to originate. In a sense, I have touched on these preconditions already by arguing that the presumed "superfluousness" of gossip is
more apparent than real. By being oriented to fulfilling distinct functions,
gossip inevitably transmits, or becomes converted into, a social value that
governs, manifests, or enhances the relationship between the participants
(Lebra, 1975). In any reciprocal relationship, the gossipy subset of
exchange is inseparable from the relational context. One essential precondition of gossip in interpersonal relations, then, is sociability. There must
be a level of amiable familiarity between participants, or a desire to establish such a level, which is directed toward promoting social interaction.
Conversational gossip rarely occurs among strangers or among acquaintances whose relationship is based on maintaining a strict aloofness with
one another (Almirol, 1981).

To gossip with another person may inevitably reveal an intimate detail about oneself, so it is not something to be undertaken lightly if the
relationship is construed as unsociable. Some situations are defined to be
sociable so that gossiping can flourish, such as the office grapevine (Mishra,
1990; Sutton & Porter, 1968), where the predominant flow of shop talk is
usually restricted to topics of social interest (who is likely to get the next
promotion, who recently had a baby, and so forth). Other situations may
be specifically certified to encourage widespread participation—for example, social occasions like a party or a small drinking group (Szwed, 1966).
Paine (1970) made a study of the camp conversations of reindeer herdsmen
in Kautokeino, for whom gossip was a way of measuring one's success and
gauging others as competitors in an essentially anarchic situation. Talk
show radio is an example of how a situation may be specifically sanctioned
as "sociable" even though one party in the transaction (the radio person-

ality) does not know the other party personally (Turow, 1974). Here, an effort is made to create an ambience of informality (e.g., by addressing one another by first names) to encourage a spirited exchange of small talk and self-disclosure.

No matter how oblique the references contained in such an exchange, they must remain clear to the parties involved. Hence, a second precondition of gossip in interpersonal behavior is that the participants share or conform to a common frame of reference (Almirol, 1981). Members of communities and social groups, especially, value conformity of attitudes and beliefs, although not every member agrees with every other member on all issues. Nonetheless, presence in such a group tends to modify one's beliefs and feelings so that they are more conforming with those of other members. This results in a stock of knowledge that can serve as the backdrop against which gossip may develop and be shared in a meaningful way. The more exclusive the group, the greater is the amount of gossip in it (Gluckman, 1963).

Social psychologists have made extensive studies of group membership, and their findings throw additional light on the effects of efforts to achieve conformity on individual perceptions. For example, Solomon Asch (1956) found that conformity may come about for a variety of reasons. By analogy, the shared perceptions that are a precondition to give, accept, or return gossip may also materialize for a variety of reasons when group members try to establish a common frame of reference. Although certain group members may intentionally try to achieve conformity (Jaeger et al., 1994; Jaeger et al., 1998), it can also come about through more subtle processes, as classic autokinetic research by Muzafer Sherif (1936) showed. In this research, those who made their first judgments in groups tended to acquire a norm from the group, so that when they were tested individually, they responded similarly to others who were also in the group. We might suppose that strangers thrust together in a social milieu have a tendency to displace their judgments toward a shared interpretive framework in the way that Sherif's research participants modified their judgments toward the mean group judgment and retained this judgment when they were later tested individually.

A third precondition of gossip in interpersonal behavior is that the situation presents, if only superficially, a feeling of secrecy, privacy, or protection. The reason is that gossiping generally involves exchanging information about an individual or a group that the individual usually wishes to keep as his or her own exclusive possession (Blumenthal, 1937). It could be embarrassing, even costly, to be caught red-handed dipping into that private pool of information. Privacy gives a place for emotional release without the feeling of being culpable or held liable for one's remarks. This is not to say, however, that the situation is always perceived accurately or that one can have blind faith that there will be no breach of trust. The question of privacy is of particular concern in the helping professions, as therapy subjects patients to a situation in which they may be obliged to disclose the most personal details about themselves (Caruth, 1985; Francis, 1982). Thus, classical medical ethics presents an exacting standard, both outside and inside the profession. The Hippocratic Oath states, "What I may see or hear in the course of the treatment or even outside of the treatment in regard to the life of men, which on no account one must spread abroad, I will keep to myself holding such things shameful to be spoken about" (Hippocratic Oath, 1995, p. 239). Nevertheless, difficult choices can arise both in research and in clinical practice when the implications of what has been disclosed and the reluctance to divulge privileged communication are in conflict (Rosnow, 1997).

CONCLUSION

It is remarkable that although both rumor and gossip are as ubiquitous as the air we breathe, they are seldom examined in social psychology or general textbooks. This is surprising because we have come to learn a great deal about their nature and the limitations of earlier speculative conclusions. The dark side of rumor and gossip can sometimes destroy reputations or devastate relationships. However, whether people are motivated by an intended or a subtle conformity to the group, the community, or the culture, the consequences of rumor and gossip also reflect the extent to which social norms can be enforced on individuals who ostensibly threaten or violate them. In small groups, for example, gossip may be a way of shepherding the herd by saying "These are the boundaries, and you're crossing them" (cf. Jaeger et al., 1994; Jaeger et al., 1998; Westen, 1996). More broadly, I have tried to show that, although gossip and rumor often appear to be aversive, their underlying value lies in their multiple functions in the marketplace of social exchange. Both are socially construed phenomena, whose characteristics merge with the features of those phenomena that appear as intrinsic aspects of the life of a culture and the structure of a society. The dictionary describes gossip as idle talk and gives rumor as a synonym for certain gossip, but the idleness of these forms is only a reminder of the tricks that the social world affords for its observers.

REFERENCES

Adams, J. T. (1932). Our whispering campaigns. *Harper's Monthly Magazine, 165,* 444–450.

Addams, J. (1914). A modern devil-baby. *American Journal of Sociology, 20,* 117–118.

Aditya, R. (1997). *Toward the further understanding of managerial success: An exploration of interpersonal acumen.* Unpublished doctoral dissertation, Temple University, Philadelphia.

Allport, F. H., & Lepkin, M. (1945). Wartime rumors of waste and special privilege: Why some people believe them. *Journal of Abnormal and Social Psychology, 40,* 3–36.

Allport, G. W., & Postman, L. (1947). *The psychology of rumor.* New York: Holt, Rinehart & Winston.

Almirol, E. B. (1981). Chasing the elusive butterfly: Gossip and the pursuit of reputation. *Ethnicity, 8,* 293–204.

Altman, I., & Taylor, D. A. (1973). *Social penetration: The development of interpersonal relationships.* New York: Holt, Rinehart & Winston.

Ambrosini, P. J. (1983). Clinical assessment of group and defensive aspects of rumor. *International Journal of Group Psychotherapy, 33,* 69–83.

Anthony, S. (1973). Anxiety and rumor. *Journal of Social Psychology, 89,* 91–98.

Anthony, S. (1992). The influence of personal characteristics on rumor knowledge and transmission among the deaf. *American Annals of the Deaf, 137,* 44–47.

Anthony, S., & Gibbins, S. (1995). Believability and importance as determinants of rumor among deaf college students. *American Annals of the Deaf, 140,* 271–278.

Asch, S. E. (1956). Studies of independence and conformity: I. A minority of one against a unanimous majority. *Psychological Monographs, 70*(Whole No. 416).

Back, K., Festinger, L., Hymovitch, B., Kelley, H., Schachter, S., & Thibaut, J. (1950). The methodology of studying rumor transmission. *Human Relations, 3,* 307–312.

Baron, R. S., David, J. P., Brunsman, B. M., & Inman, M. (1997). Why listeners hear less than they are told: Attentional load and the teller–listener extremity effect. *Journal of Personality and Social Psychology, 72,* 826–838.

Bartlett, F. C. (1932). *Remembering.* Cambridge, England: Cambridge University Press.

Belgion, M. (1939). The vogue of rumour. *Quarterly Review, 273*(3), 1–18.

Bentham, J. (1988). *The principles of morals and legislation.* Amherst, NY: Prometheus. (Original work published 1781)

Blumenthal, A. (1937). The nature of gossip. *Sociology and Social Research, 22,* 31–37.

Bok, S. (1983). *Secrets: On the ethics of concealment and revelation.* New York: Vintage.

Bordia, P. (1996). Studying verbal interaction on the Internet: The case of rumor transmission research. *Behavior Research Methods, Instruments, & Computers, 28,* 149–151.

Bordia, P., & Rosnow, R. L. (1998). Rumor rest stops on the information highway: Transmission patterns in a computer-mediated rumor chain. *Human Communication Research, 25,* 163–179.

Brissey, F. L. (1961). The factor of relevance in the serial transmission of information. *Journal of Communication, 11*, 211–219.

Buckhout, R. (1968). Through a bag, darkly. *American Psychologist, 23*, 832–833.

Buckner, H. T. (1965). A theory of rumor transmission. *Public Opinion Quarterly, 29*, 54–70.

Butler, S. D. (1931). Dame rumor: The biggest liar in the world. *American Magazine, 111*, 24–26, 155–156.

Cantril, H., Gaudet, H., & Herzog, H. (1940). *The invasion from Mars.* Princeton, NJ: Princeton University Press.

Caruth, E. G. (1985). Secret bearer or secret barer? Countertransference and the gossiping therapist. *Contemporary psychoanalysis, 21*, 548–562.

Chelcea, S., Motescu, M., & Tighel, V. (1993). Locul controlului si emergenta zvonurilor [The locus of control and the emergence of rumors]. *Revista de Psihologie, 39*, 201–215.

Cheng, S.-T. (1997). Epidemic general retraction syndrome: Environmental and personal risk factors in southern China. *Journal of Psychology and Human Sexuality, 9*, 57–70.

Chorus, A. (1953). The basic law of rumor. *Journal of Abnormal and Social Psychology, 48*, 313–314.

DeClerque, J., Tsui, A. O., Abul–Ata, M. F., & Barcelona, D. (1986). Rumor, misinformation and oral contraceptive use in Egypt. *Social Science and Medicine, 23*, 83–92.

DiFonzo, N., & Bordia, P. (1997). Rumor and prediction: Making sense (but losing dollars) in the stock market. *Organizational Behavior and Human Decision Processes, 71*, 329–353.

DiFonzo, N., Bordia, P., & Rosnow, R. L. (1994). Reining in rumors. *Organizational Dynamics, 23*, 47–62.

Dunbar, R. (1997). *Grooming, gossip, and the evaluation of language.* Cambridge, MA: Harvard University Press.

Esposito, J. L., & Rosnow, R. L. (1983). Corporate rumors: How they start and how to stop them. *Management Review, 71*(4), 44–49.

Festinger, L. (1954). A theory of social comparison processes. *Human Relations, 7*, 117–140.

Festinger, L., Cartwright, D., Barber, K., Fleischl, J., Gottsdanker, J., Keysen, A., & Leavitt, G. (1948). A study of rumor: Its origin and spread. *Human Relations, 1*, 464–485.

Fine, G. A. (1977). Social components of children's gossip. *Journal of Communication, 27*, 181–185.

Fine, G. A., & Rosnow, R. L. (1978). Gossip, gossipers, gossiping. *Personality and Social Psychology Bulletin, 4*, 161–168.

Fisher, D. R. (1998). Rumoring theory and the Internet: A framework for analyzing the grass roots. *Social Science Computer Review, 16*, 158–168.

Francis, H. W. S. (1982). Of gossip, eavesdroppers, and peeping Toms. *Journal of Medical Ethics, 8*, 134–143.

Galen, B. R., & Underwood, M. K. (1997). A developmental investigation of social aggression among children. *Developmental Psychology, 33*, 589–600.

Gluckman, M. (1963). Gossip and scandal. *Current Anthropology, 4*, 307–316.

Goldsmith, D. J., & Baxter, L. A. (1996). Constituting relationships in talk: A taxonomy of speech events in social and personal relationships. *Human Communication Research, 23*, 87–114.

Goodman, R. F., & Ben-Ze'ev, A. (Eds.). (1994). *Good gossip.* Lawrence: University Press of Kansas.

Goodwin, M. H. (1982). "Instigating": Storytelling as social process. *American Ethnologist, 9*, 799–819.

Hall, M. (1965). The great cabbage hoax: A case study. *Journal of Personality and Social Psychology, 2*, 563–569.

Hall, M. (1977, Fall). That cabbage regulation which business loves to hate. *Business and Society Review*, pp. 74–75.

Hannerz, U. (1967). Gossip, networks, and culture in a black American ghetto. *Ethnos, 32*, 35–60.

Harrington, C. L., & Bielby, D. D. (1995). Where did you hear that? Technology and the social organization of gossip. *Sociological Quarterly, 36*, 607–628.

Hart, B. (1916). The psychology of rumor. *Proceedings of the Royal Society of Medicine (Psychiatry), 9*, 1–26.

Hippocratic Oath. (1995, Vol. 9). *World Book Encyclopedia*, p. 239.

Iyer, E. S., & Debevec, K. (1991). Origin of rumor and tone of message in rumor quelling strategies. *Psychology and Marketing, 8*, 161–175.

Jaeger, M. E., Anthony, S., & Rosnow, R. L. (1980). Who hears what from whom and with what effect. *Personality and Social Psychology Bulletin, 6*, 473–478.

Jaeger, M. E., Skleder, A. A., Rind, B., & Rosnow, R. L. (1994). Gossip, gossipers, gossipees. In R. F. Goodman & A. Ben-Ze'ev (Eds.), *Good gossip* (pp. 154–168). Lawrence: University Press of Kansas.

Jaeger, M. E., Skleder, A. A., & Rosnow, R. L. (1998). Who's up on the lowdown: Gossip in interpersonal relationships. In B. H. Spitzberg & W. R. Cupach (Eds.), *The dark side of close relationships* (pp. 103–117). Mahwah, NJ: Erlbaum.

Johnson, B. T., & Eagly, A. H. (1989). Effects of involvement on persuasion: A meta-analysis. *Psychological Bulletin, 6*, 473–478.

Johnson, S. (1994). A game of two halves? On men, football and gossip. *Journal of Gender Studies, 3*, 145–154.

Jones, D. (1980). Gossip: Notes on women's oral culture. *Women's Studies International Quarterly, 3*, 193–198.

Jung, C. G. (1959). A visionary rumor. *Journal of Analytical Psychology, 4*, 5–19.

Kamins, M. A., Folkes, V. S., & Perner, L. (1997). Consumer responses to rumors: Good news, bad news. *Journal of Consumer Psychology, 6*, 165–187.

Kapferer, J.-N. (1990). *Rumors: Uses, interpretations & images*. New Brunswick, NJ: Transaction.

Kerner, O., Lindsay, J. V., Harris, F. R., Brooke, E. W., Corman, J. C., McCulloch, W. M., Abel, I. W., Thornton, C. B., Wilkins, R., Peden, K. G., Jenkins, H. (1968). *Report of the National Advisory Commission on Civil Disorders*. New York: Bantam.

Kimmel, A., & Keefer, R. (1991). Psychological correlates of the transmission and acceptance of rumors about AIDS. *Journal of Applied Social Psychology, 21*, 1608–1628.

Kirkpatrick, C. (1932). A tentative study in experimental social psychology. *American Journal of Sociology, 38*, 194–206.

Klapp, O. (1972). *Currents of unrest: An introduction to collective behavior*. New York: Holt, Rinehart & Winston.

Klemke, L. W., & Tiedeman, G. H. (1981). Toward an understanding of false accusation: The pure case of deviant labeling. *Deviant Behavior, 2*, 261–285.

Knapp, R. H. (1944). A psychology of rumor. *Public Opinion Quarterly, 8*, 22–27.

Knopf, T. A. (1975). *Rumors, race and riots*. New Brunswick, NJ: Transaction Books.

Koenig, F. (1985). *Rumor in the marketplace: The social psychology of commercial hearsay*. Dover, MA: Auburn House.

Koller, M. (1992). Rumor rebuttal in the marketplace. *Journal of Economic Psychology, 13*, 167–186.

Koller, M. (1995). Authoritarianism, perception, and person perception: What do authoritarians infer from another's attempt to rebut a rumor? *Basic and Applied Social Psychology, 17*, 199–212.

Larsen, O. N. (1954). Rumors in a disaster. *Journal of Communication, 4*, 111–123.

Leaper, C., & Holliday, H. (1995). Gossip in same-gender and cross-gender friends' conversations. *Personal Relationships, 2*, 237–246.

Lebra, T. S. (1975). An alternative to reciprocity. *American Anthropologist, 77*, 550–565.

Le Gallienne, R. (1912, October). The psychology of gossip. *Munsey's Magazine*, pp. 123–127.

Lerner, A. W. (1978). On ambiguity and organization. *Administration and Society, 10*, 3–32.

Levin, J., & Arluke, A. (1985). An exploratory analysis of sex differences in gossip. *Sex Roles, 12*, 281–186.

Levin, J., & Arluke, A. (1987). *Gossip: The inside scoop*. New York: Plenum Press.

Levin, J., & Kimmel, A. J. (1977). Gossip columns: Media small talk. *Journal of Communication, 27*, 169–175.

Loewenberg, R. D. (1943). Rumors of mass poisoning in times of crisis. *Journal of Criminal Psychopathology, 5*, 131–142.

Lumley, F. E. (1925). *Means of social control*. New York: Century.

Mathur, L. K., Mathur, I., & Rangan, N. (1997). The wealth effects associated with a celebrity endorser: The Michael Jordan phenomenon. *Journal of Advertising Research, 37,* 67–73.

McGregor, D. (1938). The major determinants of the prediction of social events. *Journal of Abnormal and Social Psychology, 33,* 179–204.

Mihanovic, M., Jukic, V., & Milas, M. (1994). Rumors in psychological warfare. *Socijalna Psihijatrija, 22,* 75–82.

Miller, D. E. (1992). "Snakes in the greens" and rumor in the inner city. *Social Science Journal, 29,* 391–393.

Mishra, J. (1990). Managing the grapevine. *Public Personnel Management, 19,* 213–228.

Morin, E. (1971). *Rumour in Orléans.* New York: Pantheon.

Naughton, T. J. (1996). Relationship of personal and situational factors to managers' expectations of organizational change. *Psychological Reports, 78,* 313–314.

Nevo, O., Nevo, B., & Derech-Zehavi, A. (1993a). The development of the tendency to gossip questionnaire: Construct and concurrent validation for a sample of Israeli college students. *Educational and Psychological Measurement, 53,* 973–981.

Nevo, O., Nevo, B., & Derech-Zehavi, A. (1993b). Gossip and counselling: The tendency to gossip and its relation to vocational interests. *Counselling Psychology Quarterly, 6,* 229–238.

Nevo, O., Nevo, B., & Derech-Zehavi, A. (1994). The tendency to gossip as a psychological disposition: Constructing a measure and validating it. In R. F. Goodman & A. Ben-Ze'ev (Eds.), *Good gossip* (pp. 180–189). Lawrence: University Press of Kansas.

New York Stock Exchange, Inc. (1966, July). Circulation of rumors (Exchange Rule 435). In *Miscellaneous rules and provisions* (paragraph 2435). New York: Author.

Nkpa, N. K. U. (1977). Rumors of mass poisoning in Biafra. *Public Opinion Quarterly, 41,* 332–346.

Noon, M., & Delbridge, R. (1993). News from behind my hand: Gossip in organizations. *Organization Studies, 14,* 23–36.

Ojha, A. B. (1973). Rumour research: An overview. *Journal of the Indian Academy of Applied Psychology, 10,* 56–64.

Paine, R. (1970). Lappish decisions, partnerships, information management, and sanctions—A nomadic pastoral adaptation. *Ethnology, 9,* 52–67.

Pendleton, S. C. (1998). Rumor research revisited and expanded. *Language and Communication, 18,* 69–86.

Peterson, W. A., & Gist, N. P. (1951). Rumor and public opinion. *American Journal of Sociology, 57,* 159–167.

Pomeroy, A. (1998). *Constructing a gossip questionnaire.* Unpublished master's thesis, Temple University, Philadelphia.

Pound, J., & Zeckhauser, R. (1990). Clearly heard on the street: The effect of takeover rumors on stock prices. *Journal of Business, 63,* 291–308.

Prasad, J. (1935). The psychology of rumour: A study relating to the great Indian earthquake of 1934. *British Journal of Psychology, 26,* 1–15.

Prasad, J. (1950). A comparative study of rumours and reports in different earthquakes. *British Journal of Psychology, 41,* 129–144.

Rose, A. M. (1951). Rumor in the stock market. *Public Opinion Quarterly, 15,* 461–486.

Rosenthal, M. (1971). Where rumor raged. *Trans-Action, 8*(4), 34–43.

Rosnow, R. L. (1974). On rumor. *Journal of Communication, 24,* 26–38.

Rosnow, R. L. (1977). Gossip as marketplace psychology. *Journal of Communication, 27,* 158–163.

Rosnow, R. L. (1980). Psychology of rumor reconsidered. *Psychological Bulletin, 87,* 578–591.

Rosnow, R. L. (1988). Rumor as communication: A contextualist approach. *Journal of Communication, 38,* 12–28.

Rosnow, R. L. (1991). Inside rumor: A personal journey. *American Psychologist, 46,* 484–496.

Rosnow, R. L. (1997). Hedgehogs, foxes, and the evolving social contract in psychological science: Ethical challenges and methodological opportunities. *Psychological Methods, 2,* 345–356.

Rosnow, R. L., Esposito, J. L., & Gibney, L. (1988). Factors influencing rumor spreading: Replication and extension. *Language and Communication, 8,* 29–42.

Rosnow, R. L., & Fine, G. A. (1974). Inside rumors. *Human Behavior, 3*(8), 64–68.

Rosnow, R. L., & Fine, G. A. (1975). *Rumor and gossip: The social psychology of hearsay.* New York: Elsevier.

Rosnow, R. L., & Georgoudi, M. (1985). "Killed by idle gossip": The psychology of small talk. In B. Rubin (Ed.), *When information counts: Grading the media* (pp. 59–73). Lexington, MA: Lexington Books.

Rosnow, R. L., & Kimmel, A. (1979). Lives of a rumor. *Psychology Today, 13*(1), 88–92.

Rosnow, R. L., Skleder, A. A., Jaeger, M. E., & Rind, B. (1994). Intelligence and the epistemics of interpersonal acumen: Testing some implications of Gardner's theory. *Intelligence, 19,* 93–116.

Rosnow, R. L., Yost, J. H., & Esposito, J. L. (1986). Belief in rumor and likelihood of rumor transmission. *Language and Communication, 6,* 189–194.

Rumors of Satanism lead to a P.&G. suit. (1995, August 29). *The New York Times,* p. D10.

Rysman, A. (1977). How the "gossip" became a woman. *Journal of Communication, 27,* 176–180.

Sabini, J., & Silver, M. (1982). *Moralities of everyday life*. New York: Oxford University Press.

Scanlon, T. J. (1977). Post-disaster rumor chains: A case study. *Mass Emergencies, 2*, 121–126.

Schachter, S., & Burdick, H. (1955). A field experiment on rumor transmission. *Journal of Abnormal and Social Psychology, 50*, 363–371.

Sherif, M. (1936). *The psychology of social norms*. New York: Harper & Row.

Shibutani, T. (1966). *Improvised news: A sociological study of rumor*. Indianapolis: Bobbs-Merrill.

Sinha, D. (1952). Behaviour in a catastrophic situation: A psychological study of reports and rumours. *British Journal of Psychology, 43*, 200–209.

Smith, G. H. (1947). Beliefs in statements labeled fact and rumor. *Journal of Abnormal and Social Psychology, 42*, 80–90.

Smock, C. D. (1955). The influence of psychological stress on the "intolerance of ambiguity." *Journal of Abnormal and Social Psychology, 50*, 177–182.

Solomon, J. B. (1984, November 8). Procter & Gamble fights new rumors of link to Satanism. *Wall Street Journal*, pp. 1, 18.

Spacks, P. M. (1985). *Gossip*. New York: Knopf.

Stern, W. (1902). *Zur Psychologie der Aussage* [On the psychology of testimony]. Berlin: J. Guttentag.

Stirling, R. B. (1956). Some psychological mechanisms operative in gossip. *Social Forces, 34*, 262–267.

Suczek, B. (1972). The curious case of the "death" of the Paul McCartney. *Urban Life and Culture, 1*, 61–76.

Sugiyama, M. S. (1996). On the origins of narrative: Storyteller bias as a fitness-enhancing strategy. *Human Nature, 7*, 403–425.

Suls, J. M. (1977). Gossip as social comparison. *Journal of Communication, 27*, 164–168.

Suls, J. M., & Miller, R. L. (Eds.). (1977). *Social comparison processes: Theoretical and empirical perspectives*. Washington, DC: Hemisphere.

Sutton, H., & Porter, L. W. (1968). A study of the grapevine in a governmental organization. *Personnel Psychology, 21*, 223–230.

Szwed, J. (1966). Gossip, drinking, and social control: Consensus and communication in a Newfoundland parish. *Ethnology, 5*, 434–441.

Taylor, H. J. S. (1977). Teaching your pupils to gossip. *English Language Teaching Journal, 31*, 222–226.

Tucker, J. (1993). Everyday forms of employee resistance. *Sociological Forum, 8*, 25–45.

Turner, P. A. (1992). Ambivalent patrons: The role of rumor and contemporary legends in African-American consumer decisions. *Journal of American Folklore, 105*, 424–441.

Turner, R. H., & Killian, L. M. (1957). *Collective behavior*. Englewood Cliffs, NJ: Prentice Hall.

Turow, J. (1974). Talk show radio as interpersonal communication. *Journal of Broadcasting, 18*, 171–179.

Virgil. (1990). *The aeneid* (R. Fitzgerald, Trans.). New York: Random House. (Original work circa 19 A.D.)

Walker, C. J., & Beckerle, C. A. (1987). The effect of anxiety on rumor transmission. *Journal of Social Behavior and Personality, 2*, 353–360.

Watkins, S. C., & Danzi, A. D. (1995). Women's gossip and social change: Childbirth and fertility control among Italian and Jewish women in the United States, 1920–1940. *Gender and Society, 9*, 469–490.

Wells, H. G. (1946). *The war of the worlds*. Harmondsworth, UK: Penguin.

Westen, R. (1996). The real slant on gossip. *Psychology Today, 29*(4), 44–48, 80–81.

Westrum, R. (1979). Knowledge about sea-serpents. In R. Wallis (Ed.), On the margins of science: The social construction of rejected knowledge. *Sociological Review Monograph* (Serial No. 27).

White, D. M. (1950). The "gate keeper": A case study in the selection of news. *Journalism Quarterly, 27*, 383–390.

Yerkovich, S. (1977). Gossiping as a way of speaking. *Journal of Communication, 27*, 192–196.

Zerner, E. H. (1946). Rumors in Paris newspaper. *Public Opinion Quarterly, 10*, 382–391.

Zivney, T., Bertin W. J., & Torabzadeh, K. M. (1996). Overreaction to takeover speculation. *Quarterly Review of Economics and Finance, 36*, 89–115.

9

INTERPERSONAL TRANSGRESSIONS AND BETRAYALS

WARREN H. JONES, DANNY S. MOORE, ARIANNE SCHRATTER, AND LAURA A. NEGEL

A great deal has been written in recent years about the importance of close personal relationships and the benefits of their attendant states and processes (e.g., love, companionship, intimacy). Ironically, however, acknowledgment and documentation of the centrality of relationships has also led to the emerging recognition that, at the very least, relationships comprise the context in which much of the annoying and more severe trauma of life unfolds and, at the worst, that relationships are the primary source of much of the pain and suffering experienced by people in their day-to-day lives. Accordingly, the central focus of this chapter is on interpersonal betrayals between relationship partners.

We have been interested for some time in the dark side of relationships, examining incidents of betrayal, the circumstances in which they occur, and their consequences both for the relationship partners involved and for their relationships. In our research, we have conceptualized betrayal as a broad range of incidents in which betrayers have violated the expectations of the betrayed. In some cases, we have elicited responses to standardized stimuli assessing various aspects of betrayal, whereas in other studies we have not imposed restrictions on what should be considered an actual violation; instead our respondents' judgments of the most important betrayal incident in their lives have been accepted as the operational definition of the phenomenon under investigation.

It is ironic that betrayals apparently most often occur in the relationships to which people turn for their most intimate interpersonal needs, most frequently involving close relationship partners (Jones & Burdette, 1994). These interpersonal transgressions involve friends of the same sex, spouses, those with whom people work, children, parents, and siblings. Furthermore, it is clear that instances of betrayal, particularly the most painful ones, often linger as painful interpersonal memories for as long as 30 or 40 years after the fact (Hansson, Jones, & Fletcher, 1990).

We begin this chapter by defining interpersonal transgression and betrayal and by discussing the similarities and differences between these two concepts. Next we briefly review prior research in selected areas of interpersonal betrayal including rejection, jealousy, anger, deception, and infidelity. We then turn to our own generic approach to betrayal, which includes three operationalizations of this concept: betrayal narratives, betrayal as an individual difference variable, and betrayal as a feature of the social network. We conclude the chapter by summarizing the major trends in our research and by drawing parallels between the extant literature on specific acts of betrayal and our work as well as a recent theoretical statement on rejection and hurt feelings.

DEFINING TRANSGRESSION AND BETRAYAL

Leaving aside physical assault, theft, and other illegal behavior, the major form of harm-doing experienced by people is what might be called *interpersonal transgressions*. This refers to actions taken by others against a person that go beyond the limits of normative social intercourse and, therefore, violate various social and moral codes (e.g., treating others with proper consideration, with respect, even-handedly). Although such transgressions may be visited by anyone on another person, a particularly damaging type of interpersonal transgression is what we term an *interpersonal betrayal*, by which we mean instances of rudeness, abuse, treachery, deceit, and rapaciousness directed toward partners in various kinds of relationships.

Thus, one might conceptualize a continuum of interpersonal transgressions ranging from those committed by strangers and mere acquaintances to those committed by one's closest intimates. Actions illustrative of the interpersonal transgressions among strangers include people who "cut in line," behave in a loud and obnoxious manner, become verbally abusive, are impolite, and so on. Among relationship partners, betrayals are more likely to be deceptions, infidelities, emotional abuse, and the like. What is changing with movement along this continuum? Generally, the norm violated in the former instance is some global rule of public behavior whereas, in a relationship, the rule often reflects an understanding unique to the relationship bond. Moreover, the impact and the strength of the reaction to the transgression becomes greater as one moves from transgressions among strangers to transgressions among interpersonal partners. As angry as one might become with surly service people, the experience is typically less devastating than a piece of treachery from among one's circle of friends. Similarly, transgressions among strangers may generate emotional expressions, but betrayals among intimates may threaten one's confidence and self-esteem.

We have previously argued (Jones, 1988; Jones & Burdette, 1994) that betrayals may be conceptualized as violations of the psychological underpinnings on which relationships are established, especially violations of (a) rules or expectations, (b) trust, and (c) commitment. Because these concepts are fundamental to our definition, we elaborate on what we mean by them. First, part of what allows a relationship to develop in the first place is a kind of understanding in which participants learn to expect that their partners live up to the expectations of their role and "play by the rules" of the relationship. There are two types of relevant rules or role expectations. As suggested above, there are general expectations that are culturally conditioned and pertain to almost any interaction or any relationship. For example, one typically expects the partner in a relationship to be responsive, pleasant, and at least generally attentive, and one does not expect to be subjected to excessive emotional upheaval or criticism. In addition, expectations may develop out of the specific pattern of interactions and the history of the relationship itself (e.g., not revealing embarrassing information about one's partner to others, coming straight home from work, observing birthdays). Violation of such role expectations may also lead to judgments of betrayal on the part of relationship partners even though there is often considerable uncertainty regarding such rules, for example, whether they are explicitly or implicitly expressed and the circumstances under which they may be applied (Metts, 1989). In any case, if these expectations are violated, one is likely to feel let down by the partner and this, in turn, may stimulate thoughts about the motives of the partner's failure to live up to these "rules."

Second, relationship trust means that a partner can depend on the other to fulfill his or her promises and to remain faithful to the relationship (Rempel, Holmes, & Zanna, 1985). It also means freedom to "be oneself" or to speak openly and frankly without fear of rejection or fear that one's pique is taken too seriously or that one's unguarded confidences are betrayed (Couch & Jones, 1997). Trust and its components (e.g., predictability, dependability, and faith) are antidotes to the dangers of interpersonal involvement—rejection and betrayal. Relational trust is built on the hope that the partner remains faithful and loving and continues to manifest special feelings of love and respect. By contrast, a betrayal threatens that faith as well as the predictability and dependability assumptions relied on in order to make the relational "leap of faith" (Rempel et al., 1985). Furthermore, research suggests that at least a modicum of trust is necessary to maintain a sense of normality in relationships and other interpersonal endeavors.

Finally, enduring relationships are characterized by feelings and expressions of commitment toward the partner and the relationship. Behaviors that may be interpreted as lessening the partner's degree of commitment to a relationship are critical events in the course of a relationship because their implications extend beyond the incident in question to the future of the relationship. For example, with respect to marital relationships, research (Adams & Jones, 1997; Johnson, 1991) indicates that such commitment takes the form of (a) commitment to and satisfaction with the spouse, (b) commitment to the marriage or to the sanctity of one's vows, and (c) barriers to dissolution. A *barrier to dissolution* refers to considerations that may perpetuate one's involvement in a relationship even though it is dissatisfying and even though one might otherwise consider leaving the relationship. Such barriers include, for example, fear of others' disapproval, the "hassles of divorce," difficulty of establishing alternative relationships, loss of income, and child custody concerns. Regardless of its specific form, psychological commitment is an intention to remain in the relationship and, as such, is a promise to one's relationship partner and to oneself. Consequently, violations of relationship rules and actions taken in bad faith are threatening not only because they involve breaking the rules and violating trust, but also because of what they may auger for the future of the relationship and one's intention to remain faithful to it in the future.

Transgressions may vary from actions that are merely annoying or unpleasant—of which strangers are also capable—to more serious actions that threaten one's relationships and sense of identity and well-being. Except in rare instances, these latter transgressions occur exclusively in important relationships and are subsumed by our definition of betrayal. Betrayals, then, are a type of interpersonal transgression that are particularly disruptive and stressful not only because they involve an unpleasant incident, but because they are precipitated by someone who is trusted to not engage in behaviors leading to such events. Finally, the severity of the perceived betrayal presumably reflects several factors including which partner draws the conclusion that a betrayal has occurred, attributions regarding motives and intentionality, and the type and degree of intimacy of the relationship (Metts, 1989).

SELECTED INTERPERSONAL BETRAYALS

Researchers have devoted a great deal of attention to studying a multitude of aversive social processes occurring within interpersonal relationships. Any aversive event may constitute a betrayal if it is sufficiently provocative, that is, if it is taken as seriously threatening the status and continuity of the relationship. In this regard, illustrative processes that have been the focus of previous investigations include rejection and hurt, jealousy, expressions of anger, deception, and infidelity. Research on these processes provides an initial basis for exploring the general realm of interpersonal transgressions and, more specifically, relationship betrayals.

Rejection and Hurt

Interpersonal rejection is a debilitating force in human experience. It lowers both one's feelings of self-worth (self-esteem) and the quality of one's interpersonal relationships beyond the one involving the rejection itself, and it is associated with strong negative emotions (Nezlek, Kowalski, Leary, Blevins, & Holgate, 1997). Rejection is illustrated by abandonment, unreciprocated romantic overtures, jilting, expulsion from social groups, ostracism, disavowal, and a lack of interest in maintaining a given relationship. The mere perception of social exclusion is enough to decrease state self-esteem, to increase motivation to obtain acceptance or social approval, and to affect social perceptions and subsequent interactions with others (Leary & Downs, 1995; Nezlek et al., 1997).

Similarly, people feel hurt when they believe they have been harmed or violated either directly or symbolically (Vangelisti, 1994; Vangelisti & Sprague, 1998). Furthermore, previous research has shown that feelings of interpersonal rejection are moderately to highly correlated with hurt feelings (Leary, Springer, Negel, Ansell, & Evans, 1998). The link between these two cognitive–affective phenomena appears to be the occurrence of relational devaluation, or the judgment that another individual does not regard his or her relationship with the person to be as important, close, or valuable as the person desires (Leary et al., 1998). In fact, hurt feelings and feelings of rejection appear to be related in a circular fashion. The events that cause hurt feelings naturally involve real, imagined, or implied interpersonal rejection; conversely, the degree of hurt one experiences is related to the degree to which he or she feels excluded or rejected by another individual or group.

Interpersonal rejection also has been linked to social anxiety. Socially anxious individuals are particularly sensitive to interpersonal rejection, and, consequently, they tend to have smaller social networks, fewer close friends, and fewer romantic relationships than people who are not socially anxious (Jones & Carpenter, 1986; Jones & Russell, 1982). In fact, Papsdorf and Alden (1998) have found that judgments of similarity mediate the relationship between social anxiety and social rejection. Socially anxious people tend to display more anxious and awkward behaviors and experience greater difficulty in self-disclosing to their relational partners, making them appear dissimilar to their nonanxious counterparts and thereby increasing their likelihood of interpersonal rejection.

Jealousy

White and Mullen (1989) defined *jealousy* as the thoughts, emotions, and actions following the loss or threat of loss to self-esteem or a relationship. This threat to self-esteem or a relationship may be either real or imagined. Guerrero and Anderson (1998) emphasized three important facets of this and other conceptualizations of jealousy: (a) The cognitive and emotional components of jealousy are not independent of jealous actions and communications; (b) jealousy most often occurs within interpersonal relationships, and relationships tend to either intensify or diffuse feelings of jealousy; and (c) perceptions of rival relationships often are rooted in real and imagined social situations. De Silva (1997) described the behaviors commonly associated with jealousy, including verbal accusations, interrogations, attempts to control one's partner's freedom of action, spying, threats, and violence. According to De Silva, jealous cognitions may range from strong and explicit conclusions ("My husband is having an affair with his secretary") to less distinct perceptions ("My wife doesn't love me anymore").

The most common form of jealousy is experienced in romantic relationships. However, jealousy also occurs among siblings, friends, and co-workers. Furthermore, Parrott (1991) argued that jealousy need not involve love, and the rival need not necessarily be a person. For example, a wife may be jealous of her husband's love of cars, or a husband may resent his wife's devotion to her work. Various psychological tendencies including inherited personality traits, socially ascribed gender roles, acquired personality, and a composite of emotions have been proposed as antecedent conditions of jealousy (Buss, Larsen, Westen & Semmelroth, 1992; DeSteno & Salovey, 1994).

Jealousy constitutes a betrayal when it is manifested in such a way as to make the partner feel uncomfortable, trapped, and not worthy of trust. Surprisingly, research indicates that relationship status (e.g., married vs. dating), intimacy or relationship stage, and length do not consistently relate to the propensity to experience jealousy (White & Mullen, 1989). However, relationship satisfaction and degree of relational commitment are often associated with low levels of jealousy because both are related to high levels of investment, relationship rewards, and self-esteem (White & Mullen, 1989). Dating and cohabiting couples in committed relationships are more likely to experience jealousy than those in other types of relationships (e.g., married, casually dating, friends, divorced; Guerrero, Eloy, Jorgenson, & Anderson, 1993). Individuals who appear dependent on the relationship because of the high degree of perceived rewards may be more likely to infer threat from rival relationships. This vulnerability may increase their susceptibility to subsequent feelings of jealousy (Metts & Bowers, 1994).

Expressions of Anger

The expression of anger becomes a betrayal when it exceeds its justification. Yelling and screaming at a partner in response to minor annoyances, mistakes, or disagreements are likely to be perceived as a violation of the expectation for fair and compassionate treatment and as an assault on emotional well-being. Shaver, Schwartz, Kirson, and O'Connor (1987) described *anger* as a multifaceted emotion composed of rage, irritation, exasperation, disgust, envy, and torment. In addition, Storm and Storm (1987) include jealousy, revenge, rebelliousness, distrust, suspicion, hatred, contempt, loathing, and revulsion as components of anger. Shaver et al. described the antecedents of anger, including a predisposition to anger related to having experienced the same provocation previously, or because of stress, fatigue, or other psychological state. Additionally, these authors described a sudden loss of power, status, or respect; frustration; violations of expectations; and real or threatened psychological or physical pain as the situational antecedents of anger.

A threat to one's relationship (e.g., unfaithfulness) can easily provoke anger and is often precipitated by jealousy (Canary, Spitzberg, & Semic, 1998). Furthermore, romantic situations perceived as unfair are more likely to arouse anger than other romantic situations (Salovey & Rodin, 1986). An unfair situation, resulting in malicious envy, may be manifested through anger.

Deception

Research indicates that a variety of lying and deceitful behaviors are common within relationships (DePaulo, Kashy, Kirkendol, Wyer, & Epstein, 1996). People may lie to protect others; avoid rejection, punishment, or conflict; obscure misdeeds; manipulate others; hide or deny emotions; or to gain favor, attention, or rewards (Saarni & Lewis, 1993). Miller, Mongeau, and Sleight (1986) have classified the following types of lies: (a) "blatant lying;" (b) "omission," which is considered as deliberately misleading as an outright lie, although not factually false; (c) "distortions," in which the truth is "bent" in that information is either exaggerated or minimized with the intent to mislead, or (d) "white lies," which serve to protect the feelings of the target (Peterson, 1996). Moreover, strong emotions, such as shame, fear, threat, empathy, or sympathy, appear to stimulate virtually all forms of deceit (Saarni & Lewis, 1993). Even so, research reveals that individuals are twice as likely to tell a lie that is self-serving as compared to telling a lie to benefit another person (DePaulo et al., 1996).

DePaulo et al. (1996) reported that, on average, adult respondents reported telling one lie for every five social interactions in which they engaged, whereas participants in a college study reported telling two lies every day. According to this research, the content of these lies depended on the type of relationship (e.g., casual vs. close friend); people told more lies to casual acquaintances as compared to close friends and romantic partners (DePaulo & Kashy, 1998). Furthermore, people reported themselves to be less likely to tell lies to the people they interacted with often or had known for a long time (DePaulo & Kashy, 1998). However, this pattern did not occur without exceptions—mothers and nonspousal romantic partners are lied to approximately once in every three interactions, according to this research. These authors explained that nonmarried romantic partners may demonstrate a stronger inclination to impress their partner for the sake of image preservation. In addition, individuals may be motivated to lie to their mothers if they perceive their mothers to be in a relative position of power (e.g., controlling resources) or more likely to enforce family or moral rules (DePaulo & Kashy, 1998). In addition, Peterson (1996) found that a high level of satisfaction within interpersonal relationships negatively correlated with self-reported lying in the context of the relationship. However, individuals involved in a highly intimate relationship may be less capable of detecting deceit than those in less intimate relationships. For example, according to relevant research, the likelihood of a lie being detected within a close relationship is less than in a casual relationship (McCornack & Parks, 1990).

Infidelity

Infidelity, typically involving deception and often associated with jealousy, apparently is prevalent in the United States (Lampe, 1987). Empirical evidence reveals that approximately 50% of all marriages involve some degree of infidelity. Lampe (1987) reported that adultery is found cross-culturally and is prevalent throughout all classes, religions, and ages. Furthermore, Lampe noted that, although men historically have been considered more adulterous than women, the degree of this distinction is declining. At present, it appears that men and women are more or less equally likely to engage in infidelity (Buss & Shackelford, 1997).

However, controversy still exists regarding gender differences in the responses to emotional infidelity (e.g., falling in love with another person) versus sexual infidelity (Buss et al., 1992; Harris & Christenfeld, 1996). Women appear to be more troubled by emotional infidelity, whereas men are more troubled by sexual infidelity. Emotional infidelity represents an extramarital affair based on affection, which may pose a greater threat to a marriage than an affair based on sexual relations.

Evidence suggests that both men and women are likely to anticipate infidelity if they are experiencing marital or sexual dissatisfaction (Buss & Shackelford, 1997). Evidence also indicates that socioeconomic status and income do not consistently predict an individual's propensity to have an extramarital affair. However, women with high or low levels of education are more likely to have an affair than moderately educated women (Buunk & van Driel, 1989). Similarly, high and low levels of religiosity are associated with a higher propensity for infidelity (Buss & Shackelford, 1997). Moreover, Buss and Shackelford found that narcissism, low conscientiousness, and psychoticism were all strong antecedents of infidelity. Consequently, individuals who are unable to demonstrate high levels of self-control, delayed gratification, or dependability are prone to extramarital affairs. In addition, Buss and Shackelford found that relational partners who are more likely to engage in extramarital affairs exhibit high levels of sexualization toward others, experience high levels of jealousy and possessiveness, withhold sex in a patronizing manner, and abuse alcohol.

Summary and Conclusions

These respective approaches to chicanery and treachery clearly document the frequency and seriousness of interpersonal transgressions. They also suggest that transgressions in and outside relationships stimulate negative emotions as well as vigilance for subsequent transgressions. Thus, such transgressions not only threaten the viability and quality of the relationship in which they emerge, but they also threaten the self-esteem and well-being of those who are victimized. Finally, research on anger, jealousy, and deceit suggests that these transgressions encourage not only restorative behaviors (e.g., making amends, apology) that may repair a damaged relationship, but also avoidant and retaliatory actions that may escalate tension and damage the relationship further. One limitation of this research, however, is that the focus has often been on the isolated behavior rather than on the interpersonal context in which it occurs. For example, a lie told to a partner in a close relationship may have a very different consequence if detected than the detection of the same lie told to someone who is a mere acquaintance. Another limitation is that each of these phenomena has been studied in relative isolation from the others. However, it seems unlikely that relationship partners experience (for example) infidelity without also experiencing jealousy, expressions of anger, deceit, and so on. Consequently, another approach to understanding transgressions and betrayals would be to assess them generically with less regard for the specifics of the actions in order to explicate the similarities and differences between these classes of aversive behaviors. We have been engaged in a program of research using this strategy, and we now turn to our relevant findings.

RESEARCH ON BETRAYAL

Individual Differences in Betrayal

To study betrayal as an individual difference variable, we developed the Interpersonal Betrayal Scale (IBS; cf. Jones & Burdette, 1994), which originally consisted of 15 items requiring respondents to indicate the frequency with which they engage in everyday transgressions (e.g., "making a promise to a family member with no intention of keeping it"; "lying to a friend"; "gossiping about a friend behind his or her back"). Items were derived from common themes in narrative accounts elicited from respondents who had been asked to describe an instance in which they had betrayed a relationship partner. An item pool representing more than 90 such narrative themes was subjected to standard scaling procedures, and items were selected for the final version of the scale on the basis of psychometric criteria (e.g., item–total correlations, item–criterion correlations). Subsequently, a companion version of the scale, also with 15 items, was developed to assess the frequency with which respondents reported falling victim to the same transgressions on the part of their relationship partners (e.g., "having a family member make a promise to you with no intention of keeping it"; "being lied to by a friend"). Thus, two versions of the IBS, a betrayal of others scale (IBS–O) and a betrayal of self by others scale (IBS–S), were developed. For both scales, respondents answer each item using a 5-point, Likert-type format anchored by frequency of occurrence statements (e.g., "I have never done this," "This has happened to me several times," "I have done this many times"). Both subscales have been demonstrated to be internally reliable and reliable over time, and the validity of scale interpretations has been supported by analyses involving a variety of respondent populations (cf. Jones & Burdette, 1994).

Several studies examining the demographic, personality, and interpersonal correlates of tendencies toward betraying and being betrayed have been conducted (Carver, 1990; Hansson et al., 1990; Jones, 1988; Jones & Burdette, 1994; Jones, Cohn, & Miller, 1991; Jones, Couch, & Scott, 1997; Monroe, 1990; Montgomery & Brown, 1988). For example, IBS–O scores were significantly and inversely correlated with age, education, and frequency of attendance at religious observations and services. Among college students, White American participants yielded higher scores on the IBS–O and IBS–S than did members of minority groups and international students from various foreign countries. Interestingly, work environment or type of job has been related to self-reported betrayal. For example, psychotherapists, school teachers, attorneys, college professors, and salespersons tended to score higher on IBS–O than, for example, factory workers, computer operators, service personnel, carpenters, and nurses. Similarly, college students majoring in psychology, social science, education, business, and the humanities scored higher on the IBS–O and, hence, presumably betrayed their relationship partners more frequently than students enrolled in the physical sciences, biology, engineering, and technical majors (Jones & Burdette, 1994). It is also possible that people in certain professions or majors are more sensitive to interpersonal issues, resulting in a greater likelihood to perceive and report betrayals.

Other studies using these measures suggested that higher scores were associated with dispositional characteristics and personal problems likely to interfere with mature, mutually satisfying relationships. In psychological terms, persons who report more frequent betrayal of their relationship partners were more likely to describe themselves in negative and interpersonally inept terms. For example, among college students, IBS–O scores were significantly related to personality and emotional traits such as guilt, shame, suspiciousness, cynicism, resentment, depression, anxiety, and anger and inversely related to trust, commitment, well-being, self-control, tolerance, responsibility, and intimacy (Jones & Burdette, 1994). IBS–O scores were more strongly (inversely) related to global trust (i.e., trust in human nature or people in general) than to network trust (trust in the members of one's social network) or partner trust (trust of one's primary relationship partner), whereas ratings of having been betrayed by others (IBS–S) showed higher inverse correlations with network trust as compared to partner and global trust (Couch, 1994; Couch & Jones, 1997).

Comparisons across samples indicated that IBS–O scores were higher among groups experiencing major life problems: psychiatric inpatients and outpatients, psychotherapy clients, adjudicated adolescents, and self-identified alcoholic individuals (cf. Carver, 1990). In this regard, IBS–O scores were systematically related to measures of several dimensions of Axis II personality disorders such as borderline, paranoid, histrionic, narcissistic, and dependent personalities, among psychiatric patients (Negel, Moore, & Jones, 1997).

IBS–O scores were higher also among people experiencing disruptions in their interpersonal lives (e.g., divorced and separated adults). Among married respondents, although unrelated to marital satisfaction, IBS scores have been found to be negatively related to being satisfied with the family in which one was raised, and, for men only, marital commitment (Carver & Jones, 1992; Monroe, 1990). Dispositional betrayal was also related to the reported frequency of experiencing marital problems among married respondents (e.g., infidelity, deception, emotional abuse, loss of interest) and the tendency to blame one's spouse for the problems one perceives in one's marriage. Among adolescents, IBS–O scores were related to the number of social network members betrayed by the respondent as would be expected, but also to the proportion of network relationships described as involving jealousy, disagreements, and regret (Jones et al., 1991).

Studies among college students suggested the importance of perceptions of betrayal in the development of both romantic and platonic relationships. For example, in one study (Couch, 1996), a significant effect was observed for IBS–O scores in conjunction with satisfaction with nonromantic relationships. Respondents indicating satisfaction with relationship partners scored significantly lower than those who reported not being satisfied. Moreover, a significant effect was found for happiness in one's current romantic relationship, with individuals reporting being happy in their romantic relationship scoring significantly lower on the IBS–O than those who indicated that they were not happy. Furthermore, a significant effect was also found for experience with multiple painful breakups of romantic relationships. Respondents reporting many painful breakups scored significantly higher on the IBS–S (i.e., perceived betrayal by others) than persons reporting none or only one painful breakup. Experience as the victim of common betrayals was related to disgust, fear, and shame when responding to prototypical vignettes of betrayal and contempt and shame when responding to less prototypical vignettes (Couch, 1997). In general, experience as having been a victim of betrayal was related to higher scores for fear and shame.

Social Network Analyses

Beyond the generalized self-reported tendencies assessed by IBS–O and IBS–S, betrayal also may be conceptualized—and hence measured—as a characteristic or proportion of one's circle of friends and family members. The *social network* is defined as the people with whom a person has relatively frequent contact, who are important to the person, and who provide social support (i.e., information, help, and companionship, especially during times of stress; cf. Sarason, Sarason, & Pierce, 1990) to the person in question. To study betrayal within the social network, we have modified the Social Network List (cf. Jones & Moore, 1987) to include the identification of people in the network whom the respondent indicates having betrayed as well as people whom the respondent claims have betrayed him or her. Our version of the Social Network List instructs participants to list members of the social network and to indicate age, gender, type of relationship (e.g., friend, spouse, brother, sister, mother, work colleague), and length of acquaintance with each person listed and to rate various interpersonal dimensions for each. These dimensions include reciprocity, satisfaction with the relationship, jealousy, love, conflict, disagreements, and so on.

One study of this type surveyed more than 200 noncollege adults representing various demographic and occupational categories (cf. Jones et al., 1997). Results suggested that almost half (45%) of the respondents revealed that they had engaged in a *betrayal*—defined as a serious violation of the relationship—of at least one member of their current social network, and a similar proportion of respondents (52%) indicated that they had been the victim of a betrayal perpetuated by a member of their social network. On average, 20% of network members were identified as victims of respondents' betrayals, and 19% were classified as having betrayed the respondent. These results, therefore, suggest that betrayals are likely to involve at least some of one's closest relationship partners including spouses, family members, romantic partners, and close friends.

Furthermore, identification of a network member as having betrayed the respondent was associated, not surprisingly, with differential perceptions of that person. Specifically, network member perpetrators were rated significantly lower by respondents on positive interpersonal dimensions (e.g., satisfaction with the relationship, reciprocity of the partners, love of the partner, dependability of the partner, confidence in turning to the partner for help) and significantly higher on negative descriptive dimensions (e.g., regret, conflict, and jealousy). These results were consistent with those reported above assessing presumed relationship consequences association with vignettes of betrayal. Moreover, IBS–O and IBS–S scores were significantly related to the proportion of the network identified as victims and instigators of betrayal, respectively, a finding that supports the validity of both approaches.

Similar patterns of results were also observed at the network level of analysis in this and related studies. For example, respondents who reported having been betrayed by a greater proportion of their close associates also reported that smaller proportions of their networks were available to turn to for help and to confide in, and larger proportions of network relationships were identified as involving disagreements, conflict, and regret. Similarly, the proportion of network members betrayed by the respondent was related to the proportion of disagreements and regret within the network.

Accounts of Betrayal

Our final strategy for assessing betrayal has involved asking participants to describe their experiences of relationship treachery. Specifically, we elicited autobiographical "mini-narratives" (cf. Baumeister, Stillwell, & Wotman, 1990) by asking participants to describe an actual betrayal they experienced from each of two perspectives: (a) the most significant event in their experience in which they betrayed someone else and (b) the most significant experience in which the respondent had been the victim of an interpersonal transgression. We also asked participants to provide certain details of each event by asking them to respond to open-ended questions, for example, about their relationship to the other person (i.e., the victim or perpetrator), when the event took place, whether the victim was aware of what the respondent had done, the respondent's motives for the betrayal or the respondent's guess as to the motives of the person who betrayed him or her, and the effect, if any, on the relationship. We have administered these questions to a wide variety of participants including, for example, college students, noncollege adults, elderly people, children and adolescents, delinquent and neglected adolescents, psychiatric patients, and so on (Carver, 1990; Carver & Jones, 1992; Couch, 1997; Couch, Jones, & Moore, 1999; Hansson et al., 1990; Jones, 1988; Jones et al., 1991; Jones, Sanchez, & Merrell, 1989; Monroe, 1990; Moore, 1997a).

One issue addressed in this approach concerned types of betrayal. In what ways did relationship partners transgress against one another? Although a variety of types of betrayal were described by respondents, as would be expected, the majority of betrayals described concerned violations of relationship expectations, trust, and commitment. The most frequent type of betrayal reported by adult men involved betraying their partners or being betrayed by their partners by virtue of an extramarital sexual affair. Next in frequency for male individuals were lying, jilting a girlfriend or fiancée, betraying a confidence, two-timing girlfriends and sweethearts, and not providing emotional support. For female respondents, extramarital sexual affairs and telling lies were comparable in frequency, followed by betraying secrets. Two-timing boyfriends, excessive criticism, ignoring, avoiding, not supporting relationship partners, and jilting romantic partners were comparable in frequency.

Several respondents described being betrayed by virtue of their spouse having an extramarital affair with their best same-sex friend, or what might be called a compound betrayal. Not surprisingly, these accounts suggested even stronger emotional and other reactions; for example, one woman claimed to have worn her best friend's wedding ring as an act of revenge after finding it in her own bed.

For college students responding to the same questions, two-timing one's steady dating partner or fiancé and rejecting or jilting dating partners replaced extramarital affairs as the most common incidents by which participants indicated they had betrayed or been betrayed by an important relationship partner (Jones, 1988). Numerous students described going out with, kissing, and engaging in sexual intercourse with someone else while at home on vacation from school during a time when they were ostensibly committed to (in their own words) an exclusive or steady relationship. Students also frequently described lying and emotional turmoil between themselves and both their friends and their parents. For example, many students confessed to lying, especially to their mothers, "for their own good." Otherwise, the types of betrayal were very similar for both college students and adults. Among the elderly population, similar types of betrayal were also elicited except that these narratives often referred to an event that had taken place several years previously when the respondents were young (Hansson et al., 1990). Not surprisingly, adjudicated delinquents and psychiatric patients tended either to describe very serious forms of betrayal (e.g., physical abuse, abandonment by parents) or to argue that they had never been betrayed because they had experienced few if any close and intimate relationships (Carver, 1990).

As suggested above, the most common examples of the types of relationships involved in interpersonal betrayals—as both victims and perpetrators—are spouses and romantic partners (Jones, 1988; Jones & Burdette, 1994). This is particularly so for adults. For college students, romantic partners and friends predominated, followed by parents and siblings. Among children and adolescents, friends were more commonly cited, as were parents and siblings. For psychiatric patients, parents and ex-spouses were most frequently described as the perpetrators and the victims of betrayal.

Some interesting gender differences emerged in these studies (Jones et al., 1997). For example, men were more likely to indicate that they had betrayed their wives as compared to women saying they had betrayed their husbands. Women were more likely than men to cite betrayals between themselves and their best friends and siblings. For example, one woman indicated that she had betrayed her sister by telling their mother that her sister was a lesbian, whereas another women described her seduction of her sister's fiancé, resulting in the termination of their engagement. By contrast, men were more likely to recount betrayals involving business and occupational partners, co-workers, and employers, such as the man who told of a lifelong friend and business partner who absconded with their business funds or another male respondent who described a boss who "built a ladder to success without any rungs." Women tended to see criticism, angry outbursts, and "stonewalling" (i.e., refusing to speak during an emotional exchange) as betrayals; men did so less frequently (Moore, 1997b).

Several aspects of the betrayal descriptions are strongly related to the perspective of the respondent, that is, whether the respondent was describing an incident as the victim or the perpetrator. For example, "victim" narratives tended to be more serious violations of relational expectations (as judged by third party raters) and tended to have occurred further in the past than has been the case for "perpetrator" narratives (Jones et al., 1997). Another difference concerns the motives attributed to one's partner when one is the victim as compared to the causal attributions made for one's own behavior when one is the perpetrator. Interestingly, even in those instances where the type of betrayal was identical or similar, perpetrators tended to ascribe their actions to external, transitory, and unintentional factors, whereas, when respondents have been victimized, they attributed the behaviors of their relationship partners to internal, stable, and intentional causes (Jones, Sanchez, & Merrell, 1989). Thus, according to a majority of our respondents, one's own misdeeds derive from momentary lapses such as temporary stress, a bad mood, or intoxication, whereas transgressions on the part of partners are more likely to represent dispositional weakness, a "mean streak," deliberate selfishness, and so on. More specifically, respondents who might dismiss their own affair as the result of "pressure at work" would often attribute the affair their spouse had to perversity, or worse, to perversion.

Moreover, when asked to account for the impact of the betrayal on the relationship, respondents were far more likely to indicate that the net result was negative (e.g., resulting in termination, smoldering ill-will) when describing the sins of their partners, whereas their own misbehavior was more frequently seen as having a neutral or, in some cases, even a positive effect (Jones et al., 1997). For example, several men, whose extramarital affairs had gone undetected, claimed that their sexual relationships with their spouses had improved as a result of their betrayal. Others claimed that the threat to their relationship represented by their betrayal led to a passionate and enjoyable sexual reconciliation, although this occurred almost always for respondents describing their betrayals of others rather than respondents describing having been betrayed.

Consequences of Betrayal

With the possible exception of the type of incident cited above, the consequences of betrayal appear to be extensive and more or less universally negative and unpleasant. In the open-ended narratives, respondents describe reactions including feeling devastated, furious, depressed, anxious, disoriented, angry, stunned, enraged, overwhelmed, hopeless or, in their words, "like the rug had been pulled out from under me" or "like I had been hit in the chest with a baseball bat!" On the other hand, even the accounts of betrayal that were judged to be the most serious by raters did not always lead to the termination of the relationship. There were differences based on perspective, but even when describing having been betrayed by others, respondents indicated that the relationship ended as a result of the betrayal, on average, in only slightly more than 50% of the instances and, predictably, these tended to be friendships and romantic relationships rather than family relationships (e.g., parent–child, sibling). In most of the remaining cases, the respondent indicated that the relationship was harmed by the betrayal and that the harm is manifested by continuing mistrust, suspicion, or feelings of ill-will. In some cases, however, the issue of the betrayal was resolved through restorative processes such as apologizing and seeking forgiveness, and these are the mechanism to which we now turn.

Apology and Forgiveness

Recently we have studied factors that might influence the outcomes of interpersonal transgression by applying methods similar to those used to study betrayal. Specifically, this has involved an examination of the causal attributions made for betrayals; apology and its effect on forgiveness, retaliation, and the recapitulation of incidents; the quality of relationships after experiences of betrayal have occurred; and the lasting effects of incidents on the victim of betrayal (Moore, 1997a, 1997b; Moore & Jones, 1996; Schratter, Jones, & Negel, 1998). In other words, these studies have dealt with subsequent relationship events that may prevent betrayals from terminating or permanently damaging a relationship.

In general, these studies suggest that, although apologies and forgiveness represent an interpersonal sequence that may overcome the effects of betrayal, the effectiveness of these strategies is not necessarily guaranteed. On the one hand, there is evidence that retaliation for betrayal is relatively uncommon: In several samples fewer than 25% of the respondents reported retaliation both from the perspective of the victim and the perspective of the offender. Moreover, in one large survey among college students (Moore, 1997b), evidence suggesting that apology has a mitigating effect on forgiveness was observed. Forgiveness was almost twice as likely to occur, according to our respondents, when apologies were given.

On the other hand, forgiveness in the wake of apology did not appear to be automatic in these studies. For example, in one study (Moore, 1997a), those who received an apology within 1 week or less of the offense said they forgave the partner who offended them almost 100% of the time, whereas the rate of forgiveness fell with increasing time between offense and apology. Similarly, the manner in which apologies were delivered appeared to be important. For example, more respondents said they forgave when the perpetrator admitted he or she was wrong than when he or she did not admit wrongdoing. Apologizing with what the victim interpreted to be sincerity also made forgiveness more likely, according to our respondents. However, delivering excuses and "begging for forgiveness" were associated with lower rates of forgiveness according to these participants. There was little or no advantage gained by saying that one was sorry many times or asking for forgiveness repeatedly, as opposed to simply saying that one was sorry, or simply asking once for forgiveness.

Moreover, results from these studies may be interpreted as suggesting that, in some cases, there is no recourse from the negative consequences of having betrayed a relationship partner. For example, according to the respondents (Moore, 1997a, 1997b), although the base rate for retaliation was low, whether an apology was delivered was unrelated to whether or not the offended party sought revenge. Moreover, the old idea that forgiving is not the same as forgetting appears to have been confirmed in these studies. For example, apologies were associated with greater recapitulation of the betrayal (i.e., retelling the story of the incident, reminding the offender of what he or she had done, etc.); specifically, recapitulation was twice as likely in incidents where the offender apologized (Moore & Jones, 1996).

There also was evidence that, even though respondents often said they had forgiven the person who offended them, on closer examination their expressions of forgiveness were sometimes qualified with statements that suggested that they may not have forgiven at all. For example, in a sample of college students who were asked to recount betrayals and the subsequent sequence of events, one-third of the respondents indicated that they had forgiven the offender along with negative characterizations and indications of relationship disruption (Schratter et al., 1998). This pattern is illustrated by such statements as "I forgave him, but I hope he dies"; "I forgave her for what she did, but I never again spoke to her." This has been termed *conditional* or *pseudo-forgiveness* (Hebl & Enright, 1993). Furthermore, respondents who described their forgiveness in conditional terms indicated that the relationship in question declined in quality following the betrayal, similar to respondents who indicated that they had not forgiven the offending relationship partner, despite their ostensible forgiveness. By contrast, respondents who reported what might be termed *unconditional forgiveness* ("I forgave her so I have never thought about the incident since"; "I forgave him and it is all behind us now") reported that their relationship improved following the incident.

Summary and Conclusions

Major results from these studies that were replicated across various respondent samples may be summarized as follows: (a) many of the most common consequences of betrayal and most certainly how one feels about it appear to vary largely as a function of perspective—whether one is the victim or the offender—in the incident; (b) betrayal is a relatively common feature of relationships; (c) betrayal occurs primarily among one's closest relationships and, apparently, the most devastating betrayals occur among the most important and most intimate relationships; and (d) although betrayal often leads to apology and forgiveness, these processes sometimes mask a pattern of continuing ill-will and disruption.

Several questions remain with respect to the origins and consequences of interpersonal transgressions and betrayals. For example, the complexity of social organization would seem to make interpersonal transgressions more or less inevitable from time to time, but the question arises as to whether betrayals are inevitable in relationships because of their subjectivity and the natural ebb and flow of relationship satisfaction (cf. Couch, Jones, & Moore, 1999). Similarly, do betrayals occur because the potential benefits of such actions simply outweigh their negative consequences, or are they more likely the result of situational cross-pressures or the unintended results of at least partially acceptable motives? The consequences of betrayal seem remarkably variable. In some cases, even drastic breaches of relationship values lead to forgiveness and reconciliation, whereas in other cases, relatively trivial offenses augur poorly for the continuation of the relationship. On average, people clearly understand better and are more tolerant of their own offenses against others than they are of the offenses of others perpetrated against them. Even so, there appear to be relevant individual differences for both betrayal and forgiveness; some people appear less likely to take offense and are more empathic and forgiving when an offense occurs, whereas others are more likely to betray their relationship partners and more likely also to receive or perceive betrayal from those relationship partners. Are these dispositions regarding betrayal and forgiveness related, as would be expected, and to what degree do they predict feelings and behaviors in situations with actual relationship partners?

In this regard, it is interesting to note that self-reported betrayal of others (i.e., IBS–O) is highly correlated with perceived betrayal by others (i.e., IBS–S). One explanation for this is that betrayed relationship partners may respond in kind. Another possibility is latent in a recently proposed account of rejection and hurt feelings. According to the sociometer theory proposed by Leary and Downs (1995), self-esteem acts as an internal gauge that automatically monitors the social environment for cues denoting interpersonal rejection, disapproval, or exclusion, and triggers negative affect when such cues are detected (Leary et al., 1998; Nezlek et al., 1997). This, in turn, impels behaviors of reconciliation and affiliation in an attempt to restore social acceptance. As a consequence, the more one experiences rejection in his or her interpersonal relationships, the more likely he or she is to develop low trait self-esteem and an increased awareness, or sensitivity, to cues indicative of social exclusion. Previous research has shown that trait self-esteem moderates individuals' reactions to social inclusion and exclusion, and researchers have proposed three possible mechanisms accounting for this mediation effect (Nezlek et al., 1997). First, people with high trait self-esteem may possess a higher threshold for negatively responding to threats to their inclusionary status. Conversely, a lack of response to exclusion on the part of persons with high self-esteem may reflect a defensive reaction of minimizing such ego threats in order to maintain a positive sense of self-worth. Finally, the lack of response to exclusionary status may reflect a self-presentation tactic to convince others that the individual was not bothered by being excluded. Because of relational devaluation, hurt feelings are also theorized to result from the affective component of the sociometer, suggesting that the more rejected that one feels the more likely one is to experience negative affect.

Correspondingly, people in close interpersonal relationships are more likely to react more strongly to hurting their relational partners as well as being hurt by them because their behaviors are more consequential to their overall well-being (Leary et al., 1998). For example, in one study examining the self-fulfilling prophecy in close relationships, Downey, Freitas, Michaelis, and Khouri (1998) hypothesized that expectations of interpersonal rejection lead people to behave in ways that elicit rejection from others. Specifically, they found that high rejection sensitivity in women, or the dispositional tendency to anxiously expect, readily perceive, and overreact to rejection from significant others is more likely to result in relationship dissolution because it leads to becoming increasingly dissatisfied with a relationship and behaving in such a manner as to erode the partner's relational satisfaction and commitment.

Thus, ironically the betrayal of relationship partners may be more likely among persons who can least afford its negative outcomes. Moreover, the characteristic patterns of interaction and partner orientation among those who are less confident—and perhaps also less competent interpersonally—may inhibit the restorative relationship processes of apology, forgiveness, and reconciliation.

REFERENCES

Adams, J. M., & Jones, W. H. (1997). The conceptualization of marital commitment: An integrative analysis. *Journal of Personality and Social Psychology, 72*, 1177–1196.

Baumeister, R. F., Stillwell, A., & Wotman, S. R. (1990). Victim and perpetrator accounts of interpersonal conflict: Autobiographical narratives about anger. *Journal of Personality and Social Psychology, 59*, 994–1005.

Buss, D. M., Larsen, R. J., Westen, D., & Semmelroth, J. (1992). Sex differences in jealousy: Evolution, physiology, and psychology. *Psychological Science, 3*, 251–255.

Buss, D. M., & Shackelford, T. K. (1997). Susceptibility to infidelity in the first year of marriage. *Journal of Research in Personality, 31*, 193–221.

Buunk, B., & van Driel, B. (1989). *Variant lifestyles and relationships.* London: Sage.

Canary, D. J., Spitzberg, B. H., & Semic, B. A. (1998). The experience and expression of anger in interpersonal settings. In P. A. Andersen & L. K. Guerrero (Eds.), *Handbook of communication and emotion: Research, theory, applications, and contexts* (pp. 189–213). San Diego: Academic Press.

Carver, M. L. (1990). *Personality disorder dimensions and relational functioning.* Unpublished doctoral dissertation, University of Tulsa, Tulsa, OK.

Carver, M. L., & Jones, W. H. (1992). The Family Satisfaction Scale. *Social Behavior and Personality, 20*, 71–83.

Couch, L. L. (1994). *The development of the Trust Inventory.* Unpublished master's thesis, University of Tennessee, Knoxville.

Couch, L. L. (1996, August). *The perceived seriousness of interpersonal betrayal.* Paper presented at the International Conference on Personal Relationships, Banff, Alberta, Canada.

Couch, L. L. (1997, April). *Interpersonal betrayal: Assessment and emotional reactions.* Paper presented at the meeting of the Southeastern Psychological Association, Atlanta, GA.

Couch, L. L., & Jones, W. H. (1997). Conceptualizing levels of trust. *Journal of Research in Personality, 31,* 319–336.

Couch, L. L., Jones, W. H., & Moore, D. S. (1999). Buffering the effects of betrayal: The role of apology, forgiveness, and commitment. In J. M. Adams & W. H. Jones (Eds.), *Handbook of commitment and relational stability* (pp. 451–469). New York: Plenum Press.

DePaulo, B. M., & Kashy, D. A. (1998). Everyday lies in close and casual relationships. *Journal of Personality and Social Psychology, 74,* 63–79.

DePaulo, B. M., Kashy, D. A., Kirkendol, S. E., Wyer, M. M., & Epstein, J. A. (1996). Lying in everyday life. *Journal of Personality and Social Psychology, 70,* 979–995.

De Silva, P. (1997). Jealousy in couple relationships: Nature, assessment, and therapy. *Behavior, Research, and Therapy, 35,* 973–985.

DeSteno, D. A., & Salovey, P. (1994). Jealousy in close relationships: Multiple perspectives on the green-eyed monster. In A. L. Weber & J. H. Harvey (Eds.), *Perspectives on close relationships* (pp. 217–242). Boston: Allyn and Bacon.

Downey, G., Freitas, A. L., Michaelis, B., & Khouri, H. (1998). The self-fulfilling prophecy in close relationships: Rejection sensitivity and rejection by romantic partners. *Journal of Personality and Social Psychology, 75,* 545–560.

Guerrero, L. K., & Anderson, P. A. (1998). Rejection experience and expression in romantic relationships. In P. A. Andersen & L. K. Guerrero (Eds.), *Handbook of communication and emotion: Research, theory, applications, and contexts* (pp. 155–188). San Diego: Academic Press.

Guerrero, L. K., Eloy, S. V., Jorgensen, P. F., & Andersen, P. A. (1993). His or hers? Sex differences in the experience and communication of jealousy in close relationships. In J. Kalbfleisch (Ed.), *Interpersonal communication in evolving interpersonal relationships* (pp. 109–131). Hillsdale, NJ: Erlbaum.

Hansson, R. O., Jones, W. H., & Fletcher, W. L. (1990). Troubled relationships in later life: Implications for support. *Journal of Social and Personal Relationships, 7,* 451–463.

Harris, C. R., & Christenfeld, N. (1996). Gender, jealousy, and reason. *Psychological Science, 7,* 364–366.

Hebl, J., & Enright, R. D. (1993). Forgiveness as a psychotherapeutic goal with elderly females. *Psychotherapy, 30,* 658–667.

Johnson, M. P. (1991). Commitment and personal relationships. In W. H. Jones & D. Perlman (Eds.), *Advances in personal relationships: A research annual* (Vol. 3, pp. 117–143). London: Jessica Kingsley.

Jones, W. H. (1988, July). *Psychological and interpersonal issues in betrayal and treachery*. Paper presented at the International Conference on Personal Relationships, Vancouver, British Columbia, Canada.

Jones, W. H., & Burdette, M. P. (1994). Betrayal in relationships. In A. L. Weber & J. H. Harvey (Eds.), *Perspectives on close relationships* (pp. 243–262). Boston: Allyn and Bacon.

Jones, W. H., & Carpenter, B. N. (1986). Shyness, social behavior, and relationships. In W. H. Jones, J. M. Cheek, & S. R. Briggs (Eds.), *Shyness: Perspectives on research and treatment* (pp. 227–238). New York: Plenum Press.

Jones, W. H., Cohn, M. G., & Miller, C. E. (1991). Betrayal among children and adults. In K. J. Rotenberg (Ed.), *Children's interpersonal trust: Sensitivity to lying, deception and promise violations* (pp. 119–134). New York: Springer-Verlag.

Jones, W. H., Couch, L. L., & Scott, S. (1997). Trust and betrayal: The psychology of trust violations. In R. Hogan, J. Johnson, & S. R. Briggs (Eds.), *Handbook of personality* (pp. 465–482). New York: Academic Press.

Jones, W. H., & Moore, T. L. (1987). Loneliness and social support. *Journal of Social Behavior and Personality, 2,* 145–156.

Jones, W. H., & Russell, D. (1982). The Social Reticence Scale: An objective instrument to measure shyness. *Journal of Personality Assessment, 46,* 629–631.

Jones, W. H., Sanchez, D., & Merrell, J. (1989, April). *Attributions for betrayal*. Paper presented at the meeting of the Southwestern Psychological Association, Tulsa, OK.

Lampe, P. E. (1987). *Adultery in the United States: Close encounters of the sixth or seventh kind*. Buffalo, NY: Prometheus Books.

Leary, M. R., & Downs, D. L. (1995). Interpersonal functions of the self-esteem motive: The self-esteem system as a sociometer. In M. H. Kernis (Ed.), *Efficacy, agency, and self-esteem* (pp. 123–144). New York: Plenum Press.

Leary, M. R., Springer, C., Negel, L., Ansell, E., & Evans, K. (1998). The causes, phenomenology, and consequences of hurt feelings. *Journal of Personality and Social Psychology, 74,* 1225–1237.

McCornack, S. A., & Parks, M. R. (1990). What women know that men don't: Sex differences in determining the truth behind deceptive messages. *Journal of Social and Personal Relationships, 7,* 107–118.

Metts, S. (1989). An exploratory investigation of deception in close relationships. *Journal of Social and Personal Relationships, 6,* 159–179.

Metts, S., & Bowers, J. W. (1994). Emotion in interpersonal communication. In M. L. Knapp & G. R. Miller (Eds.), *Handbook of interpersonal communication* (2nd ed., pp. 508–541). Thousand Oaks, CA: Sage Publications.

Miller, G. P., Mongeau, P. A., & Sleight, C. (1986). Fudging with friends and lying to lovers: Deceptive communication in personal relationships. *Journal of Social and Personal Relationships, 3,* 495–512.

Monroe, P. R. (1990). *A study of marital problems, marital satisfaction, and commitment*. Unpublished doctoral dissertation, University of Tulsa, Tulsa, OK.

Montgomery, R. L., & Brown, E. O. (1988, July). *Betrayal, treachery, the CPI and the Jenkins Activity Survey*. Paper presented at the International Conference on Personal Relationships, Vancouver, British Columbia, Canada.

Moore, D. S. (1997a, March). *Interpersonal betrayal: Forgiveness and the delivery of apologies*. Paper presented at the meeting of the Southeastern Psychological Association, Atlanta, GA.

Moore, D. S. (1997b). *Interpersonal betrayal: Self-serving biases, cynicism, and the mediating effects of apology and forgiveness*. Unpublished master's thesis, University of Tennessee, Knoxville.

Moore, D. S., & Jones, W. H. (1996, March). *Apology: Mediator of retaliation and recapitulation in interpersonal betrayal*. Paper presented at the meeting of the Southeastern Psychological Association, Norfolk, VA.

Negel, L., Moore, D. S., & Jones, W. H. (1997, November). *Betrayal in psychiatric patients*. Paper presented at the meeting of the Society of Southeastern Social Psychologists, Research Triangle Park, NC.

Nezlek, J. B., Kowalski, R. M., Leary, M. R., Blevins, T., & Holgate, S. (1997). Personality moderators of reactions to interpersonal rejection: Depression and trait self-esteem. *Personality and Social Psychology Bulletin, 23*, 1235–1244.

Papsdorf, M., & Alden, L. (1998). Mediators of social rejection in social anxiety: Similarity, self-disclosure, and overt signs of anxiety. *Journal of Research in Personality, 32*, 351–369.

Parrott, W. G. (1991). The emotional experiences of envy and jealousy. In P. Salovey (Ed.), *The psychology of jealousy and envy* (pp. 3–30). New York: Guilford Press.

Peterson, C. (1996). Deception in intimate relationships. *International Journal of Psychology, 31*, 279–288.

Rempel, J. K., Holmes, J. G., & Zanna, M. P. (1985). Trust in close relationships. *Journal of Personality and Social Psychology, 49*, 91–112.

Saarni, C., & Lewis, M. (1993). Deceit and illusion in human affairs. In M. Lewis & C. Saarni (Eds.), *Lying and deception in everyday life* (pp. 1–29). New York: Guilford Press.

Salovey, P., & Rodin, J. (1986). The differentiation of social-comparison jealousy and romantic jealousy. *Journal of Personality and Social Psychology, 50*, 1100–1112.

Sarason, I. G., Sarason, B. R., & Pierce, G. R. (Eds.). (1990). *Social support: An interactional view*. New York: Wiley.

Schratter, A. K., Jones, W. H., & Negel, L. A. (1998, March). *Betrayal, apology, and the quality of forgiveness*. Presented at the annual meeting of the Southeastern Psychological Association, Mobile, AL.

Shaver, P., Schwartz, D., Kirson, D., & O'Connor, C. (1987). Emotion knowledge: Further exploration of a prototype approach. *Journal of Personality and Social Psychology, 52*, 1061–1086.

Storm, C., & Storm, T. (1987). A taxonomic study of the vocabulary of emotions. *Journal of Personality and Social Psychology, 53*, 805–816.

Vangelisti, A. L. (1994). Messages that hurt. In W. R. Cupach & B. H. Spitzberg

(Eds.), *The dark side of interpersonal communication* (pp. 53–82). Hillsdale, NJ: Erlbaum.

Vangelisti, A. L., & Sprague, R. J. (1998). Guilt and hurt: Similarities, distinctions, and conversational strategies. In P. A. Anderson & L. K. Guerrero (Eds.), *Handbook of communication and emotion: Research theory, application, and contexts* (pp. 123–153). San Diego, CA: Academic Press.

White, G., & Mullen, P. (1989). *Jealousy: Theory, research, and clinical strategies.* New York: Guilford Press.

10

AVERSIVE BEHAVIOR AND AGGRESSION IN CULTURAL PERSPECTIVE

JAMES T. TEDESCHI AND MICHAEL HARRIS BOND

In this chapter we take a theoretical conceptualization of aggressive behavior, developed by Tedeschi (1981) and elaborated most recently by Tedeschi and Felson (1994), and we integrate this approach with the available cross-cultural data. As Segall, Ember, and Ember (1997) pointed out, there is relatively little cross-cultural data on aggressive behavior, despite its significance in human social life. The available cross-cultural studies are predominantly "hologesic" or focused on social units like nations or states as the unit of analysis. In consequence, findings from such studies are about these units, not about people and their psychological functioning. Their results must then be "translated" or "unpackaged" at the individual level for psychologists to understand the personal or interpersonal dynamics that lead to aggressive behavior (Bond, 1998; Clark, 1987; Whiting, 1976). After all, individuals threaten, curse, betray, punch, execute, and rob others, even when they act on behalf of their groups or as group members. It

We thank Herman Aguinis, Dov Cohen, and Richard Wilkinson for their helpful, insightful comments on earlier drafts of this chapter.

is at this individual level that we, as social psychologists, attempt to understand and predict human behavior.

An example of the hologesic approach is Archer and Gartner's (1984) examination of post–World War II variations in country homicide rates. They found that homicide increased in combatant nations "regardless of whether they had won or lost the war, regardless of whether their economies had improved or not, and regardless of the age or gender groups of the perpetrators" (Smith & Bond, 1998, p. 87). Based on these findings, Archer and Gartner (1984) argued for a legitimation of violence model whereby the prosecution of a war required nations to socialize their members to be more violent as a matter of national interest. This socialization then had a residual impact after wartime; citizens were generally less inhibited about killing one another.

This legitimation of violence can be translated at the individual level to some measurable construct like Caprara, Barbaranelli, and Zimbardo's (1996) construct, positive evaluation of violence, that reflects individual differences in the propensity to inflict physical harm on others. Positive evaluation of violence may have been elevated in the population of the warring nations studied by Archer and Gartner (1984) as a result of their socializing citizens for war through parenting practices, educational indoctrination, and media presentations. Heightened value for violence would then generalize to disinhibiting homicide against one's own nationals after the war had ended.

The social interactionist theory of coercive actions (SITCA) proposed by Tedeschi and Felson (1994) is framed at this individual level. It describes and explains individual-level processes that result in behavior labeled *aggressive*. In this chapter, we explain SITCA and describe how its constructs operate at the level of the individual actor. We attempt to broaden the range of the theory by incorporating findings from a variety of cultural groups that suggest the importance of constructs often overlooked by theories that ignore culture.

AGGRESSION AND HOW IT IS STUDIED

Aggression consists of behaviors perpetrated by an actor who targets people experienced as aversive. These behaviors that are perceived as aggressive are often justified by actors as provoked by aversive actions of the target person. An actor's behavior is perceived as aggressive when observers attribute harmful intentions to the actor and when the actor's behavior is perceived as illegitimate or wrong (R. C. Brown & Tedeschi, 1976). Whereas the target person may perceive proactive and intentional harmdoing as illegitimate, actors often believe that their punitive action was provoked by the aversive behavior of the target and is thus legitimate and not aggressive. Thus, aggression, like the perception of aversiveness, is often in the eye of the beholder.

In some situations, observers may agree with an actor's reasons for punitive actions against a target. In such cases, the actor is not considered to be aggressive, even though she or he engaged in the same behavior as another person who cannot justify his or her action (and is, therefore, regarded as aggressive). For example, a parent may punish a child because the child has misbehaved. In this case, the parent's punitive act is a response to an aversive behavior of the child. Most people accept that parents have both the right and the responsibility to punish their children for misbehavior, although there are limits on the form and degree of punishment that are considered legitimate across cultures (Levinson, 1989; Zern, 1984) and also across social classes within nations (D. Gil, 1970).

Two important social psychological questions arise from an examination of aversive behaviors: Why do people act in such negative ways, and how do others respond to them? These questions are not independent of one another; interactions between persons seldom are so clearly independent of one another that it can be said that Actor A did something first and that Actor B simply reacted to what Actor A did. In laboratory situations, however, sequences can be contrived (using confederates) in which one of the actors clearly engages in unprovoked aversive behavior toward the other. This type of experiment is characteristic of research on human aggression. However, as we discuss, there are serious limitations imposed by the procedures that have been used to study human aggression in the laboratory.

Limitations of Research Procedures

Both theory and research indicate an instigative function for aversive social behavior. Attack and retaliation are the focus of most laboratory studies, with independent variables manipulating the presence or the intensity of attack and dependent variables measuring the target's reactions. Other factors that are manipulated, such as heat and physical exercise, typically occur during or following instigation and are interpreted as facilitating, inhibiting, or disinhibiting aggressive behavior. In a critical examination of laboratory procedures for studying aggression, Tedeschi and Quigley (1996, 2000) indicated why it is difficult to unambiguously interpret the results of experiments that study the effects of physical and social aversiveness on aggressive behavior.

Typically, a confederate insults a research participant in the waiting room prior to the arrival of the experimenter (e.g. Sebastian, 1978). The participants are given a cover story about their roles during the rest of the experiment. In the teacher–learner paradigm, the previously insulted participants are assigned the role of teacher, and the confederate the role of a learner. The learner is provided a list of pairs of word associations and is given only a brief opportunity to scan them. The two persons are then placed in separate cubicles or rooms. The teacher is provided with an intercom to communicate with the learner and with a Buss aggression machine, which is a box that contains buttons to represent 10 intensities of electric shock that can be delivered to the learner through a finger electrode. The teacher reads the first word of a paired association, and the learner must provide the correct second word. If the confederate (whose responses are predetermined by the experimenter) gives a correct association, the teacher says "good" or "correct" over the intercom. However, if the learner makes an error, the teacher is told that he or she must punish the learner by delivering an electric shock. As many as 30 word association pairs may be used in the procedures with as many as 20 occasions when the teacher must shock the learner. The average intensity of shock chosen by the teacher is the measure of aggression used in these experiments.

In the essay writing paradigm (Berkowitz, Corwin, & Heironimus, 1962), the confederate and participant are asked to create some product —an essay, a construction out of paper, or something else. They are then asked to rate each other's product by delivering from 1 (for excellent work) to 10 (for poor work) shocks to the other person. The confederate makes a rating first and is programmed to give few or many shocks, and the participant follows by evaluating the confederate's product. Of course it is possible in both the teacher–learner and essay writing paradigms to introduce other variables, such as riding stationary bicycles, being exposed to pornography, and viewing violent films between the negative behavior of the confederate and the use of shocks by the participant, and so forth.

These two sets of procedures account for a sizeable amount of aggression research. Tedeschi and Quigley (1996) noted that these two paradigms have the following features in common:

> (a) the research participant is subjected to an unprovoked attack; (b) the experimenter requires that some level of noxious stimulation be administered to the provocateur; (c) the experimenter rationalizes the use of noxious stimulation by the research participants as a necessary factor related to the purposes of the experiment; and (d) the episode takes place under the watchful eye of a person with authority in the situation—that is, the experimenter. (p. 168)

It should be noted that participants have no choice in these paradigms whether or not to administer electric shocks to the other person; they are told to do so by the experimenter. In the teacher–learner situation, participants must shock the learner whenever he or she makes an error, and in the essay writing paradigm participants must shock the other person as a means of evaluating his or her product. Tedeschi and Quigley (1996) concluded from this analysis that the instigation to "aggression" (or the use of shock) is the experimenter's instruction to do so. Thus, it can be argued that, in experiments using the teacher–learner or essay evaluation procedures, the instigation to aggression consists of experimenter commands, and results can be interpreted in terms of obedience (see Milgram, 1974). Of course participants can vary the intensity, duration, or frequency of shock, but they cannot choose not to use shocks. Factors that affect the intensity of aggression once it has been instigated are referred to as facilitators, and this is why we have argued that most laboratory research has examined facilitators rather than instigators of aggression.[1]

Aversiveness and Reactive Aggression

In the literature on aggression, little distinction is made between physical and social sources of aversiveness. Indeed, in the most dominant theory of aggression in social psychology (Berkowitz, 1993), it is assumed that reactions to physical sources of discomfort are no different than reactions to social sources of aversiveness. Taking a cue from Lorenz's (1966) ethological theory of instincts, Berkowitz argued that animals innately experience some physical stimuli as aversive. For example, exposure to high or very low temperatures, loud noises, and electric shock is experienced as aversive by humans. In Berkowitz's theory of reactive (or emotional) aggression, aversive stimuli arouse negative affect in the individual, which in turn creates a desire to hurt a suitable target. If the aggressive instigation is stronger than a fear reaction, the organism then carries out an attack against the target.

This mechanism involving aversive stimuli, negative affect, the desire to hurt, and aggressive behavior is innately prewired in the inexperienced (young) individual. The theory proposes that the organism learns to appraise stimuli and that such appraisals determine whether stimuli are experienced as aversive by the mature individual. Thus, aversiveness is at first innately associated with physical stimuli not needing appraisals, but as the animal matures, what is experienced as aversive comes to be based on subjective evaluations. Through such learning, verbal or physical attacks may be appraised as aversive and instigate aggressive behavior. An enormous amount of research has been carried out over the past 35 years that has been interpreted by Berkowitz (1993) and others (e.g., Baron & Richardson, 1993; Geen, 1990) as supporting the proposed instigative function of aversive stimuli on aggressive behavior.

---

[1]See Tedeschi and Quigley (1996, 2000) for more extensive criticisms of laboratory paradigms for studying aggression. In addition to the procedures discussed here, they have also critically examined the competitive reaction time game (Taylor & Epstein, 1967), Bandura's (1973) Bobo procedures, and Cherek's point subtraction aggression paradigm (Cherek, Spiga, & Egli, 1992). In each case questions are raised about the construct validity of these procedures in measuring human aggression.

Reviews of the literature have raised serious questions about such conclusions. For example, Anderson (1989) reviewed field, archival, and laboratory studies of heat effects on violent crimes and aggressive behavior. Although he found positive relationships between temperature and violent crimes across various geographical areas, his review of laboratory studies indicates a general failure to confirm that relationship at the level of individuals. Indeed, several experiments find the opposite relationship (e.g., Baron & Bell, 1975; Bell & Baron, 1976).

It is worth noting at this point that the findings relating heat to aggression at the level of nations or city levels thus do not "translate" to the individual level. Evidently some other factor is associated with higher average temperatures, and that factor then affects aggressive responses. One possibility is that heat is associated with subsistence practices like the use of hunting or herding. These subsistence practices require socialization for independence and assertiveness (Berry, 1979). These personality traits then predispose the individual toward higher levels of aggressive behavior. Thus, the psychological characteristic of independence or assertiveness, and not higher ambient heat, might account for the greater use of interpersonal violence.

Another hypothesis is that temperature is related to routine activities of people. According to routine activity theory (L. E. Cohen & Felson, 1979), crime and violence are more likely to occur in situations where there is a motivated offender, a vulnerable target, and an absence of guardians. Time spent in routine activities, such as work and school, place the individual in social situations where there are guardians, such as supervisors and teachers. Discretionary time may place the individual in bars, parks, and other unsupervised settings, where there is an absence of guardians. As temperatures rise, individuals may more often visit such unsupervised settings and, as a result, more crime and violence occur. Evidence consistent with the routine activity theory was found by Cohn and Rotton (1997) and Rotton and Cohn (1999). They reported that the heat–violence relationship in both Milwaukee and Dallas occurred only during evening and night hours, especially on Fridays and Saturdays. Thus, when people are engaged in discretionary activities rather than obligatory activities, temperature is significantly correlated with violent behavior. Presumably, the type of discretionary activities chosen by people is strongly affected by temperature and season of the year.

Whereas heat may not either instigate or facilitate aggression, it appears that noxious noise at least sometimes increases the intensity of aggressive behavior (see reviews by Baron, 1977; Mueller, 1983; Rule & Nesdale, 1976a, 1976b). However, close scrutiny of the procedures used in the experiments finding positive results reveals that noxious noise facilitates but does not instigate aggressive behavior. Mere exposure to loud noises does not by itself increase levels of aggressive behavior, but, if some other factor such as an attack or frustration instigates aggressive behavior, noxious stimuli may have the effect of intensifying aggression. In light of these results, Tedeschi and Felson (1994) have argued that any extraneous source that increases arousal when the individual has already been instigated to aggress may facilitate aggression.

A number of researchers have related personal stress to abusive behavior (e.g., Straus, 1980). According to physiologists, stressors include sudden alarm, intense cold or heat, or serious injury. Such stimuli produce a complex hormonal defense response that allows the body to cope with the danger. This defense reaction is vital for survival, but if it continues for prolonged periods it can be dangerous to the person's well-being. People who experience prolonged stress suffer physical ailments and depression and become abusive to others (spouses, children). This notion of stressor appears to be similar if not identical to what Berkowitz (1993) referred to as *aversive stimuli*. In our view, however, this is too limited an approach to studying aversive social behaviors and how people react to them. Stressors for most people most of the time include aversive behaviors of others that produce concerns about job security, spousal fidelity, social esteem, and other important aspects of daily social life. It is important, therefore, to develop a more differentiated theory of what constitutes aversive behaviors and the conditions under which they provoke aggressive responses by the "stressed" person.

In Berkowitz's (1993) theory of reactive aggression, aversive stimuli are the primary causes of aggressive behavior. Berkowitz does not distinguish between physical and social sources of aversiveness. As we have indicated, *physically aversive stimuli* refer to ecological, external stimuli that produce unpleasantness in the perceiver, such as heat, loud noises, and sources of physical pain. Social sources of aversiveness are insults, attacks, rejections, or other behaviors by others that create negative affect in the person. Although the evidence does not support the assertion that aversive physical stimuli can instigate aggressive behavior, we believe that under some circumstances aversive social behaviors do instigate aggressive behavior. Unlike Berkowitz, we maintain that it is not general aversiveness per se that instigates aggressiveness, but rather the emotional–motivational processes set in motion by another person's aversive behavior that do so. Anger, humiliation, and a desire for social control may serve as bases for aggressive behavior. Furthermore, aversive behaviors by others can lead to nonaggressive responses in the target like depression, guilt, fear, and anxiety. The focus of laboratory research on aggression has been on the harmdoer. This research is nonrecursive, and effects on the harmed person are ignored. The interactive features of aggressive episodes have been reduced to a type of one-man chess, taking into account what one player does without consideration of the potential moves of the other player. In contrast, we need to specify the conditions under which aversive behavior from another person instigates an aggressive response rather than some other reaction by the target person.

SOCIAL INTERACTIONIST THEORY OF COERCIVE ACTIONS

Given the limitations of laboratory experiments, particularly the absence of research on proactive aggressive behavior and the general failure to examine instigators of reactive aggression, it is important to look outside the laboratory to validate findings and extend our knowledge of such behavior. Tedeschi and Felson (1994) took this approach when they reviewed evidence obtained by a variety of other methods, including field experiments, interviews, case studies, longitudinal studies, surveys, laboratory experiments, and archives of crime statistics.

According to Tedeschi and Felson (1994), aggression theorists have focused too myopically on intrapsychic factors, such as frustration, negative affect, drive states, and physiological–biological factors (including brain centers, androgens, instincts, and genetic factors) and have tended to ignore the social factors. So, Tedeschi and Felson proposed a theory, SITCA to explain the available evidence. This theory reconceptualizes aggression as various forms of threats and punishments that people use to compel compliance or to harm others. Usually, people targeted by the threats and punishments view them as aversive, but actors may also find them aversive to administer, even when such actions are considered necessary and justified. Parents may very much dislike punishing a child for misbehavior, or teachers may dislike expelling a student for rule violations but, because of a sense of social responsibility, they carry out the punishment in the spirit of "this hurts me more than it hurts you."

Social interactionist theory assumes that individuals are interdependent with one another for their outcomes. Each person depends on others for respect, love, safety, food, money, status, and almost every other kind of reinforcement. Because the person wants to achieve goals that require mediation by other people, it is necessary to do something to get the target persons to do what is needed. Among the influence tactics available to a person are persuasion, promises, threats, rewards, punishments, exhortation, and pleas. The focus of SITCA is an examination of the conditions under which persons choose to engage in the coercive actions of threatening and punishing others rather than in noncoercive forms of influence to achieve interpersonal goals.

SITCA proposes that three major motives instigate most coercive actions: social control, justice, and identity. Actors motivated by social control occasionally use threats and punishments proactively to compel targets to do what they want. The threatener's goal is to gain compliance to some demand. Compliance is a short-term goal that is desired because it is believed by the coercing actor to mediate his or her terminal goals. A robber threatens a victim with bodily harm to compel compliance to demands, he or she desires compliance because it leads to money, and the money is to be used to satisfy other goals (e.g., peer-group status). The justice motive is activated by perceptions of injustice that cause the perceiver to redress the injustice or "to get even." An identity motive may be manifested in two ways: as proactive behavior to establish an identity and as a defensive action intended to maintain a desired identity or to restore it in the face of identity-threatening acts of other people. We examine the social control, justice, and identity motives and the processes associated with them in generating coercive actions. Central to these processes and serving as instigators of these actions are the aversive social behaviors of others.[2]

Social Control Motivation

Coercive actions are usually experienced as aversive by targets or victims. This form of aversive behavior is resorted to primarily to control other people. Coercion is more likely to be used when targets do not respond to other positive means of social influence. For example, Sun and Bond (in press) found that managers were more likely to use tactics of "coercive control" when facing a recalcitrant subordinate than when facing a cooperative subordinate.

A schematic of factors affecting the choice of coercive forms of influence is shown in Figure 10.1. As a decision maker, the actor assesses the probability of success for noncoercive means of influence, the value of the goal that successful influence would achieve, and the probability and value of costs that are likely to accrue from using that means of influence. Furthermore, people positively or negatively value particular means of influencing others, which may provide secondary value or additional costs to those means. All of these factors are considered by the actor, who attempts to maximize outcomes or minimize costs.

Power Bases and Coercion

Tedeschi and Felson (1994) postulated that low intelligence, poor social skills, inarticulateness, and lack of such power bases as expertise, attractiveness, and credibility are associated with lack of confidence in noncoercive forms of influence (see also Farrington, 1997). These factors decrease the person's ability to effectively use argument and persuasion or to promise rewards or induce trust in the target person. When an actor

---

[2]Aversive actions of others are not the exclusive instigators of threats and punishments, but they are the focus of this chapter. See Tedeschi and Felson (1994) for a thorough examination of other instigators of coercive actions.

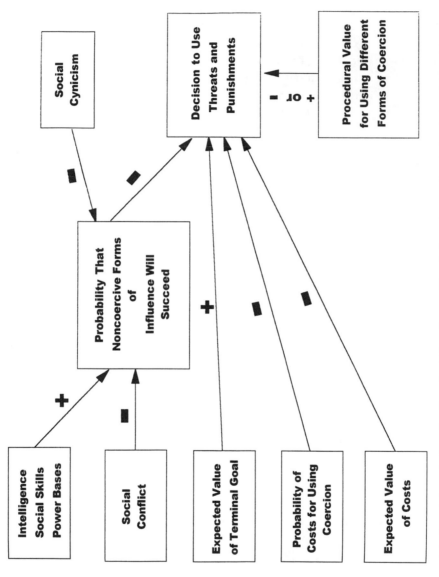

Figure 10.1. A model of social control motivation depicting the positive (+) and negative (−) relationships of factors involved in a decision to use threats and punishments.

lacks confidence in noncoercive forms of influence or when positive forms of influence fail, the actor can either decide to give up the goal that others can mediate or can try more coercive means to obtain compliance. A rather sizeable research literature indicates that these factors are related to the use of coercive actions (cf. Tedeschi, Lindskold, & Rosenfeld, 1985).

Social Conflict and Distrust

Social conflicts in which two or more interdependent parties vie for scarce resources (incompatible goals) reduce confidence in the effectiveness of positive forms of influence and make resolution difficult (Deutsch, 1994). In conflict situations, the person can either give in to the desire of the other person, try to impose his or her own solution, or seek a compromise. Each party to the conflict is aware that the communications of the other are based on self-interest and are hence suspect as a basis for the actor's own behavior. That is, distrust is induced by conflict situations (Deutsch, 1994). Distrust reduces the expected probability that noncoercive forms of influence succeed as a means of resolving the conflict, thus encouraging the use of coercion. This type of conflict situation is the focus of research using experimental games like the Prisoner's Dilemma, which are known to induce competitive and exploitative behavior (Pruitt & Rubin, 1986).

Competition for scarce and valued resources is the source of most conflicts. What is scarce and what is valued vary across cultures as a function of their ecologies and their socialization practices. Among the Mbuti, men fight over hunting territories (Turnbull, 1965). The scarcity of women is an important source of fighting and killing among the Yananomo men of Brazil (Chagnon, 1976; Knauft, 1987). Social organization within societies also affects the types of conflicts that arise. Co-wives in polygynous societies quarrel over access to husbands and resources in the family, as well as the disciplining of children (Levinson, 1989). Social organization can also reduce conflicts. In communal societies where property is shared, conflicts about property seldom occur (Knauft, 1987).

There are cross-cultural differences in both goals and tactics used in conflict situations. In multicultural research, S. H. Schwartz (1994) located 37 cultural groups at different positions on the value (goal) domains of hierarchy, benevolence, egalitarianism, and so forth. Differing strengths in endorsing S. H. Schwartz's (1992) value domains have been found to explain or "unpackage" cultural differences in the individual's choice of influence tactics for conflict resolution (Bond, Leung, & Schwartz, 1992). Ohbuchi, Fukushima, and Tedeschi (1999) found that Japanese people were more motivated by a concern for relationships with others in conflict situations, whereas Americans were more strongly oriented to achieving justice for themselves. Furthermore, Japanese people engaged in more avoidance tactics, whereas Americans preferred assertive tactics. These results can be interpreted as indicating that, in collectivist societies (like Japan), where social harmony is a salient value, people are inhibited by obvious displays of personal interest and avoid behaviors that are aversive to others. However, in individualistic societies (like the United States), pursuit of one's own interests is legitimate and even admired; hence actions that are aversive to others may be justified. These plausible speculations need to be assessed directly by using some individual-level measure of individualism–collectivism, like Gudykunst et al.'s (1996) measure of independent–interdependent self-construals, to "unpackage" (Bond, 1998) this average Japanese–American difference in tactic choice.

An important goal for all social groups is to achieve an adequate level of security, another of S. H. Schwartz's (1992) domains of value. Where there has been a history of intergroup hostility between groups, ideologies of antagonism (Staub, 1988) develop within each group. Mirror-image stereotypes (Bronfenbrenner, 1961) of mutual dislike develop and members of each group are likely to feel insecure and to perceive a high level of threat in interpersonal encounters across group lines (Stephan & Stephan, 1985). If the intergroup hierarchy is unstable, the potential for the mutual use of coercive exchanges is high (Schelling, 1963).

Social Cynicism

General beliefs about how the social world functions probably also relate to one's choice of influence tactics. That is, a social actor develops expectations about how potential targets of influence are likely to respond in interdependent encounters and so gears his or her behavioral initiatives accordingly. Leung and Bond (1998) identified five identical sets of social axioms in three cultural groups. They labeled one of these sets *social cynicism*. This factor consists of items reflecting an assessment of interpersonal and organizational life as competitive, hostile, and exploitative. We expect that both individual-level and cultural-level endorsements of this belief complex would be associated with using influence tactics characterized by coercive control (Sun & Bond, in press) earlier and more frequently in one's daily exchanges with others. Holding these cynical beliefs about the social world, an actor would pre-emptively engage in more assertive interpersonal tactics, probably setting in motion a confirmatory interpersonal cycle (see Snyder & Swann, 1978, for an example of this dynamic).

In general, whatever the source of conflict, if several people want the same resource and cannot or are not willing to share it, coercion will probably be used by the stronger on the weaker to establish hierarchies regulating access to these resources. However, in societies characterized by established hierarchies (see e.g., Hofstede, 1980, chap. 3 on power distance), external agencies of control, like the police and the military, inhibit the use of intergroup coercion to change these hierarchies. In societies characterized by high levels of human rights observance (Humana, 1986), the use of coercive tactics for re-establishing individual control is reduced, because coercion is strongly sanctioned and its use limited to societal agents, like the judiciary.

Expected Value of Terminal Goals

Expected value is a product of the perceived probability that an action leads to a particular outcome and the value of that outcome. The model presented in Figure 10.1 predicts that when actors do not believe positive means help them achieve their goals, they are more likely to use coercion, all else being equal. If goals cannot be achieved by positive forms of influence, the actor can choose either to forgo pursuit of the desired goal or use other means. Under such conditions the higher the perceived probability that coercion helps achieve the goals and the higher the value of the goal, the more likely it is that actors decide to use coercion.

Procedural Values

Ends do not always and for everyone justify the means used. A negative value for using physical violence, for example, would lower the likelihood that such means would be used. Mahatma Ghandi and Martin Luther King are examples of men who believed in fighting against oppression but used only nonviolent forms of coercion. Religious groups, like the Quakers and the Amish, socialize for nonviolence. On the other hand, there are people who positively value violent means and hence are more apt to use them. Male infants among the Yanomamo are taught to hit, kick, and bite others (Chagnon, 1976).

Inhibitory Factors

The probability and value of costs are inhibitory factors in the model shown in Figure 10.1. The higher the estimated probability of costs and the greater the negative value of those costs, the less likely the actor is to perform a coercive action. Costs may take the form of effort, financial investment, stress, or pain and may be assumed to be associated with performing the action or anticipated in terms of target or third-party retaliation. One reason that boys use more physical coercion than girls is that boys have a lower expectation of resistance and retaliation than do girls (Boldizar, Perry, & Perry, 1989). Furthermore, aggressive boys have been shown to be less concerned about retaliation than nonaggressive boys. Overconfidence about being able to avoid punishment may be a factor among habitual criminals, disinhibiting their violent conduct (Claster, 1967).

Summary

According to social interactionist theory, one motive underlying aggressive behavior is to control the behavior of other people. The individual may use threats or punishments to force compliance from a target person. The actor is more likely to choose coercive forms of influence when the value of the goal is high and other (more positive) forms of influence are expected to be ineffective. Individuals lack confidence in positive modes of influence when they are low in power bases, intelligence, education, and articulateness and are involved in conflicts over scarce resources. However, when individuals expect that the costs of using coercion outweigh the gains, they are inhibited from engaging in coercive actions.

The Justice Motive

SITCA proposes that the justice process begins with a perception by a person that an action by another did or probably could have brought about negative consequences for self or associated others. If the person attributes responsibility to an agent for bringing about the negative event, anger is experienced and a grievance is formed. A grievance constitutes a motive to restore justice to the situation. SITCA proposes that five response alternatives are available to a grievant. Figure 10.2 depicts this sequence of events.

Perceived Injustice and Attribution of Blame

Central to the justice process is a negative and blameworthy action by a perceived offender. Research has catalogued the types of injustices people experience. Mikula, Petri, and Tanzer (1989) asked respondents from Germany, Austria, Finland, and Bulgaria to report incidents when they had been treated unjustly. Analyses indicated that people experience three types of injustice: distributive, procedural, and interactional. *Distributive justice* refers to a fair allocation of positive and negative resources among people or between groups. *Procedural justice* refers to the means used to decide the outcomes, rules, standards, and scope of authority. *Interactional justice* refers to norms about benevolence, respect, and neutrality in dealing with other people. Leung (1997) found a similar pattern for the three forms of injustice among Hong Kong Chinese, as did Quigley and Tedeschi (1996) for Americans. In the Mikula et al. study, interactional injustice was by far the most important and frequent category of unjust incidents experienced by respondents, involving selfishness, failure to keep agreements, hostility, lack of regard for the feelings of others, lack of loyalty, and leveling of accusations or censure. In a study by Messick, Bloom, Boldizar, and Samuelson (1985), participants listed vicious gossip, rudeness, and lack of punctuality as unfair things that other people did.

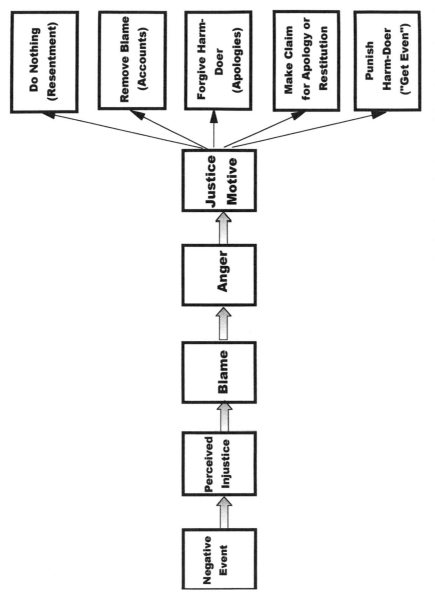

Figure 10.2. A model depicting the process by which negative events evoke justice motivation and the choice alternatives subsequently available to the grievant.

Episodes may occur in which both actors believe the other person has violated norms of interpersonal conduct. Perceptual biases and divergent perspectives may contribute to an episode in which both parties blame the other and each perceives the other as acting unjustly (see Ross & Ward, 1996, for an analysis of this social dynamic). When neither actor takes responsibility for unjust actions and each blames the other, it difficult to reach any resolution of issues that both perceive as fair. The tendency of each party in hostile interactions is to view his or her own behavior as provoked by the other (Mummendey, Linneweber, & Loschper, 1984). Furthermore, offenders view the focal events as less serious and unjust than do victims (Baumeister, Stillwell, & Wotman, 1990; Mikula & Heimgartner, 1992), further fueling the cycle of hostile or coercive exchanges. Blaming the other for one's own unjust actions can also serve as a justification for one's own aversive behavior that is then often rationalized as a defensive counterattack (Ryan, 1971). The tendency for people to weigh negative information about others more than positive information (Kanouse & Hanson, 1971) may contribute to a widening of perspective differences between interactants.

Stereotypes, first impressions, and prior expectations about individuals or groups may also affect how a person allocates responsibility and blame for another's behavior. Such anticipatory expectations may also affect which norms are activated for making such judgments and how to respond to perceived offenses. For example, Duncan (1976) found that White Americans viewed an African American protagonist who pushed another man as being more violent than a White protoganist who engaged in the same action. This result was obtained irrespective of the racial identity of the person who had been pushed. Similarly, Schruijer et al. (1994) found that members of the Italian Communist Party attributed more blame to a Fascist than to a Communist for an identical aggressive action described in a scenario. This general tendency to blame members of the out-group may, however, be moderated or even reversed, depending on political and social relations between the groups. Cultural collectivism exaggerates this group-serving bias (Gudykunst & Bond, 1997).

Any general tendency toward perceiving others as engaging in antagonistic or provocative behavior may produce defensive or retaliatory actions. Toch (1969) noted that incarcerated violent men had a paranoid style of attributions that caused them to engage in what they conceived of as pre-emptive attacks. Likewise, studies of children have found that aggressive boys attribute hostility to others in ambiguous social interactions (Dodge & Newman, 1981; Dodge & Somberg, 1987; Nasby, Hayden, & DePaulo, 1979). This evidence indicates that a "hostility bias" among some people may predispose them to interpret the behavior of others as aversive and as requiring an aggressive reaction. This bias may be a component of low "Big Five Agreeableness" that Caprara et al. (1996) found related to that component of the predisposition to aggression they labelled *positive evaluation of violence*.

There are cross-gender differences with respect to the kinds of behaviors that are experienced as instances of interactional injustice. Among couples, men were more likely to be upset about women being moody, whereas women were more apt to complain about men being inconsiderate, neglectful, and condescending (Buss, 1989). Among dating partners, women complained more about demands for sexual intimacy and the touching of their bodies without permission than did men. Levinson (1989) found that allegations of adultery were a common source of grievances leading to wife-beating in small-scale and peasant societies. In these societies, a man was more likely to beat his wife when she did not perform her duties or when she did not show him enough respect. In many societies wife-beating is seen as a legitimate method for men to use to maintain their authority in the household and to punish misbehavior.

An aversive action by an offender may violate more than one form of justice. A physically harmful action may be perceived as undeserved and as violating distributive fairness; it may simultaneously be perceived as disrespectful and hence violating standards of interactional justice. The impact that different types of justice have on each other was shown by Tyler (1988). He found that people who had been summoned to traffic court and were found guilty of violations perceived the procedures to be more fair if they had been treated with respect by the police and by the court. Thus, the experience of interactional justice contributes to the perception of procedural justice.

It is axiomatic that for every norm there is the potential for a norm violation. Norms vary across cultural groups (Argyle, Henderson, Bond, Iizuka, & Contarello, 1986). This implies that the sources of grievances vary according to cultures. Argyle et al. found that rules regarding emotional restraint were stronger in Chinese and Japanese culture than in Italian and English culture, so that the respect component of interactional justice could be more easily violated in these Asian groups. The sensitivity to affronts and the desire of people to avoid conflicts may account for the greater display of politeness and social harmony in collectivist cultures. The potential for cross-cultural conflict when people from cultures with different norms for social interaction interact is obvious (Smith & Bond, 1998, chap. 9). At a more general level norm violations form the primary basis for grievances in all cultures. The need for cataloging social norms becomes important in light of this conclusion (Moghaddam & Studer, 1997), and its continued absence from the literature is puzzling.

Grievance Motivation and Remedial Actions

When a person has a grievance, he or she may choose among a number of ways of reacting. The grievant may do nothing. Suburbanites are reluctant to express grievances against their neighbors (Baumgartner, 1988), and college students often do not express their anger against those who offend them (Averill, 1983). Grievants do nothing because of the anticipated costs of confronting offenders. Respondents in one study reported that they often do not express their grievances because they do not want to damage the relationship with the offender and they wish to avoid the effort, anxiety, and uncertainty of further conflict (Deshields, Jenkins, & Tait, 1989).

Cross-cultural research has documented that people in individualistic cultures prefer to use assertive and confrontational tactics for resolving conflicts, whereas people in collectivistic cultures prefer collaborative or avoidance tactics (Burgoon, Dillar, Doran, & Miller, 1982; Leung & Morris, in press; Ohbuchi & Takahashi, 1994). Collectivist Costa Ricans reported being more uncomfortable expressing any negative emotions than individualistic Americans, probably because of the divisive potential that negative emotions carry (Stephan, Stephan, & De Vargas, 1996). The expression of anger and contention is perceived as antisocial by the Gebusi and by Central Eskimo groups (Knauft, 1987). With such culturally variable display rules (Mesquita & Frijda, 1992), the open expression of grievances may itself be considered antisocial in some societies, and anticipated social costs would inhibit any remedial action.

A second possibility is that the grievant reconsiders the behavior of the offender, often in the light of subsequent accounts (excuses and justifications) offered by the other person. The explanation offered by the perceived offender may provide a different frame for the behavior and lead the grievant to remove blame or perhaps to mitigate the degree of blame (Riordan, Marlin, & Kellogg, 1983). The result may be the withdrawal or weakening of the grievance to the point where the costs of redressing the injustice are perceived as greater than the value of getting even.

A third possibility is that the grievant forgives the offender. A number of studies have shown that apologies often have the effect of reducing or removing the blame and punishment otherwise directed at an offender (Schlenker & Darby, 1981; G. S. Schwartz, Kane, Joseph, & Tedeschi, 1978). Apologies, if perceived as sincere, may satisfy the grievant's desire for justice because the offender reaffirms the grievant's values and judgments, admits guilt, expresses negative feelings about harming the grievant, and promises not to act in a similar manner again. One test of sincerity is the voluntary provision of compensation to the grievant be it money, goods, or service. These sacrifices by the offender are costly and constitute aspects of "restorative" justice (Moore, 1993). More elaborate apologies may also indicate greater sincerity to a grievant. Complex apologies have been found to be more effective than simpler apologies (Braaten, Cody, & Bell, 1990; Holtgraves, 1989).

A fourth possible reaction by a grievant to the norm violation of an offender is to make some claim. The claim may be a demand for restitution or an apology, which, if given, satisfies the grievant and restores justice to the situation. However, if claims are resisted by the offender, the grievant may interpret the refusal as a challenge to his or her accusations, standards of justice, or worth as an individual. The target of the claim may believe that the accusation is false or exaggerated and that the grievant is attempting to seek some exploitative advantage with the claim. A refusal thus tends to expand the scope and intensity of a grievance and may lead to an escalation of hostilities.

The way these kinds of disputes are settled varies across cultures. Trial by combat is used by the male Chukchee of Siberia (Sverdrup, 1938). The grievant's accusations against the alleged offender include a loud and insulting tirade. If the recipient rejects the accusation, he responds in kind. The two men then grapple and try to throw the other to the ground. The one who succeeds beats the other until he gives in and accepts the winner's point of view. The winner then lights a pipe and offers it to the loser as a peace-making gesture. In American society, Felson (1984) found that disputes originating with a reproach by a grievant and in which the alleged transgressor did not give an account frequently led to physical violence and harm to one or both of the actors. At this point external social agents and institutionalized procedures are often engaged to resolve the dispute and repair the damaged social fabric.

Finally, the grievant may punish the offender for the antinormative action. One way of restoring justice is to punish the offender. The oldest law of justice (*lex talionis*) is an eye for an eye, and the rule is that punishment should be equal to the offense. Norms exist in societies for when it is legitimate to punish other people and what the form and magnitude of punishment should be (Pepitone, 1984). Among the Dafla hill tribes of northeast India (Furer-Haimendorf, 1967) and of precolonial New Guinea society (DuBois, 1961), people immediately attacked anyone who offended them. In these societies a person who did not seek immediate redress for affronts and injuries was perceived as weak and indecisive and became subject to further attacks by others. In societies that have effective formal institutions of social control, there is a distinction between the types of actions that should be carried out by legal authorities and those that individuals can legitimately carry out themselves (Black, 1983).

The level or intensity of punishment roughly fits the seriousness of the offense. A variety of punishments can be used to redress injustices, and preferences are affected by culture. The Javanese handle disputes by not speaking to each other—the "satru" pattern (Geertz, 1961), and litigous Americans frequently do so by suing. The goal of the grievant is to level the scales of justice—in the English vernacular, to "get even," although the push for matching the punishment to the offense is probably determined by cultural considerations. Leung and Morris (in press) observed that little is known about these cultural considerations in "retributive justice."

We need to understand much more about remedial actions to prevent violence between contending parties in the grievance process, including the role of third parties and cultural variations in conflict resolution tactics, peace making, and forgiveness and their psychological dynamics (Keltner, Young, & Buswell, 1997). Cultural differences can range from the public glare of South Africa's recent Truth and Reconciliation Commission to a private handshake between two former disputants. Cultural groups that attach a greater importance to group concerns (Triandis, 1995) should deploy more social resources, such as mutually known, third-party mediators, to restore relationship harmony between disputants. Individuals with higher interdependent self-construals or higher levels of Big Five agreeableness (Kwan, Bond, & Singelis, 1997) should be more likely to accede to such social initiatives.

Leung and Morris (in press) concluded that the dynamics involved in attaining procedural and interactional (and possibly restorative) justice are culturally invariant, even if their specific forms may vary. The exception is distributive justice, where the press toward equitable allocations varies with the culture of the allocators and their relationship to the receiving parties (Leung, 1997). This cultural variation becomes important for the study of aggressive behavior because of Wilkinson's work on relative inequality of income (Wilkinson, 1996; Wilkinson, Kawachi, & Kennedy, 1998).

Wilkinson and his collaborators have found that the incidence of both homicide and of violent assault across the 50 states of the United States and the countries of the European Union increases with the relative inequality of incomes between the top and bottom strata of that social unit. These effects for relative inequality have been found across other types of society despite strong cultural differences (Hsieh & Pugh, 1993). This variable of relative inequality is a true societal-level variable, not formed by averaging the responses of the individuals in that society to paper and pencil measures of values or beliefs. As such, the dynamics of its action must be "unpackaged" at the individual level, so that we may understand why individuals in unequal societies are killing and assaulting one another at greater rates.

Identity Motivations

The successful use of coercion can bring prestige to an actor. Skill in insulting, abusing, and fighting others may gain respect and power for a person who uses fear as a way of gaining compliance from others. Toch (1969) described violent male prisoners as self-image promotors, akin to young gunslingers in the mythology about the American West. It is important for self-image managers to precipitate incidents so that they can enhance and maintain their reputations as "tough guys." Typically, this concern for a "macho" identity is associated with the cultural (or subcultural) definition of what it means to be a man.

"Macho Maleness" and Violence

Segall et al. (1997) catalogued the extensive evidence from a variety of cultures using numerous measures of aggression (e.g., rough-and-tumble play, verbal attack, hostile driving, homicide). They found that male individuals universally show more aggression than female individuals and that the size of this difference varies from culture to culture. They argued that cross-cultural evidence supports the explanation of this gender difference and its size in terms of socialization differences for aggression, differential assignment of tasks to girls and boys, and the greater amount of time spent by boys and young men in the company of peers rather than adults.

It is, however, also possible to examine the male–female difference in aggressive behavior and the size of this difference in terms of social pressures to establish an active, assertive, dominant, and powerful identity. The work of Schlegel and Berry (1991) shows consistent differences across 186 societies between the sexes in the socialization for boys to be more aggressive, self-reliant, and aggressive than girls. We believe that this pressure for a "macho" identity in a given culture may be indexed by gender differences in self-concepts.

Multicultural work by Best and Williams (1994) provided suggestive evidence for connotative differences in information processing by male and female individuals. They found a consistent difference across their sample of 14 nations for male compared to female individuals to perceive themselves as higher on two of Osgood, Suci, and Tannenbaum's (1957) three broad dimensions of meaning: potency and activity. This elevation on potency in particular, but also on activity, is consistent with the argument that the pressure to establish a powerful identity is related to the use of assertive and dominant tactics of social influence. These tactics spill over to include coercive behaviors, including violence.

Best and Williams (1994) were able to relate the size of the difference in male and female self-concepts of activity and potency to measures of national difference. They found that the size of this difference was greater in less socioeconomically developed countries, in countries where literacy and the percentage of women attending a university was low, and where Hofstede's (1980) factor of power distance, which means the dispersion of power in a society and the degree of obedience required, was high. In light of these results, we likewise predict that the size of gender differences in various forms of aggressive behavior correlates with the same and with similar measures.

Cross-cultural indices of aggression like homicide show that male individuals universally show much higher rates of homicide that female individuals, with that ratio increasing as the overall homicide rate increases (Lester, 1996, chap. 10). Consistent with the argument that socialization for power motivation is associated with violence, Hofstede (1980) reported that the power distance of a country correlated with the incidence of domestic political violence. Moreover, Bond and Chan (1995) reported that homicide rates correlated positively with S. H. Schwartz's (1994) country measure of hierarchy and negatively with its level of egalitarian commitment. Thus, various country-level measures of an emphasis on power and ranking seem to be related to the incidence of violent behaviors.

Cultures of Violence

The tendency of individuals to convert identity concerns into violent behavior may be especially strong in particular segments of society. Among the poor and the underclass, it is often the case that a man's identity is associated with being viewed as aggressive, tough, dangerous, and able to control women (Katz, 1988; Lewis, 1961). Miller (1958), a historian, proposed a list of focal concerns distinctive to lower class culture that are related to violent conduct. There is an emphasis on toughness, on being fearless and skilled in combat. There is a search for excitement that is associated with the boring nature of work in the lower class and a tendency to believe that fate determines outcomes. A person who believes outcomes are a matter of chance is not apt to be inhibited by threats of future punishments and is, therefore, less subject to social control measures. Finally, there is an exaggerated concern for autonomy and freedom of action, which takes the assertive stance that "no one is going to push me around." This set of beliefs, along with violent conduct, has sometimes been referred to by criminologists as the *subculture of violence* (Wolfgang & Ferracuti, 1956).

Wilkinson et al. (1998) argued that the sense of shame and humiliation associated with low relative status in one's society drives the high levels of violence in social units marked by relative inequality. Poor people develop chronically low levels of self-esteem as they are continually reminded of their personal failure by the daily exposure to the power, success, and status of wealthy others. They become driven by a need to restore pride in themselves by acquiring material goods and confronting any perceived disrespect with status-garnering violence.

The view that low self-esteem is the basis of violence is not supported by the available evidence. For example, although lower class African Americans in the United States are responsible for 50% of all violent crimes, evidence indicates that the self-esteem of lower class African Americans is as high or higher than that of middle-class White Americans (Kohr et al., 1988). Furthermore, Baumeister and Boden (1998) have reviewed evidence that self-esteem uncertainty, particularly among people with moderately positive self-esteem, is more strongly related to violent behavior than is low self-esteem. If we re-interpret Wilkinson et al.'s (1998) position in terms of self-esteem uncertainty, it could be argued that disadvantaged people, because of their material circumstances, are rendered uncertain about their self-esteem and are thus more sensitive to any sign of disrespect from others. Violent reactions to perceived affronts tend to reaffirm the person's sense of control and power, hence reducing uncertainty about worth and social standing.

Evidence of regional differences in both the legitimation and incidence of violence within the United States is consistent with the concept of a culture of violence (D. Cohen, 1996; D. Cohen & Nisbett, 1994). In these regions, "laws relating to the owning and use of guns, to the defense of self and property, to spousal abuse, to corporal and capital punishment" (Smith & Bond, 1998, p. 88) were weaker and attitudes more approving of violence (D. Cohen & Nisbett, 1994). This cultural condoning of violence is derived from a culture of honor (Peristiany, 1965) that requires individuals to defend their familial and personal integrity against external slights. Cultures of honor are found in herding economies where legal institutions are weak, requiring herders to be willing and able to defend their property against depredations by others. In addition, D. Cohen (1996) argued that the culture of violence in the southern states of the United States was augmented by their history of controlling slaves (see D. Cohen, Vandello, & Rantilla, 1998, for an overview on cultures of honor and of violence).

Defense of Identities

Affronts, insults, and other challenges to desired identities motivate the individual to engage in actions to maintain or restore face. A perceived *affront* humiliates the person, which in turn causes anger. Humiliation is an emotion experienced following a loss of power and status, whereas anger is an active emotion that motivates the person to take some action to regain control over the situation. Insulting or otherwise "putting the other person down" is a typical punitive response by the affronted person.

An insult is a derogatory labeling of another person or of something associated with that person. People use insults against others as a way of provoking and punishing and controlling them. Furthermore, they are as easy to deliver as the flick of a tongue. Insults may be described as pedogogical tools because they are often used to punish undesirable behavior of others, and hence they are intended to change the miscreant. In addition to social control, insults can be used to punish unjust conduct of others and to redress grievances. The implicit threat of violence associated with insults may restrain a person from misbehaving further.

Insults and other attacks on a person's identity are resisted because they lower the target's status, and in consequence they often lead to retaliation (Felson, 1978). In their theory of politeness, P. Brown and Levinson (1987) distinguished between threats to negative and positive face. A desire to maintain autonomy and to be free of interference from other people is the basis of negative face. Acts such as orders, threats, and other obvious attempts to control the person threaten negative face and are likely to be resisted, especially in freedom-valuing cultures (Ting-Toomey, 1988). Positive face refers to the identities valued by the person. Disapproval, criticism, disagreements, complaints, reprimands, accusations, insults, challenges, interruptions, lack of attention, and blatant noncooperation are actions that threaten positive face, especially in harmony-valuing cultures (Ting-Toomey et al., 1991). In American culture, threats to positive face are commonly referred to as *disrespect*, or in the vernacular as *dissing*.

Any attack on a person's identity, if left unanswered, may thereby validate the loss of identity and leave the impression of the target as weak and ineffectual. Retaliation communicates strength and asserts that the person cannot be treated with disrespect. If successful, the counterassertion leaves the impression that the original attacker is weak and incompetent. Neither party wants to be perceived as being "one down," and a character contest is likely to ensue. A character contest represents an escalating verbal interchange, which may often be converted into a physical battle. Indeed, it is this type of conflict spiral that often results in physical assaults and homicide (Felson & Steadman, 1983).

However, identity contests may take different forms across cultures. A public exchange of insults is ritualized by Eskimos in song duels (Hoebel, 1954). Each party ridicules the other in improvised lyrics, and applause by an audience indicates the winner. These ritualized song duels are sometimes accompanied by head-butting or wrestling. Although a song duel may be based on a justice issue, complaints and grievances tend to get converted into identity contests. Among the Kwakiutl Indians of the Pacific Northwest, reactions to insults take the form of a *potlatch*, a feast given by a host for a targeted offender. During the feast, the offended party bestows possessions on the offender. If the latter cannot respond by holding a subsequent potlatch and giving even more back to the former, he loses face within the tribe (M. D. R. Gil & Brown, 1981). The potlatch may be characterized as an attempt to kill another person's character with kindness. These ritualized forms of identity contest restrain the potential of interpersonal violence in such societies.

Politeness Norms

All societies have norms of politeness to prevent identity contests from occurring. These interpersonal guidelines are meant to restrain the incendiary potential in social life for perceiving and retaliating to insults. Ironically, Cohen, Vandello, Puente, and Rantilla (1999) have argued that this socialization for politeness prevents interactants from intervening early in the cycle of perceived insult and retaliation. So, warning communications are inhibited until even greater provocations occur and the retaliation required is much stronger. The conflict then escalates sharply and surprisingly.

Socialization for politeness need not always result in such escalation. First of all, the frequency of insults probably is lower in polite societies because of the dangerous potential attached to passing such remarks. Second, many of these societies have strong sanctions against direct forms of face-to-face counterattack. Gossip, third-party intervention, and legal modes of redress are possible alternative strategies for redress in cultural systems that have more stable residential patterns and institutions of enforcement. Such systems, like the Chinese, develop in ecologies where agriculture forms or has traditionally formed the basis of subsistence practices (Berry, 1979). In these cultures, people are socialized to conformity and restraint (Barry, Child, & Bacon, 1959). Indeed, in such societies the intensity of angry feelings is less (Matsumoto, Kudoh, Scherer, & Walbott, 1988), the likelihood of reacting to experienced emotions is lower (Gudykunst & Ting-Toomey, 1988), and the tendency to displace anger is greater (Redford, 1998). Perhaps, then, the cycle of dramatic escalation described by Cohen et al. (1999) for southerners from the United States is only characteristic of individualistic social systems based on herding traditions.

In collectivist cultures, people are relatively more concerned about their group than about themselves. Because of this collective emphasis, insults of a group-oriented form may be most effective. Semin and Rubini (1990) found that insults in individualistic northern Italy were characteristically directed toward individuals, but in collectivist southern Italy insults more often referred to members of the target's family. Bond and Venus (1991) found that Chinese students from Hong Kong were much more likely to verbally retaliate for a gratuitous insult when that insult included their group than when the insult only targeted themselves as individuals. We expect that any individual with a more interdependent self-construal (Gudykunst et al., 1996) or a more collective sense of self (Crocker, Luhtanen, Blaine, & Broadnax, 1994) is likewise more reactive to insults directed toward his or her groups.

Politeness theory suggests that some inadvertent social actions (or inaction) may be perceived as impolite or insulting. For example, a person who is preoccupied with some problem may be less attentive to other people, who may take this inattentiveness as disrespect or indifference. Similarly, negative emotions or moods may lead a person to be more self-focused and less attentive to others, and, as a consequence, that person may inadvertently violate politeness norms. The offended party may reproach the offender, who might then be offended by the other person's reproach, which he or she may perceive as unjustified. In this way, a fight that neither party sought gets under way and may escalate to a rather intense level. This process is suggested by Felson's (1992) finding that a stressed person is more likely to be the target than the initiator of physical coercion. Felson also found that being targeted mediates the relationship between stressful life events and the use of physical coercion.

The behaviors that may be directed toward others without communicating disrespect are related to the relative status of the interactants. Insubordination and rebellion undermine the legitimacy of an authority. Attempts by authorities to placate or accommodate challenges or dissent tend to legitimate the disruptive behavior and convey an identity of weakness to others. Public rebukes and punishments by authorities serve the purpose of showing that the dissident is acting illegitimately and that the authorities are strong and willing to act. Such interventions can also communicate to others that disobedience by them will similarly be punished. So, for example, the most frequent justification that police officers gave for using force is disrespect or verbal challenges to their authority (Westley, 1970). A participant observer study indicated that assaults against police officers often occurred during incidents that were precipitated by challenges to their authority (Toch, 1969). In a typical incident, a police officer might ask young men standing on a street corner to move on. If they balk and argue that they have a right to stand there and that they are not doing anything wrong, the police officer might feel his authority is being challenged and become more adamant, increasing the resistance to the point that the young men might attack the officer. Likewise, Kipnis and Consentino (1969) found in a laboratory simulation that supervisors tended to use threats and punishment against workers who rejected their authority. Parents, too, frequently use coercion when confronted by challenges to their authority by children.

The same verbal input may be differently construed by people from different cultures, resulting in different perceptions of challenge to the authority and hence of the need for reprisals. In societies characterized by high-power distance or hierarchy, people respond to insults by subordinates with greater sanctions and to insults from superiors with less animosity (Bond, Wan, Leung, & Giacalone, 1985). Inputs from those lower in status risk being perceived as insulting to the position of a superior in authority-ranking cultures (Fiske, 1991). So, suggestions in such cultures must be delivered carefully, using indirect, authority-acknowledging language or through intermediaries (Bond & Lee, 1981).

"Unpackaging" Aggression in Response to Insults

Social psychologists want cross-cultural social psychology to develop universal theories of interpersonal behavior (Messick, 1988). To do so, theories are needed that posit constructs mediating between the insult and the hostile response. This mediation must operate in all the cultural groups explored to give the model universal status. With such a model, the average difference between cultural groups in the hostile response could be explained by different average intensities of the mediating variable in the two cultural groups (Bond, 1998).

The work of Cohen and his collaborators (see D. Cohen & Vandello, 1997, for a review) has consistently shown that southerners from the United States react with greater aggressiveness to others than do northerners when insulted by an experiment participant. On average, these insulted southerners also showed greater levels of testosterone and of cortisol; felt more angry; had more violent cognitions; and believed an audience to the insult considered them less tough, courageous, strong, and manly. Such a pattern of outcomes is consistent with a "culture of honor."

These results are carefully and thoughtfully derived. They tempt one to construct a model that uses physiological, emotional, and cognitive reactions to insult as mediators of consequent hostile behavior. The elevation in hostile behavior by the insulted southerners compared to the insulted northerners would then be explained by their heightened physiological, emotional, or cognitive reactions.

The problem is that the model has not yet been tested by examining individual correlations between the mediators and the hostile outcome behavior; instead, only average differences between the southerners and northerners are presented. Structural equation models (Reis, 1982) are needed to test these relationships, and then one can select a model consistent with the data and prior theory. Quigley and Tedeschi (1996) provided an example of such a sophisticated and microscopic approach in the study of aggression. They examined data derived from reports of individuals who had been harmed by others. These data led them to propose a model where anger and blame were the reciprocally influencing outcomes of the victim's "attributions concerning the provoker's intentions to harm, his or her justification in harming, and the amount of harm done" (p. 1280).

Had Quigley and Tedeschi (1996) been examining cultural differences in blame or anger, they could then have used regression equations to identify the individual-level mediators responsible for producing the observed cultural difference. Indeed, along with Bond, Ohbuchi, Madi, and Mummendey they are currently following this strategy in a cross-cultural study of anger and aggression in Hong Kong, Japan, Germany, and the United States. Similarly, work on intergroup conflict by Stephan (see, e.g., Stephan, Ybarra, & Bachman, 1998) has focused on the perception of threat as a key mediating variable that drives hostility toward out-group persons. This mediator could apply equally well to the use of coercive behaviors in interpersonal relations. If so, its use could help integrate research in the interpersonal and intergroup traditions of social psychology.

CONCLUSION

The social interactionist theory presented here interprets aversive behaviors in terms of the motives of asserting social control, re-establishing justice, and asserting or protecting a valued identity. The interdependence of the individual with others for outcomes makes it necessary to use social influence to attain personal goals. Among the means available to control the behavior of others are threats and punishments, actions that surely are perceived as aversive to the target persons. Punishments may also be administered to norm violators as a means to redress a perceived injustice and to deter further conduct of the same kind either by the offender or by prospective offenders. A desire to assert or to defend identities can also be the basis for aversive behavior. Some people want an identity as tough, strong, powerful, or dominant, and they engage in self-promoting behaviors to achieve such a reputation. People are also motivated to defend desired and valued identities from threats and attacks by others, and they may get involved in identity contests leading to coercive actions.

Although these three motives have been treated as if they were independent for purposes of exposition, it is probably the case that most coercive (or aggressive) episodes are overdetermined—that is, all three motives may be simultaneously activated. The most prevalent form of perceived injustice is interactional injustice, which clearly overlaps with infractions of politeness norms and identity attacks. Furthermore, if a person could control events, presumably he or she would not be treated unfairly or with disrespect. Hence, social control motivation is activated by such acts of others. Similarly, Wilkinson's (1996) work on relative inequality, an issue of distributive justice, leads to coercive actions calculated to establish an esteemed but questioned identity.

Our frequent references to cross-cultural research indicate that the conditions we have specified for the use of coercion may be the same in all cultures—to gain compliance, to redress injustice, and to assert and defend identities. People use threats and punishments to gain compliance from others in all societies and more often when conflicts arise between people. However, the form, frequency, and intensity of conflicts vary as a function of the scarcity of resources and the type of social organization associated with a culture. People in all societies are aggrieved when they experience injustice and may punish the norm violator as a means of redressing the injustice (P. Brown, 1990). The form that punishment takes varies across cultures, but the justice process appears to occur similarly everywhere. Every society develops politeness norms to protect vulnerable social identities. Attacks on identity may nevertheless occur, perhaps because of reproaches based on perceptions of unjust behavior or out of divergent interests in conflict situations or even inadvertently. Whatever the basis of perceived identity attacks, individuals are highly motivated to defend their identities and character contests may ensue.

The social interactionist view of aggressive behavior attempts to specify what it is about aversiveness that leads to the use of threats and punishments by a person. Evidence indicates that physical forms of aversiveness are chiefly facilitative of aggressive behavior, but socially aversive behaviors that are related to concerns for social control, social justice, and identity serve as instigators of what has been called "aggression."

REFERENCES

Anderson, C. A. (1989). Temperature and aggression: Ubiquitous effects of heat on occurrence of human violence. *Psychological Bulletin, 106*, 74–96.

Archer, D., & Gartner, R. (1984). *Violence and crime in cross-national perspective.* New Haven, CT: Yale University Press.

Argyle, M., Henderson, M., Bond, M. H., Iizuka, Y., & Contarello, A. (1986). Cross-cultural variations in relationship rules. *International Journal of Psychology, 21*, 287–315.

Averill, J. R. (1983). Studies on anger and aggression: Implications for theories of emotion. *American Psychologist, 38*, 1145–1160.

Bandura, A. (1973). *Aggression: A social learning analysis.* Englewood Cliffs, NJ: Prentice Hall.

Baron, R. A. (1977). *Human aggression.* New York: Plenum Press.

Baron, R. A., & Bell, P. A. (1975). Aggression and heat: Mediating effects of prior provocation and exposure to an aggressive model. *Journal of Personality and Social Psychology, 31*, 825–832.

Barry, H., Child, I., & Bacon, M. (1959). Relation of child training to subsistence economy. *American Anthropologist, 61*, 51–63.

Baumeister, R., & Boden, J. M. (1998). Aggression and the self: High self-esteem, low self-control, and ego threat. In R. Geen & R. Donnerstein (Eds.), *Human aggression: Theories, research, and implications for social policy* (pp. 111–137). San Diego, CA: Academic Press.

Baumeister, R. F., Stillwell, A., & Wotman, S. R. (1990). Victim and perpetrator accounts of interpersonal conflict: Autobiographical narratives about anger. *Journal of Personality and Social Psychology, 59*, 994–1005.

Baumgartner, M. P. (1988). *The moral order of a suburb.* New York: Oxford University Press.

Bell, P. A., & Baron, R. A. (1976). Aggression and heat: The mediating role of negative affect. *Journal of Applied Social Psychology, 6*, 18–30.

Berkowitz, L. (1993). *Aggression: Its causes, consequences, and control.* New York: McGraw-Hill.

Berkowitz, L., Corwin, R., & Heironimus, M. (1962). Film violence and subsequent aggressive tendencies. *Public Opinion Quarterly, 27,* 217–229.

Berry, J. W. (1979). A cultural ecology of social behavior. In L. Berkowitz (Ed.), *Advances in experimental social psychology* (Vol. 12, pp. 177–206). New York: Academic Press.

Best, D. L., & Williams, J. E. (1994). Masculinity/femininity in the self and ideal self descriptions of university students in fourteen countries. In A. M. Bouvy, F. J. R. van de Vijver, P. Boski, & P. Schmitz (Eds.), *Journeys into cross-cultural psychology* (pp. 297–306). Lisse, the Netherlands: Swets & Zeitlinger.

Black, D. (1983). Crime as social control. *American Sociological Review, 48,* 34–45.

Boldizar, J. P., Perry, D. G., & Perry, L. C. (1989). Outcome values and aggression. *Child Development, 60,* 571–579.

Bond, M. H. (1998). Social psychology across cultures: Two ways forward. In J. G. Adair, D. Belanger, & K. Dion (Eds.), *Proceeding of the 26th International Congress of Psychology: Vol. 1. Advances in psychological science: Social, personal and cultural aspects* (pp. 137–150). Hove, UK: Psychology Press.

Bond, M. H., & Chan, S. C. N. (1995, July). *Country values and country health.* Paper presented at the 7th European Congress of Psychology, Athens, Greece.

Bond, M. H., & Lee, P. W. H. (1981). Face saving in Chinese culture: A discussion and experimental study of Hong Kong students. In A. Y. C. King & R. P. L. Lee (Eds.), *Social life and development in Hong Kong* (pp. 288–306). Hong Kong: Chinese University Press.

Bond, M. H., Leung, K., & Schwartz, S. H. (1992). Explaining choices in procedural and distributive justice across cultures. *International Journal of Psychology, 27,* 211–225.

Bond, M. H., & Venus, C. K. (1991). Resistance to group or personal insults in an ingroup or outgroup context. *International Journal of Psychology, 26,* 83–94.

Bond, M. H., Wan, K.-C., Leung, K., & Giacalone, R. A. (1985). How are responses to verbal insult related to cultural collectivism and power distance? *Journal of Cross-Cultural Psychology, 16,* 111–127.

Braaten, D. O., Cody, M. J., & Bell, K. (1990, June). *Account episodes in organizations: Remedial work and impression management.* Paper presented at the annual meeting of the International Communication Association, Dublin, Ireland.

Bronfenbrenner, U. (1961). The mirror image in Soviet–American relations: A social psychologist's report. *Journal of Social Issues, 17,* 45–56.

Brown, P. (1990). Gender, politeness, and confrontation in Tenejapa. *Discourse Processes, 13,* 123–141.

Brown, P., & Levinson, S. C. (1987). *Politeness: Some universals in language usage.* New York: Cambridge University Press.

Brown, R. C., Jr., & Tedeschi, J. T. (1976). Determinants of perceived aggression. *Journal of Social Psychology, 100,* 77–87.

Burgoon, M., Dillar, J., Doran, N., & Miller, M. (1982). Cultural and situational influences on the process of persuasive strategy selection. *International Journal of Intercultural Relations, 6*, 85–100.

Buss, D. M. (1989). Sex differences in human mate preferences: Evolutionary hypotheses in 37 cultures. *Behavioral and Brain Sciences, 12*, 1–49.

Caprara, G. V., Barbaranelli, C., & Zimbardo, P. G. (1996). Understanding the complexity of human aggression: Affective, cognitive, and social dimensions of individual differences in propensity toward aggression. *European Journal of Personality, 10*, 133–155.

Chagnon, N. A. (1976). *Yanomamo, the fierce people.* New York: Holt, Rinehart & Winston.

Cherek, D. R., Spiga, R., & Egli, M. (1992). Effects of response requirement and alcohol on human aggressive responding. *Journal of the Experimental Analysis of Behavior, 58*, 577–587.

Clark, L. A. (1987). Mutual relevance of mainstream and cross-cultural psychology. *Journal of Consulting and Clinical Psychology, 55*, 461–470.

Claster, D. S. (1967). Comparison of risk perception between delinquents and nondelinquents. *Journal of Criminal Law, Criminology, and Police Science, 58*, 80–86.

Cohen, D. (1996). Law, social policy, and violence: The impact of regional cultures. *Journal of Personality and Social Psychology, 70*, 961–978.

Cohen, D., & Nisbett, R. E. (1994). Self-protection, insults and the culture of honor: Explaining southern homicide. *Personality and Social Psychology Bulletin, 20*, 551–567.

Cohen, D., & Vandello, J. (1997). Meanings of violence. *Journal of Legal Studies, 17*, 567–584.

Cohen, D., Vandello, J., Puente, S., & Rantilla, A. (1999). *Interaction styles that perpetuate violence: How norms for politeness and aggression work.* Manuscript submitted for review.

Cohen, D., Vandello, J., & Rantilla, A. K. (1998). The sacred and the social: Cultures of honor and violence. In P. Gilbert & B. Andrews (Eds.), *Shame, interpersonal behavior, psychopathology, and culture* (pp. 261–282). New York: Oxford University Press.

Cohen, L. E., & Felson, M. (1979). Social change and crime rate trends: A routine activity approach. *American Sociological Review, 44*, 588–608.

Cohn, E. G., & Rotton, J. (1997). Assault as a function of time and temperature: A moderator-variable time-series analysis. *Journal of Personality and Social Psychology, 72*, 1322–1334.

Crocker, J., Luhtanen, R., Blaine, B., & Broadnax, S. (1994). Collective self-esteem and psychological well-being among White, Black, and Asian college students. *Personality and Social Psychology Bulletin, 20*, 503–513.

Deshields, T. L., Jenkins, J. O., & Tait, R. C. (1989). The experience of anger in chronic illness: A preliminary investigation. *International Journal of Psychiatry in Medicine, 19*, 299–309.

Deutsch, M. (1994). Constructive conflict resolution: Principles, training, and research. *Journal of Social Issues, 50,* 13–32.

Dodge, K. A., & Newman, J. P. (1981). Biased decision-making processes in aggressive boys. *Journal of Abnormal Psychology, 90,* 375–379.

Dodge, K. A., & Somberg, D. R. (1987). Hostile attributional biases among aggressive boys are exacerbated under conditions of threats to self. *Child Development, 58,* 213–224.

DuBois, C. (1961). *The peoples of Alor.* New York: Harper & Row.

Duncan, B. L. (1976). Differential social perception and attribution of intergroup violence: Testing the lower limits of stereotyping blacks. *Journal of Personality and Social Psychology, 34,* 590–598.

Farrington, D. P. (1997). Human development and criminal careers. In M. Maguire, R. Morgan, & R. Reiner (Eds.), *The Oxford handbook of criminology* (pp. 361–408). Oxford, England: Clarendon Press.

Felson, R. B. (1978). Aggression as impression management. *Social Psychology Quarterly, 41,* 205–213.

Felson, R. B. (1984). Patterns of aggressive interaction. In A. Mummendey (Ed.), *Social psychology of aggression: From individual behavior to social interaction* (pp. 107–126). Berlin: Springer-Verlag.

Felson, R. B. (1992). "Kick 'em when they're down:" Explanations of the relationship between stress and interpersonal aggression and violence. *Sociological Quarterly, 33,* 1–16.

Felson, R. B., & Steadman, H. J. (1983). Situational factors in disputes leading to criminal violence. *Criminology, 21,* 59–74.

Fiske, A. P. (1991). *Structures of social life: The four elementary forms of human relations.* New York: Free Press.

Furer-Haimendorf, C. von. (1967). *Moral and merit: A study of values and social controls in South Asian societies.* London: Weidenfeld and Nicholson.

Geen, R. G. (1990). *Human aggression.* Pacific Grove, CA: Brooks/Cole.

Geertz, H. (1961). *The Javanese family.* New York: Free Press.

Gil, D. (1970). *Violence against children: Physical child abuse.* Cambridge, MA: Harvard University Press.

Gil, M. D. R., & Brown, B. (1981). Face saving among West Coast (Kwakiutl) Indians. *Journal of Psychological Anthropology, 3,* 297–308.

Gudykunst, W. B., & Bond, M. H. (1997). Intergroup relations across cultures. In J. Berry, M. Segall, & C. Kagitçibasi (Eds.), *Handbook of cross-cultural psychology* (Vol. 3, pp. 119–161). Needham Heights, MA: Allyn & Bacon.

Gudykunst, W. B., Matsumoto, D., Ting-Toomey., S., Nishida, T., Kim, K., & Heyman, S. (1996). The influence of cultural individualism-collectivism, self construals, and individual values on communication styles across cultures. *Human Communication Research, 22,* 510–543.

Gudykunst, W. B., & Ting-Toomey, S. (1988). Culture and affective communication. *American Behavioral Scientist, 31,* 384–400.

Hoebel, E. A. (1954). *The law of primitive man*. Cambridge, MA: Harvard University Press.

Hofstede, G. (1980). *Culture's consequences: International differences in work-related values*. Beverly Hills, CA: Sage Publications.

Holtgraves, T. (1989). The form and function of remedial moves: Reported use, psychological reality, and perceived effectiveness. *Journal of Language and Social Psychology, 8*, 1–16.

Hsieh, C. C., & Pugh, M. D. (1993). Poverty, income inequality, and violent crime: A meta-analysis of recent aggregate data studies. *Criminal Justice Review, 18*, 182–202.

Humana, C. (1986). *World human rights guide*. London: Pan.

Kanouse, D. E., & Hanson, L. R. (1971). Negativity in evaluations. In E. E. Jones, D. E. Kanouse, H. H. Kelley, R. E. Nisbett, S. Valins, & B. Weiner (Eds.), *Attribution: Perceiving the causes of behavior* (pp. 47–62). Morristown, NJ: General Learning Press.

Katz, J. (1988). *Seductions of crime: Moral and sensual attractions of doing evil*. New York: Basic Books.

Keltner, D., Young, R. C., & Buswell, B. N. (1997). Appeasement in human emotion, social practice, and personality. *Aggressive Behavior, 23*, 359–374.

Kipnis, D., & Consentino, J. (1969). Use of leadership powers in industry. *Journal of Applied Psychology, 53*, 460–466.

Knauft, B. M. (1987). Reconsidering violence in simple human societies: Homicide among the Gebusi of New Guinea. *Current Anthropology, 28*, 457–497.

Kohr, R. L., Coldiron, J. R., Skiffington, E. W., Masters, J. R., et al. (1988). The influence of race, class, and gender on self-esteem for fifth, eighth, and eleventh grade students in Pennsylvania schools. *Journal of Negro Education, 57*, 467–481.

Kwan, V. S. Y., Bond, M. H., & Singelis, T. M. (1997). Pancultural explanations for life satisfaction: Adding relationship harmony to self-esteem. *Journal of Personality and Social Psychology, 73*, 1038–1051.

Lester, D. (1996). *Patterns of suicide and homicide in the world*. New York: Nova Science.

Leung, K. (1997). Negotiation and reward allocation across cultures. In P. C. Earley & M. Erez (Eds.), *New perspectives on international industrial/organizational psychology* (pp. 640–675). San Francisco: New Lexington Press.

Leung, K., & Bond, M. H. (1998, August). *Cultural beliefs about conflict and peace*. Paper presented at the 24th International Association of Applied Psychology, San Francisco, CA.

Leung, K., & Morris, M. W. (in press). Justice through the lens culture and ethnicity. In J. Sanders & V. L. Hamilton (Eds.), *Handbook of law and social science: Justice*. New York: Plenum Press.

Levinson, D. (1989). *Family violence in cross-cultural perspective*. Newbury Park, CA: Sage Publications.

Lewis, O. (1961). *The children of Sanchez: Autobiography of a Mexcian family*. New York: Random House.

Lorenz, K. (1966). *On aggression*. New York: Harcourt, Brace & World.

Matsumoto, D., Kudoh, T., Scherer, K., & Wallbot, H. G. (1988). Emotion antecedents and reactions in the US and Japan. *Journal of Cross-Cultural Psychology, 19*, 267–286.

Mesquita, B., & Frijda, N. H. (1992). Cultural variations in emotions: A review. *Psychological Bulletin, 112*, 179–204.

Messick, D. M. (1988). On the limitations of cross-cultural research in social psychology. In M. H. Bond (Ed.), *The cross-cultural challenge to social psychology* (pp. 41–47). Newbury Park, CA: Sage.

Messick, D. M., Bloom, S., Boldizar, J. P., & Samuelson, C. D. (1985). Why we are fairer than others. *Journal of Experimental Social Psychology, 21*, 480–500.

Mikula, G., & Heimgartner, A. (1992). *Experiences of injustice in intimate relationships*. Unpublished manuscript, University of Graz, Austria.

Mikula, G., Petri, B., & Tanzer, N. (1989). What people regard as unjust: Types and structures of everyday experiences of injustice. *European Journal of Social Psychology, 20*, 133–149.

Milgram, S. (1974). *Obedience to authority: An experimental view*. New York: Harper & Row.

Miller, W. (1958). Lower class culture as a generating milieu of gang delinquency. *Journal of Social Issues, 14*, 5–19.

Moghaddam, F. M., & Studer, C. (1997). Cross-cultural psychology: The frustrated gadfly's promises, potentialities, and failures. In D. Fox & I. Prillentensky (Eds.), *Critical psychology* (pp. 185–201). Newbury Park, CA: Sage.

Moore, D. B. (1993). Shame, forgiveness, and juvenile justice. *Criminal Justice Ethics, 12*, 3–25.

Mueller, C. W. (1983). Environmental stressors and aggressive behavior. In R. G. Geen & E. I. Donnerstein (Eds.), *Aggression: Theoretical and empirical reviews* (Vol. 2, pp. 51–76). New York: Academic Press.

Mummendey, A., Linneweber, V., & Loschper, G. (1984). Actor or victim of aggression: Divergent perspectives—Divergent evaluations. *European Journal of Social Psychology, 14*, 291–311.

Nasby, W., Hayden, B., & DePaulo, B. M. (1979). Attributional bias among aggressive boys to interpret unambiguous social stimuli as displays of hostility. *Journal of Abnormal Psychology, 89*, 459–468.

Ohbuchi, K., Fukushima, O., & Tedeschi, J. T. (1999). Cultural values in conflict management: Goal orientation, goal attainment, and tactical decision. *Journal of Cross Cultural Psychology, 30*, 51–71.

Ohbuchi, K., & Takahashi, Y. (1994). Cultural styles of conflict. *Journal of Applied Social Psychology, 24*, 1345–1366.

Osgood, C. E., Suci, G. J., & Tannenbaum, P. H. (1957). *The measurement of meaning*. Urbana: University of Illinois Press.

Pepitone, A. (1984). Violent aggression from the multiple perspectives of psychology. *Journal of Social and Economic Studies, 1,* 321–355.

Peristiany, J. G. (Ed.). (1965). *Honor and shame: The values of Mediterranean society.* London: Weidenfeld & Nicolson.

Pruitt, D. G., & Rubin, J. Z. (1986). *Social conflict: Escalation, stalemate, and settlement.* New York: Random House.

Quigley, B. M., & Tedeschi, J. T. (1996). Mediating effects of blame attributions on feelings of anger. *Personality and Social Psychology Bulletin, 22,* 1280–1288.

Redford, P. (1998, August). *Self-construal and anger action tendencies in Hong Kong and the United Kingdom.* Paper presented at the 14th Congress of the International Association for Cross-Cultural Psychology, Bellingham, WA.

Reis, H. T. (1982). An introduction to the use of structural equations: Prospects and problems. In L. Wheeler (Ed.), *Review of personality and social psychology* (Vol. 3, pp. 255–287). Beverly Hills, CA: Sage.

Riordan, C. A., Marlin, N. A., & Kellogg, R. T. (1983). The effectiveness of accounts following transgression. *Social Psychology Quarterly, 46,* 213–219.

Ross, L., & Ward, A. (1996). Naive realism in everyday life: Implications for social conflict and misunderstanding. In E. S. Reed, E. Turiel, & T. Brown (Eds.), *Values and knowledge: The Jean Piaget Symposium series* (pp. 103–135). Mahwah, NJ: Erlbaum.

Rotton, J., & Cohn, E. G. (1999, February). *Cold facts about heat and aggression.* Paper presented at the Nag's Head Conference on Affect, Hostility, and Aggression, Highland Beach, FL.

Rule, B. G., & Nesdale, A. R. (1976a). Emotional arousal and aggressive behavior. *Psychological Bulletin, 83,* 851–863.

Rule, B. G., & Nesdale, A. R. (1976b). Environmental stressors, emotional arousal and aggression. In I. G. Sarason & C. D. Spielberger (Eds.), *Stress and anxiety* (Vol. 3, pp. 87–103). Washington, DC: Hemisphere.

Ryan, W. (1971). *Blaming the victim.* New York: Random House.

Schelling, T. C. (1963). *The strategy of conflict.* New York: Oxford University Press.

Schlegel, A., & Berry, H. (1991). *Adolescence: An anthropological inquiry.* New York: Free Press.

Schlenker, B. R., & Darby, B. W. (1981). The use of apologies in social predicaments. *Social Psychology Quarterly, 44,* 271–278.

Schruijer, S., Tedeschi, J. T., Blanz, M., Mummendey, A., Banfai, B., Dittmar, H., Kleibaumhter, Mahjoub, A., Mandrosz-Wroblewska, J., Molinari, L., & Petillon, X. (1994). The group-serving bias in evaluating and explaining harm-doing behavior. *Journal of Social Psychology, 134,* 47–54.

Schwartz, G. S., Kane, T. R., Joseph, J. M., & Tedeschi, J. T. (1978). The effects of post-transgression remorse on perceived aggression, attribution of intent, and level of punishment. *British Journal of Social and Clinical Psychology, 17,* 293–297.

Schwartz, S. H. (1992). The universal content and structure of values: Theoretical advances and empirical tests in 20 countries. In M. Zanna (Ed.), *Advances in experimental social Psychology* (Vol. 25, pp. 1–65). New York: Academic Press.

Schwartz, S. H. (1994). Beyond individualism/collectivism: New cultural dimensions of values. In U. Kim, H. C. Triandis, C. Kagitcibasi, S. C. Choi, & G. Yoon (Eds.), *Individualism and collectivism: Theory application and methods* (pp. 85–119). Newbury Park, CA: Sage Publications.

Sebastian, R. J. (1978). Immediate and delayed effects of victim suffering on the attacker's aggression. *Journal of Research in Personality, 12,* 312–328.

Segall, M. H., Ember, C. R., & Ember, M. (1997) Aggression, crime, and warfare. In J. W. Berry, M. H. Segall, & C. Kagitcibasi (Eds.), *The handbook of cross-cultural psychology* (Vol. 3, pp. 213–254). Needham Heights, MA: Allyn & Bacon.

Semin, G. R., & Rubini, M. (1990). Unfolding the concept of person by verbal abuse. *European Journal of Social Psychology, 20,* 463–474.

Smith, P. B., & Bond, M. H. (1998). *Social psychology across cultures* (2nd ed.). London: Prentice Hall.

Snyder, M., & Swann, W. B., Jr. (1978). Behavioral confirmation in social interaction: From social perception to social reality. *Journal of Experimental Social Psychology, 14,* 148–162.

Staub, E. (1988). The evolution of caring and nonaggressive persons and societies. *Journal of Social Issues, 44,* 81–100.

Stephan, W. G., & Stephan, C. W. (1985). Intergroup anxiety. *Journal of Social Issues, 41,* 157–176.

Stephan, W. G., Stephan, C. W., & De Vargas, M. C. D. (1996). Emotional expression in Costa Rica and the United States. *Journal of Cross-Cultural Psychology, 27,* 147–160.

Stephan, W. G., Ybarra, O., & Bachman, G. (1998). *Prejudice toward immigrants.* Manuscript submitted for publication.

Straus, M. A. (1980). Stress and child abuse. In C. H. Kempe & R. F. Helfer (Eds.), *The battered child* (3rd ed., pp. 86–103). Chicago: University of Chicago Press.

Sun, H., & Bond, M. H. (in press). Interactant's personality and status as determinants of influencer's choice of tactics. In J. P. Li, A. Tsui, & E. Weldon (Eds.), *Management and organizations in China.* New York: Macmillan.

Sverdrup, H. V. (1938). *With the people of the Tundra* (Human Relations Area Files, Trans.). Oslo: Gyldendal Norsk Forlag.

Taylor, S. P., & Epstein, S. (1967). Aggression as a function of the interaction of the set of the aggressor and the set of the victim. *Journal of Personality, 35,* 474–485.

Tedeschi, J. T. (Ed.). (1981). *Impression management theory and social psychological research.* New York: Academic Press.

Tedeschi, J. T., & Felson, R. B. (1994).*Violence, aggression, and coercive actions.* Washington, DC: American Psychological Association.

Tedeschi, J. T., Lindskold, S., & Rosenfeld, P. (1985). *An introduction to social psychology*. St. Paul, MN: West.

Tedeschi, J. T., & Quigley, B. M. (1996). Limitations of laboratory paradigms for studying aggression. *Aggression and Violent Behavior: A Review Journal, 1*, 163–177.

Tedeschi, J. T. & Quigley, B. M. (2000). A further comment on the construct validity of laboratory aggression paradigms: A response to Giancola and Chermack. *Aggression and Violent Behavior: A Review Journal, 5*, 127–139.

Ting-Toomey, S. (1988). A face-negotiation theory. In Y. Kim & W. B. Gudykunst (Eds.), *Theory in intercultural communication* (pp. 213–235). Newbury Park, CA: Sage Publications.

Ting-Toomey, S., Gao, G., Trubinsky, P., Yang, Z., Kim, H. S., Liu, S. L., & Nishida, T. (1991). Culture, face maintenance, and styles of handling interpersonal conflict: A study in five cultures. *International Journal of Conflict Management, 2*, 275–296.

Toch, H. H. (1969). *Violent men: An inquiry into the psychology of violence*. Chicago: Aldine-Atherton.

Triandis, H. C. (1995). *Individualism and collectivism*. Boulder, CO: Westview Press.

Turnbull, C. (1965). *Wayward servants: The two worlds of the African Pygmies*. Garden City, NY: Natural History.

Tyler, T. R. (1988). What is procedural justice? Criteria used by citizens to assess the fairness of legal procedures. *Law and Society Review, 22*, 103–135.

Westley, W. A. (1970). *Violence and the police: A sociological study of law, custom, and morality*. Cambridge, MA: MIT Press.

Whiting, B. B. (1976). The problem of the packaged variable. In K. F. Reigel, & J. A. Meacham (Eds.), *The developing individual in a changing world* (pp. 303–309). The Hague, The Netherlands: Mouton.

Wilkinson, R. G. (1996). *Unhealthy societies: The afflictions of inequality*. London: Routledge.

Wilkinson, R. G., Kawachi, I., & Kennedy, B. P. (1998). Mortality, the social environment, crime and violence. *Sociology of Health and Illness, 20*, 578–597.

Wolfgang, M., & Ferracuti, F. (1956). *The subculture of violence: Toward an integrated theory of criminality*. London: Tavistock.

Zern, D. S. (1984). Relationships among selected child-rearing variables in a cross-cultural sample of 110 societies. *Developmental Psychology, 20*, 683–690.

IV

CONCLUSION

11

THE AVERSIVE SIDE OF SOCIAL INTERACTION REVISITED

ROBIN M. KOWALSKI

Given a choice between being stranded on a deserted island alone for the rest of their lives or being stranded in the company of at least one other person, most people would choose to be stranded with other people. One reason for electing the company of another person would be survival. Relative to living alone, a person's chances for survival in an unfamiliar, potentially threatening environment increase substantially when in the presence of others. Beyond simple survival, however, people would also likely choose to be stranded with another individual because relationships with others provide meaning for people's lives (Klinger, 1977) and are a source of psychological well-being. In fact, people's need to be included by others is so strong that some researchers consider it to be a fundamental human motive (Baumeister & Leary, 1995).

Given the importance of relationships to people's lives, it is ironic that the same relationships that people seek so eagerly are the source of many, perhaps most, of their greatest frustrations and unhappiness. One key reason that people seek therapy involves problems with their personal relationships (Horowitz, 1986; Rook, 1994). People rank conflicts with others as one of the most significant daily stressors that they encounter (Bolger,

297

DeLongis, Kessler, & Schilling, 1989). How is it that we can need others so much, indeed rely on others for our survival and well-being, yet often find it so difficult to maintain satisfying relationships with them?

The answer may lie in the fact that our desire to be connected to other people reflects not simply an indiscriminate desire to be around other people but rather a need for "frequent, *nonaversive* interactions within an ongoing relational bond" (Baumeister & Leary, 1995, p. 497). People desire to be in relationships with others, but not just any kind of relationship. Rather, they want those relationships to be relatively free of pain, annoyance, tension, and conflict. Unfortunately, most aversive interactions occur within the context of our closest connections with others. The person whom you love the most is the one you are most likely to hurt and the one most likely to hurt you (Miller, 1997). The person who raises your spirits by leaving flowers or a love letter one day is the same individual who, the next day, behaves like an insensitive jerk. The spouse in whom you have placed complete trust is the one who later betrays that trust. The friend whom you respect is the same individual with whom you engage in disrespectful breaches of propriety.

Because the study of aversive behaviors is relatively new, much remains to be learned about them. However, as the chapters in this book illustrate, certain features appear to be common to most if not all negative social behaviors. These features are discussed in the sections that follow.

AVERSIVE BEHAVIORS ARE AN INEVITABLE PART OF RELATIONSHIPS

Despite their aversiveness, relational transgressions and negative social interactions are an inevitable and frequent part of relating to others (Duck, 1994; Duck & Wood, 1995). Indeed, Miller (chapter 2) acknowledged that some breaches of propriety are now so commonplace that some people do not recognize them as inappropriate or aversive at all. Winters and Duck (chapter 3) discussed profanity as being "extremely prevalent." Leary and Springer (chapter 6) stated that the incidence of hurt feelings is "surprisingly common," and Rosnow (chapter 8) discussed rumor and gossip as something that people do all of the time. W. H. Jones, Moore, Schratter, and Negel (chapter 9) labeled betrayals as a relatively common feature of relationships. Clearly, regardless of the specific type of transgression, aversive behaviors are a common and inevitable feature of relationships.

What accounts for the inevitability of negative social behaviors? Why do people engage in aversive behaviors so frequently with those who are closest to them? In large part, the answer lies in the needs, desires, histories of relating, and relationship expectations that two people bring with them when they enter a relationship. In an effort to satisfy their needs or to bring others' behaviors in line with their own expectations, people sometimes engage in behaviors that others find objectionable. The more time that is spent with someone and the closer the relationship, the greater the likelihood that one or both parties insult, offend, embarrass, or hurt the other. With time, people gain increased access to psychological weaponry (Miller, 1997) that can be used against their relational partners. For example, people may unwittingly reveal their partner's secrets or intentionally embarrass their partner in the presence of others.

Given the inevitability of aversive interactions, we should perhaps ask "Why are they not more common than they are?" For example, why do interaction partners not hurt our feelings more than they do? Why do people refrain from intentionally embarrassing us when they are inclined to do so? Why do we not induce guilt in our friends and relationship partners more often in order to bring their behavior in line with our expectations? Indeed, according to Miller (chapter 2) "cultural changes have probably made people generally less willing to temper their actions and restrain their impulses in the service of the collective good" (p. 34).

The answer to the question of why there is not more aversiveness in our interpersonal interactions is self-control (Baumeister, 1997). In his examination of evil, Baumeister stated that "regardless of the root causes of violence, the immediate cause is often a breakdown of self-control. . . . You do not have to give people reasons to be violent because they already have plenty of reasons. All you have to do is take away their reasons to restrain themselves" (p. 14). Thus, aversive behaviors do not occur more frequently than they do because of constraints that people put on their own behavior. Ironically, however, this self-constraint may, over time, actually enhance the inevitability of relational transgressions. The strength model of self-regulation suggests that ego depletion underlies lapses of control. Following an act of self-control, self-regulatory resources are weak. Any other immediate attempts at self-control will, therefore, be less successful (Dale & Baumeister, 1998; Muraven, Tice, & Baumeister, 1998). Thus, following an extended period of withholding biting comments directed toward one's partner, for example, the ability to refrain from engaging in other aversive behaviors, such as hurting the partner's feelings or inducing guilt in the partner, may be diminished.

NEGATIVE SOCIAL BEHAVIORS HAVE POSITIVE FEATURES

That people frequently engage in behaviors that might threaten their connections with others suggests that aversive behaviors must be perceived as having some redeeming value, at least from the perspective of the perpetrator. The belongingness hypothesis (Baumeister & Leary, 1995) posits that many of people's behaviors are motivated by their desire to establish or maintain connections with others. Although this immediately brings to mind positive overtures that people might make toward others, behaviors that have potentially negative consequences may also be used to establish and maintain social connections. For example, some people use teasing to increase relationship solidarity or to socialize people into a group (Kowalski, 2000; Kowalski, Howerton, & McKenzie, chapter 7). Swearing (Winters & Duck, chapter 3) may be used to indicate familiarity, acceptance, and relational connections with others. Many self-presentational behaviors, such as playing dumb, have both self-serving and other-serving qualities (Vonk, chapter 4). People may downplay their own traits and abilities to make other people feel comfortable. Thus, even though they have the potential to be perceived aversively by targets, many negative social behaviors are perpetrated with the intent of showing closeness and solidarity with the target.

In addition to using aversive behaviors to establish or maintain connections with the target of the behaviors, people sometimes behave aversively toward one person (i.e., the target) because they are trying to establish a relationship with someone else. For example, betrayals, such as infidelity, gossip, and breaches of confidentiality, often occur so that the betrayer may establish a connection with another person. Hurt feelings sometimes occur because an individual chooses to spend time with one individual over another. People may tease someone to be accepted by members of their peer group even if the individual being teased rejects them. Thus, aversive behaviors may be used to establish or maintain connections with the target, or they may be directed toward the target to establish a relationship with some other person or group.

REPETITIVE AVERSIVE BEHAVIORS ARE PARTICULARLY UNPLEASANT

Although annoying and irritating, many aversive interpersonal behaviors that occur in isolation are easily tolerated and quickly forgotten. Repeated relational transgressions, however, are quite another matter, because aversiveness increases with the frequency of unpleasant behaviors. Cunningham, Barbee, and Druen (1997) used the term *social allergen* to refer to obnoxious, annoying behaviors that produce unpleasant reactions in others. Just as the physical response to a single exposure to a physical allergen, such as dust, is relatively minor, so the emotional and social response to infrequent exposure to a social allergen, such as teasing, is often negligible. However, repeated exposure to social allergens produces a social allergy that Cunningham et al. defined as "a reaction of hypersensitive disgust or annoyance to a social allergen" (p. 191).

Examples of the process by which social allergens develop into social allergies through repeated exposure to the noxious stimulus abound. For example, isolated instances of teasing may be perceived as funny or at least as not maliciously motivated. However, constant and persistent teasing despite requests that the teaser terminate the behavior becomes very unpleasant for the victim and detrimental for his or her relationship with the teaser. Similarly, Katz and Joiner (chapter 5) noted that reassurance-seeking itself is seldom problematic. Rather, it is the repetitive, persistent nature of excessive reassurance-seeking that makes it aversive. Given that we all, on occasion, hurt others' feelings, we generally forgive occasional hurtful slights perpetrated against us. However, when a relational partner continues to engage in behaviors that we indicate are hurtful, the partner's behavior cannot be explained away as simple carelessness or mindlessness, and its hurtfulness increases.

Not surprisingly, then, repetitive negative social behaviors create formidable relationship challenges. Even when targets do not believe that the perpetrator is intentionally engaging in an aversive behavior, its repetition shows that the perpetrator is doing nothing to stop the behavior. To the target, the perpetrator's lack of effort in stopping his or her offending behavior may suggest relational devaluation, that is, the perpetrator does not value his or her relationship with the target enough to stop the troubling behavior (Leary, Springer, Negel, Ansell, & Evans, 1998).

One by-product of repeated exposure to another's aversive behaviors is that the target may develop a heightened vigilance and sensitivity to such behaviors. As a result, the target may begin to interpret even innocuous behaviors by friends or relational partners as aversive (W. H. Jones et al., chapter 9; Leary & Springer, chapter 6). For example, persistent negative evaluations from one's spouse may lead one to interpret any comment from the spouse as criticism.

JUDGMENTS OF AVERSIVENESS ARE IDIOSYNCRATIC

People differ in their perceptions of the aversiveness of behaviors, such that a behavior that one person perceives to be funny may be regarded as hurtful and demeaning by another. Research that has examined differences in the perceptions of victims and perpetrators shows that, relative to victims, perpetrators minimize the negative impact of their behavior, view the behavior more benignly, perceive the behavior as rationally motivated, and see the consequences of the behavior as limited (Baumeister, 1997; Baumeister, Stillwell, & Wotman, 1990; Besag, 1989; Kowalski, 2000; Leary et al., 1998). Along these lines, W. H. Jones et al. (chapter 9) found that victim narratives of betrayal reflected more serious violations of relational expectations and that the betrayals tended to have occurred further in the past than perpetrator narratives. Similarly, Kowalski (2000) discovered that perpetrators perceived instances of teasing as more humorous and less annoying than victims.

Despite the research attention that has been devoted to victims' and perpetrators' perceptions of aversive behaviors, the reactions of third parties to negative social behaviors have been neglected. We know little about people's reactions to seeing others being teased, having their friends betrayed, or knowing that others' feelings are hurt. In some instances, observers may find behaviors more aversive than targets. For example, the target of ingratiation may enjoy being flattered whereas observers evaluate it negatively (Vonk, chapter 4).

People are sometimes the unintended recipients of others' aversive behaviors. For example, a driver picking his nose at a stoplight or an individual walking down the street scratching his crotch presumably do not intend their behaviors to be either seen by others or evaluated as negative or aversive. Nevertheless, observers may find such behaviors offensive and disconcerting (Miller, chapter 2). Similar evaluations of offensiveness may occur when people witness others' excessive use of profanity, even when that profanity is not directed toward them.

Because victims, perpetrators, and observers may have different perspectives on and reactions to aversive behaviors, the consequences of the behaviors for each also differ. Relative to perpetrators, victims generally experience more negative and more long-term consequences of others' aversive behaviors. For example, victims of teasing report more detrimental, long-lasting effects of the teasing than perpetrators (Kowalski, 2000). A recent episode of the Maury Povich show illustrates this phenomenon well. A female guest on the show recounted how her life had been ruined because of the relentless teasing she received in high school. One male classmate whom she remembered as the ringleader of the teasing also appeared on the show. Unlike the woman who had been devastated by the teasing, however, the male guest had no recollection at all of having teased her.

As in the case of this woman who had been teased, the effects of aversive behaviors can last for many years. Indeed, as noted by W. H. Jones et al. (chapter 9), "instances of betrayal . . . often linger as painful, interpersonal memories for long periods of time, even 30 or 40 years after the fact" (p. 234). In many of the narrative accounts of interpersonal transgressions discussed in this volume, participants recalled events that occurred some years earlier. For example, Leary and Springer (chapter 6) noted that some of the instances of hurt feelings recounted by participants in their studies occurred up to 10 years previously. Similarly, Kowalski (2000; Kowalski et al., chapter 7) found that most instances of teasing that were recounted by college students had occurred during elementary and junior high school.

Although the effects of aversive behaviors on victims can clearly be devastating and of greater magnitude than those experienced by perpetrators, perpetrators are not completely immune from the ill-effects of their actions. Some perpetrators of teasing, for example, reported feeling embarrassment, guilt, and regret about what they had done (Kowalski, 2000; Kowalski et al., chapter 7; Tedeschi & Bond, chapter 10). Perpetrators who tease, hurt the feelings of others, or engage in other aversive behaviors may experience any of a number of negative emotions, including shame, guilt, and remorse. Their behavior may reveal undesired aspects of themselves and their capacity to harm others. In addition, perpetrators may worry about the social implications of their relational transgressions. Problems in relationships make good material for the rumor mill. The betrayer may worry about the broader interpersonal network implications of his or her behavior. On the positive side, however, human foibles and the awareness of undesired aspects of ourselves may lead people to constructively alter their behavior in the future (Spitzberg & Cupach, 1998).

Although observers would be expected to be affected the least by others' aversive behaviors, there are nonetheless consequences for them as well. For example, simply witnessing aggression increases one's risk for negative mental health consequences (Katz & Joiner, chapter 5). Some observers may feel ineffective in their attempts to support friends who have been betrayed. Parents may feel unable to intervene on behalf of their child who is being bullied at school, creating feelings of guilt. Others may experience empathic embarrassment at the seeming obliviousness some people have while engaging in breaches of propriety.

PEOPLE DISH IT OUT FAR BETTER THAN THEY TAKE IT

Given that victims and perpetrators often differ in their perceptions of the aversiveness of particular behaviors, it is not surprising that people evaluate their own behaviors very differently than they evaluate the same behaviors performed by others, that is, people dish it out far better than they take it. One reason for this is that individuals who behave aversively know why they do so, whereas when these same individuals are victims, they cannot be certain of the motives behind others' behavior. In addition, differences in the attributions made for our own and others' aversive behaviors reflect a simple case of the actor–observer bias. We are more likely to make dispositional attributions for the negative actions of others and situational attributions for our own untoward behavior (E. E. Jones & Nisbett, 1972).

PEOPLE USUALLY DO NOT INTEND TO BE AVERSIVE

Although some perpetrators maliciously engage in aversive behaviors with the intention of hurting other people, in point of fact most perpetrators do not intend to hurt others (Leary et al., 1998). Many perpetrators are not even aware that their behaviors are annoying or bothersome to other people, suggesting an interesting feature of human behavior: People often do not have a clue regarding how aversive they really are. In Leary et al.'s (1998) study of hurt feelings, most of the perpetrators (over 80%) indicated that they had not intended to hurt another person's feelings, that the hurt had been an accident or the result of inconsiderateness and insensitivity. As noted by Miller (chapter 2), people often engage in aversive behaviors out of sheer ignorance. They are simply unaware of the appropriate relational rules either because the rules have not been completely clarified within the context of a particular relationship (Metts, 1994) or because of some type of social skill deficit on the part of the perpetrator (Miller, chapter 2). As an indication of people's lack of awareness regarding the aversive nature of some of their behaviors, imagine the chagrin of an individual confronted with the fact that he has just been observed relentlessly picking his nose.

AVERSIVE BEHAVIORS LEAD TO INFERENCES OF RELATIONAL DEVALUATION

Targets experience negative affect when they interpret others' behaviors as aversive. For example, breaches of propriety or repetitive teasing may produce embarrassment if the behavior is public or anger at the lack of respect connoted by the behavior. Betrayals, such as one's relational partner spending increasing amounts of time with a member of the other sex, may create jealousy or anger. Being slighted by a friend may make one feel sad and hurt. Excessive reassurance-seeking and negative feedback-seeking may lead targets to experience sadness and depression.

The reason for the experience of negative affect in response to aversive behaviors appears to lie in people's perceptions of changes in relational evaluation conveyed by the behavior, specifically people's feelings that others do not value their relationships as much as the target desires or as much as they did previously (Leary, Koch, & Hechenbleikner, in press). This idea of changes in relational evaluation explains why the relational transgressions of close others are typically more hurtful and more noticeable than those of strangers or acquaintances. Generally, we desire the approval and acceptance of close others more than of strangers. Thus, we are more likely to be hurt by indications of relational devaluation from close, as opposed to distant, others.

AVERSIVE BEHAVIORS INVOLVE ACTS OF COMMISSION AND ACTS OF OMISSION

When asked to report aversive behaviors, people mention both acts of commission and acts of omission. Most of the annoying, mundane, behaviors that have been discussed in this book as well as in other books of a similar theme (Cupach & Spitzberg, 1994; Kowalski, 1997; Spitzberg & Cupach, 1998) have focused primarily on acts of commission, things that the perpetrator does, such as teasing someone (Kowalski et al., chapter 7) or inducing guilt in a relational partner (Sommer & Baumeister, 1997), that the victim finds annoying and bothersome. Acts of omission—things that the perpetrator fails to do, such as forgetting a special occasion, that also annoy or offend the victim—have received less attention. However, because of their potential for conveying relational devaluation and for creating negative affect in the victim, acts of omission are just as aversive as acts of commission.

MEN AND WOMEN DIFFER IN THE PERFORMANCE AND JUDGMENT OF AVERSIVE BEHAVIORS

Many of the behaviors examined within this volume and elsewhere show gender differences. First, men and women often differ in the frequency with which particular behaviors occur. For example, men are more likely to state that they had betrayed their wives than women are to say they had betrayed their husbands (W. H. Jones et al., chapter 9). In general, men tease more than women (Alberts, 1992; Alberts, Kellar-Guenther, & Corman, 1996; Eisenberg, 1986; Kowalski, 2000), and Jay (1992) and Selnow (1985) found swearing to be more prevalent among men than women.

Second, men and women often differ in their perceptions of what constitutes a negative social exchange. For example, men report being more upset about women's moodiness, whereas women indicate disliking men's inconsiderateness and neglectfulness (Tedeschi & Bond, chapter 10). Relative to men, women are more likely to view criticism, angry outbursts, and stonewalling as betrayals (W. H. Jones et al., chapter 9). Winters and Duck (chapter 3) report that women react more strongly than men to the use of obscenity. Thus, not surprisingly, women tend to find breaches of propriety more offensive than men.

Men and women also differ in the manner in which an interpersonal transgression manifests itself. Whereas men more than women report betrayals of business partners, women more than men recount betrayals of same-sex friends. Among adolescents, boys more then girls tease through direct put-downs of others. Relative to boys, girls tease more playfully and are more likely to allow the target to join in on the tease (Eder, 1993).

Gender is also related to people's perceptions of the aversiveness of a particular social behavior. Boys who mercilessly tease and behave aggressively toward others are often viewed as just being boys. In contrast, girls who engage in the same behavior are judged as behaving inappropriately. A woman who fails to open the door for others is given no notice at all. However, a man who fails to open or hold the door open for others may be evaluated negatively (Miller, chapter 2). One exception to this seems to be swearing. Winters and Duck (chapter 3) stated that swearing is perceived negatively regardless of the gender of the swearer. However, it is probably safe to say that male swearers are generally viewed less negatively than female swearers.

Gender differences in the practice and perception of aversive behaviors may be explained primarily in terms of socialization. Whereas boys tend to be socialized for independence and activity, girls tend to be socialized for interdependence and connectedness (Myers, 1999). Because of differences in the way that men and women are socialized, some aversive behaviors are both more commonplace and more acceptable in male as opposed to female circles. For example, parents are far more likely to discourage acts of aggression among female as opposed to male children. Similarly, an adolescent boy who belches or passes gas is more likely to be reinforced by his peer group than a female adolescent who engages in the same behavior.

Gender differences in aversive behaviors may create difficulties in male–female relationships. Behaviors that are accepted within one's same-sex peer group may produce very different reactions when they occur with members of the other sex. For example, because girls generally engage in more playful teasing than boys, girls may be hurt and offended by the more direct put-downs inherent in boys' teasing. Boys, on the other hand, may perceive the girls as being overly sensitive and may therefore continue their teasing. Similarly, breaches of propriety that may be reinforced among male peer groups may be evaluated negatively by female individuals when they occur in mixed-sex groups.

CONCLUSION

Our relationships with friends, family members, and romantic partners are a source of great meaning and joy in our lives. However, these same relationships are often the source of our greatest frustrations, annoyances, and hurts. The more time people spend together and the closer they become, the more likely it is that they offend, embarrass, insult, and hurt each other through aversive behaviors such as teasing, breaches of propriety, aggression, and betrayal.

These aversive behaviors are an inevitable and frequent part of our relationships with others. No one can claim that they have never been victimized by the aversive behaviors of a close other or that they have never perpetrated betrayals against others. Given the inevitability of these negative social behaviors, it is fortunate that they sometimes have positive features and are sometimes even motivated by efforts to establish camaraderie and connections with others.

Whether referred to as aversive behaviors, relational transgressions, negative social behaviors, or social allergens, the behaviors examined within this book make their presence known in most interpersonal relationships. Although I tend to think of these behaviors as the underbelly of social interaction, they are in fact as much a part of the mainstream of interpersonal interaction as more positive, relationship-enhancing behaviors.

REFERENCES

Alberts, J. K. (1992). An inferential/strategic explanation for the social organization of teases. *Journal of Language and Social Psychology, 11*, 153–177.

Alberts, J. K., Kellar-Guenther, Y., & Corman, S. R. (1996). That's not funny: Understanding recipients' responses to teasing. *Western Journal of Communication, 60*, 337–357.

Baumeister, R. F. (1997). *Evil: Inside human violence and cruelty*. New York: W. H. Freeman.

Baumeister, R. F., & Leary, M. R. (1995). The need to belong: Desire for interpersonal attachments as a fundamental human motivation. *Psychological Bulletin, 117*, 497–529.

Baumeister, R. F., Stillwell, A., & Wotman, S. R. (1990). Victim and perpetrator accounts of interpersonal conflict: Autobiographical narratives about anger. *Journal of Personality and Social Psychology, 59*, 994–1005.

Besag, V. (1989). *Bullies and victims in school*. Buckingham, UK: Open University Press.

Bolger, N., DeLongis, A., Kessler, R. C., & Schilling, E. A. (1989). Effects of daily stress on negative mood. *Journal of Personality and Social Psychology, 57*, 808–818.

Cunningham, M. R., Barbee, A. P., & Druen, P. B. (1997). Social allergens and the reactions that they produce: Escalation of annoyance and disgust in love and work. In R. M. Kowalski (Ed.), *Aversive interpersonal behaviors* (pp. 189–214). New York: Plenum Press.

Cupach, W. R., & Spitzberg, B. H. (Eds.). (1994). *The dark side of interpersonal communication*. Hillsdale, NJ: Erlbaum.

Dale, K. L., & Baumeister, R. F. (1998). Self-regulation and psychopathology. In R. M. Kowalski & M. R. Leary (Eds.), *The social psychology of emotional and* behavioral problems: Interfaces of social and clinical psychology (pp. 139–166). Washington, DC: American Psychological Association.

Duck, S. (1994). Stratagems, spoils, and a serpent's tooth: On the delights and dilemmas of personal relationships. In W. R. Cupach & B. H. Spitzberg (Eds.), The dark side of interpersonal communication (pp. 3–24). Hillsdale, NJ: Erlbaum.

Duck, S., & Wood, J. T. (1995). For better, for worse, for richer, for poorer: The rough and smooth of relationships. In S. Duck & J. T. Wood (Eds.), Confronting relationship challenges (Vol. 5, pp. 1–21). London: Sage.

Eder, D. (1993). "Go get ya a French!": Romantic and sexual teasing among adolescent girls. In D. Tannen (Ed.), Gender and conversational interaction (pp. 17–31). New York: Oxford University Press.

Eisenberg, A. R. (1986). Teasing: Verbal play in two Mexicano homes. In B. B. Schieffelin & E. Ochs (Eds.), Language socialization across cultures (pp. 182–198). Cambridge, England: Cambridge University Press.

Horowitz, L. (1986). The interpersonal basis of psychiatric symptoms. Clinical Psychology Review, 6, 443–469.

Jay, T. B. (1992). Cursing in America. Philadelphia: John Benjamins.

Jones, E. E., & Nisbett, R. E. (1972). The actor and the observer: Divergent perceptions of the causes of behavior. In E. E. Jones, D. E. Kanouse, H. H. Kelley, R. E. Nisbett, S. Valins, & B. Weiner (Eds.), Attribution: Perceiving the causes of behavior (pp. 79–94). Morristown, NJ: General Learning Press.

Klinger, E. (1977). Meaning and void: Inner experiences and the incentives in people's lives. Minneapolis: University of Minnesota Press.

Kowalski, R. M. (1997). Aversive interpersonal behaviors: An overarching framework. In R. M. Kowalski (Ed.), Aversive interpersonal behaviors (pp. 215–233). New York: Plenum Press.

Kowalski, R. M. (2000). "I was only kidding!": Victims' and perpetrators' perceptions of teasing. Personality and Social Psychology Bulletin, 26, 231–241.

Leary, M. R., Koch, E. J., & Hechenbleikner, N. R. (in press). Emotional responses to interpersonal rejection. In M. R. Leary (Ed.), Interpersonal rejection. New York: Oxford University Press.

Leary, M. R., Springer, C., Negel, L., Ansell, E., & Evans, K. (1998). The causes, phenomenology, and consequences of hurt feelings. Journal of Personality and Social Psychology, 74, 1225–1237.

Metts, S. (1994). Relational transgressions. In W. R. Cupach & B. H. Spitzberg (Eds.), The dark side of interpersonal communication (pp. 217–239). Hillsdale, NJ: Erlbaum.

Miller, R. S. (1997). We always hurt the ones we love: Aversive interactions in close relationships. In R. M. Kowalski (Ed.), Aversive interpersonal behaviors (pp. 11–29). New York: Plenum Press.

Muraven, M., Tice, D. M., & Baumeister, R. F. (1998). Self-control as a limited resource: Regulatory depletion patterns. Journal of Personality and Social Psychology, 74, 774–789.

Myers, D. (1999). Social psychology. New York: McGraw-Hill.

Rook, K. S. (1994). Investigating the positive and negative sides of personal relationships: Through a lens darkly? In B. H. Spitzberg & W. R. Cupach (Eds.), *The dark side of close relationships* (pp. 369–393). Mahwah, NJ: Erlbaum.

Selnow, G. W. (1985). Sex differences in uses and perceptions of profanity. *Sex Roles, 12*, 303–312.

Sommer, K. L., & Baumeister, R. F. (1997). Making someone feel guilty: Causes, strategies, and consequences. In R. M. Kowalski (Ed.), *Aversive interpersonal behaviors* (pp. 31–55). New York: Plenum Press.

Spitzberg, B. H., & Cupach, W. R. (Eds.). (1998). *The dark side of close relationships*. Mahwah, NJ: Erlbaum.

AUTHOR INDEX

Numbers in italics refer to listings in the reference sections.

Carlston, D. E., 81, 104, *114*
Carnelley, K. B., 140, *142*
Carnevale, P. J. D., 81, *109*
Carpenitieri, S., 132, *142*
Carpenter, B. N., 237, *254*
Carter, S. L., 32, 34, *54*
Cartwright, D., *226*
Caruth, E. G., 224, *226*
Carver, M. L., 242, 243, 246, 247, *252*
Carver, V. H., 12, *21*
Cascardi, M., 136, *142*
Catron, T., 132, 137, *147*
Cattarin, J., 191, *201*
Chagnon, N. A., 267, 269, *287*
Chan, S. C. N., 278, *286*
Chazen, M., 184, 188, *199*
Chelcea, S., 218, *226*
Cheng, S.-T., 216, 217, *226*
Cherek, D. R., 261, *287*
Child, I., 281, *285*
Chokel, J., 166, *173*
Chorus, A., 218, *226*
Chowdhuri, I., 184, *200*
Christenfeld, N., 240, *253*
Clancy-Colecchi, K. R., 133, *145*
Clark, L. A., 154, *174*, 257, *287*
Clark, M. S., 12, *21*
Claster, D. S., 269, *287*
Clement, R. W., 35, *55*
Cloud, J., 17, *21*, 192, *199*
Cody, M. J., 274, *286*
Cohen, D., 32, *54*, 137, *142*, 279, 281, 283, *287*
Cohen, L. E., 262, *287*
Cohen, R., 68, *74*
Cohen, S., 6, *21*
Cohl, B., 64, *76*
Cohn, E. G., 262, *287*, *291*
Cohn, M. G., 242, *254*
Coldiron, J. R., *289*
Cole, D. A., 132, *142*
Collins, N. L., 122, *142*
Colvin, C. R., 12, *21*, 37, *54*
Comans, C., *76*
Consentino, J., 282, *289*
Contarello, A., 273, *285*
Cooper, J., 82, 99, *109*, *114*
Corman, J. C., *228*
Corman, S. R., 182, *199*, 305, *307*
Cornell, D. P., 139, *145*
Cortes-Conde, F., 180, 189, 196, *199*
Corwin, R., 260, *286*

Cosmides, L., 100, *110*, 167, *174*
Couch, L. L., 235, 242–244, 246, 250, 252–254
Coupland, N., 62, 68, *75*
Coyne, J. C., 64, *74*, 117–121, 131, *142*
Craik, K. H., 181, *199*
Creden, J. F., *142*
Cresser, R., 180, *200*
Crest, D., 63, 66, *74*
Crocker, J., 281, *287*
Crumley, L. P., 163, 168, *174*
Cunniff, C., 192, *201*
Cunningham, M. R., 13, *21*, 300, *307*
Cupach, W. R., 3, 5, *22*, 24, 42, *54*, 57, 303, 305, *307*, *309*
Czapinski, J., 85, *112*

Dale, K. L., 299, *307*
Daly, J. A., 36, *57*
D'Amato, J., 64, *76*
Danzi, A. D., 220, 221, *232*
Darby, B. W., 274, *291*
Daro, D., 62, *74*
Darwin, C., 166, *172*
Daubman, K. A., 82, *110*
David, J. P., 214, *225*
Davis, K. E., 104, *111*
Davis, M. S., 64, *74*
Davis, R. D., 39, *56*
Dean, D., 82, *110*
Debevec, K., 207, *227*
DeClerque, J., 216, 217, *226*
de Klerk, V., 64, 69, 71, *74*
De La Ronde, C., 128, 130, *146*
Delbridge, R., 221, *229*
DeLongis, A., xi, *xiii*, 6, *21*, 298, *307*
DePaulo, B. M., 42, *54*, 85, 93, *110*, 239, 240, *253*, 272, *290*
Derech-Zehavi, A., 204, 220, *229*
Dermer, M., 106, *109*
Deshields, T. L., 274, *287*
De Silva, P., 238, *253*
DeSteno, D. A., 238, *253*
Deutsch, M., 267, *288*
De Vargas, M. C. D., 274, *292*
Dewhurst, A. M., 133, *142*
Diener, E., 155, *173*
DiFonzo, N., 206, 207, *226*
Dillar, J., 274, *287*
Dillard, J. P., 117, *146*
Dindia, K., 72, *74*

Hill, M. G., 83, *111*
Hill, T. E., 30, *55*
Hilton, J. L., 104, *110*
Hippocratic Oath, 224, *227*
Hixon, J. G., 128, 130, *146*
Hodge, S., 30, *55*
Hodgins, H. S., 53, *55*
Hoebel, E. A., 280, *289*
Hofstede, G., 268, 277, 278, *289*
Hogan, R., 81, *111*
Hogg, A., 53, *58*
Hokanson, J. E., 119, 138, *141, 143*
Holahan, C. J., 119, *146*
Holden, G. W., 136, *143*
Holgate, S., 237, *255*
Hollander, G. R., 119, *143*
Holliday, H., 218, *228*
Holmes, J., 35, *55*
Holmes, J. G., 235, *255*
Holtgraves, T., 274, *289*
Hooley, J. M., 125, *143*
Hoover, J. H., 191, *200*
Hopper, R., 63, *75*, 182, 190, *200*
Horowitz, L., 297, *308*
Horowitz, R., 80, 81, *111*
Howell, R., 196, *200*
Hsieh, C. C., 276, *289*
Hubschmid, T., 131, *143*
Hughes, G., 60–62, 64, *75*
Hughes, M., 82, *111*
Humana, C., 269, *289*
Hurst, M., 59, *74*
Hymovitch, B., *225*

Ickes, W., 12, 19, *21, 22,* 37, *54*
Iizuka, Y., 273, *285*
Inman, M., 214, *225*
Innes, J. M., 62, *75*
Iyer, E. S., 207, *227*
Izard, C. E., 153, *173*

Jaeger, M. E., 42, *55,* 205, 206, 216, 218,
    221, 223, 224, *227, 230*
Jaffe, K., 140, *142*
Jakubaschk, J., 131, *143*
Jay, T. B., 30, 50, *55,* 59, 60, 63–68, 71,
    72, *75,* 305, *308*
Jellison, J. M., 81, 102, *111*
Jenkins, H., *228*

Jenkins, J. O., 274, *287*
Jerrold, F., 133, *145*
Johnson, B. T., 216, *227*
Johnson, F. L., 63, 65, 67, *75*
Johnson, J. G., 120, *145*
Johnson, M. P., 236, *253*
Johnson, S., 221, *227*
Joiner, T. E., Jr., 118–122, 126–130, 138,
    143–146
Jones, D., 221, *227*
Jones, E. E., 80, 81, 83, 84, 92, 93, 97,
    98, 101, 104, 106, 107, *110,*
    111, 303, *308*
Jones, S. C., 106, *112*
Jones, W. H., 81, *111,* 234–237, 242–
    250, *252–255*
Jong, E., 72, *75*
Jorgensen, P. F., *253*
Joseph, J. M., 274, *291*
Josephs, R. A., 126, *143*
Jourard, S. M., 72, *75*
Jukic, V., 217, *229*
Jung, C. G., 207, 208, 216, *227*

Kahneman, D., 53, *54*
Kamins, M. A., 206, 207, *227*
Kane, T. R., 274, *291*
Kanner, A. D., 156, *173*
Kanouse, D. E., 272, *289*
Kapferer, J.-N., 207, *228*
Kashy, D. A., 42, *54,* 85, 93, *110,* 239,
    240, *253*
Kassinove, H., 64, 69, 70, *76*
Katz, J., 118–122, 126–130, 136, 138,
    144, 145, 278, *289*
Kawachi, I., 276, *293*
Keefer, R., 217, *228*
Keith, P. M., 128, *146*
Kellar-Guenther, Y., 182, *199,* 305, *307*
Kelley, H. H., 7, *24,* 225
Kellogg, R. T., 274, *291*
Kelly, A. E., 83, *112*
Keltner, D., 42, 53, *55,* 179, 181, 182,
    187, 190, 197, *200,* 276, *289*
Kennedy, B. P., 276, *293*
Kerner, O., 205, *228*
Kernis, M. H., 138, 139, *145*
Kerr, M., 134, *145*
Kessler, J. W., 178, *201*
Kessler, R. C., xi, *xiii,* 6, *21,* 142, 298,
    307

Pound, J., 207, *230*
Powell, L., 64, 69–71, *76*
Powers, E., 82, *110*
Prasad, J., 207, 215, *230*
Pratt, S. B., 196, *201*
Predmore, S. C., 123, 138, *146*
Prentice, D. A., 36, *57*
Prinz, R. J., 133, *142*
Pritchard, B., 117, *145*
Pruitt, D. G., 81, *109*, *113*, 267, *291*
Puente, S., 281, *287*
Pugh, M. D., 276, *289*
Putnam, R. D., 32, 33, *57*
Pyszczynski, T., *145*

Quigley, B. M., 259–261, 283, *291*, *293*

Rachal, K. C., 19, *23*, *56*
Radcliffe-Brown, A. R., 177, *201*
Radford-Davenport, J., *55*
Rangan, N., 216, *229*
Rantilla, A., 279, 281, *287*
Read, S. J., 123, *147*
Reddy, V., 184, *201*
Redford, P., 281, *291*
Reeder, G. D., 81, 84, 103, 104, *113*
Reiffer, L., 139, *147*
Reis, H. T., 283, *291*
Reiss, S., 132, *146*
Rempel, J. K., 235, 236, *255*
Reynolds, J. A., III, 30, *57*
Rhodewalt, F., 97, 102, 103, *111*, *113*
Rholes, W. S., 140, *146*
Richardson, D. R., 14, *24*, 137, *143*, 152,
    174, 261, *285*
Richters, J. E., 125, *143*
Rickert, V. I., 192, *201*
Rieber, R. W., 64, 70–72, *76*
Riedel, H., 133, *147*
Rinck, C. M., 68, 69, 71, *77*, 154, *175*
Rind, B., 218, 227, *230*
Riordan, C. A., 274, *291*
Ritchie, K. L., 136, *143*
Robinson, W. L., 64, 69, 71, *77*
Rodin, J., 239, *255*
Rojahn, J., 132, *146*
Rokeach, M., 166, *174*
Rook, K. S., xi, *xiii*, 4, 5, *24*, 50, *57*,
    297, *309*

Rose, A. M., 216, *230*
Rosenberg, S., 81, *112*, *113*
Rosenfeld, P., 267, *293*
Rosenthal, M., 206, 207, *230*
Rosner, B., 189, 191, *201*
Rosnow, R. L., 42, *55*, 205–212, 214–
    221, 224, *225–227*, *230*
Ross, D. M., 7, 10, *24*, 182, 184, 186,
    188, 190, 191, 193–195, *201*
Ross, L., 272, *291*
Rossiter, C. M., Jr., 59, *74*
Rothwell, J. D., 60, 62, 63, 67–69, *76*
Rotton, J., 262, 287, *291*
Rubert, M. P., 119, *143*
Rubin, J. Z., 60, 68, 71, *76*, 267, *291*
Rubin, M. E., *22*
Rubini, M., 63, *77*, 281, *292*
Rudman, L. A., 35, *57*, 101, *113*
Rule, B. G., 262, *291*
Russell, D., 237, *254*
Russell, J. A., 155, *174*
Rutledge, L. L., 136, *143*
Rutt, D. J., 59, *74*
Ruzzene, M., 13, *24*
Ryan, W., 272, *291*
Rysman, A., 204, *230*

Saarn, C., 239, 240, *255*
Sabini, J., 204, 210, 211, *231*
Sabourin, T. C., 37, *57*
Sagarin, E., 62, *76*
Salovey, P., 238, 239, *253*, *255*
Samuelson, C. D., 270, *290*
Sanbonmatsu, D. M., 102, *113*
Sanchez, D., 246, *254*
Sandage, S. J., 23, *56*
Sanders, J. S., 64, 69, *77*
Sarason, B. R., 244, *255*
Sarason, I. G., 244, *255*
Sarnoff, I., 6, *24*
Savitsky, K., 42, *54*
Scanlon, T. J., 215, *231*
Schachter, S., 6, *24*, 215, *225*, *231*
Schafer, R. B., 128, *146*
Scheidlower, J., 62, *77*
Schelling, T. C., 268, *291*
Scher, S. J., 85, 97, *109*
Scherer, K., 281, *290*
Scherlis, W., *55*
Schieffelin, B. B., 187, 197, *201*
Schilling, E. A., xi, *xiii*, 6, 21, 298, *307*

SUBJECT INDEX

Blame, attribution of, 272–276
Body, control of, 44–45
Boorishness, 49–50
Bordia, Prashant, 215
Bragging, 42
Broken promises, 161
Brownnosing, 104
Bullying, 5
  in Japan, 198
  revenge as response to, 17
  teasing vs., 179, 180
Butler, Smedley D., 209–210

Care, lack of, 38
Carter, Jimmy, 159–160
Censorship, 204
Child Behavior Checklist, 137
Children
  aggressive behavior in, 135
  attachment styles in, 139
  teasing in, 182–188, 191–196
China, 273, 281
Chronic life strains, 10
Clinton, William Jefferson, 210
Collectivist cultures, 14, 281
Commitment, 236
Community, sense of, 32
Companions, control of, 45
Computer viruses, 34
Conditional forgiveness, 250
Conflicts, interpersonal, 297
Conflict Tactics Scale (CTS), 136, 137
Confrontation, as response to aversive
    behavior, 20
Contagious depression, 121–122
Control
  of body, 44–45
  of companions, 45
  desire for, as motivation for coercive
    actions, 265–270
  of environment, 45
  impropriety and loss of, 37
  need for, 8
  of props, 45
  teasing as means of gaining, 188–189
Couples, happy vs. unhappy, 13
Criticism, hurt feelings resulting from,
    160–161
Cronkite, Walter, 208

Crying, as response to hurtful events,
    168–169
CTS. *See* Conflict Tactics Scale
Culture(s)
  and aggressive behavior, 275–276,
    278–279
  and impropriety, 31–35
  individualistic vs. collectivist, 14, 281
  and teasing, 196–198
Cynicism, social, 268–269

Dafla hill tribes, 275
Daily hassles, 10
Deception, 239–240
Depression
  and aggressive behavior, 132–134
  "contagious," 121–122
  5-HT related depression, 132
  integrative interpersonal theory of, 128
  and negative feedback-seeking, 124–
    127
  and reassurance-seeking, 118–121
  and social functioning, 117
Depressotypic behavior(s), 117–140
  aggressive behavior as, 131–137
  and dispositional attachment style,
    139–140
  excessive reassurance-seeking as, 118–
    123
  and low/unstable self-esteem, 138–139
  negative feedback-seeking as, 123–131
Derogation, as response to hurtful events,
    169–170
Devaluation effect, 121
Development, teasing and, 184–185
"Devil-babies," 208–209
*Diagnostic and Statistical Manual of Mental
    Disorders,* 126
Disassociation, interpersonal, 158–160
Disruptional betrayal, 243–244
Dissing, 280
Distancing, as response to aversive be-
    havior, 19
Distributive justice, 270, 273
Down's syndrome, 196
Dread rumors, 216, 217
Drunkenness, 49
Dual-failure model of aggressive behavior,
    132

Eating disorders, 191
Effort, lack of, 37–38
Ejaculatory swearing, 61, 62
Elections, 159–160
Embarrassment
    intentional, 48–49
    and teasing, 191, 194–195
Emotional infidelity, 240–241
Empathic accuracy, 12
Entrainment model, 129
Environment, control of, 45
Etiquette, 30, 31
Evolution, human
    and hurt feelings, 166–168
    and sensitivity to duplicity, 100
Evolving norms, 41
Excessive reassurance-seeking, 118–123,
        138
    definition of, 118
    and depression, 118–121
    interpersonal consequences of, 121–
        122
    measurement issues with, 122–123
Expected value, 269

Fads, 33
Familiarity, and swearing, 63
Family relationships, 13–14
Fashion, 33
5-HT related depression, 132
Flattery, 106
Forgiveness
    as response to aversive behavior, 18–
        19
    as response to betrayal, 249–250
Framing, 184
Franklin, Benjamin, 219
Frequency
    of aversive behaviors, 10
    of improprieties, 50, 51

Garfield, James A., 210
Gender
    and aggressive behavior, 273, 277
    and betrayal, 240–241, 246, 247
    and gossip, 218
    and homicide, 134–135

and hurt feelings, 168
and infidelity, 240–241
and performance/judgment of aversive
        behaviors, 305–306
and standards of propriety, 35
and swearing, 70–71
and teasing, 181–183, 194
Goffman, Erving, 40
Golden, Andrew, 17
Gossip, 42
    definition of, 204
    identifying characteristics of, 210–211
    influence function of, 221
    informational function of, 220
    intimacy function of, 221–222
    and misreading of motives, 205
    moral/judgmental orientation of, 210–
        211
    nebulous forms of, 211–212
    preconditions of, 222–224
    and secrecy, 204
    and storyteller, 206–207
    transactional role of, 218–219
Gossip columns, 219
Great Britain, 79
Grief, 153
Grievances, 273–275
Grooming, individual, 44–45
Grudges, 16
Guilt induction, 42

Harris, Eric, 17
Harrison, George, 214
Hippocratic Oath, 224
Hitchcock, Alfred, 33
Homicide, 134–135, 258, 278
Hostility, 90–91
Humiliation, 191
Hurt, 153
Hurt feelings, 151–172
    from active/passive disassociation, 158–
        160
    aggressing as response to, 169
    from betrayal, 161
    from criticism, 160–161
    crying as response to, 168–169
    derogating as response to, 169–170
    as emotional experience, 153–156

Hurt feelings (*continued*)
  evolutionary underpinnings of, 166–168
  individual differences in proneness to, 165–166
  intercorrelation of, with other emotions, 155–156
  interpersonal events triggering, 152, 157
  and interpersonal rejection, 237–238
  from lack of appreciation, 162
  and maladaptive behaviors, 152
  perpetrators of, 170–171
  prevalence of, 151–152
  and relational devaluation, 156–157
  relational moderators with, 162–164
  seeking other relationships as response to, 170
  from teasing, 161–162
Hurt—Proneness Scale, 165–166
Hustling, 82

IBS. *See* Interpersonal Betrayal Scale
Idealism, 12
Ignorance of social rules, 36
Impropriety, 29–53
  bothersomeness of, 50, 51
  cultural influences related to, 31–35
  frequency of, 50, 51
  impact of, 51, 52
  of individual, 44–45
  interactive behavior, involving, 46–50
  origins of, 31–42
  personal influences related to, 35–40
  significance of, 52–53
  situational influences related to, 40–42
  types of, 42–44
Inappropriateness, 9
Inattention, 46
Incivility, 30
India, 275
Individual differences
  in betrayal, 242–244
  with impropriety, 35–36
  in perceptions of aversive behavior, 14–15
  in reactions to rumor, 209–210
Individual impropriety, 44–45
Individualism, 32
Individualistic cultures, 14, 281

Infidelity, 240–241, 246
Influence, gossip and, 221
Ingratiation, 81, 92, 104–107
Ingratiator's dilemma, 104
Injury, physical, 134–135
Injustice, perceived, 270–276
Insults, 42, 49, 63, 279–280, 283
Integrative interpersonal theory of depression, 128
Intentionality of aversive behaviors, 11, 171, 304
Interactional justice, 270
Internalized resignation, 19
International relations, 36
Internet, 33, 207, 215
Interpersonal Betrayal Scale (IBS), 242–245, 251
Interpersonal transgressions, 234–236
Interruptions, 42
Intimacy, 12–13
  gossip and, 221–222
  perceptions of risk in, 14–15
  and propriety, 43
Intimidation, 81, 96
Italy, 281

Japan, 36, 198, 267–268, 273
Java, 275
Jealousy, 8, 238–239
Job applicants, self-presentation of, 84
Johnson, Mitchell, 17
Joking, teasing vs., 180
Jung, Carl G., 208
Justice, aggression and desire for, 270–276

Kaluli, 197
Klebold, Dylan, 17

Labor force, 31–32
Language, 61. *See also* Swearing
Lazarus, R. S., 10
Leary, Mark, 84
Lennon, John, 214
Littering, 45
"Loose" settings, 40

Lying, 42

MAACL—R. See Multiple Affect Adjective Check List
Major life events, 10
Malevolence, and impropriety, 38–39
Maliciousness, 49
Manners, 30, 31, 47
Marriage, 34
Martyrs of gossip, 205
Maury Povich show, 302
McCartney, Paul, 211–212, 214, 221
McGregor, D., 212
Media
    gossip in, 219, 222–223
    rumors in, 207
    violence in, 33
Middle class, emergence of, 31
Miss Manners, 30
Morality, 83–84, 210–211
Morin, Edgar, 206
Motivation(s)
    for coercive actions, 264–265
    for self-presentation, 84–85, 89–93
    for swearing, 66–68
    for teasing, 185–186, 197–198
Motives, rumor and misreading of, 205
Multiple Affect Adjective Check List
    (MAACL—R), 154–155
Multiple audience problem, 40–41

Name-calling, 197
National School Safety Center, 17
Native Americans, 196
Negative feedback-seeking, 123–131, 138
    definition of, 123
    and depression, 124–127
    interpersonal consequences of, 128–129
    measurement issues with, 129–131
    and self-verification, 123–124
Negative self-presentation, 85–86
Neuroticism, and hurt-proneness, 166
Nonconformity, 38
Norms, 6, 9
    conflicting, 40–41
    evolving, 41

and impropriety, 40–41
    specificity of, 40

Obscene language, 59
Omission, acts of, 305
Oral communication skills, inadequate, 36–37
Outcome-relevant involvement, 215–216

PANAS. See Positive and Negative Affect Schedule
Papua New Guinea, 197, 275
Passive disassociation, 158–159
Peer rejection, 135
Perceptions of aversive behavior, 7–15
    and ambiguity, 9
    and empathic accuracy, 12
    and inappropriateness, 9
    individual differences in, 14–15
    and intentionality of aversive behavior, 11
    and interference with basic psychological needs, 8
    and presence of audience, 15
    and prevailing norms, 9
    and relational intimacy, 12–13
    and severity/frequency of transgressions, 9–11
    and social confrontation episodes, 8
    and swearing, 69–72
    teasing, 190
    and type of relationship, 13–14
Permitted disrespect, 177
Perpetrators
    of aversive interpersonal behaviors, 303–304
    of hurt feelings, 170–171
    of teasing, 181–183, 190, 194–195
Personality
    and standards of propriety, 35–36
    and swearing, 62
    and teasing, 181
Physical injury, 134–135
Physique anxiety, 191
Playfulness, excessive, 50
Playing dumb, 82–83, 92–93, 96
Playing the dozens, 196

Sadness, 155
Sandbagging, 82
Sarcasm, 184
School violence, 17
Secondary appraisal phase, 10
Self-concept
    and teasing, 185
    and use of coercion, 276–283
Self-disclosure, teasing as means of, 187–188
Self-esteem
    depressotypic behaviors and low/unstable, 138–139
    and hurt-proneness, 166
    need for, 8
    and revenge, 18
    and teasing, 191
Self-glorification, 104
Self-handicapping, 102–103
Selfishness, 39
    and impropriety, 39
Self-presentation(s), 79–109
    categories of, 80–81
    dimensions of, 81–84
    intended aversive, 86–98
    motives for, 84–85
    negative, 85–86
    and teasing, 189
    unintended aversive, 98–107
Self-promotion, 82, 85, 90, 96, 101–103
Self-regulation, 37
Self-teasing, 189
Self-verification theory, 123–125, 138
Severity of aversive behaviors, 9–11
Sex roles, 35
Sexual assault, 136
Sexual infidelity, 240–241
Sexual revolution, 34
Shame, 191
Shanabarger, Ronald, 16
Sherif, Muzafer, 223
SITCA. See Social interactionist theory of coercive actions
Slang, depiction of women in, 62–63
Slanging matches, 79
Social classes, 31
Social comparison theory, 218
Social confrontation episodes, 8
Social control, aggression and desire for, 265–270

Social cynicism, 268–269
Social disorder, 30
Social interactionist theory of coercive actions (SITCA), 258, 264–285
    assumptions of, 264
    focus of, 264
    identity motive in, 276–283
    justice motive in, 270–276
    social control motive in, 265–270
Socialization
    gossip as means of, 218
    for politeness, 281
    teasing as means of, 186–187
Social Network List, 244–245
Social networks, 244–245
Social support research, 6
Social undermining, 4
Societal norms. See Norms
Sour-grapes rationalization, 170
Southern United States, 32
Standards of decorum, 6
Starr, Ringo, 214
Stephens, Ronald, 17
Storytelling, 206–207
Stress, 10–11
    and abusive behavior, 263
    from interpersonal conflicts, 297
Subculture of violence, 278–279
Supplication, 83, 90, 96
Swearing, 59–73
    asseverative, 61, 62
    audience for, 66
    aversiveness of, 64
    categories of research on, 63–64
    classification of, 64–66
    classifications of, 61–62
    and concepts of profanity, 61
    contextual factors with, 68–69
    ejaculatory, 61, 62
    and familiarity, 63
    and groups, 62
    motivations for, 66–68
    and personality type, 62
    prevalence of, 60
    as relational activity, 72–73
    and social experience, 60
    social functionality of, 62–63
    and social perception, 69–72
    and stigmatization of groups/classes, 64–65

Synthetic benevolence, 205

Talk show radio, 222–223
Targets
    of ingratiation, 104–107
    of self-presentation, 93–97
    of teasing, 183–184, 191–194
Teasing, 10, 11, 42, 48, 177–198, 302
    audience for, 195–196
    bullying vs., 179, 180
    conceptualizations of, 178–180
    consequences of, 190–196
    cross-cultural variations in, 196–198
    and development, 184–185
    functions of, 185–189
    hidden meaning in, 179
    hurt feelings from, 161–162
    joking vs., 180
    perceptions of, 190
    and power/control, 188–189
    prevalence of, 180
    self-disclosure via, 187–188
    and self-presentation, 189
    and socialization, 186–187
    targets of, 183–184, 191–194
    and teaser, 181–183, 190, 194–195
    as term, 178
Technology, and standards of propriety,
    33–34
Temperature, and aggression levels, 262
Ten Commandments, 60
"Thick-skinned" individuals, 165
"Tight" settings, 40
Transgressions, interpersonal, 234–236

Turner's Syndrome, 192
2 Live Crew, 60
Type A personality, 62, 72

Underappreciated, feeling, 162

Vain distortion effect, 106
Violence, 133–136
    in media, 33
    revenge as form of, 17–18
    subculture of, 278–279
    and temperature, 262
Virgil, 206
Visionary rumors, 208
Vulgarity, 30, 61, 65–66

Wall Street Journal, 207
War of the Worlds (radio broadcast), 207–
    208
Washington Post, 33
Wayne, John, 32
Wells, H. G., 207–208
Western cultures, 32
Wish rumors, 216–217
Women
    depiction of, in slang, 62–63
    and teasing, 191–192
    view of, on swearing, 59–60
Woodham, Luke, 17

Yananomo, 267

ABOUT THE EDITOR

Robin M. Kowalski, PhD, is a professor of psychology at Western Carolina University in Cullowhee, North Carolina. She obtained her PhD in social psychology from the University of North Carolina at Greensboro. Her research interests include social anxiety, social–psychological factors in health and illness, gender and aggression, and aversive interpersonal behaviors (specifically complaining and teasing). She is the editor of the book *Aversive Interpersonal Behaviors*, is coeditor of the book *The Social Psychology of Emotional and Behavioral Problems*, and coauthor of the book *Social Anxiety*. Her research on complaining brought her international attention, including an appearance on NBC's "Today Show."